Understanding
TEXTILES

Phyllis G. Tortora

Chairperson, Department of Home Economics
Queens College

anding

TILES

Macmillan Publishing Co., Inc.
NEW YORK

Collier Macmillan Publishers
LONDON

Macmillan Publishing Co., Inc.
866 Third Avenue, New York, New York 10022

Collier Macmillan Canada, Ltd.

Library of Congress Cataloging in Publication Data

Tortora, Phyllis G
  Understanding textiles.

  Bibliography: p.
  Includes index.
  1. Textile fibers.   2. Textile fabrics.
3. Textile industry.   I. Title.
TS1445.T63   677   76-52754
ISBN 0-02-420940-6

Printing: 4 5 6 7 8   Year: 0 1 2 3 4

PREFACE

The purpose of this book is to provide a common background for students who are making a study of textiles. Some students may be planning to enter one of the many career areas that require some knowledge about textiles. Others may be interested in becoming better-informed consumers. Whatever may motivate students into an introductory course in textiles, certain basic concepts are essential to their understanding of the subject. It is my hope that these concepts are presented in a clear, logically developed format.

It has been my intention to emphasize the interrelationships of fibers, yarns, fabric constructions, and finishes and to apply what has been learned about each of these components to the understanding of textile behavior and performance. To this end, diagrams and photographs were carefully selected to illustrate the concepts and processes described in the text. Where possible, pictures of machinery or steps in textile processing are included to provide a visual as well as a written description.

The recommended references at the end of each chapter have been selected to complement the subject matter of the chapters. I have made a conscious effort to include both relatively elementary and highly technical material so as to introduce students to the variety of resources in the field. I have also tried to include readings from the most widely used periodicals in the field. An extensive bibliography, broken down under special subject headings, is appended to the book.

Chapters 1 and 2 establish the relationship of fiber properties to fiber behavior. Chapter 1 focuses on physical properties of fibers and Chapter 2 deals with the chemistry of textile fibers. Chapter 2, which presents in an elementary way some of the basic concepts in textile chemistry, is written for the student who has had no previous chemistry training. The student should be able to gain some understanding of these elementary concepts and to appreciate not only the integral role that chemistry plays in the manufacture and finishing of textile products, but also the role of chemistry in the use and care of textiles by consumers. Often this kind of material is integrated into varying parts of a text; I have not done so here because a separate chapter on the subject offers a better opportunity to explain elementary chemical terminology and concepts and to relate these concepts to the science of textiles. Some teachers may prefer to emphasize this chapter a great deal, whereas others may wish to discuss it briefly. Either approach may be taken.

The chapters on textile fibers (Chapters 3 to 12) are each organized in much the same way with the same topic headings being used in each chapter. These topic headings are also used in the introductory chapter dealing with textile fiber properties—to facilitate comparisons between fibers. Each chapter ends with a table summarizing some of the more important characteristics of the major fiber groups discussed in that chapter.

From fibers the text moves to yarns and their production (Chapter 13) and from yarns the text then goes on to fabric structures. Fabric structures are divided into woven fabrics (Chapter 14), knitted fabrics (Chapter 15), and other methods of fabric construction (Chapter 16.) These chapters deal with the newest processes for the manufacture of yarns and fabrics as well as the more traditional methods.

The various methods of adding color and giving special finishes to fabrics are discussed in Chapters 17 to 20. Much of the appeal of textile fabrics results from the color and decoration that are applied to them. A number of photographs selected for Chapters 17 and 18 are of historic textiles and are meant to provide a special emphasis on the aesthetic qualities of textiles.

Each of Chapters 21 to 24 fulfills a special purpose in the organization of the book. Chapter 21, "The Care of Textile Products," is included as a separate chapter, even though some material about the care of textiles is also included in preceding chapters, because of the importance of care in relation to consumer satisfaction with textiles.

Chapter 22 deals with textiles and the environment, a topic of concern to both the consumer and the textile industry. I do not believe that this area is covered in any other text currently available. The chapter is addressed not only to ways in which textile production and use affect the environment but also raises questions about the complex "trade-offs" between environmental quality and increased costs of consumer goods.

Chapter 23 provides a brief introduction to the subject of textile testing. Many colleges and junior colleges have little or no textile testing equipment. Others may have extensive and elaborate textile laboratories. For the former, this chapter provides photographs of basic equipment and some brief discussion of types of equipment used in testing, as well as descriptions of some simple tests that can be performed in the classroom or at home. For the latter, this chapter provides a very general introduction to the subject of textile testing that may be expanded in other courses. This chapter does not serve as a substitute for technical or laboratory manuals.

The last chapter provides a summary of the text. It explores some of the ways in which fiber, yarn, fabric construction, and finishes contribute to the total structure of the fabric, and how the structure of the fabric is, in turn, related to its performance.

Each college or university organizes its course work in unique ways. While it is not possible for a single text to meet the needs of all programs, I believe that this book includes all of the information essential to an introductory textiles course and offers the student and the teacher neither too much nor too little. It will be up to the faculty and students who use this book to tell me whether I have indeed reached that goal.

The contributions of a number of people to the preparation of this book should not be overlooked. To my family goes my appreciation for their encouragement and enthusiastic support for the project. My husband Vincent and my son Christopher deserve special thanks for their assistance with the photography. Thanks go to my daughter Giulia for a myriad of small tasks she performed to help me.

The readers selected by the publisher also deserve many thanks. It was through their constructive and careful criticism that the manuscript was refined to its present form and contents. These excellent readers included Dr. Norma Skaar, Oregon State University, and anonymous readers from Ohio State University, the University of Illinois, and the University of Arizona. Thanks go also to Dr. Norman Goldman, chairman of the Department of Chemistry of Queens College, CUNY for his careful reading of the chapter on the chemistry of textiles. Constance Sussman, laboratory technician in the Department of Home Economics at Queens College, was also helpful in reading and critiquing some portions of the manuscript.

Typing of portions of the manuscript was done by Nora Schwartzer, Lois Trowbridge, Diana Heijmans, Ann Denaro, and Charlotte Engel.

Finally, I owe appreciation to the many segments of the textile industry who were so generous with information and photographs and other illustrative materials. Picture sources are acknowledged with each reproduction, but it is impossible to identify all of the many firms and individuals who provided source materials and other forms of assistance.

P. T.

CONTENTS

macramé
embroidery
lace

INTRODUCTION

Each day every person makes decisions about textiles. From the simplest choice of what clothes to wear, to the commitment of a major portion of the family budget to buy a new carpet, judgments about the performance, durability, attractiveness, and care of textiles are consciously or unconsciously made. The economic implications of decisions about fibers, yarns, and fabrics obviously increase if one is professionally involved with textiles. But whether understanding textiles is required for personal or for professional purposes, the key to informed decision making is knowledge about fibers, yarns, fabrics, finishes, and the ways in which these are interrelated.

Textiles fulfill so many purposes in our lives that the study of textiles can be approached in a number of ways. Textiles may be seen as purely utilitarian, in relationship to the numerous purposes they serve. Textile products surround each of us at every moment of our lives, waking or sleeping. On awaking in the morning we climb out from under sheets and blankets and step into slippers and a robe. We wash our faces with a washcloth, dry them with a towel, and put on clothing for the day. We even brush our teeth with toothbrushes, the bristles of which are made from textile fibers. If we get into a car or bus, we sit on upholstered seats and the machine moves on tires reinforced with strong textile cords. We stand on carpets, sit on upholstered furniture, and look out of curtained windows. Even the insulation of our houses is glass textile fiber. Not only are golf clubs, tennis rackets, and ski poles reinforced with textile fibers but so are roads, bridges, and buildings. Strong, heat-resistant textile fibers in the nose cones of space ships travel to the moon with the astronauts. Physicians implant artificial arteries made of textiles or use fibers for surgery that gradually dissolve as wounds heal. Few of our manufactured products could be made without textile conveyor belts. Even our processed foods have been filtered through textile filter paper. There is truly no aspect of modern life that is untouched by some area of textiles.

On the other hand, textiles can be seen as part of a huge industrial complex. The textile industry produces about 17 billion square yards of fabric each year. About 38 per cent of the fabric produced is made into apparel, 31 per cent goes into home furnishings, 17 per cent into industrial fabrics, 3 per cent is exported, and the remaining 11 per cent is used for other consumer products that include sporting goods, home building materials, and automobile tires.[1] In the United States, the production of textiles and apparel accounts for one job out of every eight.[2] This complex network of industry and business rests on a foundation of technological and mechanical processes that are constantly being

[1] *A Profile of Textiles* (Charlotte, N.C.: American Textile Manufacturers Institute, Inc., 1975), p. 5.

[2] *Textiles from Start to Finish* (Charlotte, N.C.: American Textile Manufacturers Institute, Inc., 1975), p. 1.

expanded and improved through the development of new and more efficient technologies for manufacturing and finishing fibers, yarns, and fabrics.

Then, too, textiles may be perceived as objects of great beauty, even as works of art. The selection of specific textile products for individual and/or family use is often based on the attractiveness of the fabric. The beauty of textiles is legendary. Woven tapestries hang on the walls of museums as a reminder that the weaver was once an artist as well as the practical producer of useful items. The poetic images associated with weaving and spinning have been used by many poets.

> Whenas in silks my Julia goes. . .[3]

> Twist ye, twine ye! even so
> Mingle shades of joy and woe,
> Hope and fear, and peace and strife,
> In the thread of human life.[4]

> I broider the world upon a loom,
> I broider with dreams my tapestry;[5]

> Had I the heavens' embroidered cloths,
> Enwrought with gold and silver light.[6]

All three aspects of textiles: the utilitarian, the technological, and the aesthetic have played a part in the uses of textiles from the very earliest times. Any comprehensive view of textiles must encompass each of these facets.

Textiles in Historic Context

No one knows exactly when the spinning and weaving of textiles began, but archeologists tell us that woven wool and plant fiber fabrics were made more than 8,500 years ago in Catal Huyuk, a hunting village in what is today the country of Turkey.[7] For most of the time that people have made fabrics, the only fibers available for use were found in nature, and the processes used to make these fibers into cloth were carried out by hand.

In spite of limited technology, people created a wide variety of fabrics for themselves and for use in their homes. Some of these fabrics, such as the simple, plain homespun cloth used for every day were strictly utilitarian. Others were elaborately patterned, printed, or dyed in order to satisfy the universal human need for beauty.

As the complex social and political organizations of people evolved, some of the small hunting villages were replaced by larger towns, and eventually by cities and urban centers. Along with the growth of cities, nations, and empires, there were improvements in technology and the development of international trade, both of which involved textiles. Changes in textile technology and trade

[3] Robert Herrick, "Upon Julia's Clothes."
[4] Sir Walter Scott, "Guy Mannering."
[5] Arthur Symons, "The Loom of Dreams."
[6] William Butler Yeats, "He Wishes for the Clothes of Heaven."
[7] J. Mellaart, "Catal Huyuk in Anatolia," *Illustrated London Daily News*, (February 9, 1963) p. 196ff.

had come about as early as the time of the Roman Empire. The Romans not only traded actively with nearby Egypt to import cotton but they had developed trade in silk with faraway China by the year A.D. 1. Close to storehouses in Roman settlements excavated in India, archeologists have found facilities for dyeing and finishing cotton fabrics. In the remains of many Roman towns there is evidence of installations for finishing and dyeing fabrics.

During the Middle Ages the production and trading of the plant called *woad*, an important source of dye, was a highly developed industry. Returning crusaders brought luxurious silk and cotton fabrics from the Middle East to their homes in Europe, and these "foreign novelties" became an important item in trade. During the fifteenth century, the trade fairs of southern France provided a place for the active exchange of wools from England and silks from Persia. The economic activities surrounding these events gave rise to the first international banking arrangements.

Even the discovery of America was a result of the desire of Europeans to find a faster route not only to the spices but also to the textiles of the Orient. Once the American colonies had been established, the colonists sold native dyes such as indigo and cochineal to Europe and bought cottons from India.

Technological Advances

At the time when textiles were assuming an increasingly important role in international trade, advances were being made in the technology of textile production. Even so, the manufacture of cloth was still essentially a hand process. By 1700 in Western Europe spinning was still being done on a spinning wheel, by hand. Fabrics were woven by hand on looms for which the power was provided by the weaver.

The production of textiles was the first area to undergo industrialization during the industrial revolution, which occurred during the latter half of the 1700s in Western Europe, especially in Great Britain, France, and the Low Countries. The vast changes that took place during this period, though not only technological but also sociological, economic, and cultural, included a major reorganization of manufacturing of a variety of goods. This came about during the seventeenth and eighteenth centuries when good quality textile products, produced inexpensively in India and the Far East, were gradually replacing European goods in the international market. In England, this competition produced a severe economic crisis within the textile field, and it became imperative that some means be found to increase domestic production, to lower costs, and to improve quality of textiles. The solution was found in the substitution of machine or nonhuman power for hand processes and human power.

Many important inventions were made during this period that improved the output and quality of fabrics. The most important of these were spinning machines, automatic looms, and the cotton gin. These inventions provided the technological base for the industrialization of the textile industry. Each invention that improved one step of the manufacturing of textiles also had an effect on the parts of the process. For example, an improvement that increased the speed of weaving meant that looms consumed greater quantities of yarn. More rapid yarn production required greater quantities of fiber. The growth of the textile industry was further hastened by the use of machines that were driven first by waterpower, then by steam, and finally by electricity.

The full mechanization of the textile industry was accomplished by the early part of the nineteenth century. The next major developments in the field were to take place in the chemist's laboratory. Experimentation with the synthesis of dyestuffs in the laboratory rather than from natural plant materials led to the development and use of synthetic dyestuffs in the latter half of the nineteenth century. Other experiments proved that certain natural materials could be dissolved in chemical solvents and re-formed into fibrous form. This principle was used to produce "artificial silk" (now called rayon) from cellulosic materials such as mulberry leaves, wood chips, or cotton linters. By 1910, the first plant for manufacturing rayon had been established in the United States.

The manufacture of rayon marked the beginning of the man-made textile industry. Since that time, enormous advances have been made in the technology for making fibers, spinning them into yarns, constructing fabrics, and coloring and finishing them. Today the textile industry utilizes a complex technology based on scientific processes and a vast economic organization.

Future Directions

With the application of advanced technology to the textile field, textile use has expanded from the traditional areas of clothing and home furnishings into the fields of construction, medicine, aerospace, sporting goods, and industry. These applications have been made possible by the ability of textile chemists to "engineer" textile fibers for specific uses. At the same time that textile technology is making strides in new directions, the fabrics that consumers buy for clothing and household use also benefit from the development of new fibers, new methods of yarn and fabric construction, and new finishes for existing fibers and fabrics.

The following applications of textiles to new uses point the way to the future:

A textile company has patented a fabric which responds automatically to temperature changes. It gets thinner and cooler as the temperature rises and gets thicker and warmer as the temperature drops.

An engineer has developed a portable collapsible bridge of woven polyester for the Army. It can span a 60-foot river in 30 minutes and is strong enough to support a 20-ton tank. . . .

A rapid transit system has been devised to ferry people from perimeter parking lots into the cores of cities. It is a huge conveyer belt made of woven cotton and nylon.[8]

Chemists are also experimenting with fibers that will change color with the environment, and technologists are trying to find commercially viable proc-

[8] *A Profile of Textiles* (Charlotte, N.C.: American Textile Manufacturers Institute, Inc., 1975), p. 5.

esses that take the melted material from which fibers are made and form them directly into finished products. All of these processes are based on existing technology or on theoretical understanding of the nature and structure of textile products. Just how the field of textiles will develop in the future is uncertain. But it *is* certain that the ways in which textile products are used by our increasingly technological society will continue to expand in new and unexpected directions.

1
TEXTILE FIBERS AND THEIR PROPERTIES

Textile fibers may be found in nature or created by man. Natural fibers are taken from either animal, vegetable, or mineral sources. A few examples of widely used natural fibers include animal fibers such as wool and silk; vegetable fibers, especially cotton and flax; and asbestos, a mineral fiber.

Fibers created by man through technology are divided into two basic classifications. Regenerated man-made fibers are made from natural materials that cannot be used for textiles in their original form, but that can be regenerated (or re-formed) into usable fibers by chemical treatment and processing. These *regenerated fibers* are made from such diverse substances as wood, corn protein, milk protein, small cotton bits called linters, and seaweed. True synthetic man-made fibers are made or "synthesized" completely from chemical substances such as petroleum derivatives.[1]

Generic Fiber Classification

Groups of fibers that are related in their chemical structure may be compared to large, extended families. Each fiber family group is made up of smaller family units. These smaller family units are, in turn, composed of a number of individual units. For example, some fibers have a structure made of protein (the large extended family). Subunits of the "protein" family include silk, which has no other close relatives; animal hair fibers, including wool, mohair, cashmere, camel's hair, and the like; and regenerated protein fibers that can be made from corn, soybean, peanut, or milk protein.

Within the family are certain "family resemblances," or ways in which the members of each group are alike. Most protein fibers, for example, show these similarities: they are harmed by the same chemicals, fairly resilient, harmed by dry heat, and weaker wet than dry. Like human family members, however, each fiber has its own talents or eccentricities: silk has high luster, wool does

---

[1] In this text, the term *man-made* is used when reference is made to both regenerated and synthetic fibers. When reference is made to those fibers synthesized from chemical substances, the term *synthetic* is used.

not; vicuña and cashmere are exceptionally soft and luxurious to the touch; and the color of camel's hair cannot be removed easily.

As a result of legislation known as the Textile Fiber Products Identification Act, the Federal Trade Commission has established names and definitions for each of the families of man-made fibers. The "family" name is called the *generic* name or generic classification of the fiber. Manufacturers of man-made fibers also give each of their fibers a name that is known as the *trademark*. Mary Smith, John Smith, and George Smith may be members of the same human family, each with the same family name, but each with a different given name. In the same way, Orlon acrylic, Zefran acrylic, and Acrilan acrylic are all members of the generic group of acrylics, but each has a different trademark.

By law all manufactured items made from man-made fibers must (at the point of purchase) carry the generic name of the fiber on a label. Most manufacturers use the generic term along with their own trademark, so that the consumer will find such terms as Dacron (trademark of E. I. du Pont de Nemours & Company) polyester (generic name) or Kodel (trademark of Eastman Kodak Company) polyester on labels of textile products.

Textile Fiber Products Identification Act

Fiber manufacturers introduced ever-increasing varieties of new fibers to the public in the decade of the 1950s. No regulation was made of the use of man-made fiber names, so that each manufacturer who made his own version of a fiber gave it his own trademark. The consumer was confronted with a variety of fiber names and had no ability to distinguish one from the other. Furthermore, two or more fibers might be blended together without the consumer's knowledge. The purchaser of a man's shirt had no way of knowing whether it was made of cotton, rayon, or a cotton and polyester blend.

The consumer confusion resulting from this situation led to the Textile Fiber Products Identification Act (often abbreviated to TFPIA), which provided for fiber content labeling of all textile products. The law, which became effective March 3, 1960, has been amended several times since that date. The legislation assigned responsibility for the enforcement and drafting of rules and regulations under the act to the Federal Trade Commission.

Under the provisions of the TFPIA, all fibers, either natural or man-made, all yarns, fabrics, household textile articles and wearing apparel are subject to this law. One of the first tasks assigned to the Federal Trade Commission was the establishment of generic names or classifications for man-made fibers.

Natural fibers, which are each to be called by their own name, are defined in the act as "any fiber that exists as such in the natural state." The terms for natural fibers, such as *cotton, linen, silk,* and *wool* appear on labels. Man-made or, as the act defines them, manufactured fibers are defined as "any fiber derived by a process of manufacture from any substance which, at any point in the manufacturing process, is not a fiber." The law charged the Federal Trade Commission with the responsibility of classifying the many different manufactured fibers that had been introduced. These categories or generic classifications were based on similarities in chemical composition. Along with similarities in chemical composition, fibers in these groupings had many common physical properties, care requirements, and performance characteristics. Altogether there are now twenty-one generic fiber groupings for manufactured fibers. New generic classes may be added when manufacturers are able to demonstrate that fibers are sufficiently unique to warrant a separate classification from those already in existence, so that it is possible that further generic classes may be established in the future as new fibers are synthesized.

The TFPIA requires that all textile products have a label attached that lists the names of the fibers, either natural or generic, from which they are made.[2] Fiber listing must be done in order of the percentage of fiber by weight that is present in the product. The largest amount must be listed first, the next largest second, and so on. Thus, for example, a fabric might be labeled:

60% polyester
30% cotton
10% acetate

The manufacturer must list the generic name of the fiber, but he may also list the trademark. So, for example, the same label could also read as follows:

60% Dacron polyester
30% cotton
10% Acele acetate

Note that the trademark is capitalized, but the generic term is not.

Fiber quantities of less than 5 per cent must be labeled as "other fiber," unless they serve a specific purpose in the product. If they are listed, the function of these minor components must be stated. For example, a manufacturer could say, "96 per cent nylon, 4 per cent spandex for elasticity," because spandex is an elastic fiber and does perform a specific function. The intent of this provision is to prevent manufacturers from implying that 5 per cent or less of a fiber will produce some positive benefit. Quantities of less than 5 per cent of most fibers normally have little or no effect on fabric performance. Examples of exceptions are in the use of elastomeric fibers such as spandex or metallic fibers that control static.

Where products are made from fibers that have not been identified, for instance, from mixed reused fiber, the label may indicate that such a product is "composed of miscellaneous scraps, rags, odd lots, textile by-products, secondhand materials, or waste materials." Such a label might read, for example:

45% rayon
35% acetate
20% miscellaneous scraps of undetermined fiber content.

No trademarks or other terms may be used that imply the presence of a fiber

[2] With these exceptions: upholstery stuffing; outer coverings of furniture, mattresses and box springs; linings, interlinings, stiffenings or paddings incorporated for structural purposes and not for warmth; sewing and handicraft threads, and bandages and surgical dressings.

that is not actually a part of the product. For example, it would be illegal to use the following labels:

SILK-SHEEN Blouses
   100% nylon
          or
Woolly Warm Blankets
   100% acrylic

The law also requires that either the name of the manufacturer, a registered trademark, or a registered identification number appear on the label. All the mandated information must appear on the same side of the label, and all printing must be of the same type or size.

Imported goods are also subject to this legislation and must be labeled in conformity with provisions of the law. If textiles are sold in this country just as they were imported, they must be labeled with the name of the country of origin. For example, if woolen blankets made in Australia were sold in the United States, they would have to be labeled "Made in Australia"; however, wool fiber imported from Australia and spun and then woven in the United States would not be labeled as from Australia.

Properties of Textile Fibers

Fibers, which are the primary materials from which most textile products are made, can be defined as units of matter of hairlike dimensions, with a length at least one hundred times greater than the width. Many substances found in nature can be classified as fibers according to this definition; however, only a limited number of these materials are useful in the production of yarns or fabrics.

Whether a fiber can be utilized in the creation of a yarn or fabric depends upon the physical and chemical properties of the fiber. Many fibrous substances lack one or more essential qualities required of textile fibers. They may not, for example, be sufficiently long to be spun into a yarn. Or they may be too weak to use, too inflexible, too thick in diameter, or too easily damaged in spinning and weaving.

Comparison of fiber qualities and characteristics requires the use of certain basic terms and a technical vocabulary. Definition of these terms and of their meanings as they relate to textile performance and/or behavior is important for communication and understanding.

PROPERTIES RELATING TO APPEARANCE

Some qualities of textile fibers are related to their physical appearance. Since most single fibers are so small that they cannot be examined adequately with the naked eye, the physical appearance of these fibers is best observed under a microscope. With a microscope it is possible to observe such properties as length, diameter, surface contour, and color. The physical characteristics of each individual fiber affect the appearance and behavior of the yarns and fabrics into which they are manufactured.

Color and Luster

The color of natural fibers varies. Some, like cotton, have just enough pigment to make them yellow or off-white; others, like wool, may range from white to black. Even man-made fibers are usually off-white or yellowish in tint. If this color interfers with dyeing or printing, the color may be removed by bleaching.

Luster is the amount of light reflected by the fiber. Man-made fibers may have bright luster, which is undesirable in some products. To decrease the luster a chemical, titanium oxide, is added to the material from which the fiber is made. The small particles of the chemical break up the reflected light, giving the fiber a lower luster or "deluster" the fiber. Untreated fibers may be known as "bright" fibers, delustered fibers may be called "dull" fibers.

Shape and Luster

The shape of a fiber can be examined both in *cross section* and in its *longitudinal* form. Since cross section is a practical way in which to view the three-dimensional form of a fiber, cross sections are often used as a means of comparison. Cross sections vary from fiber to fiber, ranging from circular to oval, triangular, dog-bone shaped, U-shaped, and so on.

The cross-sectional shapes of man-made fibers are uniform. Some irregularities in shape will occur in natural fibers, but the range of these differences is slight enough that fabric appearance is not much affected.

Differences in cross section are responsible for differences in fiber characteristics such as appearance, hand or feel, surface texture, and body. Luster and covering power are also affected by cross-sectional shapes.

Fabrics are often used to cover that which is placed beneath them. The ability of a fabric to cover an object is known as its *covering power*. The covering power of fibers and fabrics have two aspects: the visual and the geometric. Visual covering power is related to the ability of the fiber to hide what is placed beneath it. The more transparent the fiber, the less covering power it has. The second aspect, that of geometric covering power, might be described as the quantity of fiber required to make a yarn that will cover a specific area.

Geometric covering power is measured by filling a standard sized container with yarn, then weighing the amount of yarn required to fill the container. When a small quantity of fiber is required to fill the container, the fiber is said to have good covering power. When a large quantity of fiber is required to fill the container, the fiber is said to have poor covering power. The better the covering power, the less expensive it will be to manufacture a yarn or fabric, because less quantity of fiber will be required.

Round, cross-sectional shaped fibers have a soft, smooth, sometimes slippery

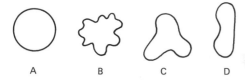

Figure 1-1. Typical variations in fiber cross-sectional shape: (a) round (nylon 6), (b) serrated (Carval rayon), (c) trilobal (Antron nylon), (d) dogbone (Orlon acrylic).

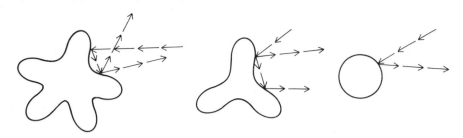

feel. Unless a special treatment has been given to the fiber to decrease its luster, the luster of round fibers is high. Covering power is, however, poor. This is because the surface area of round fibers is less than that of any other shape. Also being both round and smooth, the fiber will pack closely together into a yarn.

Dog-bone shaped and flat cross-section fibers have a harsher, less smooth handle. The covering power of these fibers is excellent. Completely flat cross sections have a high luster, and some manufacturers have produced flat fibers with a glittering luster, but those with less regular surface, such as cotton which has a somewhat flat but irregular cross section, do not have high luster.

Fibers with three- and five-lobed shapes have been manufactured. Three-lobed fibers are known as trilobal fibers and those with five lobes are known as pentalobal. The term *multilobal* is used to refer to all fibers with a number of lobes in the cross section. Trilobal fibers with triangular-shaped cross sections have increased covering power, a more silklike feel, and an increased luster. The luster results from the reflection of light not only from the surface of the fiber but also from the light being reflected from one lobe to another. Penta-lobal fibers also have this tendency to reflect light from one lobe to another, but because there are more lobes among which the light can be reflected, the fibers have a soft, subdued sheen.

When the lobes of the fiber are increased still further, light rays are broken up and the luster decreases. Octolobal fibers have been made to decrease luster or glitter.

Surface Contour

Some fibers have smooth, even contours when examined longitudinally, others are rough and uneven. Wool, for example, is covered with many small scales that cause wool fibers to cling closely together. Cotton is twisted, making it reflect light unevenly, and giving it a dull appearance. Horizontal lines or other markings may appear in the length of some man-made fibers as a result of irregularities in the cross-sectional shape of the fiber. The valleys between the lobes of multilobal fibers cause shadows, which (under the microscope) appear as dark lines and are known as *striations*.

Crimp

Some fibers possess a wavy, undulating physical structure. This characteristic is called *crimp*. Wool has a natural three-dimensional crimp. Some synthetics

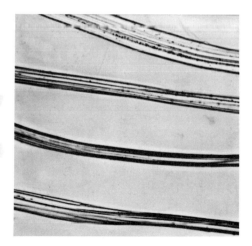

Figure 1-3. A longitudinal view of Carval rayon showing striations. Courtesy of E. I. du Pont de Nemours & Company.

are crimped during manufacture. Crimped fabrics tend to be more resilient and have increased bulk, cohesiveness, and warmth. *Cohesiveness* is the ability of fibers to cling together.

Length

By microscopic examination of textile fibers, one can readily observe the ratio (or comparison) of the length of the fiber in relation to its width. Though fibers are, by definition, always long and narrow, the length of the fiber is one basis for division or classification. Fibers of relatively short length, measured in centimeters or inches, are called *staple* fibers. Long fibers, those measured in yards or meters, are known as *filament* fibers.

All natural fibers except silk are staple fibers. Man-made fibers are manufactured in filament form but the filaments can be cut into shorter, staple lengths. Therefore, man-made fibers may be found in either staple or filament form.

The length of the fiber will have an effect on the appearance of the yarn into which it is made. Filament fibers can be made into yarns with little or no twisting. These will look smooth and lustrous. Staple fibers, being short, must be twisted together or spun in order to make them into a long, continuous yarn. Shorter fibers will produce more fiber ends on the surface of a yarn, thus creating a duller appearance.

The *hand* or *texture* of the fabric is affected by the use of either filament or staple fibers. If an untextured filament form is selected, there are fewer fiber ends on the surface of a fabric, creating a smooth, even surface. If staple fibers are used, the short fiber ends on the surface of a fabric can create a fabric that feels soft and fluffy to the touch. Judicious selection of short staple, longer staple, textured, or untextured filament yarns enables the manufacturer to vary the appearance, the texture, or other properties of fabrics.

Diameter

The diameter of the fiber is the distance across its cross section. In natural fibers the diameter usually varies from one part of the fiber to another because of irregularities in fiber size. Unless manufactured to have an uneven diameter, man-made fibers usually have a uniform diameter throughout.

In natural fibers, fineness is often an important aspect of quality. In general, thinner fibers are of higher quality because they are softer, more pliable, and have better drapability.

Man-made fibers can have any diameter that the manufacturer chooses, and the selection of diameter is generally related to the projected end use of the fiber. Clothing fibers are made in relatively small diameters, whereas heavy-duty fibers for household items or industrial uses are made with larger diameters.

Fiber diameter is measured in microns. One micron is 1/1000th of a millimeter or .000039th of an inch. Cotton fiber diameter is usually from twelve to twenty microns in width, for example.

The fineness of filament fibers is also expressed by the term *denier,* which is not a measurement of diameter but a relative measurement of yarn fineness. Nine thousand meters of yarn are weighed, and denier is the weight of this length of yarn expressed in grams. If the weight of the yarn is low, the fiber diameter is small. If the weight is high, the fiber diameter is larger. The same unit of measure is used to express yarn size for synthetic filament yarns.

PROPERTIES RELATING TO PERFORMANCE

Determination of Textile Properties and Performance

A number of specific textile properties are defined and discussed in the following pages. The determination of the properties of specific fibers is made through one or more of a variety of different fiber-, yarn-, or fabric-testing methods. Test methods are standardized by organizations such as the American Society for Testing Materials (ASTM), the American Association of Textile Chemists and Colorists (AATCC), the American National Standards Institute (ANSI), or by the government through federal test method standards.

When textile materials are tested, not only must standardized procedures be utilized but testing must be done under controlled conditions. Even the temperature or the quantity of moisture present in a room may affect the results of tests. For this reason, testing is done only under conditions of controlled humidity and temperature and samples are "conditioned" for a specific period of time prior to testing at a temperature of 70 degrees F. and 65 per cent relative humidity. The conditioning time is usually at least twenty-four hours; temperature may be plus or minus two degrees; and humidity may be plus or minus two per cent.

Strength or Tenacity

The strength of textile fibers is referred to as their *tenacity.* According to the American Society for Testing and Materials (ASTM), tenacity is determined by measuring the force required to rupture or break the fiber.[3] Tenacity is measured either in grams per denier or in grams per tex.[4] Grams per denier (abbreviated g/d) is the number of grams of weight required to break a fiber of one denier. *Grams per tex* (abbreviated g/t) is the number of grams of weight required to break a fiber of one tex.

Tensile strength measures textile strength in terms of pounds of weight required per square inch to break a yarn or fabric. This measure is more frequently applied to woven fabrics than to fibers.

[3] ASTM *Annual Book of Standards* part 33, p. 11 (American Society for Testing Materials, Philadelphia, Penna., 1976)

[4] The tex system of measurement is relatively new. Based on the metric system, the tex system is being actively promoted by ASTM in order to standardize yarn measurement systems. Instead of determining the weight of 9,000 meters for yarn as is done for denier, the tex system determines the weight of 1,000 meters.

Although measuring the tenacity of a fiber will provide some guide to potential strength in a woven fabric, many other factors will also affect the durability of the fabric into which the yarn is made. The strength of filament fibers is more comparable to the strength of yarns and fabrics than is the strength of staple length fibers. Such factors as the twist of the yarn, the closeness of the weave, the type of weave, the kind and strength of a yarn, and so on will also be important in determining the ultimate durability and strength of a woven fabric.

Specific Gravity

Density and *specific gravity* are terms that are used in relation to the weight of fibers. Both terms show a relationship, but each has a somewhat different technical definition.

Density is the ratio (relation) of a mass (quantity) of a substance (in this case, a textile fiber) to a unit of volume (in this case, cubic centimeters). Density in textile fibers is expressed in terms of grams per cubic centimeter. *Specific gravity* is the density of the fiber in relation to the density of an equal volume of water at a temperature of 4 degrees C. The specific gravity of water is 1. If a fiber has a specific gravity of more than 1, it is heavier than water; if it has a specific gravity of less than 1, it is lighter than water. Only a few textile fibers have a specific gravity that is less than that of water, so that the specific gravity of most fibers will fall in a range of from 1.0 to 2.0 or slightly above. (See Table 1.1.)

Density has significance for the consumer in a number of ways. Olefins, with a specific gravity of less than that of water, will float on the top of water during laundering. The low density of olefin fibers makes possible the manufacture of fibers from smaller amounts of raw materials. This results in lower costs for the fiber. Glass fiber has a high specific gravity. Therefore, if a cotton fabric and a glass fabric are made of yarns of comparable size and of similar weave, the glass fabric will be much heavier than the cotton.

Flexibility

Flexibility of fibers refers to their ability to be bent or folded and is an essential quality of textile fibers. Stiffness or rigidity limits the usefulness of a fiber, as it becomes difficult to spin it into yarns. Fabrics made from fibers of limited flexibility do not drape well and they are not comfortable for wearing apparel. Furthermore, the fiber must bend or flex often without breaking or splitting, as in many end products the textiles are subject to manipulation that causes fibers to bend or fold.

Elongation and Elastic Recovery

Elongation is the stretching or lengthening of a fiber. Elongation does not imply that the fiber will return to its original form, but merely that the fiber

Table 1.1

Glass fiber	2.54
Cotton	1.52
Wool	1.32
Nylon	1.14
Olefin	0.92

length can be elongated or extended. Measurement of elongation is commonly made as "elongation to break," the amount of stretch the fiber can withstand before it will break.

Elastic recovery is the ability of fibers to return to their original length after being stretched. Elastic recovery can be quantified or measured, and is calculated in numerical terms as the percentage of elastic recovery. A measured fiber (or fabric) is elongated or stretched to a specific degree, for a specified period of time. The stress is then removed, and the fiber is allowed to recover for a short period of time. After recovery, the fiber is remeasured, and the percentage of recovery is calculated. A fiber with 100 per cent recovery has returned to its original length. A fiber with 80 per cent recovery is 20 per cent longer after stretching.

Joseph points out that it is important to evaluate elastic recovery in relation to elongation. For example, fibers with high elongation but low elastic recovery may stretch out of shape. In this way the negative effect of one of these qualities may cancel out the positive effect of the other.[5]

Resiliency

Resiliency refers to the ability of a fiber to spring back to its natural position after folding, creasing, or deformation. Fibers differ in their natural resiliency, and those that are resilient are likely to recover from creasing or wrinkling more quickly. Although resiliency and elasticity are not the same, high elastic recovery is necessary for good resilience.

The term *loft* is related to resiliency. Sometimes known as *compressional resiliency*, loft is the ability of fibers to return to their original thickness after being flattened or compressed. A fabric with "loft" is one that is springy and resists flattening.

Abrasion Resistance

One of the most important physical properties of a fiber in relation to durability is its ability to withstand abrasion. *Abrasion* is the rubbing or friction of fiber against fiber, or fiber against other materials. Fibers with poor abrasion resistance break and splinter, which produces worn or broken areas in fabrics.

Abrasion of fabrics may take place when they are flat, folded, or curved, so that fibers can be subjected to three types of abrasion: flat, flexed, and edge abrasion. Furthermore, the varying conditions under which fabrics are used make abrasion resistance difficult to evaluate. Pizzuto lists five variables that must be considered in evaluating abrasion resistance. They are

a. Type of abradant.
b. Amount of pressure between fabric and abradant.
c. Position of the fabric while being abraded.

[5] M. Joseph, *Introductory Textile Science* (New York: Holt, Rinehart and Winston, Inc., 1972), p. 191.

d. Frequency and time duration of the abrading sequence.

e. Tension exerted on the fabric while it is being abraded.[6]

The several types of machines used for testing abrasion resistance work on different principles, and the results obtained on the different machines cannot be compared. Some test machines use a flat abrasion action, some use a curved abrasion action, and some use a flexing motion.

Pilling takes place when a fabric has been subject to abrasion that causes fiber ends to break, migrate to the surface, and form into a small ball that clings to the surface of the fabric. Pilling is a more serious problem in strong fibers, as weaker fibers tend to break and fall off the surface of the fabric when pills are formed, whereas the stronger fibers do not break away and the pills stay on the surface of the cloth.

Absorbency

The ability of a fiber to absorb or take water into itself affects many aspects of its use. The ability of a bone-dry fiber to absorb moisture is called *moisture regain.* In calculating the properties of textile fibers, textile technologists will take a sample of fibers or fabric, dry it thoroughly, and return the sample to a controlled atmosphere in which temperature and humidity are accurately maintained at a temperature of 70 degrees F. and 65 per cent relative humidity. The amount of moisture that is taken up by the sample is then measured. *Saturation regain* is measured at 95 to 100 per cent relative humidity.

A fiber that permits some moisture absorption is comfortable to wear, especially in hot weather. Absorbent fibers accept dyes and special finishes readily and are easy to launder. On the other hand, fibers that absorb moisture readily dry slowly and may be stained by waterborne soil.

Some fibers *adsorb* moisture rather than absorb it. When water is adsorbed, it is held on the surface of the fiber rather than being taken into the fiber itself. If such fibers have a low moisture regain, they dry more quickly than absorbent fibers and stain less readily. *Wicking* takes place when moisture travels along the surface of the fiber but is not absorbed into the fiber. Most synthetics have low absorbency, but some also have wicking properties that make them more comfortable to wear, since perspiration can travel to the surface of the fiber where it can evaporate.

The strength of some fibers is affected by the moisture that they contain. Cotton, for example, is stronger when wet than when dry, whereas rayon is weaker wet than dry. For the consumer this means that handling some fabrics during laundering may require greater care. For the manufacturer, it means that processing of fibers during dyeing or finishing must be modified.

Electrical Conductivity

Electrical conductivity is the ability of a fiber to carry or transfer electrical charges. Fabrics with low or poor conductivity build up electrical charges with

[6] J. Pizzuto, *Fabric Science* (New York: Fairchild Publications, Inc., 1974), p. 307.

the result that these fabrics cling or produce electrical shocks. Many synthetic fibers have poor conductivity, and when several layers of clothing of low electrical conductivity are worn, the problem of charge buildup is aggravated.

Poor conductivity is related to low moisture regain. Water is an excellent conductor of electricity, and fibers with good absorbency are not as likely to build up static electricity as those that are nonabsorbent. Furthermore, some fibers with fairly good moisture absorbency but poor conductivity display static buildup and fabrics "cling" only when weather conditions are dry. Treatments given to fabrics to decrease static accumulation involve finishes that enable fibers to hold moisture on the surface or to absorb more moisture. Some man-made fibers are modified in structure during manufacture so as to increase electrical conductivity.

Dimensional Stability

Dimensional stability results when fibers neither stretch nor shrink. Stretching is related to elastic recovery, as fibers with good elastic recovery retain their shape. Shrinkage is a decrease in the length of fibers and may be accompanied by an increase in the width of the fiber.

Many fabrics are subject to *relaxation shrinkage* after they have been stretched and distorted during manufacture. These fabrics, which may be made of fibers that are inherently dimensionally stable, become elongated during weaving and/or finishing, then relax to their natural size after the first few launderings. Fibers or fabrics display *progressive shrinkage* if they continue to shrink each time they are washed.

Synthetic fibers that are thermoplastic or heat sensitive may shrink when subjected to heat. Special treatment with heat called *heat setting* can, however, be used to set the fiber and make it dimensionally stable. The synthetic fibers or fabrics that have been heat-set do not shrink unless the heat setting temperature is exceeded.

Effect of Heat

Textile products may be subjected to heat not only during manufacture and processing but also in use. In home care, for example, fabrics may be pressed or dried in a hot drier. The way in which various fibers respond to the application of heat depends upon their chemical composition. Many synthetic fibers soften or melt at various temperatures. Cellulosic and protein fibers scorch or turn brown. The specific behavior exhibited by each fiber will, of course, determine the way in which the fiber must be handled during manufacture and use.

Synthetic fibers are said to be thermoplastic fibers because they soften or melt on exposure to heat. This characteristic is used to advantage in the manufacturing of some textile products because the application of the right amount of heat will permanently set pleats or shape into the fabric. Careful control of heat causes physical changes to take place within the fiber that alters its form, thereby establishing a permanent shape. In fabrics made from thermoplastic fibers, heat may be used to fuse seams and make buttonholes.

Flammability

Some fibers ignite and burn, some smoulder, and others are noncombustible. Fibers that burn when they are held in a direct flame and stop burning when the flame is removed are designated self-extinguishing.

Burning of small quantities of textile fibers may be used as a means of differentiating one fiber group from another. Although precise identification of individual fibers cannot be made by burning, burning can help establish the general fiber group to which the fiber belongs. Cellulosic fibers, for example, exhibit flammability characteristics much like that of paper, protein fibers burn in a manner similar to hair, and some synthetics melt when they burn. The odor produced when a fiber burns and the kind of ash that remains after burning may also aid in the identification of the fiber.

The flammability of textile fibers may be related to their selection for use in particular products. Certain fibers are inherently noncombustible whereas others exhibit flame-retardant or flame-resistant properties. Glass fiber draperies are often used in public places because they are noncombustible, thereby decreasing the hazards of fires. Special finishes are applied to fabrics to retard flammability. Children's sleepwear and certain household products, such as carpets and mattresses, must, by law, be tested to determine whether they pass established test standards relating to flammability.

OTHER TEXTILE PROPERTIES

Chemical Reactivity and Resistance

The chemical reactivity and resistance of textile fibers are discussed at length in the next chapter. Many of the substances used in the manufacture of fibers, in their finishing, and in the care of fabrics in the home are chemical in nature. Therefore, the behavior of textiles when they are exposed to these chemical substances is important to the consumer as well as to the textile technologist.

Sensitivity to Micro-organisms and Insects

Some fibers support the growth of micro-organisms (such as molds or mildew) that will deteriorate the fibers. Others may permit such bacterial growth without damage to the fabric. Still other fibers do not support bacterial growth at all. Fiber characteristics in this respect will affect the choice of fibers for certain uses. Boat sails made of cotton are subject to the conditions favorable to the development of mildew when they become wet. Synthetics, which resist mildew, thus compete favorably with cotton in making sails for boats. Mildew will develop on some fabrics if they are stored in warm, dark, damp areas.

Carpet beetles, clothes moths, and silverfish are the most common insect pests that attack textile fibers. Special finishes may be given some fabrics to make them resistant to insects. Proper care and storage of susceptible fabrics can prevent insect damage.

Sensitivity to Environmental Conditions

A number of general environmental conditions may have an adverse effect on textile fibers. These include exposure to sunlight and air pollution. For example, many fabrics lose strength after long exposure to sunlight, whereas others may be discolored. Acetate fibers may be discolored by air pollution, and some fabrics lose strength or degrade as they age.

Interrelatedness of Fiber Characteristics

The particular qualities that distinguish one textile fiber from another result from the combination of the characteristics that have been discussed. No one single fiber characteristic stands alone, but each property contributes to, and modifies, fiber behavior. (Fiber properties are further changed or modified by yarn and fabric.) For example, a fiber might have good tensile strength, but poor abrasion resistance. This fiber would, therefore, be less serviceable than a fiber of moderate strength with better abrasion resistance. Another fiber might possess excellent abrasion resistance but have poor resiliency, or poor elastic recovery. *In short, it is the sum of its qualities or characteristics that determines the usefulness of a fiber.*

Some of the negative qualities of fibers can be overcome through special finishes or processing. A finish is a treatment given to a fiber, yarn, or fabric in order to enhance or alter some of its qualities. It is possible to treat wool fabrics so that they become mothproof, or to treat cotton so that it gains in luster and in strength. Some finishes increase absorbency, and/or resilience, whereas others decrease flammability. Special texturizing processes for man-made yarns can increase the elasticity of the yarn or decrease pilling.

RELATION OF CARE PROCEDURES TO PROPERTIES

Care procedures that are appropriate for fabrics are determined by an evaluation of the behavior of the fiber in relation to many of the factors discussed earlier in this chapter. Laundering or dry cleaning, ironing, and storage procedures must be determined by taking into account the reaction of the fiber to the chemical substances used in home and professional cleaning, sensitivity to heat, and resistance to micro-organisms, insects, and environmental conditions. The latter consideration affects the type of care that is necessary in the storage of textiles.

PERMANENT CARE LABELING REQUIREMENTS

Since July, 1972, wearing apparel and fabrics sold by the yard must carry a permanently affixed label giving instructions for the care of this item. House-hold textiles are exempt from the ruling, as are items that sell for less than

$3 retail, footwear, headgear, and hand coverings. Also excluded from this requirement are items that, because of their appearance, would be marred by a label, and items, such as a sheer blouse, in which there is no place to affix a label inconspicuously.

The care label must be placed so that it is readily accessible to the user. For piece goods the label is given to the customer at the time of purchase. If garments are sold in packages in which the care instructions are not readily visible, the manufacturer is required to repeat the instructions on the packaging material.

When the law was first enacted, many complaints were made because of the lack of clarity of some labels. For example, one label that confused the public and outraged dry cleaners read "Dry-clean only. Do not use petroleum solvents, or the coin-operated method of dry cleaning." Dry cleaners pointed out that this instruction eliminated both coin-operated cleaning and most professional dry cleaners who generally use petroleum solvents. Dry cleaners have also complained because many of the items that are labeled "machine washable" can also be dry cleaned. If the label makes no mention of dry cleaning, customers may launder items they would normally dry-clean, assuming that dry cleaning is not safe. Sometimes manufacturers place the labels in positions that are uncomfortable for the wearer, leading the wearer to clip out the label and lose the care instructions.

Recommended References

CHAPMAN, C. B. *Fibres*. Plainfield, N.J.: Textile Book Service, 1974.

COOK, J. G. *Handbook of Textile Fibers*, vols. 1 and 2; Watford, England; Merrow Textile Books, 1975.

Encyclopedia of Textiles, American Fabrics. Englewood Cliffs, N.J.: Prentice-Hall, Inc., 1972.

HEARLE, J. W. S., and R. H. PETERS. *Fiber Structures*. London: Butterworth & Co., 1963.

HOLLEN, N. and J. SADDLER, *Textiles*. New York: Macmillan Publishing Co., Inc., 1973.

JOSEPH, M. *Introductory Textile Science*. New York: Holt, Rinehart, and Winston, Inc., 1972.

LaBARTHE, J. *Elements of Textiles*. New York: Macmillan Publishing Co., Inc., 1975.

LINTON, G. E. *Applied Textiles: The Modern Textile and Apparel Dictionary*. Plainfield, N.J.: Textile Book Service, 1972.

LYLE, D. S. *Modern Textiles*. New York: John Wiley & Sons, Inc., 1976.

MONCRIEFF, R. W. *Man-Made Fibres*. New York: John Wiley & Sons, Inc., 1975.

POTTER, M. D. and B. P. CORBMAN. *Textiles, Fiber to Fabric*. New York: McGraw Hill Book Co., 1967 5th ed.

2

THE CHEMISTRY OF TEXTILES

Those who undertake an intensive study of textile science will need to develop a solid background in organic chemistry. Many introductory courses in textiles, however, do not have chemistry prerequisites. It is, therefore, the purpose of this chapter to explore certain quite elementary concepts that relate to the chemistry of textiles and that are basic to a more complete understanding of the behavior of textiles and textile products.

In Chapter 1, a number of physical properties of textiles were outlined. It is the chemical structure of each fiber that determines what its physical characteristics will be. All matter is made up of combinations of one or more of some one hundred elements. An *element* is a substance that cannot be broken down any further by chemical means. "It might be compared to a primary color that is composed of nothing but itself."[1]

All textile fibers except glass, metal fibers, and asbestos are organic in nature. An organic material—by chemical definition—is one that contains the chemical element carbon. In natural fibers the chemical construction of the fiber has been determined by nature, whereas the structures of synthetic and regenerated fibers have been "engineered" by textile chemists.

The basic building block of an element is the *atom,* which is the smallest amount of an element that can exist. Atoms, however, do not generally exist in isolation, but can combine into larger units called *molecules.* In turn, matter, even small bits of simple substances, is composed of many millions of molecules. Each atom of an element can combine with only a limited number of atoms of other elements. Chemists, who call this combining capacity *valence,* have established the combining capacity of each element, which is expressed as an integer (1, 2, 3, 4, . . .). Oxygen, for example, has a valence of two, that is, it can combine with up to two other elements; hydrogen, which has a valence of one, can combine with only one other element; and carbon with a valence of four can combine with as many as four other elements. One molecule of water, for example, is made up of one atom of oxygen, which has two bonding points

[1]H. Mark, *Giant Molecules* (New York: Time, Inc., 1966), p. 10.

available, in combination with two atoms of hydrogen, each of which has one bonding point.

As mentioned previously, almost all fibers are organic and all organic compounds contain carbon together with a few other elements such as hydrogen, oxygen, nitrogen, the halogens (fluorine, chlorine, bromine, and iodine) and sulfur. Carbon with four valence points offers opportunity for combinations with many other elements. "The carbon atom can be imagined as a small ball with four arms sticking out of it . . . these arms represent carbon's valence bonds. Each one is a point of attachment, it can (and readily does) grasp the valence arm of another atom."[2]

A carbon atom can combine with another carbon atom by using one, two, or three of its valence points. When each carbon atom uses one valence, the bond that forms is called a single bond. When each carbon atom uses two of its valence points, a double bond is formed, and when three valence points are used from each carbon atom, a triple bond obtains. These second and third bonds between carbon atoms are very reactive. This property of carbon compounds can be used in forming new compounds by breaking some double or triple bonds between carbons in order to add on new elements. The single bond between the carbon atoms remains after this alteration takes place.

There are many thousands of different organic compounds, and all made from a relatively small number of elements. Dr. Bruce Hartsuch used the following analogy to describe organic compounds. ". . . we realize that we can take a very few types of building materials and construct an almost unlimited number of houses. All these houses differ from each other in only a very few things—the kind of structural elements, the number of them, and their arrangement with respect to each other . . . [likewise] organic compounds differ from each other not only in the number of the elements in the molecule, but also in the arrangement of the elements."[3]

The arrangement of atoms within the molecule may take a variety of forms. The most common form of molecules with which the textile chemist deals is a linear, chainlike arrangement as in the following:

Carbon to carbon to carbon to carbon

$$\longrightarrow \qquad \longrightarrow \qquad \longrightarrow \qquad \longrightarrow$$

Not only the elements that make up the molecule but also the way in which these elements are arranged determine the behavior of a specific compound. The structure of the molecule, its elements and their arrangements, are so important to the organic chemist that chemists make diagrammatic representations or formulas of the molecules. These formulas, a kind of chemical shorthand, show the positions occupied by all of the elements.

Signs and symbols represent elements and the ways in which they connect. Each of the elements has an abbreviation or symbol, usually the first letter or a combination of several letters found in the name of the element. The symbol for carbon is abbreviated C; oxygen, O; hydrogen, H; chlorine, Cl; and so on.

[2] Ibid., p. 52.

[3] B. Hartsuch, *Introduction to Textile Chemistry* (New York: John Wiley & Sons, Inc., 1950), p. 19.

The connections between elements may be shown by drawing a line between the elements:

$$C—C—C—C—\text{ and so on.}$$

If a double bond is formed between two elements, a double line may be drawn: $C=C$.

A six-carbon ring formation called a benzene ring may sometimes be shown by a simple diagram, without showing all of the carbons, as follows:

The double lines represent double bonds between carbon atoms. This compound is part of so many organic compounds that the shortened form of the formula is generally utilized by the textile chemist; it is a convention that the corners of these geometric figures represent carbon atoms.

In order to simplify the formulas somewhat more, other combinations of elements that are readily recognizable to the chemist may be written without the lines showing chemical bonding. For example, a combination of oxygen with hydrogen to form a common group, the hydroxyl group, is written as $-OH$. When more than one atom of an element is required for a compound in which the bonds and specific position of the element is not shown, a small number is written to the right and slightly below the symbol of the element. The formula for water, for example, is written H_2O, showing two atoms of hydrogen and one of oxygen. H_2SO_4 (sulfuric acid) contains two atoms of hydrogen, one of sulfur, and four of oxygen.

So far the formulas used to illustrate the "shorthand" of chemistry have been simple. Formulas of organic compounds, however, are rarely simple. The formula for cellulose, the basic material of which cotton is composed, is shown as the chemist would write it.

$$\begin{array}{c} \text{TEXTILE MOLECULAR STRUCTURE} \end{array}$$

The chemistry of textile fibers is but one branch of the field of organic chemistry. Much of organic chemistry is concerned with fairly small, complex molecules, few of which are composed of as many as one hundred atoms, whereas textile materials are composed of giant molecules known as *macro-*

molecules. Analysis of these large molecules shows that they are composed of molecular subunits containing perhaps two to twenty atoms, and that the large molecules were built up from many of these smaller units joined together. In textile fibers the molecules join together in a very special way, into long chains. The individual, subunit compounds are called *monomers* and the long-chain macromolecules made from the monomers are called *polymers.* In cellulose, for instance, the subunits are derived from glucose. Interestingly, the subunits of the constituents of another well-known macromolecule, starch, are also derived from glucose. Starch and cellulose have completely different properties, however, because the subunits are bonded to each other differently; starch is not fibrous but can be digested by humans, whereas the opposite is true for cellulose.

POLYMERIZATION

The formation of polymers, or *polymerization,* is accomplished through the joining of monomers, one to the other. In the formation of polymers, several intermediate steps take place. Two monomers (small, nonpolymerized compounds) may join to form a *dimer* (two-monomer molecule), a dimer and a monomer join to form a *trimer* (three-monomer molecule), two dimers join to form a *tetramer* (four-molecule structure), and so on.

Homopolymers are polymers made of the same substance. Not all polymers are made of uniform material. When monomers of different substances (mixed monomers) are joined together into long-chain structures, a *copolymer* is formed. Copolymerization is likely to be utilized when one polymer exhibits a negative quality in homopolymer form that can be overcome by combination with another substance.

Graft-polymers are made by attaching monomers onto long-chain polymers. The long chain forms the base structure, rather like the trunk of a tree, with the side chains branching off. Grafting makes possible the addition of qualities not present in the "mother" fiber. Grafting of monomers, for example, can reduce static electricity buildup, improve dyeability, improve soil resistance, increase strength, or decrease shrinkage. Grafting is a relatively new technique and, though not yet widely used, will undoubtedly be further developed for a variety of applications.

Linear polymers are formed either by *addition polymerization* or by *condensation polymerization.* In condensation polymerization, as a small molecule (usually water, ammonia, or hydrogen chloride) is eliminated, monomers join other molecules.

$$\text{monomer} + \text{monomer} \longrightarrow \text{dimer} + \text{water (eliminated)}$$
$$\text{dimer} + \text{dimer} \longrightarrow \text{tetramer} + \text{water (eliminated)}$$

Monomers may link up with monomers, monomers with polymers, polymers with polymers, and so on to form a growing chain, with the elimination of water or another compound during the process. Examples of this process are, among the natural fibers, cellulose from glucose, and among the man-made fibers, nylon from its components.

Figure 2-1. Amorphous arrangement of polymers within fiber.

Addition polymerization differs from condensation polymerization in that no compound is split off. Monomers with the capacity to react (unsaturated monomers) can add to each other in a chemically effected chain reaction to join into a long-chain molecule. This is generally accomplished under conditions of high pressure, high temperature, and in the presence of a *catalyst* (a substance that does not take part in the reaction but which facilitates the reaction):

$$\begin{array}{c} \text{monomer} \\ + \\ \text{activator} \end{array} = \begin{array}{c} \text{reactive} \\ \text{monomer} \\ + \\ \text{monomer} \end{array} = \begin{array}{c} \text{reactive} \\ \text{dimer} \\ + \\ \text{monomer} \end{array} \longrightarrow polymer$$

An example of this process is the polymerization of acrylonitrile to create acrylic fibers. Acrylonitrile is a nitrogen-containing three-carbon molecule.

This, in highly simplified terms, is part of the chemical process that takes place in the manufacture of synthetic fibers. Most of the specific processes utilized by companies to make their trademarked textile fibers are carefully guarded secrets. Such confidential processes are known as *proprietary processes*. Textile chemists, however, can make reasonably accurate estimates of the processes used by each company by reading research reports and by analyses of the properties and physical structure of the fibers.

Polymers and Their Arrangement

The molecules within each polymer are held together by chemical bonds formed as monomer joins monomer. But each individual fiber is made of many chemically alike polymer molecules that may occupy different positions within the fiber. The arrangement of polymers within the fiber may be either random or parallel. A random or unorganized arrangement of long-chain molecules creates an *amorphous* area within the fiber. (See Figure 2.1.) Orderly, parallel arrangement of polymers is known as *crystallinity*. Crystalline arrangements of molecules may lie in a variety of positions relative to the fiber shape. However, if the crystalline polymers are parallel to the length of the fiber, they are said to be *oriented*. (See Figure 2.2.)

Figure 2-2. Crystalline arrangement of molecules in fiber, with molecules oriented to fiber length.

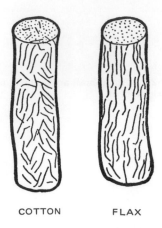

COTTON   FLAX

Figure 2-3. Orientation of molecules in cotton and flax. Reprinted from *Man-Made Fibres* by R. W. Moncrieff p. 74. Courtesy of R. W. Moncrieff.

Most fibers possess largely crystalline structures, but also have some amorphous areas. Textile chemists believe that amorphous areas are weaker than crystalline areas, and that those fibers with the highest levels of crystallinity are the strongest fibers. A high degree of orientation of crystalline areas (that is, the crystalline areas lie parallel to the length of the fiber) is said to produce still greater strength.

Moncrieff illustrates this concept by contrasting the structures of cotton and flax.

Molecules of cellulose which constitute both cotton and flax are similar . . . the reason for the difference in the physical properties of cotton and flax lies in the arrangement of the molecules. In flax, they are highly oriented, they are very well parallelised, and they lie side by side along the length of the fibre; in cotton some of the fibres lie parallel to the fibre axis, but quite a large proportion of them lie at an appreciable angle to the fibre axis. [See Figure 2.3.] When tension is applied to the fibre nearly all of the molecules in flax take their fair share of the load, and a high breaking load is the result; but in the case of cotton, the strain has to be taken by those molecules that are facing in the right direction, i.e., roughly parallel to the fibre axis—those molecules lying approximately at right angles to the fibre axis take little or none of the load. Consequently the tenacity of cotton is lower than that of flax.[4]

Some man-made fibers are quite amorphous in structure when they are formed. By stretching or "drawing" the fiber, these amorphous areas can be made more parallel and crystalline. Stretching the fiber causes the polymers within the fiber to arrange themselves along the direction of stretch.

Figure 2-4. Effect of drawing of fibers on polymer orientation.

Internal Bonds or Forces

In addition to the internal bonding that holds the individual molecules together to form the long-chain molecule, there are attractive forces that hold the polymers together within the fiber. These forces are of two primary types: *Van der Waals* forces and *hydrogen bonding*.

Van der Waals forces are relatively weak attractions based on proximity of the molecules. Chapman points out that although the forces of attraction of this type may be small individually, the cumulative effect of a large number of groups of polymers is significant. When molecules are crystalline and highly oriented, the strength of these forces is enhanced, because there is a greater area over which the polymer molecules may be in close contact.[5]

Hydrogen bonding in well-oriented fibers is a powerful force for binding molecules together. Hydrogen bonding occurs in situations where one atom of

[4]R. W. Moncrieff, *Man-Made Fibres* (New York: John Wiley & Sons, Inc., 1975), pp. 67, 68.

[5]C. B. Chapman, *Fibres* (Plainfield, N.J.: Textile Book Service, 1974), p. 19.

Figure 2-5. Cross-linking of molecules within fiber.

hydrogen links together two other atoms. In order for hydrogen bonds to be formed, molecules must be packed closely together, as occurs in textile fibers with closely packed, highly oriented molecules. Furthermore, the appropriate reactive elements must be present in the molecules. Reactive atoms are nitrogen, oxygen, and fluorine, which are small electronegative elements. Hydrogen bonds are present in natural cellulose and protein fibers, as well as in manufactured fibers that contain hydrogen and appropriate reactive atoms.

When long polymers are attracted to parallel long polymers by Van der Waals forces, hydrogen bonding, or both, fibers are stronger than if short polymers are attracted to short polymers. In longer molecules, the area over which these forces bond is greater. When the area of attraction between molecules is greater, then more force is required to break the cohesive forces. This generalization is true only up to a certain point, however. Chain length will eventually reach the point where any further increase in the length of the chains will not result in an increase in strength. At the same time, no decrease in strength takes place either.

Cross-Linkages

A third means by which molecules are held together is by *cross-linking*. Cross-linking is the attachment of one long chain molecule to another by covalent chemical bonds; these are bonds of a strength equivalent to that along the polymer chain. A small amount of cross-linking in fibers will produce such desirable properties as ability to resist creasing and increased crease recovery. In some instances, cross-linkages seem to increase chemical stability and improve resistance to attack by insects and bacteria. Wool and animal hair fibers have naturally cross-linked structures. It is thought that the cross-links in wool are one of the factors responsible for the excellent resiliency of wool.

Special chemical finishes can be used to create cross-linkages in some fibers that do not possess them naturally. Such finishes when applied to cotton, for example, improve crease resistance and wrinkle recovery, but decrease strength and abrasion resistance. It may be helpful to imagine that the cross-links serve to return the molecules to their original position within the fiber after it has been bent or folded, thus providing wrinkle recovery.

Fringed Fibril Theory

With continuous research and investigation into the chemical structure of fibers, new theories and knowledge concerning the arrangement of molecules continue to evolve. One such theory, the "fringed fibril theory," put forth by Hearle and Peters suggests that within the fiber are both highly oriented and

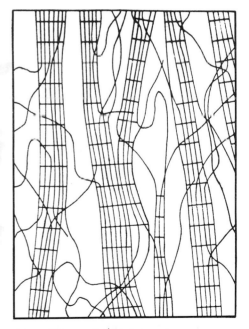

Figure 2-6. Fringed fibril structure. Reprinted from *Fiber Structures* by J. W. S. Hearle and R. H. Peters. Courtesy of Newnes-Butterworth Publishers, London, England.

Table 2.1*

Properties Common to Fibers with a High Degree of Orientation and High Crystallinity	Properties Common to Fibers with Low Degree of Orientation and Low Crystallinity
high tenacity	low tenacity
low elongation	high elongation
brittle	extremely pliable
increased luster	subdued luster
low moisture absorption	high moisture absorption
high chemical stability	low chemical stability
low dyeing affinity	high dyeing affinity
may have less pleasant handle	warm, soft handle

*R. W. Moncrieff, *Man-Made Fibres* (New York: John Wiley & Sons, Inc., 1975), p. 100 ff.

amorphous regions. "Polymer molecules may pass from a crystalline to a noncrystalline region and may also pass through a second (and more) crystalline region. Thus we develop a picture of small, ordered crystalline zones which are separated by less well-ordered amorphous regions, but which are all connected together by a random network of polymer molecules."[6]

RELATIONSHIP OF FIBER STRUCTURE TO PROPERTIES

To examine in depth the variations of fiber structure as they relate to the various properties of fibers is beyond the scope of this book. The following summary of properties common to fibers with a high or low degree of orientation may, however, be useful.

These characteristics are those associated with the extremes of molecule orientation and crystallization. Polymeric fibers possess both amorphous and crystalline regions and show characteristics that fall somewhere between these extremes.

Effect of Side Chains

Although most polymers are of straight-line formation, some polymeric substances react to form side chains as well. These side chains cause the molecules to function differently than either the long, straight molecules or the cross-linked molecules. Such polymers do not crystallize as readily as regular unbranched polymers, because the side chains prevent the polymer chains from coming in close enough contact for Van der Waals attractive forces to operate.

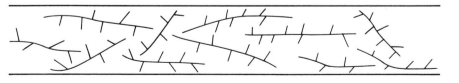

Figure 2-7. Polymers with side chains within fiber.

[6]Ibid., p. 20.

Such side chain polymers are sometimes formed purposely in the synthesis of elastic fibers or to introduce or alter other properties not inherent to a polymer.

CHEMICAL SUBSTANCES COMMONLY USED WITH TEXTILES

Fibers are composed of long-chain molecules or polymers that are arranged in positions roughly parallel to the lengthwise direction of the fiber. If one were to diagram each of the smaller molecules from which the polymers are formed, one would see precisely the elements of which they are made. When the chemist sees a molecular diagram or formula, he recognizes that there are "functional chemical groups" within the polymers, that is, places at which chemical reactions are likely to take place. Some of these reactions take place when textiles come into contact with substances used in processing or in everyday use.

Materials with which textile fibers come into contact might be divided, roughly, into these basic groups: (1) materials used in processing fibers or fabrics, such as bleaches or dyestuffs, (2) special finishing materials used to alter fabric characteristics such as crease resistance, soil resistance, flame retardancy, and so on, and (3) materials used in home or professional care or cleaning of fabrics, such as soaps, detergents, cleaning solvents, and moth repellants. Some of these substances are organic (having carbon in the compounds) and some are inorganic. Some are acid, some are alkaline, and some are neutral. Many processes in manufacturing, finishing, and care of textiles utilize the reaction of fibers to acids or alkalis.

Acids

Acids are both strong and weak, and organic and mineral. Acids are characterized by the ability to neutralize bases or alkalis, and the ability to turn a special indicator paper, called litmus paper, from blue to red. Among the better known strong inorganic acids are sulfuric acid and hydrochloric acid. Acetic acid is a weak organic acid (more commonly known as vinegar). Other organic acids include lactic acid, present in sour milk, and ascorbic acid or vitamin C. These few examples may serve to illustrate the diversity of types of acids.

Action of Acids. The action of acids when they come into contact with various textile fibers varies not only with the type of textile fiber but also with the strength and type of the acid. It is important for the textile manufacturer to be acquainted with the effect of acids on textile fibers in order to avoid damaging fibers or fabrics during finishing. Also, some specialized textile processes rely on the action of acids on various textile fibers.

Acid hydrolysis is a chemical reaction that is important for textile fibers. Hydrolysis results in the breaking of long-chain molecules into shorter chains. In these cases, the bonds connecting the subunits are unstable to acid and the result is a loss of tensile strength. If the reaction goes on for a sufficiently long time, susceptible fibers will actually be dissolved. Cellulosic fibers are damaged by strong mineral acids and are harmed even by quite diluted concentrations of these substances. This quality is not especially important to the consumer, but is utilized in the manufacture of some man-made cellulosic fibers. For example, acid hydrolysis is used to convert short cotton fibers into a substance called oxycellulose as the first step in the manufacture of rayon.

The same reaction, in a highly controlled process, is used to make permanently stiffened sheer cotton fabrics. The acid is applied so that it breaks down the outermost layer of fabric. The outer layer softens, the reaction is stopped, and the fabric is given a hard press that forms the outer fabric layer into a smooth, clear, permanently stiffened finish.

Because dilute acids do not readily harm protein fibers (the bonds connecting the subunits are relatively stable to acid), especially wool, acid treatments can be utilized in cleaning wool of vegetable matter prior to spinning. The controlled acid solution destroys the bits of wood and burrs caught in the wool, the acid is neutralized, and the wool is left unharmed. Such processes are carried out under rigidly controlled conditions to avoid any harm to the fibers. Strong mineral acids will destroy wool fiber.

Fibers that are sensitive to the action of acids cannot be dyed in dyestuffs that require the presence of strong acids.

Alkalis

Alkalis are members of a class of substances called bases and are opposite in nature to acids. Bases react with acids to form neutral compounds. Alkalis when dissolved in water are slippery to the touch, have a bitter acrid taste, and change litmus paper from red to blue. The most important strong alkali is caustic soda or lye, known in chemical terminology as sodium hydroxide or NaOH. Sodium hydroxide is used extensively in textile and related industries in making soap, in special treatments given cotton, and in manufacturing rayon fiber. Borax, baking soda, household ammonia, and washing soda are also bases.

Action of Alkalis. Alkalis, even strong caustic alkalis at high temperature, do not harm natural cellulosic fibers. Alkalis do, however, cause radical physical changes to take place within these fibers, and, as a result, a special treatment with the alkali sodium hydroxide is sometimes given to cellulosic fibers to take advantage of these changes that improve the strength and appearance of cellulosic fibers.

Sensitivity to alkalis is important in the care of protein fibers (silk, wool, and animal hair fibers) in which the bonds between the subunits are broken by alkali. Some synthetic fibers are negatively affected by alkalis. Many strong soaps and detergents have alkali material added to increase their cleaning power. These soaps and detergents should be avoided for use with fibers that are sensitive to the action of alkaline substances.

Oxidation and Oxidizing Agents

Many fibers are not white enough in their natural state or after manufacture to permit dyes to be fully effective. These colors and/or stains accumulated during spinning and weaving are removed by the action of bleaches that causes oxygen to be added to the coloring matter by a process called oxidation. This leads to the removal of the colors and the stains.

During bleaching, coloring matter is converted into a colorless substance. However, the oxidizing agent (bleach) may also react with the fiber itself. If the fiber is sensitive to the action of the oxidizing agent, the fiber may be damaged.

Chlorine bleach is an oxidizing agent that may damage protein fibers and spandex. Chlorine bleach must be carefully controlled in bleaching cellulose fabrics, but does no appreciable harm to other fibers such as polyester or nylon. Other bleaching agents made from substances such as sodium perborate will oxidize stains without damage to fibers.

Both the consumer and the manufacturer benefit from understanding the action of oxidizing agents on different fibers.

CHEMICAL REACTIONS AND THEIR IMPORTANCE TO THE TEXTILE INDUSTRY

The textile industry is the greatest consumer of industrial chemicals of all industries known today. Some 6,500 special chemicals are now manufactured for the textile industry.[7] In addition to the chemical reactions utilized in the manufacture of fibers, of which more is said in later chapters, textile manufacturers are concerned with the chemical reactions between textile chemical specialties (known as textile auxiliaries) and textile fibers. These auxiliaries are used as cleaning agents, as chemical finishing agents, and as dyestuffs.

Cleaning agents are selected for use both on the basis of their ability to remove foreign matter from the fiber and their compatibility with the fiber. As has been mentioned earlier, strongly alkaline cleaning agents cannot be used on protein fibers because of the likelihood that these substances will degrade the fibers.

Chemical finishing agents vary widely in type and purpose. In some instances the chemicals used alter the physical appearance of the fiber without changing the chemical nature of the fiber. Mercerization is an example of such a reaction. In mercerization, cotton or linen fibers are treated with a strong alkali. The action of the alkali on the cotton causes the fibers to become stronger, more lustrous, and more chemically reactive.

In other cases, the chemicals utilized react in such a way that some parts of the chemical substance become a permanent part of the fiber structure. This is true in the case of mothproofing wool. Within the wool molecule are a number of cross-links of different chemical composition. Apparently the moth larvae attack a particular cross-link called a disulphide cross-linkage. Wool is treated with a process that first breaks the disulphide linkage, then rejoins the broken ends of the links by a short hydrocarbon residue supplied by further treatment with other chemicals. The resulting linkage is different chemically than the natural linkage and will not be attractive to moths.

[7] "Textile Chemistry." *Encyclopedia of Science and Technology* (New York: McGraw-Hill, Inc., 1971), vol. 13, p. 551.

Modern dyestuffs are chemically synthesized. In dyeing, three substances of a chemical nature are utilized: the fiber, the dyestuff, and the solvent. The solvent is the material in which the dyestuff is carried and must penetrate the fiber in order to carry the dye within the fiber. Water may be used as a solvent, or other organic substances may be used.

Dyes enter fibers most easily in the amorphous regions, then as the fiber swells from the entrance of the solvent and dye, the dyestuff spreads throughout both crystalline and amorphous regions. Fibers with highly oriented, crystalline structures are, therefore, more difficult to dye, and special dyestuffs and dyeing techniques must be utilized in order to color these fibers.

Colorfastness, or the ability of a fiber to retain the color to which it has been dyed, may require further chemical treatments. If the fiber was penetrated easily to carry the dye into the fiber, then when the fiber is laundered, water may enter as easily to carry the dye back out again. During dyeing, additional treatments are sometimes given the dyed fibers in order to transform the soluble dyestuffs into insoluble compounds within the fiber.

As with other chemical finishes, the application of dyestuffs must also take into account the effect of acids, alkalis, organic solvents, and the like on textile fibers. Protein fibers, which are always sensitive to alkali, cannot be dyed in a highly alkaline medium, and cellulosic fibers cannot be dyed by highly acid dyes.

Recommended References

BELLMEYER, F. W., Jr. *Synthetic Polymers.* Garden City, N.Y.: Doubleday & Company, Inc., 1972.

COWIE, J. M. G. *Polymers: Chemistry and Physics of Modern Materials.* New York: Intext Educational Publishers, 1973.

CHAPMAN, C. B. *Fibres.* Plainfield, N.J.: Textile Book Service, 1974.

HALL, A. J. *Handbook of Textile Finishing.* 2nd ed. New York: Chemical Publishing Co., 1957.

HARTSUCH, B. *Introduction to Textile Chemistry.* New York: John Wiley & Sons, Inc., 1950.

HEARLE, J. W. S., and R. H. PETERS. *Fiber Structures.* London: Butterworth, 1963.

KAUFFMAN, M. *Giant Molecules.* New York: Doubleday & Company, Inc., 1968.

MARK, H. ed. *Giant Molecules.* New York: Life, Inc., 1966.

MONCRIEFF, R. W. *Man-Made Fibres.* New York: John Wiley & Sons, Inc., 1975.

PETERS, R. H. *Textile Chemistry.* vol 1, New York: American Elsevier Publishing Co., 1967.

"Textile Chemistry." McGraw-Hill *Encyclopedia of Science & Technology.* vol. 13, New York: McGraw Hill, Inc., 1971, p. 551 ff.

3

NATURAL CELLULOSIC FIBERS

Cellulosic fibers are composed of natural and regenerated cellulose, or of regenerated chemical variants of cellulose. Natural cellulosic fibers are derived from a wide variety of plant sources, which are classified as follows:

1. Seed hair fibers, or those fibers that grow in a seed pod on plants.

2. Bast fibers, or those fibers that are removed from the stems of plants.

3. Leaf fibers, or those fibers that are found in the leaves of plants.

4. Miscellaneous fiber from mosses, roots, and the like.

Table 3.1

Natural Fibers	Man-made Fibers
A. *Seed Hair Fibers*	A. *Rayon*
Major Fibers	1. Viscose rayon
1. cotton	2. Cuprammonium rayon
	3. High wet-modulus rayon
Minor Fibers:	
1. kapok	B. *Modified Cellulose Fibers*
2. coir	1. acetate
	2. triacetate
B. *Bast Fibers*	3. saponified rayon**
1. flax	
2. jute	
3. ramie	
4. hemp	
C. *Leaf Fibers***	
1. abaca**	
2. sisal**	
3. henequin**	
4. pina**	
D. *Miscellaneous***	
1. Spanish moss**	
2. sacaton (root fiber)**	

**Of historical or curiosity value only.

Man-made cellulosic fibers include rayon, a regenerated cellulosic fiber and acetate and triacetate, which are modified cellulosic fibers.

Cellulose Family

Table 3.1 lists fibers of the cellulose family. Included in this list are not only those fibers that have extensive commercial production and distribution but also fibers that have little or no importance to the consumer.

Each of these cellulosic fibers possesses distinctive qualities or properties that distinguish it from others and make it especially suitable for certain end uses. Most cellulosic fibers also share a "family resemblance" in their physical and chemical properties.

In all subsequent discussions of the properties of different fibers, statements about fiber characteristics are made in relation to the characteristics of other fibers. For example, when flax is said to be a relatively strong fiber, what is meant is that in comparison with other fibers, flax is fairly strong. If the strength of flax were measured against that of a strand of steel or aluminum wire, for example, it would seem relatively weak.

GENERAL CHARACTERISTICS OF CELLULOSIC FIBERS

The following discussion summarizes the general characteristics of natural cellulosic fibers and rayon as a class or group. Cellulose acetate and cellulose triacetate are chemical variants of cellulose, and, as such, do not share in many of the "family characteristics." Their specific fiber characteristics are discussed at length later in Chapter 4.

The density of cellulosic fibers tends to be relatively high, making fabrics woven from these fibers feel comparatively heavy. Cellulosic fibers have relatively low elasticity and resilience. As a result, they wrinkle easily and do not recover from wrinkling readily. Absorbency and moisture regain are generally good. Most cellulosic fibers are, therefore, slow to dry after wetting, comfortable to wear, and easy to dye.

Cellulosic fibers are good conductors of heat and electricity. As good conductors of heat, they carry warmth away from the body and are favored for use in hot weather and warm climates. Since they conduct electricity, cellulosic fibers neither build up static electricity nor produce shocks when worn.

Cellulosic fibers tend to burn easily, with a quick, yellow flame, much as paper (which is also cellulose). Most cellulosic fibers can, however, withstand fairly high dry heat or ironing temperatures before they scorch. On an electric iron, cotton and linen settings are the highest settings on the dial.

Chemical properties of cellulosic fibers include good resistance to alkalis. Excessive bleaching will harm cellulosic fibers, although carefully controlled bleaching is less detrimental. Strong mineral acids are quite damaging, and most natural cellulosic fibers will withstand high water temperatures. Such properties permit laundering of cellulosic fibers with strong detergents, controlled bleaching, and hot water temperatures. Regenerated cellulosic fibers are more sensitive to chemicals and require more careful handling and gentle agitation with lower water temperatures.

Most insects do not attack cellulosic fibers. However, silverfish are likely to attack heavily starched cellulosic fabrics. Most cellulosic fabrics are susceptible to attack by fungi, especially mildew. Extended exposure to sunlight tends to damage the fibers.

Seed Hair Fibers

Seed hair fibers belong to a class in which the fibers grow from the seeds that are formed in pods on certain plants. The most widely used seed hair fiber is cotton. Other seed hair fibers include kapok, coir, milkweed, and cattail.

Cotton

HISTORY

The cotton plant appears to have been native to the area known today as India and Pakistan, and the cultivation and use of cotton is thought to have begun there. Eventually the use of cotton spread into other areas in which the climate was compatible with its cultivation. Some archeologists and anthropologists believe that cotton was imported into South America from Asia during prehistoric times. Others, who point out that cotton plants of South America differ genetically from the Asian varieties, believe that cotton cultivation and spinning developed independently in the Western Hemisphere.

The earliest evidence of actual woven cotton fabrics was found in India during the excavation of the city called Mohenjo-Daro. The date assigned to these fabrics was 3000 B.C., so that we know that the use of cotton for fabrics was well established by this date. Fabrics of comparable age have been unearthed in excavations of Peruvian grave sites.[1]

Historians note that among the fabrics made in India were cottons so fine that they were called by names such as "flowing water" or "evening dew." One pound of cotton could be made into yarn 250 miles in length.[2] The species of cotton fiber from which these fabrics were made is now extinct and their fineness has never been equaled.

From India, cotton cultivation spread west to Egypt and east into China and the South Pacific. Roman writers speak of importing cotton fabrics from Egypt and the East. Since cotton cannot be cultivated in the cooler European climates, cotton fiber and fabrics used in the Middle Ages had to be imported. Because Europeans had never seen cotton plants, the belief was widespread that cotton came from the fleece of a beast that was half-plant and half-animal.[3]

[1] M. D. C. Crawford, *The Heritage of Cotton.* New York: G. P. Putnam's Sons, 1924.

[2] W. Born, "Spindle and Distaff as Forerunners of the Spinning Wheel," *CIBA Review,* (December 1939), p. 982.

[3] Frank Anderson, "Medieval Beasties," *Natural History* (January 1973), p. 61.

One of the purposes of Columbus' voyage was to find a shorter trade route to India in order to import the fine Indian cotton fabrics. When Columbus found the Indians of Santo Domingo wearing cotton garments he was convinced that he had, indeed, discovered a new route to India.

Large-scale cotton cultivation in the American colonies is thought to have begun as early as 1556 when cotton seeds were planted in Florida. By 1616, colonists in Virginia were growing cotton along the James River.[4]

The southern states of the United States proved especially hospitable to the cultivation of cotton, and the production of cotton soon became a major factor in the economy of the South. As the United States spread westward, the cultivation of cotton also spread west in those areas where the climate was suitable. Today the major cotton producing states are Alabama, Arizona, Arkansas, California, Georgia, Louisiana, Mississippi, Missouri, New Mexico, North Carolina, Oklahoma, South Carolina, Tennessee, and Texas.

ECONOMIC IMPORTANCE OF COTTON PRODUCTION

Worldwide, more cotton is used than any other single fiber. In 1975 almost 12,000 million metric tons of cotton were produced. By comparison, the next largest quantity of fiber produced was polyester, of which somewhat more than 3,400 metric tons were made.[5]

The United States produced about 15 per cent of the world's cotton or an estimated 8,500,000 bales in 1976. This is the third largest production of any single country, and is exceeded only by the USSR which produced more than 12,000,000 bales and mainland China which produced 11,000,000 bales. Five other countries had 1975–76 cotton crops in excess of 1 million bales each, namely: Brazil, India, Pakistan, Turkey, and Egypt.[6]

Although much of the cotton produced in the United States is used domestically, cotton is an important export crop as well. United States exports of cotton in 1974 were valued at nearly $1.3 billion.[7] The cotton industry estimates that more than 5 million Americans live wholly or in very substantial part on incomes earned directly from cotton, including 1.3 million who farm, gin, store, and/or market cotton.[8]

BOTANICAL INFORMATION

Cotton fiber is removed from the boll or seed pod that grows on a plant of the botanical genus, *gossypium.* Cotton is a member of the mallow family, related

[4] *The Story of Cotton,* National Cotton Council of America, Memphis, Tennessee, p. 2.

[5] *Textile Organon* (June 1976), pp. 65, 69.

[6] *Textile Organon* (October 1976), p. 145.

[7] *Cotton, the First Fiber.* Booklet published by National Cotton Council of America, Memphis, Tennessee.

[8] *Cotton Today,* National Cotton Council of America, Memphis, Tennessee, p. 6.

to the common garden hollyhock. The fibers are single plant cells that develop as an elongation of the outer layer of cells of the cotton seed. These seed hairs are called *lint*. A secondary growth of much shorter fibers accompanies the growth of cotton lint. These fibers, which are too short to be spun into yarn, are called *linters*.

TYPES OF COTTON

Cotton fibers are sometimes classified according to the length to which they grow. These are as follows:

1. Short, staple fiber: 3/8 to 3/4 inches in length. Short fibers come from Asiatic species of cotton that are both short and coarse.

2. Intermediate-length staple fiber: 13/16 to 1 1/4 inches in length. The variety known as American Upland is of intermediate length and coarseness. This variety of cotton makes up by far the largest quantity of cotton fiber grown in the United States.

3. Long staple fiber: 1 1/2 to 2 1/2 inches. This includes varieties known as Sea Island, Egyptian, and Pima (or American-Egyptian), all of which are used for good-quality cotton fabric. Peruvian and Brazilian fibers also fall into this classification. However, the Peruvian variety known as Tanguis has a slight crimp and rougher feel, somewhat like that of wool with which it is sometimes blended.

Figure 3-1. (*opposite, top*) Cotton flower; (*opposite, bottom*) closed boll; and (*above*) mature open boll. **Courtesy of the United States Department of Agriculture.**

CULTIVATION

For optimum growth the cotton plant requires a warm climate, with adequate rain or other water supply. A favorable distribution of rainfall is more important than the quantity of rain because the plant needs plenty of moisture during the growing season and warm, dry weather during harvesting. For this reason, cotton is also successfully grown in warm, dry climates with adequate water for irrigation.

Blooms appear on the plant from 80 to 110 days after planting. The blooms are creamy white or yellow in color when they first appear. From twelve hours to three days after the blooms have appeared, they have changed in color to pink, lavender, or red and have fallen off the plant, leaving the developing boll on the stem. Fifty to eighty days later the pod has matured, the pressure of the full-grown fiber has caused the pod to burst, and the cotton is ready to be picked. Failure to pick the ripened bolls promptly will detract from the quality of the fiber.

Picking of the cotton is done either by hand or machine. In the United States a great deal of cotton production and harvesting has been mechanized, but in underdeveloped parts of the world much of the cotton planting, cultivation, and harvesting is done by hand.

Once the cotton fiber has been picked it must be separated from the cotton seeds. This process is done by ginning. The cotton gin removes the fibers from the seeds, which are used in making cotton seed oil and fertilizer. Cotton linters, too short for spinning, are utilized in making rayons and acetates; as stuffing materials for mattresses, upholstery, and pillows; and in nontextile materials such as paper.

The quality of cotton fiber varies not only with the length and variety of fiber but also in regard to physical condition from ginning; the amount of vegetable matter, dirt, and sand present; and color.

To provide an objective means of evaluating cotton quality, the Department of Agriculture establishes a grading system in which color, brightness, the amount of foreign matter, and ginning preparation are evaluated. The standards for grading are revised from time to time. The following nine original grades were established:

1. Middling. Fair.

2. Strict Good Middling.

3. Good Middling.

4. Strict Middling.

5. Middling—all grades are compared with this type.

6. Strict Low Middling.

7. Low Middling.

8. Strict Good Ordinary.

9. Good Ordinary.

Current grading systems use only numbers 2 through 8 of these classifications, with gradations between each number, which permit up to twenty-four different classifications. An alternative method of grading is based on the micronaire fineness of the fiber, or the weight in micrograms per inch of fiber.

Individuals who work in the cotton industry in jobs where they come into contact with a great deal of cotton dust often develop a serious lung disease called "brown lung." This condition, known medically as *byssinosis*, results from inhaling the dirt and other contaminants present in cotton fiber. Research is underway to try to find methods of production that will eliminate this illness.

PROPERTIES OF COTTON

Physical Appearance

Color of Fiber. Cotton fiber is generally white or yellowish in color.

Shape. The length of an individual cotton fiber is usually from 1,000 to 3,000 times its diameter. The diameter may range from 16 to 20 microns. In

Figure 3-2. Cotton harvesting machine that picks five bales of cotton per hour. Photograph courtesy of the United States Department of Agriculture.

cross section the shape of the fiber varies from a U-shape to a nearly circular form. Seen in microscopic cross section, the fiber displays a hollow, central canal known as the *lumen*. During growth this channel carries nutrients to the developing fiber.

The fiber grows much as a tree does, with concentric rings of growth. Each layer is made up of small fibrils, or minute fibrous segments. As these fibril layers are deposited, they form a complex series of spirals that reverse direction at some points. The reverse spiral, fibril structure of cotton gives it some small degree of elasticity and is responsible for its twisted shape. The mature cotton fiber has a natural twist, called *convolutions,* which can be seen clearly when the lengthwise direction of the fiber is examined with a microscope. This twist gives the magnified cotton fiber the appearance of a twisted ribbon and it makes cotton easier to spin. Long, staple cotton has about 300 twists per inch;

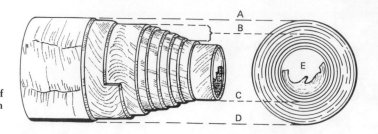

Figure 3-3. Diagram showing the structure of cotton fiber. Courtesy of the National Cotton Council of America.

short cotton has less than 200. In spite of the twisted shape of the cotton fiber, it is relatively uniform in its size.

Luster.   The luster of cotton is low, unless it has been given special treatments or finishes. This is, in part, a consequence of the natural twist of cotton and its resultant uneven surface that breaks up and scatters light rays reflected from the fiber surface.

Other Properties

Strength.   Strength of cotton on a scale of high, medium, and low would rank as medium. (Tenacity is 3 to 4.9 g/d.) In comparison with other cellulosic fibers, cotton is weaker than flax and stronger than rayon.

Cotton is 10 to 20 per cent stronger when wet than dry. Its strength can be increased by a process called *mercerization* in which yarns or fabrics held under tension are treated with controlled solutions of sodium hydroxide. The alkali causes the fiber to swell, straighten out, and to become more lustrous and stronger.

Density and Specific Gravity.   Cotton is a fiber of relatively high density, having a specific gravity of 1.54. (Compare this with that of polyester, 1.38, or nylon at 1.14). This means that cotton fabrics will feel heavier in weight than comparable fabrics made from polyester or nylon.

Elasticity and Resilience.   Like most other cellulosic fibers, the elasticity and elastic recovery of cotton are low. Not only does cotton stretch relatively little but it also does not recover well from stretching. Its resilience is low.

As a result, cotton fabrics wrinkle easily and do not recover well from wrinkling, although they drape well; special finishes can be given to cotton to overcome this disadvantage. Unfinished cotton fabrics generally must be ironed after laundering.

Absorbency and Moisture Regain.   Cotton is an absorbent fiber. Its good absorbency makes cotton comfortable in hot weather, suitable for materials where absorbency is important (such as diapers and towels), and relatively slow to dry, because the absorbed moisture must be evaporated from the fiber. For the same reason, cotton fibers take waterborne dyes readily. The percentage moisture regain of cotton is 7 to 8 per cent.

Dimensional Stability.   Cotton fibers exhibit neither shrinkage nor stretching in their natural state. Woven or knitted cotton fabrics may shrink in the first few launderings because the laundering releases tensions created during weaving or finishing. The relaxation of these tensions may cause changes in the

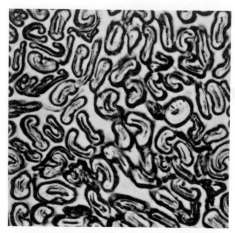

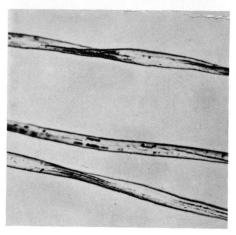

Figure 3-4.   Photomicrograph of cotton in a cross section and a longitudinal view. Courtesy of E. I. du Pont de Nemours & Company.

fabric dimensions. Cotton fabrics can be given special finishes to prevent this *relaxation shrinkage.*

Heat and Electrical Conductivity. Cotton conducts electricity, and thus does not build up static electrical charges. It has moderately good heat conductivity, which makes the fabric comfortable in hot weather.

Effect of Heat; Combustibility. Cotton is not thermoplastic and will not melt. Exposure to dry heat at temperatures above 300 degrees F., however, does cause gradual decomposition and deterioration of the fiber. Excessively high ironing temperatures cause cotton to scorch or turn yellow.

Cotton is combustible. It burns upon exposure to a flame and will continue to burn when the flame has been removed. Burning cotton fabric smells like burning paper, and a fluffy, gray ash residue remains. It is not possible to distinguish cotton from other cellulosic fibers by burning.

The Behavior of Textile Fibers in Relation to Selected Conditions

Chemical Reactivity. Cotton that has been cleaned and bleached is about 99 per cent cellulose. Its chemical reactions are typical of cellulosic materials. Table 3.2 shows the reaction of cotton to treatment with certain chemical substances in the laboratory.

Table 3.2*

Substance	Effect on Cotton Fiber
Acids	
Mineral acids such as sulfuric, hydrochloric, nitric, etc.	Concentrated acids destroy. Cold, diluted acids, if not neutralized and washed out, degrade and destroy the fiber.
Volatile organic acids: i.e., formic, acetic.	No harmful effect.
Nonvolatile organic acids: i.e., oxalic, citric, etc.	If not removed, degrade fiber slightly.
Alkalis	
Strong alkalis: sodium hydroxide, etc.	No harmful effect. Causes fiber to swell and become stronger.
Weak alkalis: borax, soap, etc.	No harmful effect.
Oxidizing Agents	
Chlorine bleaches	Destroys if uncontrolled.
Organic Solvents	
(Used in spot and stain removal) perchloroethylene naptha	No harmful effects.*

*SOURCE: J. LaBarthe, *Elements of Textiles* (New York: Macmillan Publishing Co., Inc., 1975), pp. 22–23.

IMPLICATIONS FOR MANUFACTURE. Some of the chemicals listed are utilized in the finishing of cotton. For example, acids may be employed to permanently stiffen the cotton fabric called organdy. The reaction of cotton to strong alkalis, in which the fiber swells and becomes stronger with (when the process is carried out under tension) an increase in luster as well, is used for mercerization. Dyestuffs that are too acidic in reaction cannot be applied to cotton fabrics.

IMPLICATION FOR CARE.   Chemical reactivity of the fiber also has implications for care. Cotton can be successfully cleaned using either synthetic built detergents, which are generally quite alkaline in character, or natural soaps. The alkalinity of the detergents has no effect on the fiber. Dry-cleaning solvents do not harm cotton, so where construction details or trim would make wet laundering undesirable, dry cleaning could be used.

Stains can be removed from cotton by using the stronger oxidizing bleaches as long as water temperature, concentration of bleaching agent, and time of exposure are controlled. Strong chlorine bleaches should not be poured directly on cotton since small pinholes can be formed in the fabric from direct contact with the chlorine bleach.

Resistance to Micro-organisms and Insects.   Mildew grows on cotton fibers, especially if they are stored under conditions of dampness, warmth, and darkness. This fungus stains the fiber and eventually rots and degrades it. Other bacteria and fungi that grow in soiled, moist areas will also deteriorate or rot cotton fabrics.

Moths and carpet beetles do not attack cotton, but silverfish may eat the fiber. Heavily starched fabrics are liable to be damaged by silverfish.

Environmental Conditions.   Extended exposure to sunlight will cause weakening and deterioration of cotton fabrics. Cotton draperies will last longer if lined with another layer of fabric.

Age does not seriously affect cotton fabrics; however, it is important that the fabrics be stored in clean condition and in dry areas to prevent mildew.

Special acid-free tissue paper can be used to store antique cotton garments, and cotton quilts and spreads. Ordinary tissue paper should not be used for wrapping fabrics for long-term storage, as the paper contains an acid residue that may damage the cloth.

USE AND CARE

The range of items for which cotton fabrics are used is enormous. In wearing apparel the qualities of comfort, dyeability, launderability, and moderate cost have caused cotton to be used widely in articles of apparel ranging from underwear to evening gowns. In the home, bed linens, table linens, draperies, upholstery and slipcover fabrics, and towels are frequently made from cotton.

Cotton has been increasingly blended with other fibers, especially with man-made fibers. This blending may be done to produce a lower cost fabric, or to create cottonlike fabrics with better resiliency or that require less ironing.

Along with its many positive qualities, cotton has some disadvantages such as low wrinkle recovery and combustibility. A variety of finishes for cotton have been developed that can compensate for some of these less desirable qualities. Special finishes are discussed in Chapters 19 and 20.

MINOR SEED HAIR FIBERS

Coir

Coir is a fiber obtained from the outer hull or shell of the coconut. Most of the coir produced is utilized in the geographic areas where the fiber is grown.

The production of the fiber is carried out by hand using rather primitive methods. The coconut is picked, the nut is removed, and the husks are collected.

The fibrous material of the husk is held tightly in place, so the husks must be soaked in water for a long period of time in order to facilitate fiber removal. This step of soaking is called *retting*. Husks are cut into two or three sections and remain in the water from five to six months. Salt water and tidal action seem to produce the best conditions for retting coir.

After retting, the husks are dried in the sun. Next they are placed on a plank, and are either beaten with a club to separate out the fiber or placed in a breaker drum. The breaker drum contains rollers with nails set into them that pull the fiber from the husk.

The brown coir fibers, which are from five to ten inches long, are used for brushes, ropes, and mats. Among the useful qualities of coir are resistance to rot, lightness coupled with elasticity, and resistance to abrasion.

Kapok

Kapok, like cotton, grows in a seed pod. The kapok tree, sometimes called the silk-cotton tree, is native to the tropics. Seed pods are gathered when they fall or are cut from the tree. The dried fiber is easily separated from the seeds.

The fiber has exceptional resiliency and buoyancy, but is too brittle to be spun readily into yarns. As a result, the uses of kapok are limited chiefly to stuffings and insulation materials. Because of its buoyancy and resistance to wetting, kapok has been used as a filling for life preservers. Having a hollow, air-filled structure, kapok can remain in the water for hours without an appreciable absorption of water, while holding up considerable weight.

Some kapok stuffings are used in household furnishings. The fibers have a tendency to deteriorate and to break down after a time.

Bast Fibers

Bast fibers are those that grow in the stems of plants. Located in the inner bark of the stalk, these fibers are often several feet in length. The best known of the bast fibers is flax, which is made into linen fabrics. Other important bast fibers include jute, ramie, and hemp. Minor fibers of historical interest but of no commercial importance are kenaf, urena, and nettle.

Flax

Certain plants are native to a particular geographic area. During prehistoric times, flax had the widest distribution of any of the fiber-bearing plants. The oldest archeological evidence of the use of flax shows that the flax plant stem was used in basket making long before flax fiber came into use. Techniques for removing the long fibers from flax stems were developed at a later period. At first wild flax was gathered, but subsequent cultivation of the plant spread it rapidly throughout the Mideast, Northern Africa, and Europe.

Actual samples of woven linen fabrics have been recovered from Egyptian tombs dating from 4000 B.C. The hot, dry climate of Egypt has preserved samples of both coarse and fine linen materials. Additional samples of linen fabrics have been excavated from the dried-out lake mud of prehistoric villages in Switzerland where the mineral salts of the lakes preserved the textiles. These samples are considered to be as much as 7,000 years old.[9]

In Europe, before world trade routes were developed, linen fabrics were widely utilized for most of the items in which cotton is used today. Cooler northern climates were not suited to the cultivation of cotton, but did permit the growth of flax. The widespread use of flax for many purposes is reflected in terminology still employed, such as *bed linens* or *table linens*. In modern products, bed linens and table linens are often made from fibers other than flax.

The United States does not produce flax for textiles (although flax seed is produced here), but imports the fibers, yarns, or fabrics. About 27 million pounds of flax and linen goods were imported to the United States in 1975. About 80 per cent of these imports are of finished fabrics and manufactured goods.[10] Countries that produce substantial quantities of flax are the Soviet Union, Belgium, Ireland, and New Zealand.

[9] G. Schaefer, "On the History of Flax Cultivation," *CIBA Review*, Basle, Switzerland (April 1945) 1763 ff.

[10] *Textile Organon* (November 1976), p. 169.

Figure 3-5. Photograph of flax plants in bloom. Courtesy of the United States Department of Agriculture.

Figure 3-6. Mature flax stalks after pulling. The stalks have been bundled. Threshing machines will remove the seeds which are used for linseed oil. Courtesy of the United States Department of Agriculture.

BOTANICAL INFORMATION

The botanical name of the flax plant is *linum usitatissimum*. Some varieties of the plant are grown for fiber, whereas others are grown for seeds. The plant grows to a height of from two to four feet. The varieties grown for fiber have long stems, with few branches and seeds.

CULTIVATION

In most countries the flax crop is sown in the early spring. The plant thrives best in temperate climates with adequate rainfall. Harvesting is done about eighty to one hundred days after sowing when about one half of the seeds are ripe and leaves have fallen from the lower two-thirds of the stem. In those countries where inexpensive labor is readily available, flax is still harvested by hand, but in developed countries, much of the labor of flax pulling is now done by machine. Whether done by hand or machine, the flax plant is pulled completely from the ground. Removing plants from the ground retains as long a stem as possible and prevents discoloration of fibers through wicking.

Stalks are dried sufficiently so that they can be threshed, combed, or beaten in order to remove the flax seeds, which are used for sowing future crops or for making linseed oil or livestock feed.

PREPARATION OF THE FIBER

Bast fibers require extensive processing in order to remove the fibers from the woody stem in which they are held. The procedure is similar for all bast fibers. The deseeded flax straw has to be partially rotted in order to dissolve the

Figure 3-7. The men are loading bundles of flax into retting tanks filled with heated water. The soaking action loosens the outside flax fibers from the woody center stalk. Courtesy of the Belgium Linen Association.

substances that hold the fiber in the stem. This first step in preparing the fiber is called *retting*.

Retting processes are of three types:

1. *Dew retting*. Dew retting takes place in the fields. The flax is laid out in swaths in the fields where the action of rain and dew together with soil-borne micro-organisms causes the bark of the stems to become loosened. This may take from seven to twenty-one days, depending on weather conditions. After retting, the bark is removed and retted straw bundles are set up in the fields to dry.

2. *Water retting* takes place when flax is submerged in water from six to twenty days. When water temperature is cooler, the process takes the longer amount of time. Water retting may be done in ponds, in vats, or in sluggish streams. As in dew retting, the bacterial action causes the bark to be loosened.

3. *Chemical retting* is done by using chemicals to perform the retting function. Only limited use is made of chemical retting, and often it follows a short period of "half retting" during which bacterial action on the bark is begun.

Retting only loosens the bark from the stem. Following retting, *breaking* and *scutching* finish the job of separating the fiber from the stem. In breaking, the flax straw is passed over fluted rollers or crushed between slatted frames. This breaks up the brittle, woody parts of the stem, but does not harm the fiber. In scutching, the broken straw is passed through beaters that knock off the broken pieces of stem. The fibers are baled and shipped to spinning mills.

At the mill the fibers go through yet another process before they are ready for spinning. The fibers are *hackled* or combed in order to separate shorter fibers (called tow) from longer fibers (called line fibers), and to align fibers parallel preparatory to spinning.

PROPERTIES OF FLAX

Physical Appearance

Color. Unbleached flax varies in color from a light cream color to dark tan. Different types of retting may produce differences in fiber color.

Shape. Fiber length may be anywhere from five to twenty inches, but most line (longer) fiber averages from fifteen to twenty inches, whereas tow (shorter fiber) is less than fifteen inches. Fiber diameter averages fifteen to eighteen microns.

In microscopic cross section, flax has a somewhat irregular, many-sided shape. Like cotton, it has a central canal, but this lumen is smaller and less distinguishable than that of cotton. Looking at the lengthwise direction of fiber under the microscope is rather like looking at a stalk of bamboo. Flax has crosswise markings spaced along its length that are called *nodes* or *joints*.

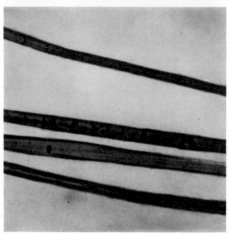

Figure 3-8. Photomicrograph of flax in a cross section and a longitudinal view. Courtesy of E. I. du Pont de Nemours & Company.

Luster. Because it is a straight, smooth fiber, flax is more lustrous than cotton. Many linen fabrics are designed to take advantage of this natural luster.

Other Properties

Strength. Flax is stronger than cotton, being one of the strongest of the natural fibers. It is as much as 20 per cent stronger wet than dry.

Density and Specific Gravity. The specific gravity of flax is about the same as that of cotton (1.52). Linen fabrics are, therefore, comparable in weight to cotton fabrics, but feel heavier than silk, polyester, or nylon, even in cloth of similar weave.

Elasticity and Resilience. Elongation, elasticity, and resilience of flax are still lower than that of cotton because linen lacks the fibril structure that gives some resilience to cotton. Linens crease and wrinkle badly unless given special finishes.

Absorbency and Moisture Regain. Moisture regain of linens is in the same range as cotton (about 8 to 12 per cent). Unlike cotton, linen has very good wicking ability, that is, moisture travels readily along the fiber as well as being absorbed into the fiber. The fiber gives up its moisture readily, making it quick-drying. Both absorbency and good wicking ability make linen useful for towels and for warm-weather garments.

Dimensional Stability. Like cotton, flax has good natural dimensional stability, neither shrinking nor stretching. However, it is also like cotton in that tension from manufacturing may result in relaxation shrinkage of fabrics. Pre-shrinkage treatments can be applied to linen fabrics to prevent relaxation shrinkage.

Heat and Electrical Conductivity. Linen conducts heat more readily than cotton and is even more comfortable for summer wear. Good conductivity of electricity prevents static electricity buildup.

Effect of Heat; Combustibility. Higher temperatures are required to scorch linen than to scorch cotton. Linen is slightly more resistant to damage from heat than is cotton. The burning characteristics of linen are similar to those of cotton; it is combustible, continues to burn when the flame is removed, and burns with an odor like that of burning paper.

Behavior of Linen in Relation to Selected Conditions

Chemical Reactivity. The chemical reactions of linen closely parallel those of cotton. Like cotton, linen is destroyed by concentrated mineral acids, not harmed by alkalis, decomposed by oxidizing agents, and not harmed by organic solvents used in dry cleaning. Linen could be mercerized, but because the flax is naturally strong and lustrous, there is little to be gained by the mercerization of flax.

Resistance to Micro-organisms and Insects. If linen is stored damp and in a warm place, mildew will attack and harm the fabric. Dry linen is not susceptible to attack. It generally resists rot and bacterial deterioration unless it is stored in wet, dirty areas. Moths, carpet beetles, and silverfish do not usually harm linen fabrics.

Environmental Conditions. Linen has better resistance to sunlight than does cotton. There is a loss of strength over a period of time, but it is gradual and not severe. Linen drapery and curtain fabrics are quite serviceable.

The resistance of linen to deterioration from age is good, especially if fabrics are properly stored. Linen, however, has poor flex abrasion resistance and should not always be folded at the same place in order to avoid abrasion at folded edges.

Care Procedures. Linen can be dry-cleaned or laundered at home with heavy-duty detergents. Being stronger wet than dry, the fabric requires no special handling during laundering. Excessive chlorine bleaching will damage linen, but linen fabrics can be whitened by the periodic, controlled use of chlorine or other bleaches.

Ironing temperatures for linen are at the highest end of the dial of electric irons. Linen fabrics can be ironed safely at a temperature of 450 degrees F. Dryer drying at the highest setting is satisfactory.

Uses

Linen fabrics are utilized in wearing apparel and in household textiles. Yarns spun from flax range from very fine for weaving into sheer, soft "handkerchief" linens to coarse, large-diameter yarns for "crash," a fabric that is frequently used for making dish towels.

Table 3.3
Comparison of the Characteristics of Cotton and Linen Fibers*

	Cotton	Linen
Specific gravity	1.52	1.52
Tenacity (grams per denier)		
Dry	3.0–5.0	5.5–6.5
Wet	3.3–6.4	6.0–7.2
Moisture regain	7–11%	8–12%
Resiliency**	poor	poor
Burning	burns, does not melt	burns, no melting
Conductivity of		
Heat	excellent	excellent
Electricity	excellent	excellent
Resistance to damage from		
Fungi	damaged	damaged
Insects	silverfish damage	silverfish may eat sizing
Prolonged exposure to sunlight	causes loss of strength	loss of strength
Strong acids	poor resistance	poor resistance
Strong alkalis	excellent resistance	excellent resistance

*Data on this and subsequent fiber characteristics charts obtained from: *Man-made Fiber Fact Book* (Washington, D.C.: Man-Made Fiber Producers Association, Inc., 1974); "Man-made Fiber Desk Book," *Modern Textiles* (March 1976); "Identification of Fibers in Textile Materials," *Bulletin X-156.* E. I. Du Pont de Nemours & Company, December 1961; *Textile Handbook* (Washington, D.C.: American Home Economics Association, 1974); R. W. Moncrieff, *Man-Made Fibres* (New York: John Wiley & Sons, Inc., 1975).

**Characteristics such as resiliency, conductivity, and resistance are compared on the following scale: poor, fair, moderate, good, and excellent.

In wearing apparel, linen fabrics are popular for summer clothing. The major disadvantage of linen clothing, its wrinkling, may be overcome by giving the fabrics special crease-resistant finishes. Blending of fabrics with synthetics may also help to overcome the tendency to wrinkle.

For household textiles, linen fabrics are often used in table linens. The launderability of linen combined with its good luster and attractive appearance make it quite popular in tablecloths and place mats. Other important uses for linen fabrics in the home include tea towels, especially those used for drying glasses. Linen produces less lint (small bits of fiber that break off from the yarn) than cotton, and is, therefore, preferred for drying glassware, as it does not leave a lint deposit on the dried glass. Linen is used alone or in blends for household products such as curtains and in slipcover and upholstery fabric.

The fabric is in relatively short supply and tends to be rather expensive. Both the cost factor and desirability in increasing wrinkle resistance have led to blending flax with other fibers.

OTHER BAST FIBERS

Ramie

Ramie or China grass is obtained from a plant in the nettle family. It is a perennial shrub. The fibers are taken from the stalk. Ramie plants are grown in semitropical regions in China, Japan, Egypt, Indonesia, Taiwan, and Russia. In the United States, the states of Florida, Louisiana, California, and Texas produce some quantities of ramie.

Ramie stalks are planted and the fiber is harvested the third year after

Figure 3-9. Ramie plants growing in Florida. Courtesy of R. V. Allison.

planting. Three crops may be cut each year. After cutting the stems, the leaves of the plant are beaten off, the stems are split lengthwise, and the bark is stripped from it. This yields "ribbons" of bast that are soaked in water until the green outer layer can be scraped off. After drying, this substance, sometimes called China grass, is bundled and shipped.

Before spinning, the fiber must be retted out of the ribbons. Both dew and wet retting, similar to that used with flax, can be done. A chemical retting process that uses caustic soda and an acid rinse has been patented, and is used in the industrially developed countries.

Ramie has a fine diameter, very good strength, and high luster. It is white in color, its absorbency is excellent, it dyes rapidly, and it has good resistance to attack by micro-organisms.

The commercial use of ramie has been limited by the difficulties of processing that increase the cost of the fiber, making it more expensive to produce than either cotton, flax, or hemp. Until the chemical retting process was developed, only hand methods could be employed to remove the fiber from the stem. The control of quality of fibers is also difficult. Researchers in Florida have developed controls for growth and processing that have made possible the production of uniform quality fibers.

Ramie is being blended with cotton, rayon, and polyester fibers. The major use of ramie is in clothing, fabrics, household textiles, tent cloth, fiber cloth, string, and cordage.

Jute

Jute fiber is taken from the stem of the jute plant. Successful cultivation of the plant requires fertile soil and a hot, moist climate. Jute plants grow from six to sixteen feet high.

The stalks are cut just after the flowers begin to fade. Like other bast fibers, separation of the fiber requires retting. After retting, the stems are broken and the fiber is removed.

Jute is shorter than most other bast fibers. Its length is only about 150 times its breadth, which makes it difficult to spin. It ranges in color from light to dark brown, and it is soft, fine, and lustrous, but not very pliable. On exposure to air, jute becomes somewhat brittle. It absorbs moisture readily, resists deterioration by micro-organisms, and is weakened by exposure to sunlight.

Jute is in demand as a cheap, useful packaging material. Between 1970 and 1975, the United States imported annually more than 800 million pounds of jute.[11] Burlap is one of the major jute bagging fabrics. Jute is also used for making carpet backings and cordage.

Hemp

Hemp is a member of the mulberry family and related to the marijuana plant. The fiber bundles come from the bast layer of the stem. Mature plants

[11] *Textile Organon* (November 1974), p. 155.

are cut off and spread on the ground where they are left to dry for five or six days. Leaves and seeds are beaten off, and bundles or sheaves of hemp are formed after additional drying. Retting, breaking, and scutching complete the fiber extraction process.

Hemp has a tensile strength comparable to that of linen; it is one of the strongest of the natural fibers. It has good absorbency and poor elasticity. In its chemical properties, hemp is similar to cotton and flax.

The major uses of hemp are in the production of industrial fabrics, twine, and ropes of great tensile strength. It finds some limited use in clothing and household textiles in some countries such as Italy.

Leaf Fibers

Leaf fibers are of limited usefulness and for the most part, are made into cordage. They are taken from a variety of plants, most of which are perennials that produce fiber for from five to twenty years. The leaves are harvested and through mechanical methods the extraneous matter is scraped and broken away from the fiber.

The most widely used leaf fibers are those from cactuslike plants such as *sisal* and *henequin,* and from the *abaca plant.* Pineapple leaves produce a fine, soft, lustrous fiber known as *pina* that is used in the Phillippine islands to make *pina cloth,* a very decorative textile.

Miscellaneous Fibers

A few fibers are obtained from roots and mosses. Sacaton, a coarse, stiff, root fiber from Mexico was used as bristle for brushes. Spanish moss, an air plant, has been used for inexpensive upholstery material and for mattress filler. In recent years synthetic fibers have, to a large extent, replaced these materials.

Recommended References

"Abaca." *CIBA Review.* vol. 1, p. 6.
"Coir." *CIBA Review,* August-September 1956.
"Cotton." *CIBA Review,* December 1952.
Cotton from Field to Fabric, National Cotton Council, Memphis, Tennessee.
Cotton Today. National Cotton Council, Memphis, Tennessee.
CRAWFORD, M. D. C. *The Heritage of Cotton.* New York: G. P. Putnam's Sons, 1924.
"Flax." *CIBA Review,* 1965, No. 2.
"Hemp." *CIBA Review,* 1962, No. 5.
"Jute." *CIBA Review,* February 1955.
LEWIS, ETHEL. *The Romance of Textiles.* New York: Macmillan Publishing Co., Inc., 1937.
ROLLINS, M. L. *Cotton Fiber Structure.* Watford, England: Merrow Publishing Company, Ltd.
"Ramie." *CIBA Review,* November 1957.
SCHAEFER, G. "On the History of Flax Cultivation." *CIBA Review,* April 1945, p. 1963 ff.
WEIBEL, A. C. *Two Thousand Years of Textiles.* New York: Pantheon Books, 1952.

4

MAN-MADE CELLULOSIC FIBERS

For thousands of years the only fibers used for textiles were those found in nature, even though, as early as 1664 Robert Hooke, an English writer, suggested that man ought to be able to create fibrous materials that had the same qualities as natural fibers. However neither Hooke nor any of his contemporaries were equal to the task.[1] In the nineteenth century, a number of scientists had begun to look seriously for techniques for creating fibers. Their search was successful, and by the end of the century Count Hilaire de Chardonnet, a Frenchman, had set up a factory for the production of rayon, the first "man-made" fiber.

Rayon

The earliest processes for making rayon utilized natural materials that were fibrous in nature, such as short cotton linters that could not be spun into yarns, or fibrous wood pulp. Chardonnet used the pulp of mulberry trees because silkworms ate the leaves. The pulp was dissolved in chemicals that broke down the molecular structure of the fiber somewhat, while still retaining a substantial quantity of long-chain molecules. The solution was forced through a metal plate that had small holes in it, exposed either to heated air or to a chemical solution, and then formed into a long, hairlike filament. This substance was called artificial silk.

Today this fiber would be classed as rayon, a regenerated cellulose. The specific process that was used is now obsolete in the United States and has been replaced by other methods of manufacture, but the basic principle of taking a natural material that is not usable in its original form and regenerating it into usable textile form remains the same. The manufacture of rayon by Chardonnet in 1891 marks the beginning of the man-made fiber industry.

The Federal Trade Commission's definition of rayon is broad, identifying rayon as "a manufactured fiber composed of regenerated cellulose, as well as

[1]R. W. Moncrieff, *Man-Made Fibres*, New York: John Wiley & Sons, Inc., 1975, p. 147.

manufactured fibers composed of regenerated cellulose in which substituents have replaced not more than 15 per cent of the hydrogen of the hydroxyl groups." The major fiber groups that fall within this definition are viscose rayon, cuprammonium rayon, high tenacity rayon, and high-wet-modulus rayon. Viscose rayon accounts for by far the largest amount of rayon manufactured.

VISCOSE RAYON

Manufacture

The following steps are employed in the process for manufacturing viscose rayon:

Purified cellulose, the base material from which viscose rayon is made, is provided, usually in the form of wood pulp, although cotton fibers, especially the short cotton linters, are also used. This material is supplied in the form of blotterlike sheets about two feet square.

The quantity of cellulose is measured carefully by weight, then placed in a "soaking press" where it remains immersed in a solution of caustic soda (sodium hydroxide) for about an hour. The excess solution is pressed out and the pulp material has been changed into a substance called alkali cellulose.

Alkali cellulose is shredded into small, fluffy particles called "white crumbs." These are aged under carefully controlled conditions for several days.

Carbon disulfide is then added to the white crumbs, which produces sodium cellulose xanthate and changes the color to bright orange. The orange "crumbs" are placed in dissolving tanks of dilute caustic soda. The resulting solution is thick and viscous, and is known as viscose. In color, it is gold with a consistency similar to that of honey.

The viscose is filtered to remove any insoluble particles. This is important because the particles would interfere with the spinning process. Now, the viscose must be aged or ripened a second time.

The final step in the formation of the fiber is the spinning. Man-made fibers are created by forcing the solution or viscous liquid through a spinneret, a metal plate with small holes arranged in a precise pattern. These holes are spaced to allow the filaments to be extruded without touching each other. The holes must be exactly the same size in order to produce uniform fibers. The metal used in the plate must be capable of withstanding high pressures. For spinning viscose, the spinneret is made of gold, platinum, or rhodium.

When man-made fibers are extruded into a liquid bath that causes the fibers to solidify or coagulate, the process is known as *wet spinning*. Viscose is wet spun into a dilute sulfuric acid bath. The dilute sulfuric acid and various salts dissolved in the bath cause the extruded solution to coagulate into long filaments when it enters the bath.

These newly formed filaments are handled differently depending on the type of fiber and yarn that is to be formed. If the fiber is to be used in filament form, the yarn is formed immediately by drawing out the coagulated viscose and winding it onto spools or making it into other types of yarn packages. If the

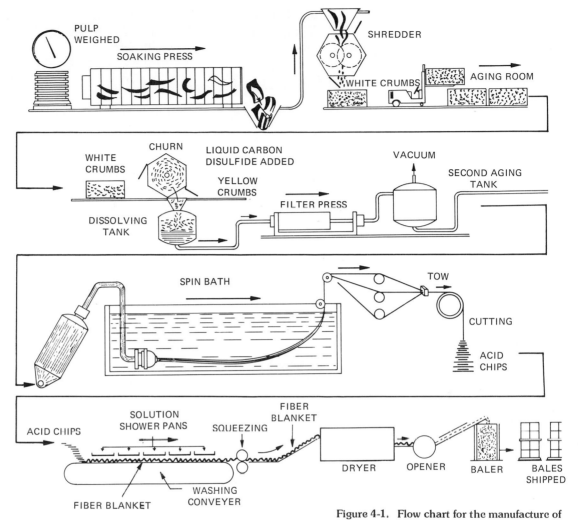

PULP WEIGHED

SOAKING PRESS

SHREDDER

WHITE CRUMBS

AGING ROOM

WHITE CRUMBS

CHURN

LIQUID CARBON DISULFIDE ADDED

YELLOW CRUMBS

DISSOLVING TANK

FILTER PRESS

VACUUM

SECOND AGING TANK

SPIN BATH

TOW

CUTTING

ACID CHIPS

ACID CHIPS

SOLUTION SHOWER PANS

SQUEEZING

FIBER BLANKET

FIBER BLANKET

WASHING CONVEYER

DRYER

OPENER

BALER

BALES SHIPPED

Figure 4-1. Flow chart for the manufacture of viscose staple fibers. Courtesy of American Enka Company.

manufacturer wishes to make staple fiber lengths, the filaments are drawn and then cut into short staple lengths. Whether the fiber is formed into filament or staple fiber, it must be washed to remove chemicals or other impurities.

Properties of Viscose Rayon

In the manufacture of man-made fibers, many qualities can be built into the fiber. For this reason it is difficult to generalize about all rayon fibers, since each manufacturer may produce viscose rayons that differ somewhat. The following discussion refers to the properties of viscose rayon that has not had any special modifications.

Rayons have generally been used in products that are competitive with cotton. When compared with cotton, rayons have displayed certain disadvantages. They are not equal in firmness and crispness; they have poorer dimensional stability, stretching and shrinking more than cotton; and they lose strength when wet so that rayons must be handled carefully both in industrial processing and in home laundering.

Physical Appearance

Color and Luster. Rayon fibers are normally white in color. Like all man-made fibers, they can have color added to the solution from which the fiber is to be spun. This provides a permanently locked-in color through a process known as *solution dyeing*. Manufacturers prefer, however, to add color to rayon fibers after they have been made into yarns or fabrics. The manufacture of the fiber is often completed many months before the fiber is made into a fabric and long before that fabric finds its way to the retail market. Fashions in color change often, and the manufacturer would have to anticipate the colors that would be popular well in advance of the time that the fabric is to be sold. For this reason, solution-dyed rayon fabrics are produced in limited, usually basic, colors.

The luster of rayon can be modified by the addition of titanium dioxide, a delustering agent, to the solution before the fibers are extruded. Delustering agents break up light rays and decrease shine. Man-made fibers that have not been delustered are called *bright* fibers; those that have been delustered are called *dull* or *semidull* fibers.

Shape. Man-made fibers can be manufactured in any length and diameter. In cross section the rayon fiber is an irregular circle with serrated edges. When lengthwise fibers are examined microscopically, longitudinal lines called *striations* are seen.

Other Physical Properties

Strength. The strength of viscose rayon is low. The lower polymer chain length of viscose when compared with polymer length of cotton and linen is responsible for this lower strength of viscose. Furthermore, rayon is weaker than cotton because its physical structure is different. During the growing process cotton develops a fibril structure, the layers or rings of which protect the fiber and provide greater strength. Ordinary rayon has no fibril layers in which the crystallinity of the physical structure is increased. Instead, rayon has a more amorphous inner structure. There is a considerable decrease in strength when the fiber is wet. Rayon fabrics must be handled carefully during laundering. Tenacity of regular viscose when dry is 0.73 to 2.6 g/d; when wet it is 0.7 to 1.8 g/d.

Density and Specific Gravity. The specific gravity of rayon is 1.5–1.53. Rayon fibers are comparable in density and specific gravity to cotton (1.54) and linen (1.5). Viscose, cotton, and linen fabrics of similar weave and construction will be of comparable weight.

Elasticity and Resilience. The elastic recovery of rayon is low, as is its resiliency. Untreated rayons tend to stretch and wrinkle badly. However, wrinkle-resistant finishes can be given to viscose in order to overcome these

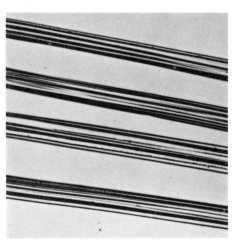

Figure 4-2. Photomicrograph of regular viscose rayon in a cross section and a longitudinal view. Courtesy of E. I. du Pont de Nemours & Company.

disadvantages. Tebilized is the trademark of one wrinkle-resistant finish applied to rayon and other cellulosic fibers.

Absorbency and Moisture Regain.　The physical structure of viscose is more amorphous than that of cotton or linen, making the viscose fibers more absorbent than the natural cellulosic fibers. Moisture regain is 13 per cent. Viscose accepts dyes readily, because of its increased absorbency. Also, fibers with larger surface area dye more readily, and the serrated edge of the rayon fiber provides greater surface area. The absorbency of the fiber makes clothing of viscose comfortable to wear.

Dimensional Stability.　Viscose rayons stretch, and having low elastic recovery tend to remain stretched. For some time after stretching, the distorted fabric tends to "creep" toward, but not completely to, its original length.

Fabrics may be stretched during processing and exhibit relaxation shrinkage upon a first laundering. Fibers may continue to shrink in subsequent launderings, as the "creep" effect continues. Tightly woven fabrics made of viscose rayon tend to shrink less than loose weaves. Special finishes can be given to viscose to overcome some of the problems of shrinkage. Treating fabrics with resin finishes has been the most commonly used means of stabilizing viscose rayon fabrics.

Heat and Electrical Conductivity.　The conductivity of both heat and electricity of viscose rayon is satisfactory, so that the fiber is reasonably comfortable in hot weather and does not build up static electricity.

Effect of Heat; Combustibility.　Viscose fabrics must be ironed at lower temperatures than cotton. Too high ironing temperatures will produce scorching. The recommended ironing temperature of viscose rayon is 250°F. Long exposure to high temperatures deteriorates the fiber.

The fibers burn with similar characteristics to those of cotton. Viscose rayon fabrics continue to burn after the source of the flame has been removed, and burning fabrics have the odor of burning paper. A soft, gray ash remains after burning.

Behavior of Viscose Rayon in Relation to Selected Conditions

Chemical Reactivity.　The amorphous physical structure of viscose makes viscose more susceptible to action of alkalis and acids. Acids attack viscose more readily than cotton or other cellulosic fibers. Viscose is more susceptible to damage from alkalis, as well.

Resistance to Micro-organisms and Insects.　Viscose is subject to damage from mildew and rot-producing bacteria. Silverfish will attack the fiber. Care in storage is necessary to prevent exposure of the fabric to conditions that encourage mildew and silverfish.

Environmental Conditions.　Exposure to sunlight will deteriorate viscose rayons more rapidly than cotton. Viscose rayon is not especially satisfactory for use in curtains or draperies unless they are lined to protect against sunlight. Age has no deleterious effect on viscose rayons if care is taken to be sure fabrics are stored in a clean, dry condition.

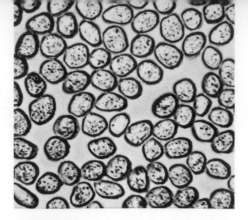

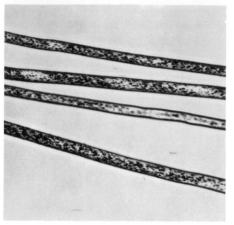

Figure 4-3. Photomicrograph of high-wet-modulus fiber in cross section and a longitudinal view. Courtesy of E. I. du Pont de Nemours & Company.

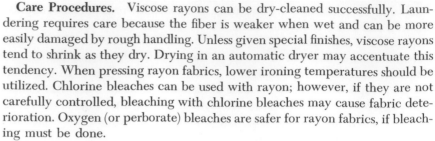

Care Procedures. Viscose rayons can be dry-cleaned successfully. Laundering requires care because the fiber is weaker when wet and can be more easily damaged by rough handling. Unless given special finishes, viscose rayons tend to shrink as they dry. Drying in an automatic dryer may accentuate this tendency. When pressing rayon fabrics, lower ironing temperatures should be utilized. Chlorine bleaches can be used with rayon; however, if they are not carefully controlled, bleaching with chlorine bleaches may cause fabric deterioration. Oxygen (or perborate) bleaches are safer for rayon fabrics, if bleaching must be done.

USES

Viscose rayon fabrics are used in wearing apparel and household textiles. Fabrics made from rayon have a broad range of quality and price. For optimum serviceability, rayons should have been given special finishes to control shrinkage and wrinkling.

There is such a great variation in the quality of these fabrics that consumers should be sure to follow care-labeling instructions closely. Some rayon fabrics require dry cleaning for best results, whereas others can be laundered quite successfully.

For apparel, viscose rayons are made into a wide variety of garments and accessories, ranging from millinery to lingerie, to suits, dresses, and sportswear. Viscose rayon is often blended with other fibers. In the home, rayon fabrics or blends of rayon and other fibers may be utilized for tablecloths, slipcovers, upholstery, bedspreads, blankets, curtains, and draperies.

Rayon fibers are now being used to manufacture a wide variety of nonwoven fabrics, both disposable and durable. The relatively low cost and ready availability of these fibers makes them especially suitable for this use.

CUPRAMMONIUM RAYON

The manufacture of cuprammonium rayon was discontinued in the United States in 1975. It is still being manufactured abroad in Italy, Japan, and East Germany.

Properties of Cuprammonium Rayon

Properties of this type of rayon are quite similar to those of viscose rayon. The fiber has a somewhat more silklike appearance and feel, and is often manufactured in finer diameters.

Under the microscope cuprammonium rayon appears to have a round cross section and a smooth longitudinal appearance. No striations, or very faint striations, appear on the surface.

The fiber can be made into very lightweight fabrics. A good conductor of heat and fairly absorbent, it is especially suitable for use in warm-weather clothing.

HIGH-WET-MODULUS RAYON

Attempts have been made to produce rayon fibers that possess some of the advantages of cotton. These experiments have centered on the development of rayon fibers with fibril structures similar to that of the natural cellulose fibers.

A Japanese researcher, S. Tachikawa, discovered a process for manufacturing rayon that develops a physical structure more like that of cotton. In this process, the severity of the chemical processing was decreased, the manufacturing time was decreased, and careful control was maintained over the chemical materials used. More specifically, Tachikawa's process eliminated the aging of alkali cellulose, dissolved the cellulose xanthate in water rather than in caustic soda, and eliminated the ripening of cellulose xanthate. A lower concentration of acid was used in the spinning bath with little or no salts.

These rayons are known as *high-wet-modulus rayons,* which means rayons that have greater resistance to deformation when wet. Trade names currently in use for high-wet-modulus rayons include Avril, Lirelle, Nupron, Xena, and Zantrel.

Properties

The microscopic appearance of high-wet-modulus rayon is similar to that of cuprammonium rayon; its cross section is round but may show grainy-looking texture in the lengthwise direction. However, the granular features are not clearly pronounced dark spots like those in delustered fibers. Fibers are made in both staple and filament form. Table 4.1 lists those properties of high-wet-modulus rayons that differ from regular viscose rayon.

Table 4.1

Property	Differences from Regular Viscose Rayon
Strength	
dry	increased strength
wet	weaker wet than dry, but has much better wet strength than viscose or cuprammonium rayon.
Elasticity and resilience	improved resilience, better elastic recovery.
Absorbency and moisture regain	decreased absorbency, making fabrics somewhat harder to dye than viscose rayons, but still easy compared with many synthetics.
Dimensional stability	does not stretch or shrink excessively.
Effect of heat	can tolerate higher ironing temperatures (slightly above those suitable for cotton).
Chemical reactivity	can be mercerized.
Resistance to sunlight	although deteriorated by sunlight, resistance is better than regular viscose rayon.

Uses

Producers of high-wet-modulus rayons say that they are suitable for use in the same kind of products as cotton. These rayons have a crisp, lofty feel. High-wet-modulus rayons, which offer better dimensional stability and strength during laundering than conventional rayons, are often made into wind jackets, sportswear, and sweaters, as well as shirts, dresses, and a variety of household fabrics. High-wet-modulus rayons are frequently blended with cotton. Typical blends would include blends with polyester in durable press fabrics, and blends with cotton.

Modified Cellulosic Fibers

In the 1920s experimentation with regeneration of cellulosic materials led to the discovery of a by-product called cellulose acetate. This substance, a chemical derivative of cellulose, was used as a coating for the fabric wings of World War I airplanes. It caused the fabric to tighten up and to become impervious to air. After the war, the demand for this material decreased, and the manufacturers of cellulose acetate sought another market for their product. Intensive research yielded a process for converting cellulose acetate into a fiber with high luster and excellent draping qualities. Like rayon, acetate was known as "artificial silk."

The resulting confusion between real silk and "artificial silk" led the Federal Trade Commission to establish a separate name for the man-made fibers. In 1924 the term *rayon* was established to include both regenerated cellulose and cellulose acetate. In 1953 an FTC ruling established separate categories for rayon and acetate and for triacetate, another modified cellulose fiber.

Cellulose acetate and cellulose triacetate are classified as modified cellulose fibers. These fibers should be distinguished from the rayons which are regenerated cellulose fibers. The production of both fibers begins with cellulose, but unlike rayon, the chemical composition of acetate and triacetate fibers is not cellulose but chemical variations of cellulose known as esters of cellulose. For this reason, the behavior of cellulose acetate and cellulose triacetate differs somewhat from the other cellulosic fibers.

The diagram of the cellulose molecule subunit shows that it possesses three —OH groups, known in chemical terminology as *hydroxyl groups*. In the chemical reactions that take place during the manufacture of cellulose acetate (and cellulose triacetate), acetyl groups are substituted for —OH groups on the cellulose molecule. This process is known as *acetylation*.

cellulose subunit

All three of the hydroxyl groups in the cellulose molecule can be acetylated. When a substance is formed from cellulose in which all three hydroxyl groups have been acetylated, the material is called cellulose triacetate. If a smaller number of hydroxyls are acetylated, the substance is called cellulose acetate. Cellulose acetate is, technically, a diacetate. Both are used in forming textile fibers.

$$CH_2OC-CH_3$$

cellulose triacetate

The initial stages of formation of both cellulose acetate and cellulose triacetate are the same. Cotton linters or wood pulp are treated to remove any impurities. In making acetate, the purified cellulose is steeped in acetic acid for a time in order to make the material more reactive. After further treatment with still more acetic acid, acetic anhydride is added. This mixture is stirred until it is thoroughly blended, but no reaction takes place until sulfuric acid is added to the mixture. The sulfuric acid begins the reaction. The temperature is kept low, and the mixture stands for seven or eight hours until it takes on a thick, gelatinlike consistency. The material formed is triacetate, also known as the primary acetate. From this point, the procedure differs, depending on whether cellulose diacetate or triacetate is being made.

CELLULOSE TRIACETATE

Cellulose triacetate having been formed, water is added to the viscous solution. The triacetate can no longer be held in this weak solution and precipitates out in the form of small, white flakes. These flakes are collected, dried, and then dissolved in a solution of methylene chloride and a small quantity of alcohol. The fibers are dry-spun through a spinneret into warm air, solidify, and are formed into yarns.

CELLULOSE DIACETATE (REGULAR ACETATE)

To follow the steps in the spinning of regular acetate, one must return to the formation of triacetate, or the base acetate. The next step is the conversion of the base acetate into a diacetate. The primary acetate (triacetate), ex-

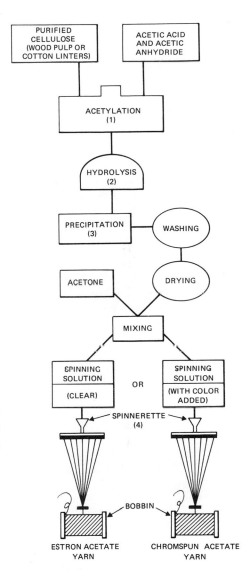

Figure 4-4. Flow chart for the manufacture of cellulose acetate. Courtesy of Eastman Kodak Company.

cess acetic acid, and acetic anhydride from the first reaction are combined with sufficient water to produce a 95 per cent solution of acetic acid. This mixture stands for twenty hours, during which time acid hydrolysis takes place and some of the acetylated hydroxyl groups are reconverted to their original form. This mixture is tested constantly so that the reaction is stopped at the appropriate point. The mixture is poured into water and the cellulose acetate precipitates into chalky white flakes that are collected, washed, and dried. This is the secondary acetate or cellulose acetate.

Flakes from different batches of cellulose acetate are mixed together to maintain a uniform quality of acetate. The flakes are soluble in acetone. Before spinning, the flakes are dissolved in acetone to form the solution or dope. This takes about twenty-four hours. The dope is filtered, then extruded through spinnerets into warm air that evaporates the acetone. In winding the fiber into yarns, fibers are given a slight stretch that orients or parallels the molecules, making the fiber somewhat stronger.

Appearance of Cellulose Acetate and Cellulose Triacetate

Shape. In microscopic appearance cellulose diacetate and cellulose triacetate are very similar. Normally both fibers are clear and have irregular, multilobed shape in cross section rather like popcorn. Acetate may be manufactured in Y-shaped or doughnut-shaped cross section as well. The hollow or doughnut-shaped fiber type is said by the manufacturer to have increased luster, a fuller, more resilient hand, and increased bulk. Y-shaped fibers are said to give the fabric maximum bulk and covering power. The hand of the fabric is stiffer and crisper than other acetates. The Y-shaped fibers are especially recommended for use in drapery fabrics.[2]

The longitudinal appearance of regular acetate and triacetate fibers shows broad striations. It is not possible to distinguish normal acetate fibers from triacetate fibers by microscopic examination.

Luster and Color. If acetate and triacetate have not been treated to decrease luster, both fibers will have a bright appearance and good luster. Fibers that have been delustered show small, black spots of pigment in the microscopic longitudinal view and cross section. Fibers are white unless they have been solution-dyed.

Other Properties

Strength. Both acetate and triacetate have very low strength. Both are weaker wet than dry. The abrasion resistance is poor. Nylon hosiery wearing against acetate satin linings in coats provides sufficient abrasion to cut these fibers.

Density and Specific Gravity. Acetate and triacetate are both lower in specific gravity than rayon or cotton at 1.32 and 1.3, respectively. Comparable

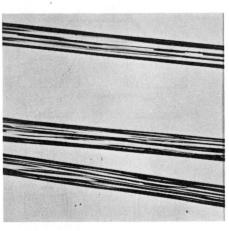

Figure 4-5. Photomicrograph of cellulose acetate fiber in a cross section and a longitudinal view. Courtesy of E. I. du Pont de Nemours & Company.

[2] *ESTRON Technical Bulletin* No. TB-A-201, p. 5.

fabrics, therefore, feel lighter when made of acetates or triacetates than if they are woven of cotton, linen, or rayon.

Elasticity and Resilience. Acetate and triacetate differ markedly in their elastic recovery and resilience. Acetate has poor elastic recovery and poor wrinkle recovery. By contrast, triacetate has increased elastic recovery, is resilient, and has good wrinkle recovery.

Absorbency and Moisture Regain. Acetate is more absorbent than triacetate. (Acetate has a moisture regain of 6.3 to 6.5 per cent, whereas triacetate regains only 3.5 per cent of moisture.) If compared with cotton, acetate has a slightly lower moisture regain (cotton regains 7 to 10 per cent), and just about half the regain of rayon. Its low absorbency makes acetate difficult to dye except with disperse dyes or before spinning.

Dimensional Stability. Triacetate fibers have good resistance to stretch or shrinkage. Acetate fabrics may exhibit relaxation shrinkage on laundering unless they are pretreated. Knit fabrics are especially prone to relaxation shrinkage with as much as 10 per cent shrinkage during laundering. Exposure to high temperatures may also cause acetates to shrink.

Heat and Electrical Conductivity. Neither heat nor electrical conductivity of acetate and triacetate are as good as the conductivity of other cellulosic fibers. Both fibers tend to build up static electricity charges, and neither acetate nor triacetate is as cool to wear as cotton, linen, or rayon.

Effect of Heat; Combustibility. Both acetate and triacetate are thermoplastic fibers; they will soften and melt with the application of heat. Triacetate can be given a special heat treatment that makes it less sensitive to heat than acetate. Permanent pleats and surface designs such as moire can be heat-set in acetate. Heat treatments given to triacetates increase the crystallinity of the molecule. Along with the increase in crystalline structure, the moisture regain decreases. Heat-treated triacetates can be permanently set into pleats or other shapes. Table 4.2 contrasts the effect of heat on each fiber.

If ignited, acetate and triacetate burn with melting. When the flame has been put out, a small, hard, beadlike residue remains at the edge of the burned area. Fire-retardant finishes can be added to acetate and triacetate fibers before spinning. The Celanese Corporation has developed a fiber called FR Arnel that is recommended for blending with polyester fibers in flame-retardant children's sleepwear. *SayFR* is a flame-retardant acetate made by FMC Corporation.

Behavior in Relation to Selected Conditions

Chemical Reactivity. Table 4.3 compares the chemical reactivity of acetate and triacetate.

Resistance to Micro-organisms and Insects. Mildew will grow on acetate or triacetate if the fabrics are incorrectly stored. The growth causes discoloration of the fabric but no serious loss of strength. Triacetate is more resistant to mildew than acetate.

Moths or carpet beetles do not attack either fiber. However, heavily starched or sized acetates are prone to attack from silverfish.

Table 4.2

Acetate	Triacetate
Sticks at 350°F. to 375°F.	464°F. (after heat treatment)
Melts at 500°F.	575°F.

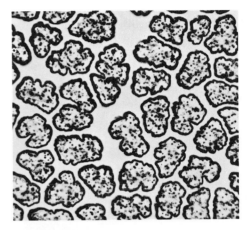

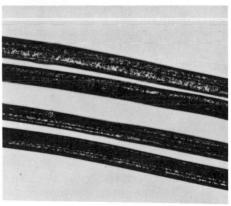

Figure 4-6. Photomicrograph of delustered cellulose triacetate fiber in a cross section and longitudinal view. Courtesy of E. I. du Pont de Nemours & Company.

Table 4.3

	Acetate	Triacetate
Effect of acids	resistant to cold, dilute acids. decomposed by strong acids; dissolves in acetric acid.	resistant to cold, dilute acids. damaged by strong acids; slightly better acid resistance than acetate.
Effect of alkalis	good resistance to weak alkalis. saponified by strong alkalis.	like acetate.
Effect of bleach	hydrogen peroxide or sodium perborate bleach recommended at temperatures below 90°F.	like acetate.
Effect of organic solvents	petroleum products safe for use; dissolved by acetone, an ingredient in some fingernail polish remover.	like acetate—partially dissolved by acetone with heat.

Environmental Conditions. Extended exposure to sunlight will cause a loss of strength and deterioration of acetate fabrics. Draperies should be lined to protect them from the sun. Triacetate has moderate resistance to sunlight. The resistance of acetate to ultraviolet light is decreased if the fiber has been delustered.

Acid fumes in the atmosphere may adversely affect some dyes used for acetates. The low absorbency of acetates requires that they be dyed with a type of dye known as "disperse" dye. Certain of these dyes are subject to atmospheric fading or "fume" fading. Blue and gray shades, after exposure to atmospheric gases produced by heating homes with gas, turn pink or reddish. Greens may turn brown.

To overcome this problem, acetate fibers maybe colored in the solution before the fiber is extruded from the spinneret. Pigment that is added to the acetate solution is locked into the fiber permanently and cannot change in color. Trademarks for solution-dyed acetates include Chromspun, Celaperm, and Colorspun.

In addition to solution dyeing, special finishing agents called diethanolamine or melamine can be applied to acetate and triacetate fabrics to stabilize colors and prevent fume fading. Also some blue dyes that are not reddened by gas fumes have been developed.

Acetate does lose some strength through aging. Triacetates resist deterioration with age.

Care Procedures

Acetate. If handled with care, acetates can be successfully laundered. However, acetates that have not had special shrink-resistant finishes should be dry-cleaned. Woven acetate goods may shrink as much as 5 per cent and knits as much as 10 per cent in laundering.

During laundering, acetate fabrics should not be subjected to undue stress through wringing or twisting. Fibers are weaker wet than dry, and acetates will wrinkle badly if creased or folded when wet.

Hydrogen peroxide or sodium perborate bleaches can be used if necessary for whitening of fabrics. Bleaching should be carefully controlled. Ironing temperatures for acetates must be kept low. The fabric will stick and melt if ironed at too high a temperature.

Acetone, a component of some fingernail polishes, will dissolve acetate. Care should be taken to avoid spilling acetone-containing substances on the fabric.

Triacetate. Triacetate fabrics can be hand- or machine washed. Hydrogen peroxide and sodium perborate bleaches can be used. They have better wrinkle recovery and crease resistance than acetates. If the fabrics require touch-up ironing after laundering, triacetates can be ironed at the rayon setting on the iron dial.

Dry-cleaning solvents will not harm triacetates. These fabrics can be successfully dry-cleaned.

Acetone will also damage triacetate fabrics. Spills from nail polish remover that contains acetone will harm the fabric.

Table 4.4
Comparison of Characteristics of Regenerated Cellulosic Fibers

	Regular Tenacity Rayon	High-Wet-Modulus Rayon	Acetate	Triacetate
Specific gravity	1.52	1.52	1.32	1.32
Tenacity (grams per denier)				
Dry	0.73–2.6	2.5–5.5	1.2–1.5	1.2–1.4
Wet	0.7–1.8	1.8–4.0	0.9–1.2	0.8–1.0
Moisture regain	11–14%	11–14%	6%	4%
Resiliency	poor	fair	poor	fair
Burning	burns, no melting	burns, does not melt	burns. melts at 500°F.	burns. melts at 575°F.
Conductivity of				
Heat	good	good	fair	fair
Electricity	good	good	fair	fair to good
Resistance to damage from				
Fungi	damaged	damaged	fair resistance	resistant
Insects	attacked by silverfish	attacked by silverfish	silverfish may eat sizing	silverfish may eat sizing
Prolonged exposure to sunlight	loss of strength	some loss of strength	some loss of strength over time	moderate resistance
Strong acids	poor resistance	poor resistance	poor resistance	poor resistance
Strong alkalis	poor resistance	excellent resistance	causes saponification and eventual loss of strength	causes saponification and eventual loss of strength

Uses

Acetate is used for many household and apparel textiles because it has an attractive appearance and pleasant hand or texture. Decorative fabrics are woven to take advantage of the high luster and wide color range available in acetate fabrics.

Acetates are used for items of clothing such as blouses, dresses, and lingerie. Handsome drapery and upholstery fabrics are often made of acetate brocade, taffeta, or satin. Acetate yarns are used in some fabrics together with yarns of other fibers in order to provide a contrast between the luster of acetate and a dull appearance of, for example, cotton or rayon.

Triacetate fabrics have the advantage of being able to be heat-set. Apparel in which pleat or shape retention is important is often made from triacetate. The major use of this fabric is in wearing apparel; however, the manufacturer recommends its use for comforters, bedspreads, draperies, and throw pillows, as well. Arnel, the only triacetate produced at present, is manufactured by the Celanese Company.

Recommended References

"Artificial Silk." *CIBA Review*, 1967, vol. 2.

"Cellulose: Rayon and Acetate." *American Fabrics*, Fall 1969, p. 51.

COOK, J. G. *Handbook of Textile Fibres*. Watford, England: Merrow Publishing Company Ltd., 1967.

Encyclopedia of Textiles, American Fabrics. Englewood Cliffs, N. J.: Prentice-Hall, Inc., 1972.

LOASBY, G. "History of Rayon and the Synthetic Fibers." *Research*, January 1952.

MONCRIEFF, R. W. *Man-Made Fibres*. New York: John Wiley & Sons, Inc., 1975.

5
PROTEIN FIBERS

Protein fibers are those fibers in which the basic chemical structure is composed of amino acids joined in polypeptide chains. They may be separated into three basic groups:

1. Those fibers that are animal hair. The major fiber in this group is sheep's wool. Other fibers of commerical importance are those obtained from animals such as the alpaca, camel, cashmere goat, llama, vicuña, and guanaco, and the fleece of the angora goat, called mohair. Also used are qiviut, hair from the musk ox, angora rabbit hair, fur fiber from animals such as beaver, mink, and rabbit; and cow and horse hair.

2. Those fibers formed from filaments extruded by caterpillars. Silk, produced by the silkworm caterpillars, is the only important fiber in this group. In the past such unusual materials as spider silk and byssus from mussels were said to have been made into fabrics.

3. Those fibers that are regenerated from vegetable or animal protein. Corn, soybeans, and milk are some of the base materials from which regenerated protein fibers have been made.

All protein fibers contain the elements carbon, hydrogen, oxygen, and nitrogen. Wool contains sulfur as well. In each protein fiber these elements are combined in different arrangements. As a result, properties of the various protein fibers may show some striking differences.

Even so, these fibers share a number of common properties. Protein fibers, except silk, tend to be weaker than cellulosic fibers, and they are weaker wet than dry. Fabrics made from protein fibers must be handled with care during laundering or wet processing.

Density and specific gravity of protein fibers tend to be lower than that of cellulose. Fabrics made from these fibers feel lighter in weight than comparable fabrics made from cellulosic fibers.

Protein fibers have greater resilience than cellulosic fibers. They are more resistant to wrinkling and hold their shape well.

Fibers from the protein family do not burn readily. When set aflame, they may extinguish themselves. Burned fibers smell like burning hair, flesh, or feathers. Protein fibers tend to be damaged by dry heat and should be ironed with a press cloth or steam. Wool and silk require lower ironing temperatures than cotton and linen, with recommended temperatures around 300 degrees F.

Chemical properties common to most protein fibers include susceptibility to damage by alkali and by oxidizing agents, especially chlorine bleach. Care in laundering is required to avoid damaging fibers through the use of strongly alkaline soaps and detergents, and chlorine bleach. Fabrics can be bleached safely with hydrogen peroxide. Acids are less damaging to protein fibers than to the cellulose fibers.

Sunlight discolors white fabrics made from protein fibers, turning them yellow after extended exposure to the sun. Although wool has better resistance to sunlight than cotton, it will degrade on prolonged exposure. Silk degrades quite readily on exposure to sunlight.

Table 5.1
Protein Fiber Family

Natural Fibers	Man-Made Fibers
ANIMAL HAIR FIBERS	REGENERATED PROTEIN OR AZLON FIBERS
MAJOR FIBERS	MINOR FIBERS
Wool (from sheep)	*Animal Protein*
	Milk protein
MINOR FIBERS	Aralac**
Camel Family	Fibrolane BX**
alpaca	Fibrolane BC**
camel's hair	Lanital**
huarizo	Merovina**
guanaco	
misti	*Vegetable Protein*
vicuña	Peanut protein
llama	Ardil**
	Corn protein
Goat Family:	Vicara**
cashmere	Soybean protein fiber**
Mohair (from the angora goat)	Chinon
qiviut (from the musk ox)	
Fur Fiber	
beaver	
fox	
mink	
chinchilla	
rabbit (especially Angora rabbit)	
Other	
horsehair	
cow hair	
EXTRUDED FIBERS	
MAJOR FIBERS	
silk (from the silkworm)	

**No longer in production.

Animal Hair Fibers

The hair of a number of different kinds of animals has been used for textile fibers for many centuries. If one looks briefly at the early history of textile fibers, it appears that the widespread use of animal hair fibers for construction of yarns may have developed later than the use of plant fiber. An analysis of fabrics that are 8,500 years old indicates that some were made of wool.[1]

However, the prehistory of northern Europe shows no evidence of the use of wool until considerably later. The belief that wool use for fabrics was developed later in Europe and South America is supported by the fact that the herding of sheep and goats was not widespread in Europe until the Bronze Age, or about 2000 to 3000 B.C., whereas in South America, herding is dated about 1000 B.C.[2]

Early hunting peoples undoubtedly made some use of wool fibers from the fleeces that hunters took from animals. After people recognized that these fibers were useful in constructing cloth, sheep, goats, and other animals such as camels, llamas, alpacas, and the like were domesticated in different parts of the world, and their hair was removed for spinning and weaving.

Of the many varieties of animal hair from which textile fibers are derived today, the fleece of the sheep is most widely used. In Central Asia, the camel is an important source of textile fiber, and South America is the home of a number of camellike animals that produce fibers used for spinning and weaving. The alpaca and llama are native to the Andes Mountains regions, and have been domesticated. Vicuña and guanaco are wild or semiwild animals from the same geographic region. Other animal hair fiber comes from domesticated goats such as the angora goat and the cashmere goat.

Hair from other wild or domesticated animals such as rabbits, musk oxen, horses, and cows have some minimal use in textile products.

Sheep's Wool

Under the Wool Products Labeling Act wool is defined as "the fiber from the fleece of the sheep or lamb or hair of the angora or cashmere goat (and may include the so-called specialty fibers from the hair of the camel, alpaca, llama, and vicuna)."[3] Fiber taken from the domesticated sheep makes up by far the largest quantity of fiber sold under the name of wool.

Approximately 200 different breeds and crossbreeds of sheep produce wool fiber. The fiber produced by these animals varies widely in quality not only because of the conditions under which the sheep may graze, and the quality of the pasture land, but also because some breeds of sheep produce finer quality wool than others.

The sheep that produces the most valuable and finest wool is the Merino variety. This type of wool accounts for about 30 per cent of wool production and the largest proportion of Merino fleeces comes from Australia. Merino sheep originated in Spain. From Spain they were exported to other countries. Their wool is fine, strong, and elastic, through relatively short—from one to five inches. French Rambouillet sheep, descendants of the Merino blood line,

[1] J. Mellaart, "Catal Huyuk in Anatolia," *Illustrated London News,* (February 9, 1963), 196 ff.

[2] J. G. Clark, *Prehistoric Europe* (New York: Philosophical Library, Inc., 1952).

[3] Rules and Regulations Under the Wool Products Labeling Act of 1939. (Washington, D.C.: Federal Trade Commission, 1964), p. 21.

were imported to the United States in 1840 and make up 27 per cent of all the sheep in the United States. These, too, produce fine, high-quality wool.

A second group of sheep that originated in the British Isles produces fibers that are not quite so fine or of such high quality as Merino and Rambouillet, but are also of quite good quality. Fibers range from two to eight inches in length. Some of the breeds of sheep from this group are Devonshire, Dorset, Hampshire, Oxford, Southdown, and Wiltshire. Like Merino sheep, these breeds are raised worldwide.

Coarser, longer fiber is produced by a group of sheep known as Long British or Long Crossbreeds. The fiber length is four to sixteen inches, and the better known breeds include Leicester, Lincoln, Cotswold, Romney Marsh, and Cheviot. Much of this fiber is made into outerwear in tweed, cheviot, homespun, and shetland fabrics.

A fourth group of sheep is made up of a variety of crossbred sheep that produce fibers of from one to sixteen inches in length, fibers that are coarse and have lower elasticity and strength. These wools are used largely for inexpensive, low-grade cloth and carpets.

Climatic conditions can have an adverse effect on the quality of the wool, as can the condition of the grazing area. Austrialian flocks are enclosed in large fenced areas where underbrush and burrs are kept to a minimum, whereas American sheep are permitted to graze on open ranges. This free grazing results in fleece in which pieces of wood, leaves, burrs, and other vegetable matter may be caught.

FLEECE REMOVAL

Sheep are sheared to remove the fleece in the spring season. Expert shearers move from place to place removing fleece or clip wool. In Australia, fleece is removed in sections with the underbelly section kept separate from the sides. This is done because the fleece from the undersection and legs tends to be inferior in quality to that of the sides, as it contains more vegetable matter and is more tangled, matted, and torn than fleece from the upper part of the body. In the United States it is customary to remove the fleece in one piece.

Fleece that is sheared from sheep at eight months of age or younger is called *lamb's wool.* Because this is the first growth of hair it tends to be softer and finer. Products made from this soft, fine wool are generally labeled as "lamb's wool."

Wool removed from animals that have been slaughtered is referred to as *pulled wool.* Wool is taken from hides by one of several methods. A chemical depilatory, a substance that loosens the wool from the hides, may be used. This material does not seriously damage the hide and is the preferred method as it allows full utilization of both hides and fleece. Another method is to allow bacterial action to loosen the fiber so that it can be pulled from the hide.

Pulled wool is inferior in quality to fleece or clip wool as it is less lustrous

Figure 5-1. Champion Merino sheep. Courtesy of the United States Department of Agriculture.

and elastic. Because it includes the closed end of the fiber that has been pulled from the hide, pulled wool absorbs dye less evenly. Pulled wool is generally blended with other types of wool.

Grading

Grading of wool is done at the time the fleece is sheared. In grading, the fleece is judged for its overall fiber fineness and length. An alternative to grading is found in *sorting*, in which the fleece is divided into sections of differing quality. The best fiber comes from the sides and shoulders, the poorest comes from the lower legs.

PREPARATION FOR SPINNING

The first step taken to prepare the fleece for use is *scouring*, which removes oil, grease, perspiration, and some of the dirt and impurities from the fleece. The fleece is washed a number of times in a warm, soapy, alkaline solution. A fleece of about eight pounds in weight will be reduced by scouring to about three to four pounds. Much of the weight loss results from the removal of lanolin, a natural oil secreted by the sheep, which keeps the fleece soft and waterproof.

This lanolin is recovered for use in cosmetics and other oil-based preparations. Even though lanolin can be recovered, the refuse produced by scouring of wool may be a cause of water pollution in areas where wool is processed.

If wool retains significant quantities of vegetable matter after scouring, it must be carbonized to remove this substance. *Carbonization* is the treatment of the fleece with sulfuric acid that destroys burrs, sticks, or other woody material. Careful control is maintained to assure that fibers are not damaged by the process. An alternative method is to lower the temperature of the fleece below freezing so that dirt, burrs, or vegetable matter becomes brittle and can be knocked or brushed from the fleece.

As a result of these processes the wool may become overly dry and brittle. To avoid this, a small amount of oil is added to the fiber to keep it flexible, and the wool is kept somewhat moist during handling.

All wool fibers are carded. Fine wire teeth, mounted on a cylinder, separate the fibers and make them somewhat, although not completely, parallel. This procedure also helps to remove remaining vegetable matter from the fiber. Yarns that have been carded are called *woolen* yarns.

Combing is an additional processing procedure that further aligns longer fibers in a parallel manner so that the resulting *worsted yarns* are smoother and stronger. Worsted yarns may have a tighter twist but it is not necessary that they do because of the longer fiber length used. Worsted yarns are more lustrous, less fuzzy, and often smaller in diameter than woolen yarns. Further discussion of woolen and worsted yarns is found in Chapter 13.

WOOL PRODUCTS LABELING ACT OF 1939

Wool fabrics can be made from new or from used wool, but one cannot tell by looking at the fabric whether the wool it contains is new or reused. In order to assure that products made from used fibers are clearly labeled as such, the Wool Products Labeling Act of 1939 was enacted. This legislation regulated the labeling of sheep's wool and other animal hair fibers. The provisions of this act are as follows:

All wool products must be labeled.

The fibers contained in the product, except for ornamentation, must be identified.

The following terms used in identifying wool products are defined by the statute.

Wool . . . "the fiber from the fleece of the sheep or lamb or hair of the Angora or Cashmere goat (and may include the so-called specialty fibers from the hair of the camel, alpaca, llama, and vicuña) which has never been reclaimed from any woven or felted wool product."

Reprocessed wool . . . "the resulting fiber when wool has been woven or felted into a wool product which, without ever having been utilized in any way by the ultimate consumer, subsequently has been made into a fibrous state."

Reused wool . . . "the resulting fiber when wool or reprocessed wool has been spun, woven, knitted, or felted into a wool product which, after having been used in any way by the ultimate consumer, subsequently is made into a fibrous state."[4]

The terms *new wool* or *virgin wool* may be used "only when the product or part (of a product) referred to is composed wholly of new or virgin fibers which has (sic) never been reclaimed from any spun, woven, knitted, felted, bonded or similarly manufactured product."[5]

Reprocessed wools are often made from the cutting scraps left from the manufacture of wool items. The fibers are pulled apart and returned to the fibrous state through a process known as *garnetting*. In the garnetting procedure, fibers may be somewhat damaged, and can, therefore, be lower in quality than some new wool. Reused wool products are returned to the fibrous state by garnetting. Because these fibers have been subject to wear not only from the garnetting process but also by the normal wear and tear of a garment or product in use, these are the lowest quality of the three types of fibers. Reused

[4] Text of the Wool Products Labeling Act of 1939 as amended effective June 20, 1964. Reported in *Rules and Regulations under the Wool Products Labeling Act of 1939* (Washington, D.C.: Federal Trade Commission, October 17, 1974), p. 14.

[5] "Questions and Answers Relating to Textile Fiber Products Identification Act and Regulations" (Washington, D.C.: Federal Trade Commission, October 17, 1974), p. 14.

Figure 5-2. A line of sheep shearers remove fleece from sheep. Courtesy of the United States Department of Agriculture.

wools are often made into interlining materials for coats and jackets, or other inexpensive wool products. They are sometimes referred to as *shoddy*.

Although the terms *virgin* or *new* wool guarantee that fabrics are made from wool that has not been previously fabricated, the terms carry no guarantee of quality. It is possible that a poor quality of virgin wool may be inferior to a fabric made from excellent quality reprocessed wool.

In pile fabrics the face and the backing may be made of different fibers. The contents of the face and the backing are listed separately, such as: "100% wool face, 100% cotton back." The proportion of these fibers must be indicated in percentage, so that in addition to the designation of 100% wool face, 100% cotton back," the label must also say "Back constitutes 60% of the fabric and pile 40%."

The contents of paddings, linings, or stuffings are designated separately from the face fabric, but must be listed.

MOLECULAR STRUCTURE

Wool is made of a protein substance known as *keratin*. A careful examination of the diagram showing the molecular structure of wool will reveal that in addition to its long-chain, polyamide structure, wool has covalent cross-linkages called *cystine* or *sulfur linkages*, and ion-to-ion bonds called *salt bridges*. Like other fibers, wool also possesses hydrogen bonds.

Chemists are still trying to determine the exact effect the chemical structure of wool has on the behavior of the fibers. Some of the findings can be summarized in simplified form as follows:

A. Diagrammatic representation of the fiber is usually made in the form of a ladder, showing the cross-links. Although this format is visually clearer, recent evidence indicates that the wool structure may actually be more in a helical form rather like a coil or spiral, like that of DNA. It is supposed that this coiled form of the molecule permits the marked elongation that is characteristic of wool fibers.[6]

B. Wool can be pressed into pleats or creases by the application of heat, moisture, and pressure. Hydrogen bonds are thought to permit this shaping of wool. Because hydrogen bonding takes place when molecules are close together, and because these bonds can be broken and re-formed in other areas, it is thought that shape can be set in this way: heat and moisture break the hydrogen bonds in one area, the fabric is shaped, heat is applied, and new hydrogen bonds are formed that hold the fabric in the new shape. This shape will remain only until the fabric is dampened again, at which point the molecular structure reverts to its former shape.[7]

C. The cross-linkages in wool are thought to provide the resiliency of the fiber, by pulling the fiber back to its original shape after it has been distorted through stretching or folding.

[6] J. W. S. Hearle and R. H. Peters, *Fiber Structure* (London: Butterworth & Co., 1963), p. 58.

[7] "What Happens When Setting Wool," *Textile Industries* (October 1966), p. 344.

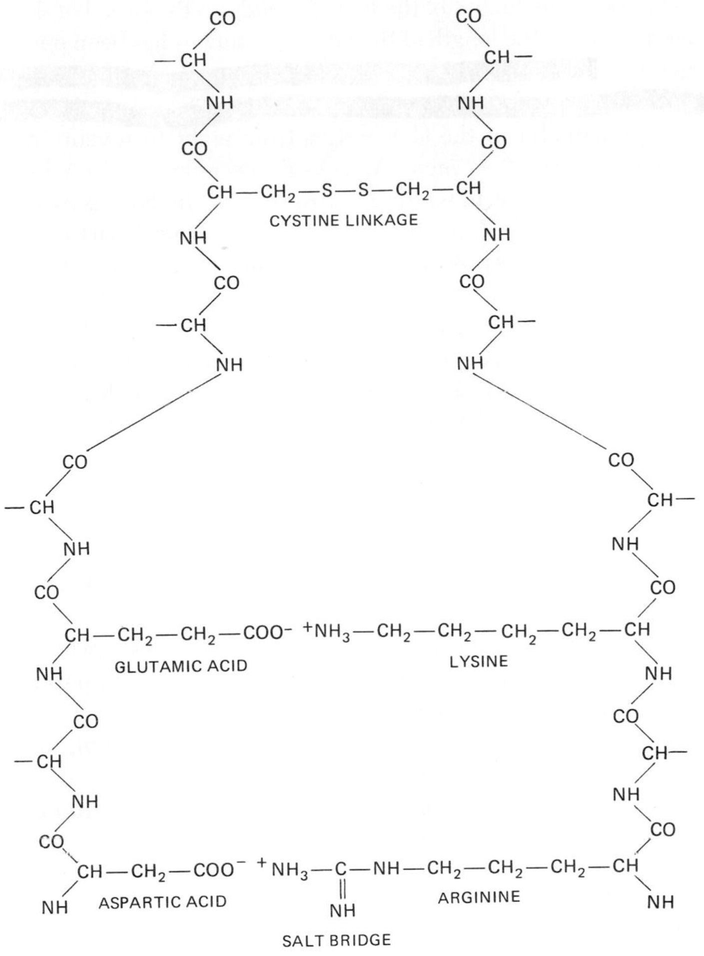

CO
—CH   CH—
  NH   NH
  CO   CO
CH—CH_2—S—S—CH_2—CH
       CYSTINE LINKAGE
NH   NH
  CO   CO
—CH   CH—
  NH   NH

CO   CO
—CH   CH—
  NH   NH
  CO   CO
CH—CH_2—CH_2—COO$^-$ $^+NH_3$—CH_2—CH_2—CH_2—CH_2—CH
     GLUTAMIC ACID   LYSINE
NH   NH
  CO   CO
—CH   CH—
  NH   NH
  CO   CO
CH—CH_2—COO$^-$ $^+NH_3$—C—NH—CH_2—CH_2—CH_2—CH
NH   ASPARTIC ACID   ‖   ARGININE   NH
            NH
      SALT BRIDGE

Figure 5-3. Structural formula for the wool molecule.

D. The cystine linkages in wool are chemically reactive to such substances as alkalis, bleaches, heat, sunlight, and certain finishing agents such as those used in mothproofing and shrink-resistant finishes.

E. The salt bridges of wool are reactive to acids and dyestuffs.

PROPERTIES OF WOOL FIBERS

Physical Appearance

Color. Wool fibers vary in natural color from white to creamy white to light beige, yellow, brown, and black. Wool may be dyed easily; however, it is difficult to keep white wool snow-white. The fiber tends to yellow from exposure to sunlight and with age. Bleaching is not a satisfactory means of keeping wool white, as chlorine bleaches are harmful to the fiber and bleaching itself tends to cause some yellowing.

Shape. The length of the fiber depends on the breed of sheep from which it comes and on the length of time during which it has been permitted to grow. In general, the range of fiber length is from one inch to fourteen or more inches, with finer fibers being shorter and coarser fibers being longer.

The diameter of the fiber ranges from eight to seventy microns (1 micron equals .00004 of an inch). Merino fleece fibers are usually about fifteen to seventeen microns in width. In cross section the fiber is oval or elliptical. The cross section may show three parts: The innermost part is called the *medulla*. Not all wool fibers possess a medulla, which is the section in which the pigment or color is carried and which provides air space. Most finer wools do not have a medulla. The next segment is the *cortex*. Research has shown that the cortex is made up of microscopic fibrils that pack this area. The outer layer is made up of a fine network of small overlapping scales. The scale structure is responsible for the behavior of wool in felting and in shrinkage, and for its insulating qualities.

Because the scales on the surface of the fiber are attached to the fiber at only one end, the open end of the scales can catch onto the scales of other fibers. When subject to conditions of heat, moisture, and friction, the interlocked scales can hold the fibers so closely together that felt, a simple type of nonwoven fabric, is formed. They also "shrink" together in water and account for a substantial amount of shrinkage that can take place in wool.

Wool fiber possesses one further quality that is important in its physical appearance and behavior; it has a natural crimp, or curly, wavy shape. This crimp increases the elasticity and springiness of wool, and makes it quite resilient. It also makes wool fiber relatively easy to spin into yarns.

Mixed into wool fleece are a number of *kemp* hairs. Kemp hairs are coarse, straight hairs that are often white and shiny and do not absorb dye easily. A large proportion of kemp hairs lowers the quality of the fleece.

Other Properties

Luster. The luster of wool varies, although sheep's wool does not have a great deal of luster. Luster varies among different breeds of sheep, different sections of the fleece, and the conditions under which the animal has been raised. In general, the luster of poor quality wool is greater than the luster of better grades of wool.

Density or Specific Gravity. The specific gravity of wool is 1.32. This relatively low density makes wool fabrics feel light in relation to their bulk. The ability of wool fibers to trap and absorb air also gives them an ability to provide warmth without excessive weight. This is fortunate since wool is so weak that a large amount of fiber is usually necessary to make fabrics of adequate strength.

Elasticity and Resilience. The elasticity and resilience of wool are excellent. These qualities contribute to the appearance of wool products by giving them very good resistance to, and recovery from, wrinkling. Wrinkles will hang out of wool garments, especially if they are hung in a damp atmosphere, as will creases, pleats, or other shape provided by pressing.

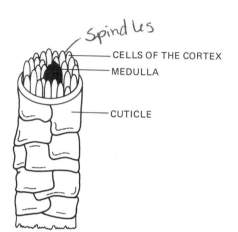

Spindles

CELLS OF THE CORTEX
MEDULLA

CUTICLE

Figure 5-4. Wool fiber structure.

Absorbency and Moisture Regain. Wool is a very absorbent fiber. However, it absorbs moisture without feeling wet on the surface. This makes it possible to wear a wool garment that is actually rather damp but does not feel especially wet. Wool also gives up its moisture slowly. Paradoxically, wool is also water repellent. Spilled liquids run off wool, because the scale structure of wool inhibits wicking of moisture along the fiber surface. Surface moisture is absorbed slowly. One can summarize the behavior of wool in relation to moisture by saying that wool is naturally water repellent but upon prolonged exposure to moisture the fiber does absorb substantial quantities of water. The moisture is held inside the fiber, not on the surface, making wool feel relatively dry even when it is holding a good deal of water.

Dimensional Stability. Wool has poor dimensional stability. As mentioned previously, the tendency of wool to shrink and felt can cause fabrics and garments to decrease in size. The shrinkage of wool is progressive. In the first laundering, fabrics stretched in the weaving process tend to relax. But wool will continue to shrink with subsequent launderings if it is not washed in cool water with a minimum of handling.

Consumers should preshrink wool fabrics before sewing unless the fabric is labeled as having been treated to prevent shrinkage. Purchasers of wool ready-to-wear should look for labels indicating shrinkage control. Finishes can be given to wool to render the fabric washable. Such finishes are discussed at length in Chapter 20.

Conductivity of Heat and Electricity. The conductivity of wool of both heat and electricity are low. Both the poor heat conductivity of wool fiber and its ability to trap air between the fibers contribute to its excellent qualities for cold-weather clothing. Even though the electrical conductivity of wool is rated as poor, wool fibers do not build up static electrical charges unless the atmosphere is very dry. The ability of the fiber to absorb moisture improves its conductivity when humidity is present in the atmosphere. For this reason wool garments sometimes generate static electrical charges indoors in winter when central heating of homes makes them warm and dry.

Combustibility; Effect of Heat. Wool will burn if a flame is held to the fabric, but it burns slowly, and when the flame is removed the fabric may self-extinguish. The danger of flammability exists, but is not so great as with many other fabrics. Wool can be treated for fire retardancy. Dry heat damages the fiber, producing a negative effect on both appearance and strength.

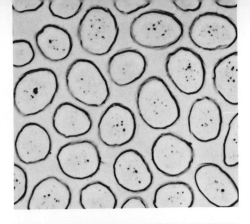
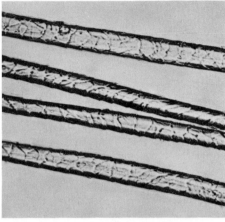

Figure 5-5. Photomicrograph of Merino wool fiber in a cross section and a longitudinal view. Courtesy of E. I. du Pont de Nemours & Company.

Wool Fabrics and Their Behavior in Relation to Selected Conditions

Chemical Reactivity. Wool fibers are quickly damaged by strong alkali solutions and even relatively weak alkalis have a deleterious effect on wool. Strong laundry detergents and soaps have "free" alkali added to increase their cleaning power and extended exposure to this additional alkali may be harmful to wool. Wool fabrics should be washed with special mild detergents.

Acids do not harm wool except in very strong concentrations. This makes it possible to carbonize wool fleece to remove vegetable matter without harming the wool fiber.

Chlorine compounds used for bleaching damage wool. Hydrogen peroxide or sodium perborate bleaches can be used safely. Organic dry-cleaning solvents will not harm the fiber.

Insects.   One of the major problems in the care of wool is its susceptibility to damage from insect pests. Moths and carpet beetles are particularly destructive because the chemical structure of the cross-linkages in wool is especially attractive to these insects. Care in the storage of wool is required to minimize attack by insects. Soiled clothing is more readily damaged than clean fabrics, as the insects may attach the spilled food as well as the wool. Fabrics of wool that have special finishes that prevent moth attack are referred to as being "mothproofed." Some of these finishes can be applied at the time of dry cleaning. Other moth-repellent substances can be placed in storage containers in closets or sprayed on fabrics. Paradichlorobenzene crystals or napthalene flakes may be used in an airtight container with garments. Chemicals should be placed above the garments since their vapors are heavier than air (see U.S.D.A. Bulletin no. 113).

Micro-organisms.   Mildew will not form on wool unless the fabric has been stored in a damp condition for an extended period of time. Fabrics should be put away only after they are completely dry.

Environmental Conditions.   Exposure to sunlight will cause deterioration of wool, although it is less severely affected than cotton. Sunlight also yellows white wool fabrics.

Age will not affect wool adversely. However, because of their susceptibility to attack by moths, wool fabrics require careful storage.

CARE PROCEDURES

Wool fabrics can be either laundered or dry-cleaned, although dry cleaning is preferable for wool fabrics that have not been specially finished to make them "washable." Dry cleaning minimizes shrinkage problems. Also, dry-cleaning solvents may include mothproof finishes that will protect wool garments from moth attack during storage.

Fabrics that have been given special finishes to render them "washable" should be laundered according to care directions attached to the fabric. Fabrics without special finishes must be handled gently, because the fabric is weaker wet than dry and also to prevent felting of fibers because of friction. Water temperatures used in washing wool products should be lukewarm, and synthetic detergents may be used. Washing can be done by hand or machine provided the wool fabrics are not agitated for more than three minutes. Knitted garments, such as sweaters, should be measured before laundering, and while the garments are drying they can be gently reshaped into their original size.

Wool fabrics should not be dried in an automatic dryer. The pounding action caused by tumbling damp fabrics in the dryer may cause excessive felting shrinkage of the fabrics. The dryer provides all of the conditions conducive to felting: heat, moisture, and friction. Drying fabrics flat will prevent strain on any one part of the garment.

Chlorine bleaches must not be applied to wool because this type of bleach will damage the fabric. Hydrogen peroxide may be used for bleaching.

Solvents used for spot and stain removal do not harm wool fabrics. However, care should be taken in the application of spot remover. Excessive friction or rubbing on the surface of the fabric may cause matting and felting of fibers in the treated spot. Pat the fabric gently, rather than rubbing hard.

Because of the detrimental effect of heat on wool fibers, ironing temperatures should not exceed 200 degrees F., and fabrics should always be pressed with a press cloth or steam.

WOOL USE

The excellent insulating qualities of wool leads to its use for cold weather clothing. Winter coats, warm sweaters, and men's and women's suits are frequently made of worsted or woolen fabrics, or blends of wool and other fabrics.

Tailored garments utilize the qualities of wool that make it possible to shape the garment through pressing techniques that depend on wool's capacity for shrinkage. By using different kinds of wool yarns, and variations in weave, a wide variety of attractive garments and accessories are manufactured from wool.

In the home, wool fabrics are made into carpets, blankets, upholstery fabrics, and sometimes draperies. Special coarse, resilient, durable wool fibers are produced for manufacture into carpets. Blankets of wool are warm without excessive weight and have the advantage of inherent flame retardancy. The durability of upholstery fabrics will depend upon the construction of the yarn and fabric, and those fabrics made from tightly twisted yarns with close, even weaves are most serviceable.

The disadvantages of wool used for apparel and in the home center on the tendency of the fiber to shrink and the susceptibility of wool to moth damage. Fabrics that have been finished to overcome both of these problems are available and appropriate handling during use and care will minimize these disadvantages. A disadvantage of wool for some individuals is that they may have allergic reactions from contact with the fiber.

Minor Hair Fibers

Many minor hair fibers possess qualities similar to those of wool. These fibers are produced in comparatively small quantities, but do have an important place in the textile industry.

CASHMERE

Cashmere fiber is obtained from the fleece of the Cashmere (or Kashmir) goat, an animal that is native to the Himalaya Mountains region of India, China, and Tibet. Iran and Iraq also produce cashmere fiber.

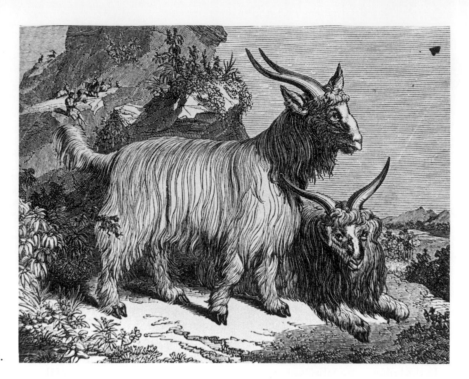

Figure 5-6. Cashmere goat.

The animals are domesticated, and fiber is gathered by combing hairs from the fleece during the shedding season. Only the fine underhair is useful for cashmere fabrics and one goat produces about four ounces of useable fiber each year.

The softest fibers are one and one-half to three and one-half inches in length. Coarser and stiffer fibers range from two to five inches. The natural color of cashmere is gray, brown, or, less often, white.

Microscopically, cashmere displays a scale structure like that of wool but the scales are spaced more widely apart. Fibers are finer than wool, about fifteen microns in diameter. The cross section of cashmere fibers is round.

The chemical and physical behavior of cashmere is much like that of wool, although cashmere is more quickly damaged by alkalis.

The softness and luster of cashmere combined with its scarcity put this fiber in the category of luxury fibers that are quite expensive. The fiber abrades easily, because of its softness, and since many of these fabrics are constructed with napped or fleecy surfaces, they require careful handling. Sweaters, coatings, and soft luxurious fabrics and yarns account for the largest proportion of the items made from cashmere.

CAMEL'S HAIR

The two-humped Bactrian camel of Central Asia is the source of the camel's hair fiber. In the spring when the weather begins to warm, the camel begins to

Figure 5-7. Bactrian camel.

shed. (Although some hair is collected at other times of the year, the largest quantity is taken in the spring.) A trailer follows the camel caravans as they move from place to place. As the hair drops, the trailer collects it, placing it in a basket that is carried by the last camel in the caravan. It has been estimated that one camel produces from five to eight pounds of hair each year. When sufficient quantities of hair have been collected, they are baled and prepared for shipping.

Within the collected hair are found both fine, soft down or *noils*, and coarse, bristly hairs. The soft noils are used for making cloth. Coarser hairs are separated out before processing.

Under the microscope, camel's hair shows a scale structure similar to that of wool, but the scales are less visible and less distinctly seen. The cortex is distinct, the medulla is discontinuous. Both the cortex and medulla are pigmented. This pigment produces the light brown or tan color associated with camel cloth, and because it is such an integral part of the fiber it cannot be removed by bleaching. Therefore, camel fabrics are usually left in their natural color or dyed to darker shades.

Camel's hair provides excellent warmth without weight. It is said to have better insulating qualities than any of the other hair fibers. It is a relatively weak fiber and subject to damage from abrasion because of its softness. Other physical and chemical properties of camel's hair are like those of wool.

Most fine camel's hair fiber is used for clothing, especially coating fabrics. Like other hair fibers there is great variety in quality of camel's hair fibers, and the consumer must evaluate these products carefully. Because it is easy to dye wool camel color and blend it with camel's hair, there may be misrepresentation of the final product as "camel's hair" when, in fact, the quantity of camel's hair is relatively low. Camel's hair fabric is expensive and should not be selected for its durability, as it tends to wear readily. Coarse camel's hair is used for industrial fiber, ropes, and paintbrushes.

Mohair

Mohair fiber is taken from the angora goat. The United States produces the largest quantity of mohair, much of it in Texas. Other important sources of the fiber are South Africa and Turkey where the angora goat originates.

Goats are sheared in the same way as sheep. Fleece is removed twice a year. Each animal yields from three to five pounds a year of four- to six-inch fiber. In order to obtain a supply of slightly longer fiber, some goats are sheared only once a year in which case the fibers are nine to twelve inches in length.

The natural color of unscoured fleece is yellow to grayish white. In cleaning, 15 to 25 per cent of the weight is removed. The clean fibers are white in color, silky, and fine in feel and appearance. Fibers are graded, and kids' or young goats' fleece are especially valued for their fineness. The cross section of the fiber is round, with the medulla being only rarely visible. Small air ducts are present between the cells of the fiber, which give it a light, fluffy feeling. The microscopic appearance of mohair is similar to that of wool.

Most of the physical and chemical properties of mohair are very similar to

Figure 5-8. Angora goat. Courtesy of the United States Department of Agriculture.

those of wool. The major differences between wool and mohair are the very high luster of mohair and its slippery, smooth surface. Mohair is especially resistant to abrasion. When viewed under the microscope, mohair shows fewer scales than wool. As a result, the fiber sheds dust and soil and neither shrinks nor felts as readily as wool. Mohair is easier to launder, as well.

Its excellent resistance to abrasion led to the extensive use of mohair in railroad and automobile upholstery. The development of synthetics has replaced the fiber in this use largely because synthetics are less expensive and not susceptible to moth damage.

The current uses of mohair include men's and women's suitings, upholstery fabrics, carpets, and draperies. Novelty yarns, such as looped or boucle yarns, are often made of mohair, and it is blended with other fiber.

The cost of mohair fabrics tends to be higher than that of wool. The quality of mohair can vary a good deal, so the consumer must evaluate mohair products carefully.

Q I V I U T

Qiviut is the underwool of the domesticated musk ox. Herds of musk oxen are cultivated in Alaska where Eskimo women have been taught to spin and knit Qiviut into articles for sale. The fiber is similar to cashmere in texture and softness. One half pound of Qiviut will make a large, warm sweater. An equivalent garment in sheep's wool would require six pounds of fiber.

Figure 5-9. Musk ox.

Figure 5-10. Alpaca.

Figure 5-11. Llama.

Figure 5-12. Vicuña herd. Foto by William L. Franklin.

ALPACA

Native to Peru, Bolivia, Ecuador, and Argentina, the domesticated alpaca produces a fleece of fine, strong fibers that have a glossy luster. The alpaca is sheared once every two years in the spring (November and December in the Southern Hemisphere). Hairs average eight to twelve inches in length, and range in color from white to brown to black.

Alpaca fiber is used in suits, dresses, and upholstery fabrics. It may be made into blends with other fibers.

LLAMA

Another domesticated Andean animal, the llama, produces a fine, lustrous fleece, similar to alpaca. Its colors are predominantly black and brown, but some lighter colors are found. Slightly weaker than alpaca or camel's hair, llama fleece is used by many Indian craftsmen to produce decorative shawls, ponchos, and other products.

The fibers are often blended. Llama fiber is used for coatings, suitings, and dress fabrics.

HUARIZO AND MISTI

Llamas and alpacas have been crossbred, and the resulting animals have fleece with many of the same qualities and characteristics as those of the parents. The Huarizo has a llama father and an alpaca mother. The Misti has a llama mother and an alpaca father.

VICUÑA

A wild animal, the vicuña lives at very high altitudes in the Andes mountains. Although attempts are being made to domesticate this animal, most of the fiber must be obtained by hunting and killing the vicuña. One vicuña yields four ounces of very fine fiber and ten to twelve ounces of less fine fiber. The Peruvian government sets a limit on the number of vicuña that can be taken in any year, so that the fiber is in very short supply.

One of the softest fibers known, vicuña is also the costliest. A vicuña coat would be comparable in cost to a good fur coat. Its use is limited to luxury items. The natural color—a light tan or chestnut brown—is usually retained, as the fiber is hard to dye.

GUANACO

Another wild animal, the guanaco, has been successfully domesticated. Although supplies of the fiber are more readily available than vicuña, it remains a relatively expensive fiber.

It has a soft, fine fleece of reddish brown color. Often blended, guanaco is similar to alpaca in its qualities.

FUR FIBER

Fiber from the pelts of fur-bearing animals is sometimes blended with other wool fibers. It provides interest, and softness, in texture. Fur fibers from animals such as the beaver, fox, mink, chinchilla, rabbit, and the like are used.

Angora rabbits have long, fine, silky, white hair. These rabbits are raised in France, Italy, Japan, and the United States. The fiber is obtained by combing or clipping the rabbits. Angora rabbit fiber is exceptionally fine (13 microns) and is very slippery and hard to spin. Angora is used chiefly in novelty items, and is often knitted. The fibers tend to slip out of the yarns and increase in length on the suface of fabrics so that some persons have the mistaken notion that angora hair "grows."

Fur Products Labeling Act of 1951

Although relatively small quantities of fur fibers are used in the production of textiles, Congress has acted to prevent deception in the sale of fur products by enacting the Fur Products Labeling Act of 1951. This legislation requires that all fur products carry the true English name of the fur-bearing animal from which the fur comes. It also requires that furs be labeled with the country of their origin.

COW HAIR AND HORSEHAIR

Small quantities of cow hair and horsehair are used. Cow hair is sometimes blended with wool in low-grade fabrics used for carpeting and blankets, and in felts. Horsehair is utilized as a filling or stuffing material for mattresses and upholstered pieces. In the past, it was woven into a stiff braid for use in millinery or dressmaking, but has been replaced in this use, for the most part, by synthetic fibers. Rubberized horsehair has been used to make carpet underlays.

HISTORY OF SILK CULTURE

Silk originates in China, the first habitat of the silkworm, which grew wild and lived on the leaves of a species of mulberry tree. Although some animal hair and flax fibers can grow to considerable length, silk is the only natural fiber that is hundreds of meters long.

Silk is made by the silkworm as it builds its cocoon. The substance is *extruded* from its body in one continuous thread from beginning to end. It is possible to unwind the cocoon and obtain this long, silk filament. The Chinese discovered this process and, recognizing the potential value of the fiber it produced, guarded the method closely for hundreds of years. Because of the natural beauty of silk, its history has been surrounded by legends. Chinese folklore credits the discovery of silk to Princess Si Ling Chi, who reigned about 2650 B.C. According to legend, after watching a silkworm spin its cocoon in her garden, she attempted to unwind the long filaments. After much experimentation she succeeded. She instructed her serving women in the art of weaving rich and beautiful fabrics from the long, silk threads. So grateful for her discovery were the Chinese that they transformed Princess Si Ling Chi into a goddess and made her the patron deity of weaving.[8]

History agrees with legend at least insofar as the approximate dates for the first use of silk by the Chinese. In spite of the close guarding of the secret of *sericulture* or the controlled production of silk, other countries managed, often by somewhat devious means, to obtain silkworms. The Japanese supposedly abducted four Chinese maidens who were experts in sericulture and forced them to disclose the process. Another princess carried silkworm eggs and the seeds of the mulberry tree in her headdress when she left China to marry a prince of another kingdom. Even as late as the sixth century A.D., the secrets of silk manufacture were sought by the Byzantine emperor Justinian who sent two

[8] Ethel Lewis. *The Romance of Textiles* (New York: Macmillan Publishing Co., Inc. 1937), p. 31 ff.

monks to the East to discover how to produce and weave these handsome fabrics. The monks returned from a lengthy trip bringing back silkworm eggs and mulberry seeds in their hollow bamboo walking sticks. From these seeds a flourishing silk industry developed in Byzantium. The cultivation of the silkworm spread to Italy and later to France.[9]

SILK PRODUCTION

Cultivation of the Silkworm

Silk is the only natural filament fiber that has significant commercial value. Produced by a caterpillar known as a "silkworm," silk can be obtained either from cultivated silkworms (Bombyx Mori) or wild species.

Silk from wild species is limited in quantity and produces a coarser, stronger, short fiber known as *tussah silk*. Tussah silk has short fibers because the cocoons from which it is taken have been broken or pierced. When wild silk is spun by caterpillars that feed on oak leaves, the silk is light brown or tan in color and cannot be bleached.

By far the largest quantity of silk is obtained through sericulture, or the controlled growth of domesticated silkworms in order to produce the silk fiber. Whether the silkworms be domesticated or wild, they go through four basic stages of development.

1. Laying of the eggs by the silk moth.

2. Hatching of the eggs into caterpillars.

3. Spinning of a cocoon by the adult caterpillar.

4. Emergence of the silk moth from the cocoon.

The science of sericulture has been perfected over many thousands of years. Today all stages of development are carefully controlled and only the healthiest eggs, worms, and moths are used for the production of silk.

Selected moths of superior size lay from 400 to 600 eggs or seeds on prepared cards or strips of cloth. Each seed is about the size of a pinhead. These eggs can be stored in cool, dry places until the manufacturer wishes to begin their incubation.

Incubation is done in a mildly warm atmosphere and requires about thirty days. At the end of this time the silkworms hatch. They are about one-eighth of an inch in length. The young silkworms require constant care and carefully controlled diets. Shredded or chopped young mulberry leaves are fed to the worms five times each day. Worms that appear to be weak or deformed are discarded, and the areas in which they are grown are kept scrupulously clean. For about a month the worm grows, shedding its skin four times. When fully grown, worms are about three and a half inches in length.

When its size and activity show that the worm is about ready to begin to spin

[9] Ibid.

a cocoon, the silkworm is transferred to a surface of twigs or straw. From two sacs located in the lower jaw, the worm extrudes a substance made up of two stands of silk (fibroin) and a gummy material (sericin) that holds them together. Moving its head in the shape of a figure eight the worm surrounds itself with a cocoon of perhaps 1,000 meters of fiber. The completed cocoon is about the size of a peanut shell, and takes two to three days to spin. If the worm is permitted to live, it will change into a pupa or chrysalis and then to a moth. After two weeks the moth breaks through the cocoon and emerges, mates, lays eggs, and begins the cycle again.

Only those moths selected as breeding stock are permitted to complete the cycle. These are selected from the largest and heaviest cocoons. The remainder of the cocoons are subjected to dry heat that kills the pupa.

Occasionally two silkworms will spin a cocoon together. This produces a cocoon made of a double strand of silk and is known as *doupion* silk.[10]

[10] *Doupioni,* in Italian.

Figure 5-13. (*Upper left*) silk moth laying eggs; (*upper right*) silkworms on a bed of mulberry leaves; (*lower left*) silkworm beginning to spin cocoon; (*lower right*) completed cocoon. Photographs courtesy of The Japan Silk Association.

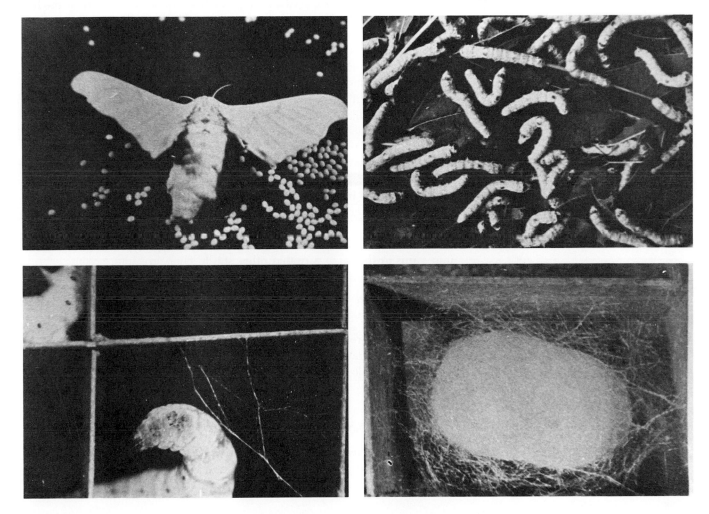

Reeling of Silk

The whole, unbroken cocoons are sorted according to color, texture, size, shape, and other factors that will affect the quality of the fiber. Reeling of silk is, to a large extent, a hand operation done in a factory called a *filature*. Several cocoons are placed in a container of water of about 140 degrees F. This warm water serves to soften the gum or sericin that holds the filaments of silk together. Very little gum is actually removed in reeling. The outer fibers are coarse, short, and not useful in filament silk. They are separated and used for spun silk, which is made from short fiber lengths.

The filaments from four or more cocoons are held together to form a strand of yarn. As the reeling continues, a skilled operator adds or lets off fibers as needed to make a smooth yarn of uniform size. A number of skeins of silk weighing fifty to one hundred grams each are combined into bundles. Each bundle is called a *book* and weighs from five to ten pounds. These are packaged into bales for shipping.

Most of the finest silk comes from Japan where the science of sericulture has been most carefully developed. Because the culture of silkworms requires so much hand labor, sericulture has been most successful in countries where labor is less expensive. Other major silk-producing areas include India, Southeast Asia, and China. European countries such as France and Italy that once had thriving silk industries no longer produce a great deal of silk fiber. These countries may still weave silk fabrics, but most of the silk fiber is produced elsewhere. No silk is produced in the United States.

Silk Yarns

The making of silk yarns is called *throwing*. Reeled silk filaments can be made into yarns immediately. Short, staple length silk fibers must be spun. Short, outside fibers of the silkworm's cocoon, the inner fibers from the cocoon, and the fiber from pierced cocoons are known as *frisons* and are made into spun silk yarns. Fibers are cut into fairly uniform lengths, combed, and twisted into yarns in the same way that other staple fibers are spun.

Gum Removal

The sericin or gum that holds the silk filaments in place in the cocoon is softened but not removed in reeling. This material makes up about 25 per cent of the weight of raw silk. It is removed either before throwing, after throwing, or after the fabric has been woven. A soap solution is used to wash the gum from the silk.

Regulation of Silk Weighting

During the latter part of the nineteenth century, the technique of weighting was employed extensively to add body and weight to silk fabrics after removal of the gum. In passing silk through a solution of metallic salts, the salts are absorbed by the fiber, with a corresponding increase in the weight of the fabric. Silk can absorb more than its own weight in metallic salts, so that this excess weight on the fiber will, eventually, cause the fabric to break.

This practice had become so widespread that a good deal of poor quality fabric was being sold. The buyer could not tell from its appearance or hand that the silk had been weighted, so the Federal Trade Commission, in 1938, began regulating silk weighting by passing its Pure Silk regulation.

These FTC regulations are still in effect. Fabrics labeled "silk" or "pure dye silk" may, under the regulations, contain from 0 to 10 per cent of weighting. All silk fabrics that have more than 10 per cent weighting must be labeled as weighted silk, unless they are black in color. Black silks are able to hold a greater quantity of weighting than other colors without degradation, and, so, black silks can be weighted up to 15 per cent.

Today very little silk sold in the United States is weighted. Fabrics that are purchased abroad, however, may have been weighted.

PROPERTIES OF SILK FIBERS

Physical Appearance

Color. The natural color of cultivated silk is off-white to cream color. Wild silk is brown.

Shape. In microscopic cross section silk is triangular in shape. The double silk filaments lie with the flat sides of the triangles together.

The fiber has a smooth, transparent rodlike shape with occasional swelling or irregularities along its length. It is fine, having a diameter of nine to eleven microns, and filaments may be as short as 300 meters or as long as 1,000 meters. Individual filaments as long as 3,000 meters have been measured.

Luster. The luster of degummed silk is high.

Other Properties

Strength or Tenacity. Silk is one of the strongest of the natural fibers (Its tenacity is 2.8 to 5.2 g.d.). Its wet strength is slightly less than its dry strength.

Density or Specific Gravity. The specific gravity of silk of 1.25 is less than that of cellulose fibers and is similar to that of wool.[11] Lightweight fabrics can be made of silk because of the fine diameter of the fiber and its high tenacity.

Elasticity, Resilience. The elasticity of silk is good and its resilience is medium. Creases will hang out of silk but its wrinkle recovery is slower and not as good as that of wool.

Absorbency, Moisture Regain. The absorbency of silk is good (the moisture regain is 11 per cent) making it a comfortable fiber to wear. Although silk is more difficult to dye than wool, it can be printed and dyed easily to bright, clear colors if appropriate dyes are used.

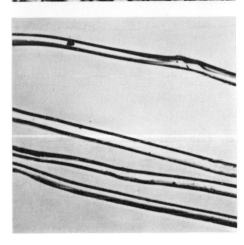

Figure 5-14. Photomicrograph of degummed silk fiber in a cross section and a longitudinal view. Courtesy of E. I. du Pont de Nemours & Company.

[11] Du Pont Bulletin X-156. Varying sources list specific gravity of silk that ranges from 1.25 to 1.34.

Dimensional Stability. The dimensional stability of silk is good. Silk does not tend to stretch or shrink to any significant extent.

Heat and Electrical Conductivity. The heat conductivity of silk is low so that densely woven fabrics can be relatively warm. However, because very sheer, lightweight fabrics can be woven from silk, it can be used for light-weight, summer clothing.

The electrical conductivity of silk is poor, and silk tends to build up static electricity charges, especially in dry atmospheres.

Combustibility; Effect of Heat. When placed in a direct flame, silk will burn, but when the flame is removed it will not continue to support combustion. Therefore, silk is not considered to be an especially combustible fabric. Like wool, silk is damaged by dry heat and should be ironed damp, at low temperatures and using a press cloth.

Effect of Selected Conditions on Silk

Chemical Properties. Like other protein fibers, silk is sensitive to the action of alkalis but is damaged more slowly than wool. Acids will harm silk more quickly than they harm wool. Chlorine bleach deteriorates the fiber, but hydrogen peroxide or other peroxygen bleaches can be used. Organic chemical solvents used in dry cleaning will not affect silk. Perspiration will cause deterioration of the fabric. Perspiration can have a negative effect on dyestuffs, causing discoloration after repeated exposure.

Insects and Micro-organisms. Mildew is not a problem with silk. Moths do not harm silk, but carpet beetles will attack the fabric.

Environmental Conditions. Sunlight deteriorates silk even more rapidly than wool, causing white fabrics to yellow. Age will lead to eventual deterio-

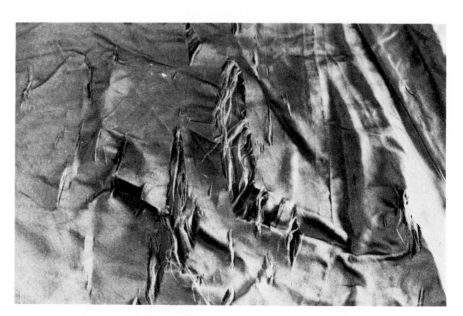

Figure 5-15. Silk fabric from the skirt of an historic costume of the 1890's that has deteriorated as a result of silk weighting.

ration of fabric strength. Silk fabrics should be stored away from light. Antique fabrics should be sealed off from the air.

Weighting of silk causes it to crack, split, and deteriorate much more quickly than would otherwise be true. Historic costumes made of silk before silk weighting was introduced are still in good condition. Silk garments made in later times, which were weighted, break apart into shreds.

CARE PROCEDURES

Most silk garments should be dry-cleaned for best results. Some of the dyestuffs used on silk are susceptible to bleeding or loss of the dyestuff into the washing water so that dry-cleaning is preferable to laundering. Small items such as silk scarves or other accessories made of silk can be laundered if mild detergents and lukewarm water are used, and if the fabrics are handled carefully. Chlorine bleaches should never be used on silk fabrics. If silk fabrics must be bleached, hydrogen peroxide can be used.

Silk fabrics should be stored away from direct sunlight, both to avoid yellowing of white fabrics and to prevent loss of strength. Long-term storage of silk wedding gowns or other items is best done in containers that are sealed against air and carpet beetles.

When ironing silk, protect the fabric with a dry press cloth. Keep ironing temperatures low, at 300 degrees F., or lower. Test silk fabrics to be sure they will not watermark before using steam or a damp press cloth. Although badly wrinkled silk fabrics will require pressing, many creases will hang out of silk fabrics without ironing.

USES

The beauty of silk fabrics is legendary. For many centuries, silk was synonymous with luxury, and was used for garments worn on feast days, festivals, and other occasions of great importance. Wall hangings of silk were used to decorate the homes of the wealthy and carpets woven of silk were used in the homes of the rich in Persia and China.

At present, the relatively smaller supplies of silk, as compared with synthetics, have tended to maintain the position of silk as a "luxury" fiber. Silk is relatively expensive and is used chiefly for dresses, blouses, and other garments and accessories that sell at fairly high prices.

Silk may also be found in some high-priced drapery and upholstery fabrics. The performance of silk fabrics in these uses is rather poor. Upholstery fabrics of silk are often made in weaves that show up the luster of the fabric, but abrade rather easily. Sunlight will deteriorate drapery fabrics of silk. Draperies made of silk should be lined with some other fabric to protect the silk from constant exposure to the sun.

Table 5.2 offers a comparison of the two major protein fibers, silk and wool.

Table 5.2

*Comparison of the Characteristics
of the Protein Fibers, Wool and Silk*

	Wool	*Silk*
Specific gravity	1.32	1.25 (boiled off)
Tenacity (GPD)		
Dry	1.0–1.7	2.4–5.1
Wet	.8–1.6	1.8–4.2
Moisture Regain	about 15%	10–11%
Resiliency	excellent	good
Burning	burns slowly, sometimes self-extinguishing when flame is removed.	burns slowly, sometimes self-extinguishing when flame is removed.
Conductivity of		
Heat	good insulator	fair
Electricity	rather poor, builds up static electricity	rather poor, builds up static electricity
Resistance to damage from		
Fungi	good	good
Insects	poor, attacked by moths, carpet beetles	fair, not attacked by moths, but is attacked by carpet beetles
Prolonged exposure to sunlight	yellows, loses strength eventually	yellows and degrades
Acids	resists action of mild or dilute acids, damaged by strong acids	more readily damaged by acids than wool, more resistant than cotton
Alkalis	damaged by even mildly alkaline substances	damaged by even mildly alkaline substances

Regenerated Protein or Azlon Fibers

With the commercially successful regeneration of cellulosic fibers, research was initiated to find suitable protein materials for regeneration in the hope of creating fibers with the highly desirable qualities of wool. As a base material, a protein was required that was readily available, as well as one that had a chemical structure similar to that of wool. Milk was selected, and in 1904 the first method for making filaments from the protein of milk (or casein) was disclosed, but the filaments were too brittle to be used. In the 1930s, a usable fiber known as Lanital was developed in Italy and one called Aralac was made in the United States. Since that time other regenerated protein fibers have been made from corn, peanuts, and soybeans.

Regenerated protein fibers had a pleasant, soft handle, but their strength was poor and their lack of durability presented a problem. Some of the milk-based proteins also developed an unpleasant odor when wet.

Except for Chinon, a Japanese graft-fiber made from milk protein and polyacrylonitrile, these fibers are only of historic significance as they are not now being produced. Moncrieff sees Chinon as "an attempt to combine protein qualities, characteristic of wool and silk, with those of acrylic fibers, viz. good stability and resistance to attack and durability."[12]

[12] R. W. Moncrieff, *Man-Made Fibres* (New York: John Wiley & Sons, Inc., 1975), p. 692.

Until the late 1960s, a few milk protein fibers were manufactured abroad. Table 5.3 depicts their period of production and the country in which they were produced. The generic name for the regenerated protein groups is *azlon*.

Worldwide shortages of foodstuffs, especially protein foods, make it unlikely that new regenerated protein fibers will be developed.

Table 5.3
Regenerated Protein Fibers

Substance	Trade Name	Country	Dates
Milk protein	Aralac	U.S.A.	1939–1948
	Fibrolane	Britain	discontinued in 1965
	Lanital	Italy	1937 into 40s
	Merinova	Italy	discontinued in late 1960s
Milk protein grafted with acrylic	Chinon	Japan	early 1970s to present
Peanut protein	Ardil	Britain	1938–1957
Corn protein	Vicara	U.S.A.	1948–1957
Soybean protein	Ford Motor Company experimented with for car seats		never in major production

Recommended References

BERGEN, W. B. *Wool Handbook*. Plainfield, N. J.: Textile Book Service. 1963.

COOK, J. G. *Handbook of Textile Fibers*. Vol. 1. Watford, England: Merrow Publishing Company, Ltd., 1968.

Encyclopedia of Textiles. London: Ernest Benn, Ltd., 1928.

Encyclopedia of Textiles, American Fabrics. Englewood Cliffs, N. J.: Prentice-Hall, 2nd ed.

FRANKLIN, W. L. "Turnabout in the Andes." (Vicuña) *International Wildlife*, May-June 1975, p. 42.

JOSEPH, M. *Introductory Textile Science*. New York: Holt, Rinehart, and Winston, Inc., 1972.

LEWIS, ETHEL. *The Romance of Textiles*. New York: Macmillan Publishing Co., Inc., 1937.

"The Musk Ox Project." *American Fabrics and Fashions*, Fall 1972, p. 40.

POTTER, M. D. and B. P. CORBMAN. *Textiles, Fiber to Fabric*. New York: McGraw-Hill Book Co., 1967, 5th ed.

"Spun Silk." *CIBA Review*. 1967, vol. 2.

VARRON, A. "The Origins and Use of Silk." *CIBA Review*, July 1938, p. 350.

WEIBEL, A. C. *Two Thousand Years of Textiles*. New York: Pantheon Books, 1952.

"Wool." *CIBA Review*, 1962, vol. 6.

6

MINERAL AND CARBON FIBERS

Asbestos

The small number of fibers that can be classified as mineral fibers might also be called inorganic fibers, because these fibers lack carbon, the essential element in the chemical composition of organic fibers. Of these fibers only asbestos is found in the fibrous state. The others, glass and metallic fibers, are considered to be man-made fibers because they are subjected to a re-formation in order to make them into fibrous form.

Asbestos fiber is obtained from mineral deposits. There are several types of asbestos fiber, but the one used for woven textiles is known as chrysotile or hydrated magnesium silicate.

Asbestos has the characteristic of being fireproof. Through the ages stories have been told of a cloth that could be placed in the fire without being consumed. One can only conclude that these fabrics were made from asbestos, the only natural fiber with this characteristic.

PRODUCTION

The largest deposits of chrysotile are found in Canada. In addition to Canada, South Africa, the Soviet Union, the United States, and Cyprus also produce asbestos.

The rocks that bear asbestos are removed from the earth by mining. Before shipping, some of the looser rock that adheres to the fibers is removed by beating or cobbing. The remainder of the fiber is separated from the rock at the factory where the fibers are spun.

Spinnable asbestos fiber is from three-eighth to three-fourth of an inch long. Because it is slippery and hard to handle alone, asbestos is often blended with from 5 to 20 per cent cotton or rayon fiber. Fabrics of asbestos made into blends with cotton and rayon are not, of course, fireproof.

Fibers alone, or in blends, are carded, then spun into yarns, and woven into

Figure 6-1. Asbestos fiber-bearing rock. Courtesy of Johns-Manville Corporation.

fabrics. Some unspun, staple-length asbestos fiber is used in insulation and in filters.

Characteristics of Asbestos Fiber

Asbestos fiber looks like a small, polished rod when it is viewed through the microscope. Its color varies, depending on the geographic location of the source. Canadian asbestos has a greenish tinge; other forms may be grayish, yellowish, or bluish in tint.

Asbestos is heavy, having a specific gravity of 2.2. Compare this with the specific gravity of wool, which is 1.3 or cotton, which is 1.5.

Asbestos can be heated to 750 degrees F. without damage. At still higher temperatures the fibers may fuse, but will not burn. For these reasons, asbestos is used extensively in industrial textiles that are subjected to heat and friction.

Uses of Asbestos Fiber

In addition to the aforementioned industrial textiles, asbestos is made into fire curtains for use in theaters and curtains for public buildings where fire prevention is important. Its major use, however, is in industrial textile products that are subject to heat and friction.

Continued inhalation of asbestos fiber can cause serious lung disease, and asbestos manufacturers must take precautions in processing the fiber to guard workers against this health hazard. Recent research has linked the presence of asbestos waste in water supplies with a higher incidence of cancer.[1] Because of possible links between asbestos particles and cancer, the use of asbestos is being limited to products in which persons are not exposed to asbestos fiber.

[1] "Pollution and Public Health: Taconite Case Poses Major Test," *Science* (October 4, 1974), p. 31.

Glass Fiber

During World War I, the Germans found that they were running short of asbestos fiber. In an attempt to find a substitute fiber that was noncombustible, the Germans attempted to make fibers from glass, with only a limited success.

Following World War I, researchers continued to look into ways of using glass to produce fibers. This technology had been sufficiently advanced by the late 1930s, when the Owens-Corning Glass Company initiated the mass production of glass fiber.

Glass fiber is made from glass that has been melted and extruded into long, fine filaments. Glass is made from silica sand and limestone, plus small amounts of other constituents such as soda ash, borax, and aluminum hydroxide.

PRODUCTION OF GLASS FIBER

Glass fiber is produced in both continuous filament form and in staple lengths. Both forms go through the same initial processes. Selected ingredients are

Figure 6-2. Flow chart for the manufacture of glass fiber. Courtesy of Owens/Corning Corporation.

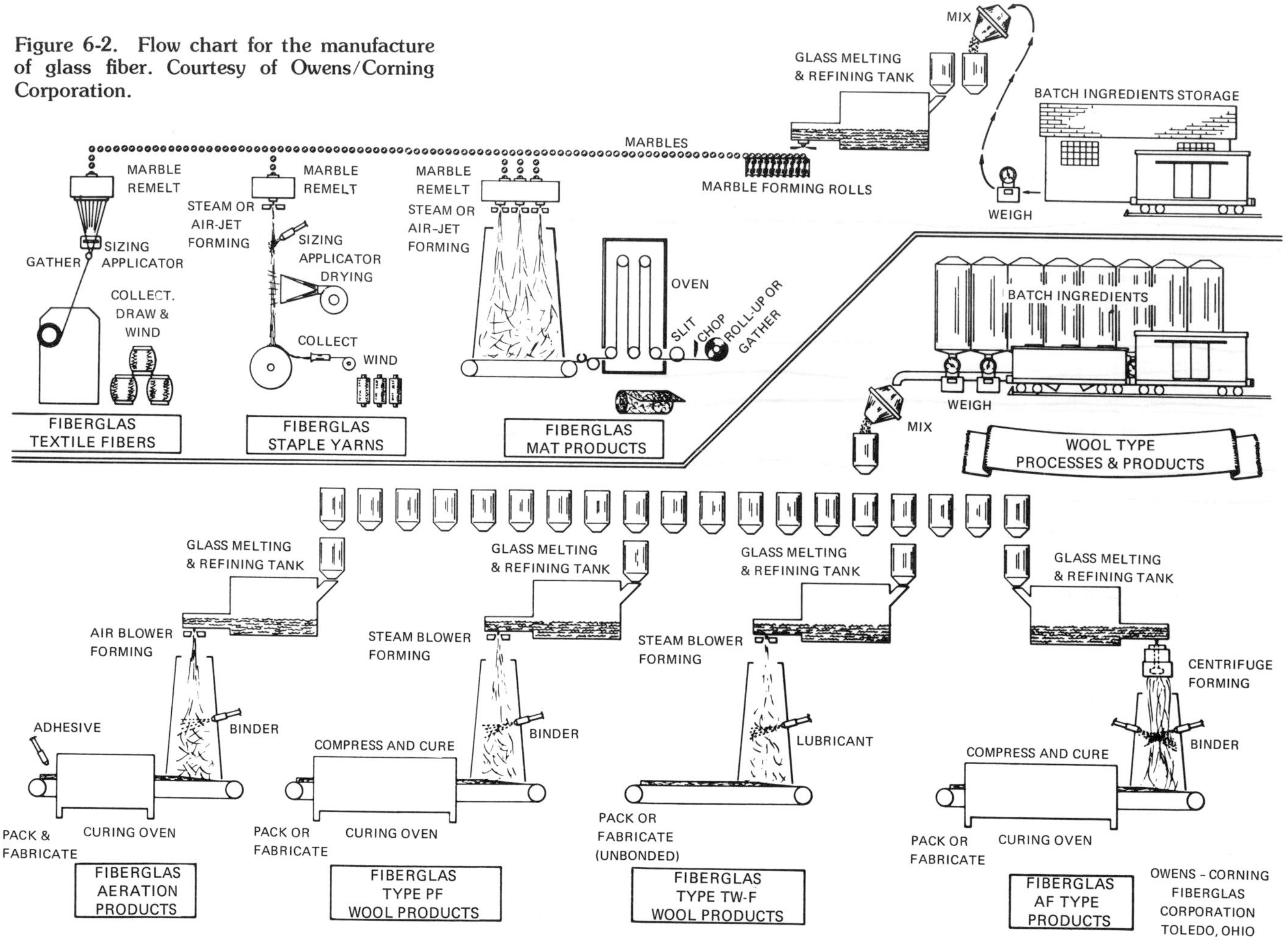

mixed together. The precise formulation is determined by the end uses of the product. The mixture of ingredients, known as the glass batch, is either formed directly into fibers in the direct melt process or made into small glass marbles about five-eighth of an inch in diameter that are called *cullet*.

The glass batch, in either bulk or marble form, is fed into an electric platinum furnace. When the furnace reaches the correct temperature, molten glass is run out of about one hundred small orifices at the bottom of the furnace. The glass hardens on contact with air, forming fine, flexible glass strands. These filaments are drawn together into a yarn or thread, lubricated, and wound. If staple lengths are desired, they are "cut" by jets of air that break the glass strands into shorter lengths of from eight to fifteen inches in length. Fibers made of glass are subject to the usual textile processes for making yarns and for weaving.

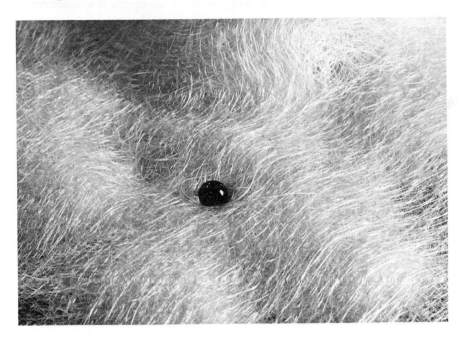

Figure 6-3. Glass marble, used in making some types of glass fiber, shown on a bed of glass fiber. Courtesy of Owens/Corning Corporation.

PROPERTIES OF GLASS FIBER

Physical Appearance of Glass Fiber

Under the microscope, glass fibers look like small, glass rods (which is just what glass fibers are). The fiber diameter is determined by the size of the orifice through which it is extruded. Size is selected according to the end use of the fiber. Finer fibers are more flexible and have certain other advantages that are discussed later.

The longitudinal view of the fiber has a very smooth, round surface that produces a high luster. The fiber is colorless, unless a ceramic pigment has been added to the glass melt before it is formed into fibers.

Properties

Strength or Tenacity. Glass fiber has exceptionally high breaking strength, and has been called the strongest fiber. Nevertheless, one of the major problems encountered in glass fabrics is their lack of flex abrasion resistance. They tend to break where creased and to wear at points where the fabric rubs against other objects.

Density or Specific Gravity. Glass fabrics have a specific gravity of from 2.5 to 2.7, which causes these fabrics to feel heavy. When made into draperies, glass fabrics must be supported with curtain rods that will withstand this increased weight.

Elasticity, Resiliency, Dimensional Stability. Glass is nonelastic and has excellent dimensional stability. At the same time, its lack of elasticity does not adversely affect wrinkle recovery, and glass fiber has excellent wrinkle resistance.

Absorbency. Glass fiber is completely nonabsorbent, and, therefore, has no affinity for dyes. For best colorfastness, color can be added to the molten glass before it is spun by incorporating ceramic pigment into the glass melt. Manufacturers, however, prefer to add color later, so as to retain flexibility in producing fabrics in colors and patterns that are fashionable. A process called *coronizing* has been developed that enables glass fiber to be colored and improves the hand, softness, and dimensional stability of glass fibers.

Coronizing is done in three stages. First, a silica dispersion is impregnated onto the fabric. The silica material helps to hold the weave firm and decreases yarn slippage. In the second step, the fabric is heat set with a slight crimp, which improves the hand. The heat treatment also causes the silica to adhere more closely. From this stage the fabric passes into a water bath that holds pigment for color and a resin that will bind the pigment to the fabric. A final treatment is given to fasten the binding resin, and the fabric is dried.

Heat and Electrical Conductivity. Glass fiber conducts neither heat nor electricity. For this reason it is used in staple form in a variety of insulation materials.

Effect of Heat, Combustibility. The fiber is completely noncombustible. When held in a flame, the finish of the fabric will darken as the pigments and resins used in finishing are destroyed, but the fibers, yarns, and woven structure of the fabric will remain intact. Glass fiber softens at 1,350 degrees F. or above.

Behavior of Glass Fiber in Relation to Selected Conditions

Chemical Reactivity. Acids do not generally affect glass fiber; however, alkalis can have a deleterious effect. Organic solvents do not affect the fiber, but some dry-cleaning solvents will adversely affect resin finishes used on glass fibers. Chlorine bleach does not harm glass fiber, but bleaching is not required because the fibers do not discolor or stain.

Resistance to Insects, Micro-organisms, Sunlight, and Aging. Glass fiber is attacked by neither mildew nor insect pests. Sunlight does not damage the fabric, nor is it harmed by aging.

Care Procedures. Glass fiber fabrics should not be dry cleaned, as the tumbling fabrics undergo in a dry-cleaning machine may damage glass fiber fabrics. Broken fibers will contaminate other fabrics cleaned with glass fabric. As has been mentioned before, some dry-cleaning solvents will damage resin finishes given to some glass fabrics. Hand laundering is the recommended method of cleaning. As a general rule, items made from glass fiber should not be laundered in a washing machine as the action of the washer may cause some fiber breakage. These broken fibers remain in the washer and may be picked up by other clothing during subsequent launderings. When clothing in which the fibers are embedded are worn, the small bits of glass can cause severe skin irritations. For the same reasons, glass fabric should not be tumble-dried.

Instead, glass fiber fabrics can be hand-washed in soapy water or detergent and rinsed. In summer, drapery fabrics can be hung on a clothesline outside and rinsed off with a garden hose. Soil will be removed easily, as the fiber is totally nonabsorbent and all soil is held on the surface of the fabric. When glass fiber fabrics are hung to dry they should be supported at several points in order to avoid putting too much pressure on the fabric at one place. Glass fiber fabrics do not require ironing.

USES

Glass fiber is not used for wearing apparel primarily because, as the ends of the fibers break, they scratch or irritate the skin, and also because of its poor resistance to abrasion, lack of absorbency, and lack of elasticity. For the most part, glass fiber is utilized in draperies, curtains, lamp shades, window shades, and table linens. Industrial uses are more varied, with glass fiber being utilized for products in aerospace, construction, electrical industries, transportation, recreation, packaging, filtration, and for insulation purposes.

Manufacturers of glass fiber are continuing to experiment with modifications of glass fiber that would make it useful for additional products. *Beta Fiberglass* is manufactured by Owens-Corning, and has an exceptionally fine diameter—as little as three microns. This low-diameter fiber is more flexible and has better abrasion resistance. The manufacturer suggests that it may eventually prove useful in new products.

METALGLASS FIBER

A fiber made of a glass core covered with a very thin metal layer is being manufactured for use in specialized applications for the military and for weather control. It has been woven into fabrics on a research and development basis, but no specific commercial applications have been explored as yet.

Made with a glass core of from .6 to 2.7 millimeters and a metal sheath of thicknesses ranging from .1 to .3 millimeters, the fiber has been made with coverings of zinc, aluminum, aluminum alloys, or lead. Other metals may also be used. It is generally used in staple form, and is handled in the same way as glass fiber.

Table 6.1
Chart of Selected Characteristics of Glass Fiber

Specific Gravity	2.54
Tenacity g/d	
Dry	6.3 to 9.6
Wet	5.4 to 6.0
Moisture regain	none
Resiliency	very good
Burning	will not burn; softens at 1,350°F.
Conductivity	
Heat	poor
Electricity	poor
Resistance to damage from	
Fungi	excellent
Insects	excellent
Prolonged exposure to sunlight	excellent
Acids	attacked only by hot phosphoric and by hydroflouric
Alkalis	attacked by strong alkalis and by hot solutions of weak alkalis

Applications thus far have included dropping these fibers along with chemicals used to seed clouds to produce rain. The fibers can be tracked on radar, whereas the chemicals cannot. By tracking the path of the fibers, researchers can determine the effects of cloud seeding on weather patterns. The military has used clouds of the fibers to confuse radar systems during bombing attacks. In attempts at weather control, the fibers were seeded into thunder clouds to neutralize the electrical field of the storm and thereby decrease the severity of lightning.[2]

Metallic Fibers

Metallic fibers were the first man-made fibers. Gold and silver "threads" have long been used to decorate costly garments, tapestries, carpets, and the like. These threads were made either by cutting thin sheets of metal into narrow strips and weaving these strips into decorative patterns, or by winding a thin filament of metal around a central core of another material.

Examination of historic costumes and fabrics reveals the disadvantage of using metals in this way. Except for gold, the metals tended to tarnish and become discolored. Threads were relatively weak, and broke readily. Durability was limited and, of course, the cost of precious metals was very high.

Fashion fabrics today make use of a wide variety of metallic fibers that are both inexpensive and decorative. Other metallic fibers are used for purely practical purposes.

DECORATIVE METALLIC FIBERS

Aluminum is the base metal used in most decorative metallic fibers. The aluminum is coated with a plastic material, either *acetate-butyrate*, a material similar to cellulose acetate, or *Mylar*, a polyester film manufactured by the DuPont Company, which is similar to Dacron polyester fiber. Mylar is the superior coating material.

A thin roll of aluminum foil, .00045 inches thick and twenty inches wide, is made. A heat-sensitive (thermoplastic) adhesive is coated on both sides. When color is required, the pigment is added to the adhesive. A yellow-gold color is used for gold fiber, the natural color of the aluminum is retained for silver, and other metallic or nonmetallic colors can also be produced. The outer layer of plastic is laminated to the metal by passing metal, adhesive, and plastic through heated pressure-squeezer rollers.

This sheet is then slit into filaments of the required width. The resultant fiber is bright in color. The fibers can be heat set into different textured effects.

The strength of these fibers is only fair. Mylar-coated fibers are stronger than those with acetate-butyrate coatings. If additional strength is required, the

[2]B. Schneider, "Pompano Firm Producing Chaff," reprinted from *Ft. Lauderdale News* (October 1, 1972). The Lundy Technical Center, Pompano Beach, Florida 33064.

fibers may be wrapped around a core of a stronger fiber. Some elastic fibers are created by wrapping the metallic fibers around an elastic core.

Acetate-butyrate coated metallic fibers will delaminate or separate if laundered at washing temperatures higher than 150 to 160 degrees F. Mylar-coated fibers are safely washed at temperatures as high as boiling.

A process used by Dow Badische to produce a metallic fiber called *Lurex* differs slightly from that described previously. In the manufacture of Lurex yarns, a metal deposit is placed on a central core of polyester film. Clear or colored resin is coated over the metal. The material is then slit into yarns of from 1/69th to 1/100th of an inch in width. The manufacturer claims that the central core of polyester film increases the strength and flexibility of the fiber.

Metallic fibers of this sort are used to add decorative touches to apparel and household textiles.

OTHER METALLIC FIBERS

A second group of metallic fibers has been developed primarily for industrial and aerospace uses; however, some of these fibers are being introduced into certain household textile products. Superfine filaments of stainless steel and aluminum are made and added to fabrics in any one of a number of ways. Sometimes metal fibers are used as the core of yarns, sometimes they are wrapped around other core yarns, and sometimes they are used alone. Steel and aluminum fibers are being blended into some industrial carpets where they cut down on static electricity buildup and have the side effect of decreasing flammability. As the heat of a fire increases, the metallic fibers conduct some of the heat away from the fire, thereby decreasing the heat of the flame. This tends to slow the rate of burning or to lower temperatures below the kindling point. Other projected end uses for metal fibers include upholstery, blankets, and work clothing and in blends with polyester for hospital gowns.

Several other types of fibers have been developed for use in the aerospace and aircraft industries. These fibers are not used for commercial textile products for the home or in garments. They include the following:

1. Aluminum silicate fibers. Uses: high temperature insulation, filters. Spinning is similar to that of glass fiber.

2. Ceramic fibers. Used in the aerospace program or in aircraft. A modification of the viscose process is used to spin a fiber with a proportion of cellulose and of metal oxides. The cellulose is burned off to yield ceramic fiber.

3. Boron fibers. Used in the aerospace program, these fibers are made by depositing boron vapor onto a fine tungsten wire.

Other Inorganic Fibers

Exotic used in very sm. amounts

Carbon Fibers

Carbon fibers, also known as graphite fibers, like many other inorganic fibers, find their major application in industrial use.

MANUFACTURE

Graphite fibers are made from rayon or polyacrylonitrile fibers that are treated with heat in four separate stages under carefully controlled conditions. The final product is a fiber from which all of the elements but carbon have been driven off.

CHARACTERISTICS

Carbon fibers are black in color, with a silky appearance. They have a stiff hand, possess high strength, and are light in weight.

USES

The application of graphite fibers to a variety of uses is expected to increase as they decrease in price. They could be used in many of the same ways that glass and high strength polyamide fibers are now used, but graphite fibers are not yet competitive in cost with either glass or polyamide fibers.

Graphite fibers have been used in lightweight structures for aircraft and spacecraft and as brake discs for jet airplanes. Graphite fibers are beginning to see wider use in such diverse areas as sporting goods, the construction industry, and medicine. For example, the spinnaker pole of the yacht *Intrepid* contained twenty-three miles of graphite yarn. A new golf club has been made with graphite fibers in the handle and the head. Graphite fibers are used for the reinforcement of bridges, buildings, and the like, and graphite materials have been used for implantation to replace bone.

Summary

Because inorganic and carbon fibers have less use in ready-to-wear and household textiles, they are generally assigned a position of less importance in the study of textiles. Except for glass fiber, they are not of major interest to the average consumer. These fibers, however, do demonstrate clearly the enormous range of textile fiber uses in a technological society.

Recommended References

BARRY, G. F. "Static Control Metal Yarns in Carpets." *Modern Textiles*, January 1973, p. 46.
COOK, J. G. *Handbook of Textile Fibers*, vol. 2. Watford, England: Merrow Publishing Company, Ltd., 1968.
"Glass Fibers." *CIBA Review*, 1963, vol. 5.

MONCRIEFF, R. W. *Man-Made Fibres*. New York: John Wiley & Sons, Inc., 1975.

Textile Fibers for Industry. Owens-Corning Fiberglas Corp., Toledo, Ohio, 43659.

TOWNE, M. K., and M. B. DERVELL. "Properties and Uses of Carbon Fiber Cloth." *Modern Textiles*, May 1976, p. 51.

WARLICK, S. "Carpet of Glass." *Textile Industries*, January 1975, p. 40.

"Weaving Engineered Fabrics" (Graphite). *Textile Industries*, February 1975, p. 88.

WESTENDORF, B. "Guidelines for Knitting Lurex Yarns." *Knitted Outerwear Times*, November 7, 1966.

7

SYNTHETIC FIBERS: NYLON AND ARAMID FIBERS

Man-made fibers, both regenerated and synthetic, dominate the modern textile industry. In 1975, man-made fibers supplied 70 per cent of the raw materials used by American textile industries.[1] In 1950, only 20 per cent of the fibers utilized were man-made.[2]

Although the processes used in producing man-made, regenerated fibers relied on the reactions between these substances and certain chemical materials, especially solvents, no attempts were made to create fibers from chemicals until the 1930s. All of the early procedures (in the man-made fiber industry) started with materials similar in structure to natural fibers. These materials were chemically dissolved, then re-formed into long, filament fibers. It was not until chemists came to understand the chemical structure of fiber molecules that they realized that it might be possible to create fibers entirely from chemical substances.

An analytical process called X-ray diffraction revealed that fibrous qualities depended on the presence of long-chain polymers. This understanding led to attempts to put together long-chain polymers in the laboratory from chemical materials. Chemists had synthesized a type of large molecule known as a *polypeptide*. A polypeptide is any polymer containing an abundance of amide linkages, that is, linkages made up of carbon, oxygen, nitrogen, and hydrogen (CONH). Silk and wool are, chemically speaking, polypeptides. Scientists believed that synthesis in the laboratory of polypeptides might lead to the invention of a totally synthetic fiber that was not derived from any natural substance.

E. I. du Pont de Nemours & Company, a chemical company, had established an extensive basic research program and those working in this program were given wide latitude as to the areas in which they might work. W. H. Carothers, a chemist at du Pont, chose to work in the synthesis of long-chain molecules.

[1] *Textile Organon* (March 1976), p. 22.

[2] Mary Carter, "Fiber Frontiers," Paper presented at the National Symposium on Fiber Frontiers (Washington, D.C.: June 1974), p. 9.

Although Carothers was not searching for textile fibers, the work he initiated in the formation of long-chain polymers was applied widely to the creation of a number of fibers and to their subsequent manufacture. Carothers was working in a direction that might be described as follows: "Take molecules that can react at both ends, react them, and long molecules will result. If these molecules are very long in relation to their other dimensions, they will exhibit fiber-forming properties."[3]

The basic research done by Carothers resulted in the invention of nylon, the first truly synthetic fiber. Nylon, like silk and wool, is a polypeptide.

Nylon, the generic name given to this fiber by du Pont, was first marketed in 1938 and its commercial distribution was beginning when the outbreak of World War II required the diversion of nylon and its constituent materials into wartime use. It was not until after the war that commercial nylon production for the civilian market was initiated on a large scale.

The invention of nylon, and its successful marketing after the war, stimulated the synthesis of additional fibers. Gradually a wide variety of synthetic fibers was introduced for public consumption; vinyon, 1939; saran, 1941; modacrylic, 1949; acrylic, 1952; polyester, 1953; aramid, 1961;[4] olefin, 1961; anidex, 1970; and novoloid, 1972.[5]

Fiber Formation

Most synthetic polymers must be converted into liquid form in order for them to be spun. This is done either by dissolving the polymer in a suitable solvent, or by melting the polymer, then extruding the liquid polymer through a spinneret.

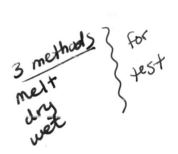

MELT SPINNING

Melt spinning utilizes the thermoplastic characteristics of fibers. Chips of solid polymer about the size of rice grains are dropped from a hopper into a melter where heat converts the solid polymer into a viscous liquid. The liquid forms a "melt pool" that is pumped through filters to remove any impurities that would clog the spinneret and delivered to the spinneret at a carefully controlled rate of flow.

The spinneret holes are usually round, but noncircular holes are also used to make filaments of various cross-sectional shapes. Melt-spun fibers may be made through Y-shaped holes that yield a three-lobed fiber, or C-shaped holes to produce a hollow filament, for example.

The diameter of the fiber is determined by the rate at which the polymer is supplied to the hole in the spinneret and the windup speed, not by the diameter of the hole. When the molten polymer emerges from the spinneret

[3]R. W. Moncrieff, *Man-Made Fibres* (New York: John Wiley & Sons, Inc., 1975), p. 319.

[4]Although the generic category of aramid fibers was established in 1974, these fibers have been produced since 1961 under the generic classification of nylon.

[5]*Man-made Fiber Fact Book* (Washington, D.C.: Man-made Fiber Producers Association, Inc., 1974) p. 14, ff.

hole, a cool air current is passed over the fiber, causing it to harden. Failure to maintain constant feeding speed of molten polymer or changes in the temperature of cooling will cause irregularities in the diameter of the fiber.[6] Nylon is a melt-spun fiber.

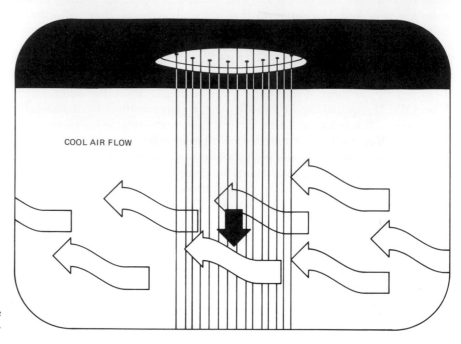

COOL AIR FLOW

Figure 7-1. Melt spinning. Courtesy of the Man-Made Fiber Producers' Association, Inc.

DRY SPINNING

Many polymers are adversely affected by heat at or close to their melting temperatures, so that they cannot be melt spun; other methods of spinning, such as dry spinning, are thus employed. Dry spinning requires the dissolving of the polymer in a solvent in order to convert it into liquid form. Substances used as solvents are chosen not only because they will dissolve the polymer but also because they can be reclaimed and reused.

The polymer and solvent are extruded through a spinneret into a circulating current of hot gas that evaporates the solvent from the polymer and causes the filament to harden. The solvent is removed and recycled to be used again.

Dry-spun filaments generally have an irregular cross section. Because the solvent evaporates first from the outside of the fiber, a hard surface skin of solid polymer forms. As the solvent evaporates from the inner part of the fiber, this skin "collapses," or folds to produce an irregular shape. If the rate of evaporation is slowed, the cross section of the filament will be more nearly round. Acetate fibers are dry-spun.

[6]C. B. Chapman, *Fibres* (Plainfield, N.J.: Textile Book Service, 1974), p. 37.

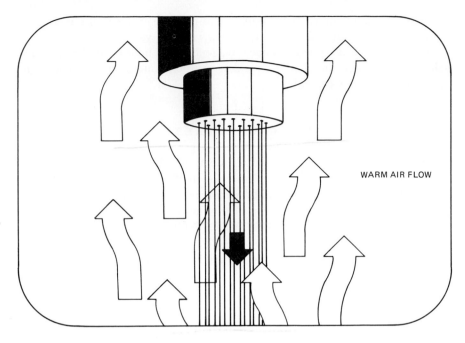

WARM AIR FLOW

Figure 7-2. Dry spinning. Courtesy of the Man-Made Fiber Producers' Association, Inc.

WET SPINNING

Wet-spun polymers are, like dry-spun polymers, converted into liquid form by dissolving them in a suitable solvent. The polymer is extruded through a jet into

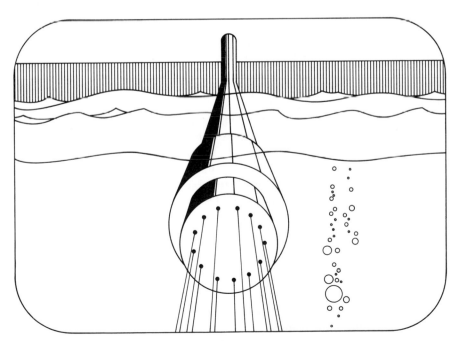

Figure 7-3. Wet spinning. Courtesy of the Man-Made Fiber Producers' Association, Inc.

a liquid bath. The bath causes coagulation of the fiber. Solvents are recovered from the liquid bath and recycled. Viscose rayon is wet-spun.

It is possible to add special chemical reagents to the liquid bath that produce selected changes in the fiber. This is done in the manufacture of some high-strength rayons, for example.

DRAWING OR STRETCHING

Both crystalline and amorphous arrangement of molecules exist within newly formed fibers. It is possible to orient these molecules to make them more parallel to the walls of the fiber, and therefore more crystalline and stronger, by stretching the fiber before it is completely hardened.

Newly formed fibers, whether formed by melt, wet, or dry spinning, are, therefore, subjected to drawing or stretching. This may be done under cold or hot temperature conditions and has the additional effect of making the fiber both narrower and longer.

HEAT SETTING

Many synthetic fibers are thermoplastic, so that when exposed to heat, they may shrink. To prevent this shrinkage, most synthetic fibers are treated with heat after spinning to "set" them into permanent shape. Not only can fibers be heat-set to make their dimensions permanent but many synthetic fabrics can also be heat-set into pleats, creases, or other permanent shaping.

The molecular structure of the fiber is involved in heat setting. Heat-sensitive fibers have not only a melting temperature but also a temperature at which the amorphous regions of the fiber become rubbery or soft. This temperature is called the glass transition temperature and is abbreviated T_g. The glass transition temperature may be reached without causing the fiber to melt.

In order for heat setting to take place the fiber is put into its new shape, the T_g of the fiber is reached, and the fiber is "locked" into the new shape by cooling in the new position. The fiber will remain in this position until the glass transition temperature is reached again. If the T_g is low, the fiber cannot be successfully heat-set for ordinary uses as hot water in washing or heat from a dryer will negate the effect of heat setting.

If, in use and care, heat-set fabrics are subject to temperatures above their respective T_gs, heat setting will be lost. Likewise, synthetic fabrics lying in a wrinkled state in a very hot dryer may have wrinkles "heat-set" if the temperature in the dryer goes above the glass transition temperature.

Yarn Types of Man-made Fibers

Man-made fibers are made into a variety of yarn types. *Monofilament yarns* are made from a single filament. Such single filament yarns are made for special purposes. Instead, most filament yarns are formed of *multifilaments* (two or more, usually many more), monofilaments twisted together. *Tow* is bundles of continuous monofilaments without twist. *Staple fibers* are shorter length fibers that have been cut from tow.

Textured fibers or yarns have had some alteration in their surface texture. Many synthetics have a crimp or twist added after drawing in order to add stretch, increase bulk, or otherwise modify the fiber (see Chapter 13).

COMMON CHARACTERISTICS OF SYNTHETIC FIBERS

Although each of the synthetic fibers has many individual qualities or characteristics, synthetic fibers as a class possess some common properties. One of the more widely shared characteristics of synthetics is *thermoplasticity* or sensitivity to heat.

When viewed under the microscope longitudinally, synthetic fibers usually appear as glass rods with either a smooth or striated surface. The fibers appear sufficiently alike that solubility tests are the only means of certain identification.

Synthetics tend to be *hydrophobic* or water resistant, and, therefore, less absorbent than the natural fibers. Lower absorbency may lead to a decrease in comfort when synthetic fibers are worn next to the skin. On the other hand, most synthetics dry quickly after laundering. Low absorbency also creates difficulties in finishing and dyeing.

Static electricity buildup is common among synthetics. Fibers that are more absorbent tend to conduct electricity more readily. More conductive fibers build up electric shocks less readily.

Many synthetics are rather smooth and slippery to the touch. Fibers may *pill*, because their strength prevents the wearing away of tangled ends. This tendency can be reduced by some of the special texturizing of yarns that is done in manufacturing.

It is usually more difficult to remove oil and grease stains from synthetics, as they have an affinity for these substances. Stain removal is made more difficult by low absorbency. Once the stain has penetrated the fiber, the fiber's resistance to water and other liquids prevents soil removal during laundering or cleaning, as the soil is held inside the fiber while the water is kept out.

Synthetics resist insects, mildew, and bacterial growth. They also tend to resist many chemicals.

Many of the aforementioned characteristics that present problems to the consumer can be overcome by special finishes or by blending fibers. Special purpose finishes for fabrics are discussed in Chapters 19 and 20.

Nylon

The generic term for polyamide fibers is nylon. Under the most recent Federal Trade Commission definition, nylon is "a manufactured fiber in which the fiber-forming substance is a long chain synthetic polyamide in which less than

85 per cent of the amide (—C—NH—) linkages are attached directly to two
$$\underset{\text{O}}{\overset{\|}{\text{C}}}$$
aromatic rings." This definition covers a variety of structures, two main classifications of which are used in the United States: nylon 6 and nylon 66.

Nylon 66

Although the processes for making both nylon 66 and nylon 6 have been known since the earliest experimentation on nylon, du Pont, which pioneered the development of nylon in the United States, chose to utilize the nylon 66 process. For this reason, until fairly recently nylon 66 was the more widely used of the two types of nylon in the United States, whereas nylon 6 predominated in Europe. Today, however, a number of United States textile companies produce nylon 6.

Manufacture of Nylon 66

The chemicals from which nylon 66 is synthesized are adipic acid and hexamethylene diamine.

Adipic Acid	Hexamethylene diamine
$COOH(CH_2)_4COOH$	$NH_2(CH_2)_6NH_2$
$1 + 4 + 1 = 6$	(6)

Note that there are six carbon atoms in each molecule of adipic acid and six carbon atoms in each molecule of hexamethylene diamine. For this reason this nylon was designated as nylon 6.6 (six carbons in each molecule of reacting chemical). In time it came to be known as nylon 66. These materials (or nylon salts) are synthesized from benzene. Benzene being in short supply, other

Figure 7-4. Flow chart showing the manufacture of nylon 66. Courtesy of E. I. du Pont de Nemours & Company.

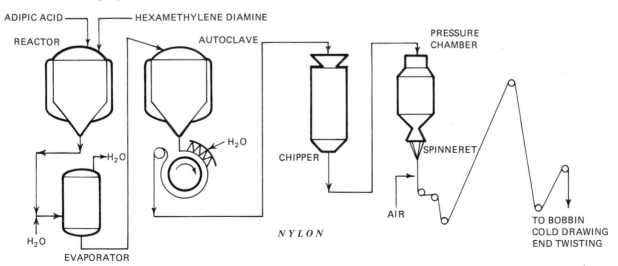

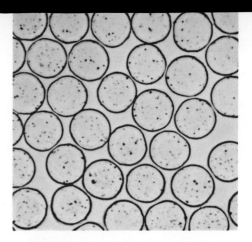

or 1.38.). Nylon

fibers, the elas-
quite as good as

sorbency, which
compatible with
r laundering.
ability at low to
of shape. At high
ving temperatures

electricity and it
lator in electrical
poor conductivity
l nylons have been
ic electricity.
nylon is about 500
ees F. If a hot iron is
er usually does not
if the molten fiber
sensitivity of nylon

ted Factors

hemically stable. Dry
sly affected by dilute
entrated hydrochloric
into adipic acid and
is made. This reaction
rmits this fiber to be
degrade nylon.
and Aging. Neither
er is degraded by long
ct if fabrics are stored
ble for use in curtains.

have been
multilobal
nd ha
es

gra
Moncr

is another basic material, but like
ages of petroleum or oil thus create
nylon is made. There is also a viable
lls and corn cobs.

nufacturing process is to cause the
ules or polymers. Nylon is formed
on of adipic acid and hexameth-
osphere. Water, which is split off
from the reacting tank. If the
nylon, titanium dioxide can be

om the tank as a ribbon, several
d water which reduces the size

ller nylon "chips." Nylon is
ated grid that is too small to
en melted. The molten nylon
any impurities. This melted
filaments are formed.
ses them to harden. Next the
low the fiber to absorb some
d state so that the fiber will
moisture.
lly strong or very lustrous.
nd thereby increase both
etched in its length. The
fiber. Coarser diameter

a long smooth cylinder.
unless it is delustered.

nylon can be excellent. It
city nylon is rated at 3.0 to
The exceptional strength of
lso for a variety of industrial
o five times that of wool. The
icity of nylon have led to its

low density fiber, the specific
n most other fibers. (Rayon, for

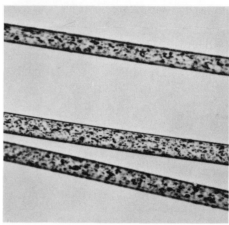

Figure 7-5. Photomicrograph of delustered, regular nylon 66 in a cross section and a longitudinal view. Courtesy of E. I. du Pont de Nemours & Company.

example, has a specific gravity of about 1.5, polyester of 1.22
can be made into very light, sheer fabrics, of good strength

Elasticity and Resilience. Contrary to most high-tenacit
ticity of nylon is very high. Its resilience is good, although no
polyester.

Absorbency. Like many synthetics, nylon is low in ab
causes the fiber to resist some dyes. Other dyestuffs that are
nylon have been developed. Nylon fabrics dry quickly aft

Dimensional Stability. Nylon has good dimensional s
moderate temperatures, neither shrinking nor stretching ou
temperatures, nylon fabrics may shrink. Washing and dr
should be kept low.

Electrical Conductivity. Nylon is a poor conductor o
builds up static electricity. Nylon serves as a good ins
materials because of its nonconducting qualities. (In part thi
is the result of the low moisture absorbency.) Some speci
manufactured to improve conductivity and decrease sta

Combustibility; Effect of Heat. The melting point o
degrees F. It will soften and may start to stick at 445 degr
used on nylons, they may glaze, soften, or stick. The fi
support combustion. However, nylon fibers do melt an
drips onto the skin, it may cause serious burns. The hea
allows it to be heat-set.

Behavior of Nylon Fibers in Relation to Selec

Chemical Resistance. Like most synthetics, nylon is
cleaning solvents will not harm the fiber. It is not serio
acids, but is soluble in strong acids. Treatment with con
acid at high temperatures will break nylon 66 down
hexamethylene diamine, the substances from which it
can be used to reclaim these basic materials and p
recycled after use. Acidic fumes from pollution will

Resistance to Micro-organisms, Insects, Sunlight,
moths, mildew, nor bacteria will attack nylon. The fi
exposure to sunlight, but age has no appreciable eff
away from sunlight. Sheer nylon fabrics are unsuita

Variations of Nylon 66

Variations of the cross-sectional shape of nylon 66
fibers are usually trilobal or multilobal in form. The
better cover with less fiber than the round nylons, a
being somewhat more like silk in feel. Some of th
luster.

Antron is one of the multilobal fibers made by du
fiber made by Monsanto.

NYLON 6

Nylon 6 is made by a slightly different process. This type of nylon is made from a chemical substance called *caprolactum*, which has the following chemical form:

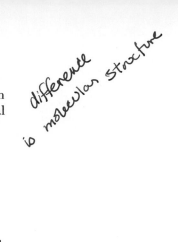

Since there are six carbons in caprolactam, the fiber is known as nylon 6.

After du Pont chose to develop nylon 66 rather than nylon 6, the development of nylon 6 was left to researchers in Europe, where it is the most common type of nylon manufactured. Nylon 6 has some advantages in processing over nylon 66, from which it differs only slightly.

Manufacture

Polymerization.   Caprolactam is polymerized by one of two methods. In one, caprolactum is liquefied, heated, and filtered under high pressure, during which process condensation polymerization takes place. In the second method, water in the amount of 10 per cent of the weight of the caprolactam is added, after which the water and caprolactam are heated to a high temperature, steam escapes, and polymerization takes place.

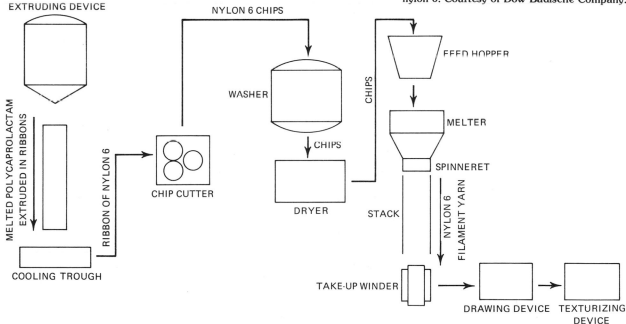

Figure 7-6. Flow chart for the manufacture of nylon 6. Courtesy of Dow Badische Company.

In both of these methods a certain amount of unchanged monomer material remains. The polymerized material is given a water bath in an extractor to remove the monomer, which, if it remained, would weaken the final fiber. The polymer is dried and made into nylon chips.

Spinning. Nylon 6 is melt spun. It has a slightly lower melting point than nylon 66. It melts at a temperature of 414–428 degrees F. The fiber is spun into air, dried, and then passed around two rollers. The first roller applies water and a wetting agent to the fiber, the second applies an oil-water conditioning material.

Drawing. The fibers are stretched to orient the molecules and to improve strength and luster. They are then dried, and wound onto a cone.

Characteristics of Nylon 6

The characteristics of nylon 6 are essentially the same as those of nylon 66 with these particular exceptions:

1. The tenacity of regular tenacity nylon 6 is 4 to 7 g/d; that of regular nylon 66 is 3 to 6 g/d.

2. The affinity of nylon 6 for acid dyes is greater than that of nylon 66, because there are more acid sites (places where the fiber combines with the dyestuff) in nylon 6 than in nylon 66.

3. Elastic recovery seems slightly better in nylon 6, as does fatigue resistance and thermal stability.[8]

Multilobal varieties of nylon 6 are also made. *Enkaloft* and *Enkalure* are multilobal nylon 6 fibers made by the American Enka Company.

CONSUMER CONSIDERATIONS CONCERNING NYLON

The availability of a wide variety of types of nylon (from fine to coarse, from soft to crisp, from sheer to opaque) has resulted in the use of nylon in an enormous range of products for apparel, the home, and industry.

Nylon has long been of major importance in the manufacture of women's hosiery because of its strength and elasticity. Sheer fabrics of nylon have been popular because of their inherent strength and abrasion resistance. Special purpose nylons have been manufactured for upholstery and carpets.

Nylon is also considered to be an "easy care" fabric. Most nylon items are machine washable; many can be tumble-dried at normal drying temperatures.

However, some aspects of the care of nylon require special attention. Like many synthetics, nylon has an affinity for oilborne stains. These should be removed with a grease solvent before laundering.

Nylon has a tendency to "scavenge" colors. Although nylon is relatively

[8]Moncrieff, *op. cit.*, p. 377.

difficult to dye, it does pick up surface color easily from other fabrics. This is why many white nylons gradually become gray or yellowed and it is, therefore, advisable to wash white nylons alone, never with other items of color.

Nylon's resilience usually precludes its ironing, but the heat sensitivity of nylon requires that it be pressed with a warm, not hot, iron, if pressing seems necessary. Also, nylon items should be removed from the drier as soon as the cycle is ended. Nylons that remain in a hot drier in a wrinkled condition may have these wrinkles "heat-set" into place if the drier is very hot.

Nylon fibers may tend to pill, as the fabric wears. Pilling on synthetics is a particular problem because the strength of the fibers causes tangled fiber ends to cling tightly. These fiber ends do not fall off, which makes wearing apparel unsightly.

OTHER TYPES OF NYLON

In addition to nylon 6 and 66, there are other types of nylon that carry other numbers. Nylon 7 is being developed in Russia. It is claimed to be more stable to heat and ultraviolet light than nylon 6. Nylon 11 is a French product made from castor oil, with a trademark *Rilsan*. It has the disadvantage of having a relatively low melting point. Rilsan has been used for fishing lines and bristles, and is a good electrical insulator.

Nylon 4

Nylon 4 was developed by the General Aniline and Film Corporation. The advantage of nylon 4 is said to be an increased moisture regain, which decreases static buildup. Nylon 4 is supposedly closer to cotton in its physical characteristics than other nylons.

Qiana

Qiana is the trademark of a nylon produced by du Pont. For some time the chemical structure of this fiber was not known, and textile scientists speculated about the possible differences in its structure from that of other nylons. It is now known to be a normal polyamide, but the intermediate materials from which it is made are somewhat different from those used in manufacturing nylon 6 and nylon 66.[9]

The marketing procedures followed in introducing Qiana were interesting. At first, the cost of the fiber was very high and the use was restricted to luxury goods. A high fashion image for the fiber was achieved by launching a major promotional campaign in which the first garments made from Qiana were designed and shown by world famous Parisian and American designers. Gradually the fiber cost was lowered and the Qiana fabrics were made into an increasingly wide variety of moderately priced garments.

An aesthetically pleasing fiber, Qiana combines a soft and luxurious hand and

[9] Ibid., p. 425.

Figure 7-7. Shirt, sweater, and pants are all made of Qiana nylon. Courtesy of E. I. du Pont de Nemours & Company.

appearance with easy care. Qiana can be laundered and dry-cleaned and has good wrinkle resistance and wrinkle recovery. Its dimensional stability is very good.

The density of Qiana is much lower than ordinary nylon, making fabrics feel light. Its tenacity is in the lower range of normal nylon strength (3.0–3.3 g/d), but is satisfactory for general use in garments. The moisture regain of Qiana is low, but the fiber has good wickability.

The fiber has a trilobal cross section, which enhances the luster. Qiana can be dyed into clear colors with good colorfastness. Like other nylons, however, Qiana tends to scavange colors. Light or white fabrics should be washed separately from other colors.

Aramid

In its most recent revision of generic fiber categories, the FTC established a separate category of fibers that it designated "aramids." Like nylon, aramid fibers are polyamides. However, in its redefinition, the FTC separated polyamides into those in which *less* than 85 per cent of the amide linkages are attached directly to the aromatic rings (nylon) and those in which 85 per cent or *more* of the amide linkages are attached to two aromatic rings (aramid). Nomex and Kevlar belong to the aramid classification.

Characteristics of aramids include high strength and good flex and abrasion resistance (comparable to nylon). Dimensional stability is good. Standard moisture regain is 5 per cent; absorbency, as with many synthetics, is relatively low.

Until a pigment dye system that was noncombustible was found for use on aramids, the color range was limited. With the increase in potential design application, the range of uses of aramid fibers has been increased.

The outstanding property of aramid fibers is their flame resistance. Aramid fibers have no melting point (they do not melt), and they have extremely low combustibility. The fiber decomposes at a temperature above 700 degrees F.

Aramids degrade and lose strength on exposure to ultraviolet rays. Their resistance to radiation from gamma, beta, and X rays is, however, excellent, and this resistance is utilized for some industrial applications. Their resistance to many chemicals and organic solvents is generally good.

Aramid fibers are used in industrial and military clothing, industrial hot-air filtration fabrics, ropes, cables, sailcloth, and marine and sporting goods. Highly temperature-resistant papers are made from Nomex aramid fibers.

Nomex aramid is being made into a variety of consumer goods, including carpets, drapery fabrics, upholstery fabrics, ironing board covers, and protective clothing. The low combustibility of the fiber makes it especially attractive for such applications.

Kevlar aramid, also made by du Pont, is being used in industrial products where reinforcement of plastic with strong but lightweight fiber material is needed. It is substituted for glass fiber in the aircraft industry because it is lighter in weight than glass. Sports equipment, such as canoes, sailboats, hockey sticks, tennis rackets, fishing rods, and golf clubs, also make use of Kevlar fibers.

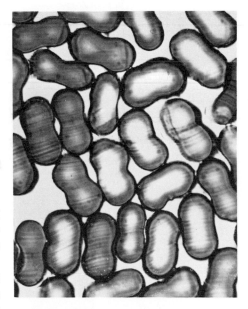

Figure 7-8. Photomicrograph of a cross section of Nomex aramid fiber. Courtesy of E. I. du Pont de Nemours & Company.

Alone or with other fibers, Kevlar may be made into bullet-resistant garments and coated fabrics.

Table 7.1

Selected Characteristics of Nylon and Aramid Fibers

	Nylon (Regular Tenacity)	Aramid Nomex (Filament)
Specific Gravity	1.14	1.38
Tenacity (g/d)		
Dry	3.0–6.0	4.8–5.8
Wet	2.6–5.4	3.8–4.8
Moisture regain	4.0–4.5%	5%
Resiliency	excellent	excellent
Burning characteristics	burns slowly with melting in flame, usually self-extinguishing after flame is removed	low flammability
Melting point	415°F. (nylon 6) 482°F. (nylon 66)	decomposes above 700°F.; does not melt
Conductivity of		
Heat	poor	poor
Electricity	poor	poor
Resistance to damage from		
Fungi	excellent	excellent
Insects	excellent	excellent
Prolonged exposure to sunlight	degrades	degrades
Acids	broken down by strong acids	degraded by hot, concentrated acids
Alkalis	good	degraded by hot, concentrated alkalis

Recommended References

"The Age of Qiana." *American Fabrics and Fashion,* Summer 1974, p. 87.

CHAPMAN, C. *Fibres.* Plainfield, N.J.: Textile Book Service, 1974.

COOK, J. G. *Handbook of Textile Fibers, Vol. 2.* Watford, England: Merrow Publishing Company, Ltd., 1968.

COLLIER, A. M. *A Handbook of Textiles.* New York: Pergamon Press, 1970.

GAGNON, R. C. *Man-made Fibers.* Scranton, Penn.: International Textbook Co., Inc., 1961.

"Kevlar: A New Concept in Fiber Strength." *American Fabrics and Fashion,* Fall 1975, p. 67.

MONCRIEFF, R. W. *Man-Made Fibres.* New York: John Wiley & Sons, Inc., 1975.

"Polyamides and Polyester." *CIBA Review,* July 1958.

"Properties of Nomex." *Technical Bulletin N-236,* E. I. du Pont de Nemours & Company, Wilmington, Delaware.

SITTIG, M. *Polyamide Fiber Manufacture.* Plainfield, N.J.: Textile Book Service, 1972.

"The Growing Multiplicity of Man-made Fibers." *American Fabrics and Fashions,* Summer 1972, p. 56.

WILFONG, R. E. and W. G. Mikell. "Kevlar Aramid." *Modern Textiles,* November 1976, p. 26

8

POLYESTER FIBERS

In his first experiments with the synthesis of polymers, W. H. Carothers concentrated his attention on compounds called polyesters. Encountering some difficulties in this research, he turned his attention to polyamides, from which he synthesized nylon.

After the discovery of nylon, a group of English researchers concentrated on the polyester group. Their experimentation led to the development and subsequent manufacture of polyester fibers. Du Pont bought the English patent and the first du Pont plant for the production of Dacron polyester in the United States opened in March, 1953.

Polyester fibers are defined as "a manufactured fiber in which the fiber-forming substance is any long-chain synthetic polymer composed of at least 85 per cent by weight of an ester of a substituted aromatic carboxylic acid, including but not restricted to substituted terephthalate units

$$p(-R-O-\underset{O}{\overset{\parallel}{C}}-C_6H_4-\underset{O}{\overset{\parallel}{C}}-O-)$$ and parasubstituted hydroxybenzoate units,

$$p(-R-O-C_6H_4-\underset{O}{\overset{\parallel}{C}}-O-)"[1]$$ (as amended September 12, 1973).

MANUFACTURE

The raw material from which most polyesters are made is petroleum. Acids and alcohols are derived from oil. The most commonly used acid is terephthalic acid. The processes that are used for manufacturing different types of polyesters vary. Many of the details of these processes are not known because the companies that hold the patents on the manufacturing processes have not released full information on precisely how these processes are carried out. A generalized description of the process for synthesizing polyesters follows.

[1]Federal Trade Commission definition quoted in *Man-made Fiber Fact Book* (Man-made Fiber Producers Association, Inc., Washington, D.C., 1974), p. 4.

Polymerization

Condensation polymerization takes place during the reaction of the acid and alcohol, in a vacuum, at high temperatures. Polymerized material is extruded in the form of a ribbon onto a casting wheel or cooling trough. The ribbon hardens, and small polyester chips are cut from the ribbon.

Spinning

The chips are dried to remove any residual moisture, and are then put into hopper reservoirs ready for melting. The melted polymer (polyester is "melt spun," like nylon) is extruded through the spinnerets, solidifies on hitting the air, and is wound loosely onto cylinders.

Drawing

Fibers are hot-stretched to about five times their original length, which decreases their width. The drawn fiber is either wound onto cones as filaments

Figure 8-1. Flow chart showing the manufacture of polyester. Courtesy of the Eastman Kodak Company.

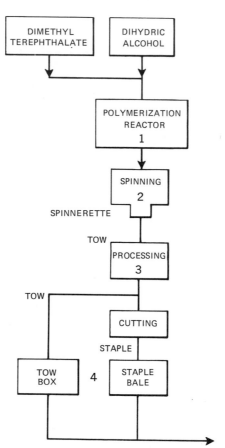

STARTING CHEMICALS: The production of KODEL polyester fiber begins with dimethyl terephthalate and a special suitable dihydric alcohol.

1 POLYMERIZATION: The dihydric alcohol and dimethyl terephthalate are placed in a polymerization reactor where, under the proper conditions, they combine to form long chain-like molecules called **polymer.**

2 SPINNING:
The liquid polymer is forced through microscopic holes in a device similar to a miniature shower head, called a **spinnerette.**
The thin strands formed by the spinnerette are cooled and gathered into bundles of continuous fiber called **tow,** which looks like untwisted rope.

3 PROCESSING:
The tow is treated to make it resist shrinking or stretching.
Lubricants are added to aid in spinning yarns.
The tow may also be crimped like a "permanent wave" to add bulk and texture to the fiber.
The tow may be cut into short lengths called **staple** fiber or it may be left uncut, in continuous tow form . . . depending upon the customer's (mill's) requirements.

4 PACKING:
Staple fiber is compressed into bales.
Continuous-form tow is packed into boxes.

SHIPPING: These forms of KODEL polyester fiber are then shipped to textile mills where the fibers are spun into yarns and woven into fabrics.

Tennessee Eastman Company produces the KODEL polyester fiber. It does not weave fabrics or make garments or home furnishings.

or crimped, and cut into staple lengths. (It is also possible in an alternative process to extrude polymerized molten polyester directly into fibers, omitting the making of polyester chips.)

CHARACTERISTICS OF POLYESTERS

Appearance

Polyester fibers are manufactured in a variety of cross sections, including round, trilobal, and pentalobal. Under the microscope, round fibers appear as long, smooth rods with spots of pigment. This pigmented appearance decreases the luster or brightness of polyesters. Longitudinally, multilobal fibers appear striated.

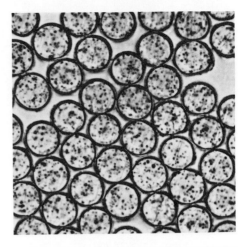

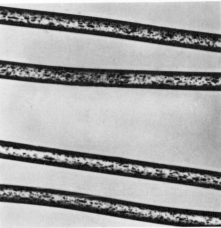

Figure 8-2. Photomicrograph of regular Dacron polyester in a cross section and a longitudinal view. Courtesy of E. I. du Pont de Nemours & Company.

Properties

Strength or Tenacity. The strength or tenacity of polyester varies with the type of fiber; however, as a general category, polyester would be considered a relatively strong fiber. Regular filaments have a breaking tenacity of 4 to 6 g/d; high tenacity filaments are rated at 6.3 to 9.5 g/d.

Specific Gravity or Density. The density or specific gravity (1.38 or 1.22 depending on type) is moderate. Polyesters have a density greater than nylon (S.G. 1.14) and lower than rayon (S.G. 1.50). Fabrics made from polyesters are medium in weight.

Elasticity, Resilience. The elasticity of polyester is generally good. Polyester recovers well from stretching, but is inferior to nylon in its elasticity. Resilience is excellent. For this reason, polyesters are often blended with less crease-resistant fibers to make easy-care fabrics.

Absorbency; Moisture Regain. The moisture regain of polyester is low, only 0.2 to 0.8 per cent. Although polyesters are nonabsorbent, they do have wicking ability. In wicking, moisture can be carried on the surface of the fiber without absorption. This quality makes polyester relatively comfortable to wear in warm weather, as perspiration is carried to the surface of the fiber and evaporated. Multilobal fiber cross sections improve the wicking qualities of polyesters.

Dimensional Stability. Polyesters that have been given heat-setting treatments have excellent dimensional stability, so long as the heat-setting temperature is not exceeded. If polyester fabrics have not been heat-set, they may shrink at high temperatures.

Effect of Heat; Combustibility. The melting point of polyester is close to that of nylon, ranging from 480 degrees to 550 degrees F. Polyesters usually need no pressing because of their excellent wrinkle recovery. If they must be pressed it should be with a warm, not hot, iron. Polyesters can be heat-set into pleats with especially good results. Not only will heat setting stabilize size and shape, but wrinkle resistance of polyesters is enhanced by heat setting.

Polyester shrinks from flame and will melt, leaving a hard black residue. The fabric will burn with a strong, pungent odor. Some polyesters are self-extinguishing. Melted polyester fiber can produce severe burns.

Polyester Fiber Behavior in Relation to Selected Conditions

Chemical Resistance. Polyesters are not harmed by solvents used in professional dry cleaning, nor are they susceptible to damage from bleaching. Although polyesters are not harmed by acids, they may be adversely affected by strong alkalis. Alkalinity encountered in detergents is not harmful.

Resistance to Micro-organisms, Insects, Sunlight, and Aging. Bacteria, mildew, and moth larvae will not attack polyesters.

Although polyesters will degrade after long exposure to sunlight, they have better sun resistance than most fibers. This resistance is enhanced when the fibers are placed behind glass that screens out some of the harmful ultraviolet rays. Polyesters are, therefore, quite suitable for use in curtains and draperies.

Age has no appreciable effect on polyesters.

Varieties of Polyesters

A number of different companies produce trademarked polyester fibers. A list of trademarked polyester fibers manufactured in the United States is included in Appendix D. In some instances, the company may manufacture several different specialized varieties of polyester fiber for different uses. Polyester fiber is made in filament, tow, or staple form. Some polyesters are used for apparel, others for home furnishings, and others strictly for industrial use. Cross-sectional shapes may be varied to alter handle and appearance. Some varieties of polyesters are solution-dyed.

CARE

Polyester fabrics are generally machine washable. Water temperatures should be warm, not excessively hot. Ordinary laundry detergents can be used. Household bleaches will not harm white fabrics. Oily stains should be removed before laundering by treatment with a grease solvent.

Polyesters should be dried at low temperatures, and items should be removed from the dryer as soon as the cycle is complete to avoid heat-setting creases. As a general rule, polyesters should not require pressing after drying, although polyester fabrics may be ironed on the wrong side with a moderately warm iron. Some blends of polyesters and cottons can be difficult to iron because the suitable ironing temperature for polyester fibers may not be high enough to press wrinkles from cotton, whereas the cotton temperature is too high for the polyester.

Most fabrics made from polyesters can be dry-cleaned safely. Some polyester double knits printed with pigment colors cannot be dry-cleaned. Care labels should be checked to determine whether dry cleaning should be avoided.

USES

Polyester either alone or in blends with other fibers is used extensively for easy-care fabrics. Many of the so-called permanent press fabrics are made by blending polyester with resin-finished cotton. The exceptional resiliency of polyester makes it especially suitable for these uses. Double knits made from polyester and polyester blends are popular because of their dimensional stability and ease of care.

In addition to being used in a wide range of wearing apparel, polyesters and their blends are used for carpets, curtains, draperies, sheets, and pillowcases for the home. Fiberfill made from polyester is used to fill pillows and comforters.

Industrial uses of polyesters include fire hoses, power belting, ropes, and nets. Tire cord for automotive uses and sails for sports are also made from polyester fibers.

Table 8.1
Selected Characteristics of Polyester Fiber

	Polyester (Regular Tenacity)	
Specific gravity	1.22 or 1.38*	
Tenacity (g/d)–filament		high tenacity
Dry	4.0–5.0	6.3–9.5
Wet	4.0–5.0	6.3–9.5
Moisture regain	0.4–0.8*	
Resiliency	excellent	
Burning and melting point	in flame, burns slowly with melting; usually self-extinguishing after flame is removed; melts at 482°–550°F.*	
Conductivity of		
Heat	poor	
Electricity	poor	
Resistance to damage from		
Fungi	excellent	
Insects	excellent	
Prolonged exposure to sunlight	good if behind glass	
Acids	good	
Alkalis	good to weak alkali	
	fair to strong alkali	

*Depending on type.

Recommended References

BROWN, A. E., and K. A. REINHART. "Polyester Fiber from Its Invention to Its Present Position." *Science*, July 23, 1971, p. 287.

COOK, J. G. *Handbook of Textile Fibers*, Vol. 2. Watford, England, Merrow Publishing Company, Ltd., 1968.

FARROW, G., and E. S. HILL. *Encyclopedia of Science and Technology*, vol. 2, New York: Interscience, 1969, p. 11.

MONCRIEFF, R. W. *Man-made Fibres*. New York: John Wiley & Sons, Inc., 1975.

PETUKOV, B. V. *Technology of Polyester Fibers*. New York: Pergamon Press, 1963.

"Polyamides and Polyester." *CIBA Review*, July 1958.

9

ACRYLIC AND MODACRYLIC FIBERS

Acrylics

Acrylic fibers are defined as "manufactured fibers in which the fiber-forming substance is any long-chain synthetic polymer composed of at least 85 per cent by weight of acrylonitrile units ($-CH_2-CH-$)."

$$CN$$

The second synthetic fiber to be produced commercially by du Pont, Orlon acrylic fiber, entered production in 1950. Acrilan acrylic was produced commercially in 1952 by Monsanto.

Early acrylic fibers were somewhat yellowish in color, and a clear white fiber was difficult to obtain. In time this problem was overcome, and the fiber is now available in a clear white, as well as being dyed a variety of other colors.

GENERAL PROPERTIES OF ACRYLICS

A number of variations in the processes used to manufacture acrylic fibers are possible. Because many of these processes are proprietary and their details are not available, it may be practical to discuss the general characteristics common to most acrylic fibers before examining what is known about their manufacture.

Appearance

The microscopic cross section of acrylic fibers may be round, bean-shaped, dog-bone shaped, or multilobal. Likewise, the longitudinal appearance of acrylics is either smooth or twisted, and may have wide striations (lengthwise markings).

Properties

Strength. The strength of acrylics is fair to good, ranging from 2.0 to 3.5 g/d, depending on the type. There is a slight decrease in strength when wet. Abrasion resistance is moderate.

Density and Specific Gravity.   The specific gravity of acrylics ranges from 1.14 to 1.19, and is comparable to that of nylon. Acrylics are often made into high-bulk but lightweight fabrics.

Elasticity and Resilience.   The elasticity of acrylic fibers varies from one trademarked fiber to another. In general, however, elastic recovery is lower than most other synthetic fibers. Resilience ranges from good to excellent.

Absorbency and Moisture Regain.   The moisture absorption of acrylics is low and moisture regain is 1.0 to 2.5 per cent.

Dimensional Stability.   Heat setting will produce good dimensional stability in fabrics made from acrylics. However, there are many varieties of acrylics with somewhat different performance in regard to their dimensional stability. For this reason, instructions on care labels should be followed carefully in laundering acrylics. For example, some fabrics are manufactured from specially crimped fibers that require dryer drying after laundering to restore the crimp. If hung wet on a line, some of these fabrics may stretch out of shape.

Electrical Conductivity.   The poor electrical conductivity of acrylics is related to their low moisture absorption. Static electricity charges are built up unless special finishes have been given to the fabrics.

Effect of Heat; Combustibility.   Untreated acrylic fibers ignite and burn readily. As fabrics of acrylic burn, flaming melt drips away and burns sufficiently long to ignite flammable surfaces on which the melt may fall. The residue is a hard, black bead at the edge of the fabric. Flame retardant finishes can be given to the fibers. The melting point of the fiber is 450 degrees F. to 497 degrees F., depending on the type of fiber. Fibers shrink in steam. Exposure to high dry heat may cause yellowing. Fibers can be heat-set.

Acrylic Fibers and Their Behavior in Relation to Selected Factors

Chemical Resistance.   The resistance of acrylics to acids is very good, except to nitric acid in which it dissolves. Resistance to alkalis is moderate and degradation by sodium hydroxide at high concentrations and/or temperatures is cited by Moncrieff for Orlon, Acrilan, Creslan, and Zefran. Solvents used in commercial dry cleaning do not affect the fiber adversely. Most acrylics are not harmed by household bleaches.

Resistance to Micro-organisms, Mildew, Sunlight, and Aging.   Neither mildew, micro-organisms, nor moths will harm acrylic fibers. Resistance to sunlight ranges from very good to excellent. Age has no detrimental effect on fabric strength.

SOME ACRYLIC TRADEMARKS

Orlon

Du Pont's acrylic, Orlon, is manufactured by a series of complex processes in which the basic material is acrylonitrile. In simplified terms, a catalyst and an activator are dissolved in water. Over a period of several hours, acrylonitrile

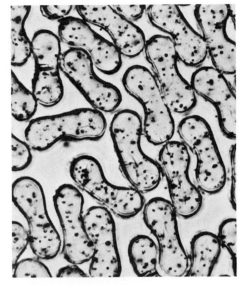

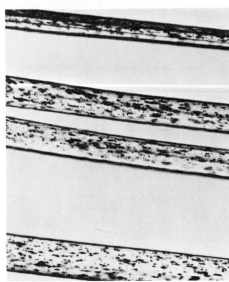

Figure 9-1. Photomicrograph of regular Orlon acrylic fiber in a cross section and a longitudinal view. Courtesy of E. I. du Pont de Nemours & Company.

and an ethylenic (ethyl-type) monomer are added and polymerization takes place in an *addition* reaction.

The polymer precipitates out of the solution, is collected, filtered, washed, and dried. The polymer is dissolved in a suitable spinning solution, heated, and extruded into a heated spinning cell. The solvent evaporates, is collected and recycled for reuse. The filaments are hot-stretched.

Orlon acrylic is made in staple or tow lengths. It has a woollike hand, and good bulking qualities, so that it gives warmth and good cover without excessive weight. In addition, it is easily laundered, can be machine dried, and is considered an "easy care" fabric. For these reasons Orlon is made (as are many acrylics) into many of the same products for which wool is used, such as sweaters, knits, socks, sportswear, pile fabrics, blankets, and carpets.

Fiber manufacturers may produce a number of specialized types of their trademarked fibers. Orlon acrylic is an excellent example of this practice. The fiber is produced in a wide variety of types for special purposes, each carrying a different number or name. Some Orlon fibers are designed for rug or carpet use; some are delustered; and some are specially suitable for apparel, hosiery, or other items.

Bicomponent Orlon

Du Pont introduced a bicomponent acrylic fiber with a permanent crimp in 1959. To form the fiber, two different types of acrylic material are extruded together as one fiber from the spinneret. Each has somewhat different shrinkage properties, and when the fiber is subjected to heat and moisture during the processing, one polymer shrinks more than the other, producing a spiral crimp that is permanent. This provides increased elasticity and resilience. The fiber is used extensively in knitted goods such as sweaters and socks. Wintuk is the certification mark given to yarns of Orlon acrylic based on bicomponent fibers. Sayelle is du Pont's certification mark for yarns made from 100 per cent bicomponent. Civona is du Pont's certification mark for yarns containing a specified amount of bicomponent Orlon.

Acrilan

Like Orlon, Acrilan is made in two stages. The first stage is the manufacture of acrylonitrile from petroleum and the second is the addition polymerization of acrylonitrile. The catalyst and activators for polymerization are added to acrylonitrile and combined in a polymerizer kettle. After polymerization, the acrylonitrile polymer is centrifuged to separate it, and dried. It goes into a mixing tank where an appropriate solvent is used to liquefy the powder. The extruded fibers are formed in a coagulating bath (wet spinning), then dried, stretched, and crimped. The fiber is made in both staple and tow lengths.

The qualities of Acrilan are like those described for acrylics in general. Monsanto also manufactures variations of Acrilan under the trademarks Bi-loft, and Acrilan 1000+, which is used for carpets.

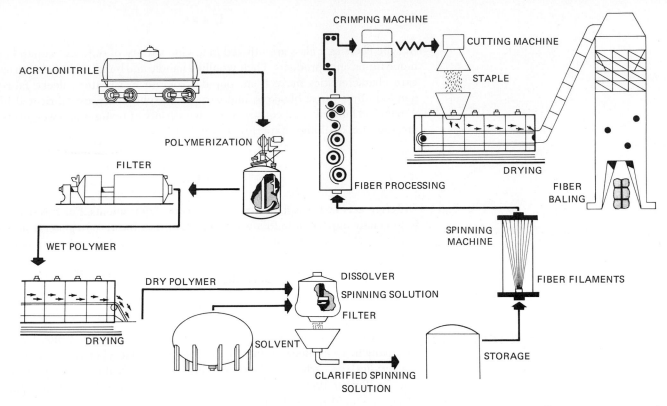

CRIMPING MACHINE

CUTTING MACHINE

ACRYLONITRILE

STAPLE

POLYMERIZATION

FILTER

FIBER PROCESSING

DRYING

FIBER BALING

WET POLYMER

SPINNING MACHINE

DRY POLYMER

DISSOLVER

SPINNING SOLUTION

FILTER

FIBER FILAMENTS

SOLVENT

DRYING

CLARIFIED SPINNING SOLUTION

STORAGE

Figure 9-2. Flow chart for the manufacture of Acrilan acrylic fiber. Courtesy of Monsanto Company.

Creslan

Creslan is the trademark given to the acrylic fiber produced by American Cyanamid Company.

Like Orlon and Acrilan, Creslan is polymerized from acrylonitrile. It is considered to be a copolymer and has a somewhat different composition from the acrylics already discussed. It is wet-spun, washed, stretched, and made into staple and tow.

Its resilience is rated slightly better than Orlon and Acrilan, but otherwise its characteristics are comparable to the other acrylics.

Zefran Acrylic

Zefran acrylic fiber is manufactured by Dow Badische. The manufacturer identifies Zefran acrylic as a "second generation acrylic textile fiber." Zefran is rated as slightly stronger than other acrylics. The rest of its characteristics are typical of the acrylics as a class, and it is used in the same types of products. (It should be noted that the trademark Zefran is applied by Dow Badische to all of its synthetic fibers. Fibers are distinguished by their generic class in accordance with TFPIA, for example, Zefran acrylic, Zefran nylon, and so forth.)

USES

Acrylic fibers as a class are utilized in a wide variety of different apparel and home furnishings products. Their woollike handle and bulk combined with easy care characteristics make them popular for use in sweaters, fleece fabrics, hand-knitting yarns, blankets, and carpets. Acrylic fibers are fabricated into woven and knitted cloth constructions in a variety of textures and weights that are used for clothing, draperies, and upholstery.

CARE

Different acrylic fibers may vary in their care requirements. For this reason it is especially important to follow care labels of these fabrics. In general, acrylic fabrics can be laundered and dry-cleaned. Acrylics may be sensitive to heat, so that when dryer drying is recommended for acrylic products, low heat settings should be used. Pressing temperatures should not exceed 250 degrees F.

Modacrylics

Modacrylic fibers were first manufactured commercially by Union Carbide Company in 1949. Because the composition of modacrylics is very similar to the acrylics, the earliest modacrylic fibers were included in the acrylic classification. But in 1960, the Federal Trade Commission ruled that a separate category should be established for them.

Modacrylics are defined as "a manufactured fiber in which the fiber-forming substance is any synthetic polymer composed of less than 85 per cent but at least 35 per cent by weight of acrylonitrile units ($-CH_2-CH-$) except

$$CN$$

fibers under category (2)[1] of Paragraph (j) of Rule 7 of the Textile Fiber Products Identification Act."

GENERAL CHARACTERISTICS OF MODACRYLICS

Appearance

The microscopic appearance of various types of modacrylics differs. Cross sections range from an irregular flat shape, through a U-shape, to a peanut shape. The longitudinal appearance usually shows some striations or it may have a grainy effect.

Properties

Strength. The strength of modacrylics ranges from 1.7 (SEF) to 2.8 (Verel),

[1] This category excepts certain synthetic rubber products that have a substantial quantity of acrylonitrile in their composition.

which makes some modacrylics weaker than acrylics and others comparable in strength. Their abrasion resistance is moderate.

Density and Specific Gravity. The specific gravity of modacrylics is 1.3, which is comparable to wool, so that the fibers feel light but also have good insulating qualities.

Elasticity and Resilience. The resilience is high, and the combination of high resilience with abrasion resistance makes modacrylic fibers especially suitable for use in high pile fabrics. Elastic recovery is good.

Absorbency and Moisture Regain. The absorbency of the fibers is low and the moisture regain is 0.4 per cent to 4 per cent. As a result, the stain resistance to waterborne soil is good.

Dimensional Stability. Modacrylics have good dimensional stability. However, their sensitivity to heat may result in some shrinkage if they are dried in a dryer at high temperatures.

Effect of Heat; Combustibility. Modacrylics are inherently fire retardant. Although they will burn when placed in a direct flame, they are self-extinguishing as soon as the flame is removed. Furthermore, the melted polymer does not drip off the fabric, so that there is no danger of burns from melted polymer. For these reasons, modacrylics are being widely used in the manufacture of children's sleepwear for which the law mandates the use of flame-retardant fabrics (see Chapter 21).

The melting point of modacrylics is low (about 370 degrees F. to 410 degrees F.). Only the olefins and saran are more sensitive to heat. If modacrylic fabrics are ironed, very low temperature settings must be used. If a dryer is used, temperatures should be set for "no heat."

BEHAVIOR OF MODACRYLIC FIBERS IN RELATION TO SELECTED FACTORS

Chemical Resistance. Dry-cleaning solvents will not affect modacrylics adversely. These fibers are soluble in acetone, and some modacrylics may be discolored by strong alkalis. Their resistance to acids is good to excellent.

Resistance to Selected Environmental Factors. The resistance to deterioration from light is fairly good. Neither moths nor mildew attack modacrylics. Age has no apparent effect.

MANUFACTURE OF MODACRYLICS

Modacrylic fibers are made from chemicals derived from natural gas, coal, air, salt, and water. Combinations of acrylonitrile and other materials, such as vinyl chloride, vinylidene chloride, or vinylidene dicyanide, are made in a polymerization reactor. The polymer formed in the reaction is dissolved in an appropriate solvent, and the fiber is spun, drawn, and cut into staple lengths. Varying degrees of crimp may be added to the fiber depending on its projected end uses.

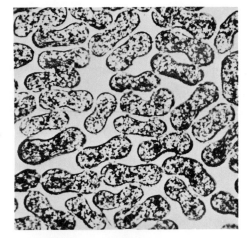

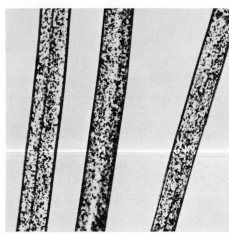

Figure 9-3. Photomicrograph of regular Verel modacrylic fiber in a cross section and a longitudinal view. Courtesy of E. I. du Pont de Nemours & Company.

USES OF MODACRYLIC FIBERS

The major areas of use for modacrylic fibers include pile and fleece fabrics for apparel, blankets, carpets, flame-resistant draperies and curtains, paint rollers, filters, wigs, and hairpieces. As a result of the fact that modacrylics have a low softening temperature and a high shrinkage potential, a variety of texturizing treatments can be given to the fibers that allow them to simulate the textures and characteristics of fur fibers. Most simulated fur fabrics are made from modacrylic or acrylic fibers. The same characteristic of modacrylics makes it possible to create hairlike fibers, which leads to their use in wigs and hairpieces.

Figure 9-4. Flow chart for the manufacture of Verel modacrylic fiber. Courtesy of Eastman Kodak Company.

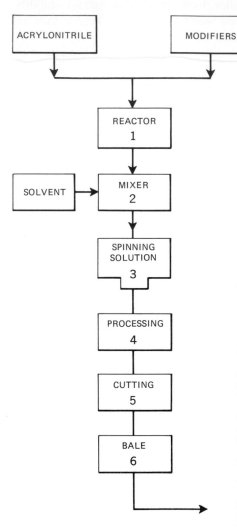

1 **POLYMERIZATION IN REACTOR:** The production of VEREL modacrylic fiber begins in a polymerization reactor where acrylonitrile and certain modifiers are combined into long chain-like molecules called **polymer.** **The type of modifier used helps give VEREL fiber properties which are distinctive from other modacrylic fibers.**

2 **MIXING:** A suitable solvent and the polymer are placed in a tank where they are stirred together until the polymer has dissolved and the mixture has a consistency similar to molasses.

3 **SPINNING:**
■ This mixture, called **spinning solution**, is forced through the microscopic holes of the **spinnerette** . . . a device similar to a miniature shower head . . . forming thin, continuous strands of solution.
■ The solvent is removed leaving the **polymer.**
■ The strands are gathered into bundles of continuous fibers called **tow**, which looks like untwisted rope.

4 **PROCESSING THE TOW:**
■ The tow is moved to the processing area where it is treated to make it resist shrinking or stretching.
■ Lubricating oils are added to aid in spinning yarns.
■ A crimp (like a permanent wave) is added to give texture and bulk.

5 **CUTTING:** The tow now moves to a cutting machine where the continuous strands are cut into short lengths called **staple fiber.**

6 **BALING:** The staple fibers, looking very much like wool, are compressed into bales and wrapped for shipment.

SHIPPING: The VEREL fiber is shipped to textile mills where it will be spun into yarn and woven into fabric.

Tennessee Eastman Company produces the VEREL modacrylic fiber. It does not weave fabrics or make garments or home furnishings.

Figure 9-5. The woman is wearing a Borgasia® coat, made to simulate seal, and constructed with 100 per cent Orlon fiber and an olefin backing yarn, while her male companion wears a coat of Borg Alaskan®. (Registered trademarks, Borg Textiles Corporation.)

As mentioned previously, modacrylics are naturally flame retardant, so that they are used in sleepwear, especially garments with fleecy or pile fabric constructions, carpets, curtains and draperies, blankets, and in some industrial fabrics where their flame resistance and good chemical resistance are both utilized.

CONSIDERATIONS IN CARE OF MODACRYLICS

Deep pile garments must be professionally cleaned in order to avoid crushing or altering the appearance of the pile. Other modacrylic fabrics are machine washable, but special care should be taken to avoid exposing them to very high temperatures because of their heat sensitivity. Low dryer temperatures must be used, and ironing should only be done with a warm, not hot, iron. Some modacrylic fibers are discolored by the use of chlorine bleaches.

TRADEMARKED MODACRYLIC FIBERS

For many years only two modacrylic fibers were made commercially: Dynel by Union Carbide Company and Verel by Eastman Kodak Company. During 1974–75, Dynel was phased out of production by Union Carbide Company. Verel continues to be an important modacrylic fiber.

Monsanto manufactures modacrylics under the trademarks Elura, and SEF. SEF has been especially recommended by Monsanto for use in flame-resistant sleepwear.

Table 9.1
Selected Properties of Acrylic and Modacrylic Fibers

	Acrylic	Modacrylic
Specific Gravity	1.14–1.19	1.30–1.37
Tenacity		
Dry	2.0–3.5	2.0–3.5
Wet	1.8–3.3	2.0–3.5
Moisture regain	1.0–2.5	.4–4
Resilience	good	good
Burning and melting point	in flame, burns with melting, continues after flame removed; softens at 450°–497°; indeterminate melting point	in flame, burns very slowly with melting; self-extinguishing after flame removed; melting point 371° (approximate) to 410°F
Conductivity of		
Heat	poor	poor
Electricity	poor	poor
Resistance to damage from		
Fungi	excellent	excellent
Insects	excellent	excellent
Prolonged exposure to sunlight	excellent	excellent
Acids	good, except nitric	good
Alkalis	good to weak alkali	good

Recommended References

"Acrylics: Dark Horse of the 70's." *American Fabrics and Fashions*, Fall 1970, p. 51.
CHAPMAN, C. *Fibres.* Plainfield, N.J.: Textile Book Service, 1974.
COOK, J. B. *Handbook of Textile Fibers,* vol. 2. Watford, England: Merrow Publishing Company, Ltd., 1968.
COLLIER, A. M. *Handbook of Textiles.* New York: Pergamon Press, 1970.
JOSEPH, M. *Introductory Textile Science.* New York: Holt, Rinehart, and Winston, Inc., 1972.
"The Mighty Modacrylics." *American Fabrics and Fashions.* Fall 1970, p. 61.
MONCRIEFF, R. W. *Man-Made Fibres.* New York: John Wiley & Sons, Inc., 1975.
SITTIG, M. *Acrylic and Vinal Fibers.* Plainfield, N.J.: Textile Book Service, 1972.

10
OLEFIN FIBERS

Although olefin monofilaments have been manufactured for specialized applications since 1949, the widespread use of olefin fibers for a variety of textile products has been a relatively recent development. (British publications may refer to these fibers as polyalkenes.)

The FTC definition of olefin fiber is "a manufactured fiber in which the fiber-forming substance is any long-chain synthetic polymer composed of at least 85 per cent weight of ethylene, propylene, or other olefin units, except[1] amorphous (noncrystaline) polyolefins qualifying under category (1) of paragraph (j) of rule 7."

Two major categories of olefin fibers exist. One is polypropylene, the other is polyethylene. Of the two, polypropylene is used more extensively for textiles and constitutes the largest quantity of olefin fibers in use today.

MANUFACTURE

Polypropylene Fibers

Polymer chips are manufactured from propylene gas. The fiber is then formed by one of two means. Polypropylene may be melt-spun or it may be mechanically fibrillated. Fibrillated fibers are created by first extruding a film of polypropylene. This film is either stretched and split or slit and drawn into a network of fibers. (See Chapter 13 for a discussion of film fibrillation.)

The properties of the melt-spun fibers and fibrillated fibers differ somewhat. The denier (size) range of melt-spun fibers is greater than that of fibrillated fibers. Fibrillated fibers have branchlike structure that may eliminate the need to add texture to the fiber. Also, fiber-to-fiber interlocking is better in fibrillated fibers, but fiber length is not so uniform, and fibrillated fibers are more likely to pill. Yarns made from the fibrillated fibers are less regular in shape than those from melt-spun fibers. Spun fibrillated yarns are smoother and softer. Less pigment is required to color fibrillated fibers than to color comparable spun yarns from melt-spun fibers.

[1] This exception refers to a type of synthetic rubber with a substantial proportion of polyolefin material.

Appearance

In microscopic appearance, the polypropylene fiber has a round cross section and a smooth, longitudinal shape.

Strength. Polypropylene olefins are strong. The breaking strength is from 4.8 to 7.0 g/d. (Regular tenacity nylon 66 is 3.0 to 3.6 g/d.) and the abrasion resistance is good.

Density and Specific Gravity. The density of polypropylene is especially low. Its specific gravity is .92, or less than that of water. As a result, olefin fabrics float on top of water when they are washed. The low density of polypropylene also is related to the relatively low cost of olefin fiber, as a small quantity of raw materials can be used to produce a large quantity of fiber.

Elasticity and Resilience. The elastic recovery of polypropylene olefin fibers is excellent. The resilience of the fiber is fair to good.

Absorbency. Almost completely nonabsorbent, polypropylene is difficult to dye. Best results in dyeing fibers are attained when the pigment is combined with the polymer before the fibers are formed. Low absorbency also makes the fiber exceptionally resistant to waterborne soil and stains. Grease and oil do stain polypropylene fabrics and since they are oleophilic (or oil-attracting), stains may be difficult to remove. Olefin fabrics have good wickability.

Dimensional Stability. The dimensional stability of heat-set polypropylene is good, as long as it is not subjected to temperatures above 250 degrees F. Elevated temperatures will result in fabric shrinkage.

Electrical Conductivity. The electrical conductivity of polypropylene is poor. Its low absorbency contributes to problems of static electricity buildup.

Effect of Heat; Combustibility. The melting point of polypropylene is quite low: 338 degrees F. Hot bacon fat dropped on olefin carpets will melt fibers. Olefins are combustible and melt as they burn. They produce a sooty smoke.

Behavior of Olefin Fibers in Relation to Selected Factors

Chemical Resistance. In general, polypropylene's resistance to alkalis and to acids is good. Some organic solvents used in dry cleaning may affect the fabrics adversely. Perchloroethylene should not be used. However, Stoddard solvent will not deteriorate the fibers. Home laundering is preferable to dry cleaning in the care of polypropylene fabrics.

Resistance to Environmental Factors. Mold, mildew, and insects do not attack olefins. Sunlight does gradually deteriorate the fabric, and age has no appreciable effect.

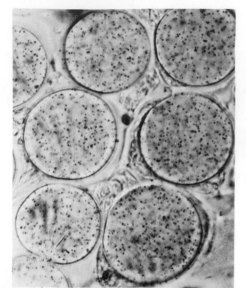

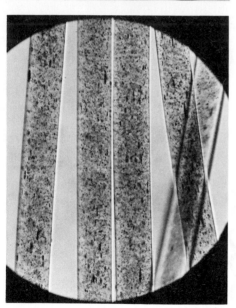

Figure 10-1. Photomicrograph of Marvess olefin fiber in a cross section and a longitudinal view. Courtesy of Phillips Fibers Corporation.

USES OF POLYPROPYLENE

Polypropylene fibers are used in the manufacture of carpets, especially indoor/outdoor carpeting. Being nonabsorbent and having good weather resistance, polypropylene can be made into carpets that will withstand exposure to outdoor conditions in areas where sunlight is not intense or prolonged. However, such carpets will deteriorate in climates like those of the American Southwest. When polypropylene is used for traditional indoor carpets, soil and waterborne stain resistance are exceptional. Other characteristics such as good abrasion resistance, good lightfastness if solution-dyed, and resistance to moths have contributed to the successful use of polypropylene for carpetings.

Upholstery fabric manufacturers have made extensive use of polypropylene. Again, stain resistance and resistance to abrasion are important in this application.

Other products made from polypropylene include knitwear, blankets, apparel, wall coverings, and replacements for jute and other bast fibers in twine, ropes, carpet backings, and the like. The wicking qualities of olefins lead to their use in diaper liners and hiking socks. In these applications, moisture is carried away from the body to evaporate.

One of the major advantages of the fiber is the low cost of production. Better-known trademarks for olefin fibers include Herculon, Vectra, and Marvess. The *Textile Organon* of June, 1977, lists more than fifty American companies that produce olefin fibers and/or films.[2]

POLYETHYLENE

Polyethylene fibers are made by the polymerization of ethylene gas. Fibers are melt-spun and then drawn to orient the molecules.

Polyethylene shares many qualities in common with polypropylene, and exhibits some differences, including a lower melting point for polyethylene and some tendency to be deformed if stretched more than 10 per cent. At this time polyethylene is not a textile fiber of major importance. It is widely used for plastic films and packaging materials.

Table 10.1
Selected Properties of Polypropylene Fibers

Specific Gravity	0.92
Tenacity (g/d)	
Dry	4.8–7.0*
Wet	4.8–7.0
Moisture regain	none
Resiliency	good
Burning and melting point	in flame, burns with melting; continues to burn after flame is removed. Melts at 325° to 335°F
Conductivity of	
Heat	poor
Electricity	poor
Resistance to damage from	
Fungi	excellent
Insects	excellent
Prolonged exposure to sunlight	slowly loses strength
Acids	excellent
Alkalis	excellent

Man-made Fiber Fact Book (Washington, D.C.: Man-Made Fiber Producers Association, Inc., 1974).

BADRIAN, W. H. "Polypropylene." *Modern Textiles.* July 1974, p. 58.
CHAPMAN, C. *Fibres.* Plainfield, N.J.: Textile Book Service, 1974.
COOK, J. G. *Handbook of Polyolefin Fibers.* Watford, England: Merrow Publishing Company, Ltd., 1967.
COOK, J. G. *Handbook of Textile Fibers,* Vol. 2. Watford, England: Merrow Publishing Company, Ltd., 1968.
"The Latest on Polypropylene." *Textile Month.* December 1975, p. 40; January 1976, p. 38; February 1976, p. 47.
MONCRIEFF, R. W. *Man-Made Fibres.* New York: John Wiley & Sons, Inc., 1975.
"Polyolefins." *CIBA Review.* 1964, vol. 3.

Recommended References

[2] *Textile Organon* (June 1977), p. 98.

11
ELASTOMERIC FIBERS

Generic Fiber
Classifications
1. spandex
2. Rubber
3. anidex

Elastomeric fibers are defined as those fibers "which have mechanical properties characteristic of natural rubber: they can be stretched to several times their original length and on release will snap back quickly to recover their original length almost completely."[1] Natural rubber has been made into fiber for many years. Natural rubber has certain disadvantages in fiber use, however. It is difficult to dye, has poor abrasion resistance, is deteriorated by sunlight, and has relatively poor chemical resistance. Textile chemists have synthesized several new fibers that compare favorably in elasticity with rubber without some of its disadvantages.

Three generic fiber classifications have been established for elastomeric fibers: spandex, rubber, and anidex. Other elastomeric fibers have been made by modifying cellulose fibers, and still other elastomers are in experimental stages of development. Of these generic fiber groups only rubber and spandex are currently being manufactured.

Rubber, Lastrile, and Anidex Fibers

RUBBER

The Federal Trade Commission has established a category that is designated as rubber fibers. The definition established is divided into three parts and includes both natural and synthetic rubber.

Natural rubber is obtained from rubber plants. From a liquid form the rubber can be extruded into fibrous form. For many years, natural rubber was used as the core for fiber-covered elastic materials. Its advantages include elasticity, flexibility, good strength, and nonabsorbency. Its disadvantages include deterioration from temperatures above 200 degrees F., from sunlight, oils, petroleum, and aging.

A variety of synthetic rubber products was marketed after World War II. These products are made from hydrocarbons such as polyisoprene, polybutadiene, and noncrystaline polyolefins. Copolymers of dienes and hydrocarbons are also used in the manufacture of some synthetic rubber.

[1]R. Meredith, *Elastomeric Fibers* (Watford, England: Merrow Publishing Company, Ltd., 1971), p. 1.

The FTC also identifies synthetic rubber made from "polychloroprene or a copolymer of chloroprene in which at least 35 per cent by weight of the fiber-forming substance is composed of chloroprene units." Synthetic rubbers exhibit similar characteristics to natural rubber in their behavior, but in general show better resistance to deterioration than rubber.

LASTRILE

Included in the FTC definitions is the term *lastrile,* which by this ruling is made of "a co-polymer of acrylonitrile and a diene (such as butadiene) composed of not more than 50 per cent but at least 10 per cent by weight of acrylonitrile units." Lastrile fibers have not been made commercially up to this time.

ANIDEX

Anidex is defined as "a manufactured fiber in which the fiber-forming substance is any long-chain synthetic polymer composed of at least 50 per cent by weight of one or more esters of a monohydric alcohol and acrylic acid (Ch_2—CH—COOH)."

Anidex fibers are no longer manufactured. For a time this elastomeric fiber was distributed by Rohm and Haas company as Anim/8.

ELASTOMERIC FIBERS BASED ON CELLULOSE

Experimentation with cross-linking and grafting of cellulose molecules has led to the development of elastomeric fibers based on cellulose. Regular viscose rayon is treated with formaldehyde, cross-linkages are formed, and the fiber is then treated to graft a copolymer to the molecule. Elastomeric behavior results. This fiber shows lower strength than spandex and lower elastic extension, although elastic recovery is higher—97 per cent recovery at 100 per cent extension as compared with 94 per cent for Lycra spandex.[2]

Spandex

Spandex fibers have attained extensive use in stretch fabrics for foundation garments, sports apparel, and other products where elasticity is important. The FTC defines spandex fibers as "a manufactured fiber in which the fiber-forming substance is a long-chain synthetic polymer comprised of at least 85 per cent of a segmented polyurethane."

Manufactured in the United States since 1959, spandex fibers are of the same composition as polyurethane foams used for mattresses and pillows. They are structured into linear polymers in combination with other substances such as

[2] R. Meredith, *Elastomeric Fibers* (Watford, England: Merrow Publishing Company, Ltd., 1971), p. 37.

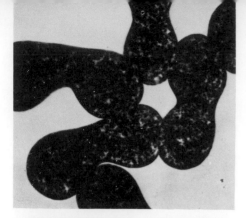

Figure 11-1. Photomicrograph of Lycra Spandex fiber in a cross-section and a longitudinal view. Courtesy of E. I. du Pont de Nemours & Company.

polyesters, polyamides, polyglycols, or copolymers of these compounds. The precise methodologies and compounds used have not been released by the manufacturers.

Appearance

The microscopic appearance of spandex fibers differs from one trademarked fiber to another. In cross section, some are round, some are shaped like peanut shells, and others are shaped like dog bones. Longitudinal views display even, smooth, though dark, surfaces.

Properties

Because spandex is selected for use in many products in which rubber might be used, it may be helpful to compare the properties of spandex to rubber as well as to other fibers.

Strength or Tenacity. Spandex is relatively weak when compared to nonelastomeric fibers. It is about twice as strong as rubber.

Density or Specific Gravity. Spandex has a moderate density, comparable to that of polyester.

Elasticity and Elastic Recovery. The most important property of spandex is its ability to stretch. It will stretch 500 to 600 per cent without breaking. This amount of stretching is comparable to an extension of six or seven times its original length, and is comparable to that of rubber. Recovery from stretching is slightly better for rubber than for spandex. The improved strength of spandex combined with its excellent stretch give it an advantage over rubber. Other properties of spandex that are described in the following paragraphs also make spandex more practical to use than rubber.

Absorbency and Moisture Regain. Although the absorbency and moisture regain of spandex fibers are low, water will penetrate the fiber, making it easy to dye. By contrast, rubber is difficult to color.

Effect of Heat; Combustibility. Spandex fibers will burn. The melting point varies from trademarked fiber to trademarked fiber, and the specific melting point is difficult to ascertain. Apparently most spandex fibers melt at temperatures of about 430 degrees to 450 degrees F. These fibers stick at temperatures around 340 degrees F.

Spandex can be heat-set. Spandex fibers can be dried safely in an automatic dryer. High water temperature tends to yellow white spandex.

Spandex Fiber and Its Behavior in Relation to Selected Conditions

Chemical Resistance. The resistance to chemicals is generally good. Chlorine compounds in strong concentrations will cause the fiber to be degraded and yellowed, but spandex will withstand chlorine concentrations such as those used in swimming pools. Chlorine bleaches should be avoided.

Sea water has no deleterious effect on spandex fibers. Perspiration and suntan oils do not seriously affect spandex, although some suntan oils may cause yellowing of white fibers. (Suntan oils *do* deteriorate rubber.)

Resistance to Micro-organisms and Light. Spandex has satisfactory resistance to micro-organisms. Exposure to light does cause yellowing of white spandex but does not deteriorate the fiber seriously.

USE OF SPANDEX FIBERS

Spandex fibers are always used in conjunction with other fibers. This combination may be made in one of several ways. The spandex fiber may be made as bare yarn, single-covered yarn, double-covered yarn, or core-spun yarn.

Bare core spandex yarns are uncovered filaments. They may be woven into fabrics in combination with other yarns to provide strength. More often, the fibers are covered with another fiber and the spandex serves as the core. Single-covered yarns are wrapped inside the filament yarn of another fiber.

Double-covered yarns are wrapped in companion filament fibers in which one layer is twisted around the core in one direction, and the second layer is twisted around the core in the opposite direction. These can be made into very sheer yarns and are often used for support hose. Where it is desirable, two different types of fibers can be used, one in each layer. Core-spun fabrics are made by holding spandex filaments at tension while a staple fiber is spun around the core.

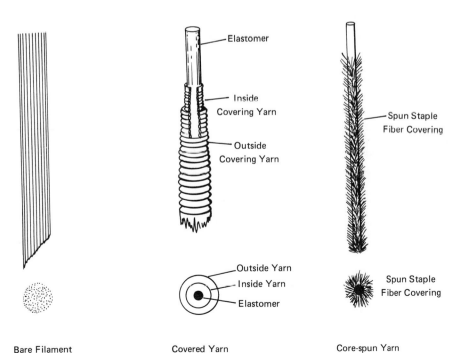

Bare Filament   Covered Yarn   Core-spun Yarn

Figure 11-2. Types of elastomeric yarns (length and cross section).

CARE OF SPANDEX FIBERS

Spandex yarns are woven or knitted into a variety of garments in which stretch is desirable. These may include power nets for foundation garments, underwear, lingerie, and for active sportswear used in sports such as swimming, skiing, golf, and tennis. Attractive stretch laces and other decorative fabrics may be made with spandex.

Spandex fibers are used in combination with other fibers, so that care must take into account not only the characteristics of spandex but also of the other fiber. Spandex should not be subject to excessive heat in ironing. It is recommended that ironing temperatures not exceed 300 degrees F. or the "synthetic" setting on a hand iron. Dryer temperatures should be moderate. Chlorine bleaches should not be used in laundering spandex. Colored lingerie, into which spandex is often made, makes bleaching unnecessary.

TRADEMARKS OF SPANDEX

Trade names for spandex fiber include Lycra, a du Pont trademark, Numa by American Cyanamid, Glospan, and Cleerspan by Globe Manufacturing Company.

In 1973, Monsanto introduced a biconstituent fiber made from spandex and nylon. Given the trademark Monvelle, the fiber is made of 50 per cent nylon and 50 per cent spandex. Monvelle is being used for support hose. Yarns made from Monvelle, either monofilament or multifilament, can be knitted into sheerer fabrics than can double-covered spandex, which has, heretofore, been used for support hosiery. (See Chapter 12 for discussion of biconstituent fibers.)

Table 11.1
Selected Properties of Spandex Fibers

Specific gravity	1.21–1.35
Tenacity (g/d)	
Dry	.6–.9
Wet	.6–.9
Moisture regain	.75%–1.3%
Breaking extension	500–600%
Burning and melting point	in flame, burns with melting; continues to burn after flame is removed. Melts at 446° to 518°F.
Conductivity of	
Heat	difficult to assess because fiber is used in combination with other fibers.
Electricity	difficult to assess because fiber is used in combination with other fibers.
Resistance to damage	
Fungi	excellent
Insects	excellent
Prolonged exposure to sunlight	resists degradation; yellows.
Acids	good—acid fumes may cause yellowing.
Alkalis	fair

Cook, J. G. *Handbook of Textile Fibers*, Vol. 2. Watford, England: Merrow Publishing Company, Ltd., 1967.

Jeffries, R. *Bicomponent Fibres.* Watford, England: Merrow Publishing Company, Ltd., 1971.

Meredith, R. *Elastomeric Fibres.* Watford, England: Merrow Publishing Company, Ltd., 1971.

Moncrieff, R. W. *Man-Made Fibres.* New York: John Wiley & Sons, Inc., 1975.

Recommended References

12

OTHER MAN-MADE, BICOMPONENT, AND BICONSTITUENT FIBERS

Saran
Vinyon
Novoloid

In addition to the man-made fibers discussed in earlier chapters, there are a number of fibers that have somewhat limited use or represent relatively recent developments in the technology of man-made fiber production. These include a number of synthetic fiber types that are manufactured in relatively small quantities either in the United States or abroad such as saran, novoloid, nytril, vinyon, vinal, and TFE fluorocarbon; alginates or regenerated fibers made from seaweed; bicomponent fibers; and biconstituent fibers.

Synthetic Fibers

SARAN

Saran is a textile fiber of limited use. It is defined as "a manufactured fiber in which the fiber-forming substance is any long-chain synthetic polymer composed of at least 80 per cent by weight of vinylidene chloride units $(-CH_2-CCl_2-)$."

Introduced by Dow Chemical Company in 1941, saran is now made in the United States by Amtech, Inc. It is a stiff, nondrapable fiber with specialized uses in agricultural and industrial fabrics. Upholstery fabrics for deck chairs and garden furniture have been made from saran.

Production and Processing

The molten vinylidene chloride/vinyl chloride copolymer is forced through the spinneret, air-spun into cold air, quenched in water, and stretched. Saran fibers can be delustered and/or solution-dyed.

Appearance

In microscopic view, filaments of saran have a round cross section. The longitudinal view shows a smooth surface. Saran can also be produced in flat and oval shapes.

Properties

Strength or Tenacity.   Saran is generally made with a large diameter, so that its strength is very good. It also has excellent tear and abrasion resistance.

Density and Specific Gravity.   A high density fiber (specific gravity is higher than most other synthetics at 1.70), the weight and inflexibility of the fiber eliminate it from use in apparel fabrics.

Elasticity and Resilience.   Fibers made of saran have excellent elastic recovery and are quite resilient.

Absorbency.   Saran is nonabsorbent. The moisture regain is less than 0.1 per cent.

Dimensional Stability.   If saran is not exposed to excessive temperatures, its dimensional stability is good.

Conductivity of Heat and Electricity.   Because of the low heat and electrical conductivity of saran, it may be used for insulation purposes.

Combustibility; Effect of Heat.   Saran burns very slowly if placed in a direct flame. The fiber is self-extinguishing after removal of the flame. The melting point of the fiber is relatively low: 335 degrees F.

Effect of Selected Conditions on Saran Fibers

Chemical Resistance.   Neither acids nor alkalis affect the fiber adversely to any extent.

Resistance to Insects, Micro-organisms, and Sun.   Saran is not attacked by moths, mildew, or bacteria. Sunlight resistance is very good, although some discoloration may take place after long exposure to the sun.

USES OF SARAN

Upholstery fabrics made from saran have been used for public conveyances, deck chairs, garden furniture, and the like. Its low absorbency, good sunlight and weather resistance, and strength and abrasion resistance make saran appropriate for this use.

Agricultural fabrics take advantage of the weather and flame-resistant characteristics of saran. Such fabrics are used to provide shade for growing plants. The chemical resistance of the fiber results in a variety of industrial uses. Saran grille fabrics are used in sound systems because they distort sound less than other materials. Some saran drapery fabrics made of saran in combination with other fibers, such as modacrylics, are used for making drapery fabrics that are flame resistant.

Furniture with saran webbing can be cleaned easily with soap and water. Because the fiber is nonabsorbent, these items will dry quickly. They do not stain readily.

VINYON

Vinyon fibers are most frequently used in industrial applications where their high resistance to chemicals is useful. Vinyon has a low melting point, and is, therefore, useful as a bonding agent in nonwoven fabric construction.

FTC defines vinyon as "a manufactured fiber in which the fiber-forming substance is any long-chain synthetic polymer composed of at least 85 per cent by weight of vinyl chloride units ($-CH_2-$ $-CHCl-$)."

Leavil, a vinyon fiber originated in Italy, is being introduced to the American market. The fiber is fire resistant, and is recommended for use in draperies, curtains, and blankets. The fiber is sensitive to heat during pressing and has a tendency to shrink during laundering. The laundry laboratory of the International Fabricate Institute recommends that allowance be made to adjust the length of Leavil draperies after repeated washings.[1]

Fabrics of leavil may be tumble dried at 120 degrees F., but drying at higher settings causes the fabric to yellow and become sleazy.

Static electricity is a problem. The use of a fabric softener will decrease static electricity buildup, however, without negatively affecting flame retardancy. The fabric can be commercially dry-cleaned. Pressing with commercial pressing equipment causes fabric shrinkage and stiffening.

The low melting point of vinyon has prevented its use to any extent in apparel. The fiber is combined with vinal, however, in making a biconstituent fiber Cordelan (see page 151).

NOVOLOID — Kynol

Novoloid fibers are manufactured fibers "containing at least 85 per cent by weight of a cross-linked novolac."

Kynol, developed by the Carborundum Company, is a novoloid fiber used in protective garments, especially for racing drivers, firemen, and military and industrial workers. It is the noncombustible nature of the fiber that makes it especially appropriate for these uses.

The manufacturer describes Kynol's characteristics as follows: tenacity though relatively low (1.7 g/d) is satisfactory for normal use, abrasion resistance is fair. It will not burn (except in high oxygen atmosphere), and it does not melt. It is not attacked by mildew and is not deteriorated by age. It will darken in color on exposure to sunlight.

The chemical resistance of Kynol is good; novoloid fiber resists acids, shows some instability in strongly alkaline environments, and is stable against almost any organic solvent.

[1] *Textile Notes*, #85. International Fabricare Institute Service Bulletin (January 1976).

The fiber is available in staple and tow. It can be woven, knitted, and needle-punched. At first, it was available in a limited color range, but the manufacturer states that recent developments have made possible a wider range of colors.

When blended with other fibers novoloids apparently confer some flame retardancy. Some protective garments for firemen are being made from a blend of Kynol and Nomex aramid.

MINOR FIBERS NOT CURRENTLY IN PRODUCTION IN THE UNITED STATES

The production of both vinal and nytril fibers has been discontinued in the United States. However, imported items made from these fabrics can sometimes be purchased.

Nytril

"A manufactured fiber containing at least 85 per cent of a long-chain polymer of vinylidene dinitrile ($-CH_2-C(CN)_2-$) where the vinylidene

Figure 12-1. Flame-resistant underwear made of 100 per cent Kynol novoloid fiber for use by racing car drivers. Courtesy of The Carborundum Company.

dinitrile content is no less than every other unit in the polymer chain," nytril fibers are soft and resilient. They have a low melting point, softening at temperatures similar to those of modacrylic fibers. Nytril fibers are most suitable for items that do not require pressing.

Major uses of nytril fibers were in garments where the softness was desirable, in pile fabrics, and in blends with wool. Like most synthetics, nytrils have low absorbency, wash and dry quickly, and have good wrinkle recovery.

Vinal

FTC definition calls vinal "a manufactured fiber in which the fiber-forming substance is any long-chain synthetic polymer composed of at least 50 per cent by weight of vinyl alcohol units ($-CH_2-CHOH-$), and in which the total of the vinyl alcohol units and any one or more of the various acetal units is at least 85 per cent by weight of the fiber."

Most of the development of vinal has taken place in Japan. The fiber has a melting point close to that of nylon 6 (c.425 degrees F.), very good chemical resistance, and is especially resistant to rot-producing micro-organisms.

The use of vinal fibers is largely in industrial applications, although some blends of vinal fiber with cotton, rayon or silk have been used abroad. Vinal scarves imported from Japan are available in the United States both in 100 per cent vinal or in blends.

In some countries vinal fibers are called polyvinyl alcohol fibers.

TFE FLUROCARBONS

Teflon, manufactured by du Pont, is a flurocarbon fiber used in industry. The Federal Trade Commission has not established a generic category for this fiber under the Textile Fiber Products Identification Act, possibly because the fiber is not available to the general consumer.

Teflon is better known to the public as a plastic coating on cooking utensils and other products. The fiber is made from the same basic material. It is noncombustible, has a very high melting point, and is highly resistant to chemicals.

Teflon has a high specific gravity, making it very heavy. The fiber has 0 per cent moisture regain, which has led to difficulty in dyeing Teflon. Thus far, the fiber has been used only in aerospace clothing and in industry.

Alginates

Alginates are regenerated textile fibers made from seaweed. They are not manufactured in the United States, at the present time, but are made abroad, particularly in England.

The generic term *alginates* is derived from the Latin word for seaweed, *alga*. The fiber is manufactured from one of the main constituents of seaweed, alginic acid.

MANUFACTURE

Seaweed is collected, dried, and milled to form a powder which is treated with chemical solutions of sodium carbonate and caustic soda. The resulting material is sodium alginate. This material is treated to additional chemical reactions to form alginic acid, which is again reacted to form sodium carbonate. The intervening processes have served to purify the substance.

An 8 to 9 per cent solution of sodium alginate is filtered and spun on a viscose spinning machine. It is wet spun into a coagulating bath in which further chemical reaction takes place, precipitating the fiber as calcium alginate.

These filaments are pulled together, given an after rinse, dried, and wound, ready for use.

CHARACTERISTICS

The microscopic cross section of the fiber is irregular but rounded. The edges are serrated. In longitudinal form it is slightly striated.

The fiber is flameproof, and is used to a limited extent for theater draperies in Great Britain. Its dry strength is similar to that of viscose rayon. However, it has very low wet strength, and in solutions of slightly alkaline, soapy water it will dissolve. This means that the fiber cannot be used for items that must be laundered. (It can be dry-cleaned.)

USES

The peculiar property alginates possess of dissolving in soapy water has limited their use in textiles. On the other hand, this quality has resulted in some interesting applications in fabric and garment manufacture.

Alginates may be used as "support" yarns in fabric construction where open, sheer, or lacelike effects are desired but not attainable through normal weaving processes. The fabric is woven, then laundered, causing the alginate yarns to dissolve, leaving only the nonalginate yarns in a lacy open pattern.

Alginate yarns may also be used when wool socks are manufactured in a continuous "string" with a few rows of stitches between the toe of one sock and the top of the next. The socks are cut apart, and when subjected to finishing processes, the remaining alginate threads dissolve out, leaving a smoothly finished edge.

Bicomponent and Biconstituent Fibers

Bicomponent and biconstituent fibers might also be called paired or twinned fibers. *Bicomponent fibers* are made from two generically similar fibers (that is, two types of nylon, two types of acrylic, and so on) whereas *biconstituent fibers* are made from two generically different fibers (that is, nylon and polyester, spandex and nylon, and so on).

Bicomponent fibers may be of two types; side-by-side bicomponent fibers or

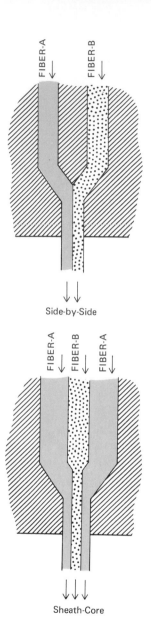

FIBER-A FIBER-B

Side-by-Side

FIBER-A FIBER-B FIBER-A

Sheath-Core

Figure 12-2. Formation of bicomponent fibers.

sheath-core fibers. In making a side-by-side bicomponent fiber, the process requires that the different polymers be fed to the spinneret orifice together so that they exit from the spinneret opening, side by side.

Sheath-core fibers require that one component be completely surrounded by the other, so that the polymer is generally fed into the spinneret as shown in the diagram (see Figure 12.2.) Variation in the shape of the orifice that contains the inner core can produce fibers with different behavioral characteristics.

Most bicomponent fibers are made in order to provide stretch or crimp to the fiber. Each of the polymers used in the bicomponent fiber has slightly different characteristics. Often one polymer is made to shrink in heat or chemical treatment more than the other, which pulls the fiber into a permanent crimp. If sufficient crimp is provided or if the fiber is elastic, the bicomponent fiber may also have increased stretchability. Cantrece nylon is a bicomponent fiber with good stretch that is used in hosiery. Other uses for bicomponent fibers have been suggested. For example, components with different melting points could be used to bond fibers together in the construction of nonwoven fabrics. When heat is applied, one fiber softens, serving as a glue to hold the other fiber in place. A less absorbent core fiber could be sheathed in a more absorbent fiber, in order to increase comfort or increase dyeability.[2]

Biconstituent fibers offer an opportunity to combine two different generic fiber types in such a way that the advantages of each can be utilized. Biconstituent fibers may be made with each constituent in continuous contact with the other. Monvelle, a stretch fiber of 50 per cent nylon and 50 per cent spandex is a biconstituent of this type that is being made into support hosiery. Microphotographs of the fiber show clearly the side-by-side nature of the two constituents.[3]

Mirafi, a non-woven fabric produced by Celanese, is made up of two types of fibers: one a polypropylene filament and the other a biconstituent fiber made with a core of polypropylene and a nylon cover. The fabric is used in civil engineering for road construction, erosion control, land reclamation, drainage, railroad roadbeds, and irrigation.

The Monsanto Company has developed an anti-static yarn for carpets. The fabric, Ultron, is composed of a blend of trilobal nylon 66 and a biconstituent filament. The biconstituent fiber in this blend is round in cross-section. It is composed of 95 per cent nylon 66 filament and 5 per cent of a very narrow stripe consisting of a combination of nylon and a conductive carbon black. The two materials are intimately bound together in a side-by-side construction.[4]

[2] R. Jeffries, *Bicomponent Fibres* (Watford, England: Merrow Publishing Company, Ltd., 1971). p. 55 FF.

[3] The American Society for Testing Materials has defined biconstituent fibers somewhat more narrowly. Under the ASTM definition, biconstituent fibers are "a continuous matrix of one polymer in which a different polymer is dispersed as a distinct, discontinuous phase." In other words, by this definition biconstituent fibers are limited to matrix fibers, as defined by the FTC. In use, however, both Monvelle and Mirifi, called biconstituent fibers by their manufacturers, are made from two different polymers but, contrary to ASTM definition, the two polymers are in continuous contact and do not utilize the matrix construction.

[4] "Ultron: Monsanto's New Static Control Nylon." *Modern Textiles* (October, 1976) p. 40.

Figure 12-3. Photomicrograph of cross section of Monvelle biconstituent fiber. The nylon portion of the fiber shows as black; the spandex is transparent. Courtesy of the Monsanto Company.

By contrast, Cordelan, a biconstituent fiber made from 50 per cent vinal and 50 per cent vinyon, is a biconstituent matrix fiber. A matrix fiber is one in which the fiber-forming components are dispersed one within the other before they are extruded through the spinneret. Cordelan is manufactured in Japan and distributed in the United States. The fiber is inherently flame retardant, neither burning nor melting, but charring. It is being recommended for use in children's sleepwear, blankets, draperies, bedspreads, mattresses, and other products where flame resistance is important.

The manufacturer claims for the fabric a soft hand, a specific gravity close to that of wool (1.32), and a high abrasion resistance. The moisture absorbency of Cordelan is higher than that of acrylics or polyesters.

Cordelan's resistance to chlorine bleaches is poor. Its low electrical conductivity causes static electricity buildup. Care instructions indicate that the fabric can be machine washed at warm settings and tumble-dried at low heat. Chlorine bleach should not be used in laundering. If the fabric is pressed, a warm setting should be used.

Under the Textile Fiber Products Information Act, biconstituent fibers must be labeled as "biconstituent or multiconstituent fiber" and the distinct constituents must be identified by their generic names. Constituents are to be listed in the order of "predominance by weight" and must state the "respective percentages of such components by weight." The ruling goes on to state, "If the components of such fibers are of a matrix-fibril configuration [like Cordelan, for example], the term 'matrix-fibril' or 'matrix fiber' may be used."

The label of a Cordelan fiber might, therefore, read as follows:

100% matrix fiber
(50% vinal 50% vinyon)

Bicomponent fibers are not covered by this regulation. They are composed of the same generic fiber type throughout, even though the different types of the same polymer may each exhibit somewhat different characteristics. Orlon Sayelle, for example, is 100 per cent acrylic and would be labeled as such.

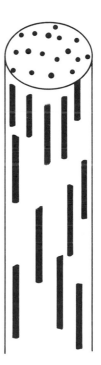

Figure 12-4. Longitude and cross section of matrix fiber structure. The black areas represent fibrils of one generic fiber; the second fiber is represented by the white.

Future Directions of Man-made Fiber Technology

Bicomponent and biconstituent fibers represent one of the newer techniques for producing man-made fibers. Some authorities refer to these fibers as "third generation man-made fibers."

The American Fabrics *Encyclopedia of Textiles* identifies the three phases or generations of man-made fiber development as being invention, diversification, and sophistication.[5]

In the first or invention phase, the basic polymer technology for man-made fibers was developed. During the diversification phase, scientists modified the various generic types of man-made fibers so that their performance would be improved and they would be more widely accepted by consumers. Now in the present phase of sophistication, fibers are being modified to make them appropriate for specialized end uses. The bicomponent and biconstituent fibers represent one aspect of this phase. The other aspect is seen in the manufacture of specialized varieties of the same generic fiber in high, medium, and low tenacities; more or less absorbent types; those for special end uses such as carpets, knits, or for nonwovens.

Representatives of the textile industry who predict the future of man-made fiber development say that they expect to see few new generic fibers based on radically different polymers from those known today.[6] Exceptions to this projection will probably occur in areas in which a specific need for new fibers has been demonstrated, such as noncombustible generic fiber types suitable for clothing and household goods.

Predicted, instead, is the continued development or refinement of special properties of existing fibers. Alteration of properties may be accomplished by varying spinning techniques, changing the cross-sectional shapes, grafting side-chain molecules onto polymers, and expanding the variety of biconstituent and bicomponent fibers.

Dr. Mary Carter, projecting future directions for textile fibers at a 1974 National Symposium on Fiber Frontiers, said that the properties of both natural and man-made fabrics are being changed so rapidly that "tomorrow we might not immediately recognize an old fiber because of today's chemistry."[7]

Recommended References

"Alginates." *CIBA Review*, 1969, No. 1, p. 3.

Cook, J. G. *Handbook of Textile Fibers*, Vol. 2. Watford: England, Merrow Publishing Company, Ltd., 1967.

Koshire, T. "A New Flame Retardant Synthetic Fiber Made by an Emulsion Spinning Process." *Modern Textiles*, February 1975, p. 22.

Moncrieff, R. W. *Man-Made Fibres.* New York: John Wiley & Sons, Inc., 1975.

Reichman, C. "Kynol: A New Fiber for Industrial Knits." *Knitting Times*, July 5, 1971.

"Third Generation of Man-made Fibers." *American Fabrics*, Spring 1969, p. 47.

"Ultron: Monsanto's New Static Control Nylon." *Modern Textiles*, October, 1976, p. 40.

[5] *American Fabrics Encyclopedia of Textiles* (Englewood Cliffs, N.J.: Prentice-Hall, Inc. 1972), p. 66.

[6] M. Carter "Fiber Frontiers," Paper presented at the National Symposium on Fiber Frontiers (Washington, D.C., June 1974) p. 10.

[7] Ibid., p. 11.

13

MAKING FIBERS INTO YARNS

For the production of cloth woven or knitted from either natural or synthetic fibers, fibers must be made into yarns. The type of yarn chosen for a fabric affects the appearance of the fabric, its durability, and its hand and draping characteristics. Yarn construction can serve either to enhance or to detract from the inherent qualities of the fiber from which the yarn is spun.

Fiber for yarns is supplied either in the form of long, continuous filaments or short, staple lengths. Being long, continuous strands themselves, filament fibers may require little more than some additional twisting to make them into yarns. Sometimes they are put through an additional process called *texturing*. Being short, staple fibers must be spun or twisted together in order to be formed into a long, continuous yarn.

HAND SPINNING

Before the invention of man-made fibers, all yarns except those made from silk had to be spun from short, staple fibers. At first these staple fibers were twisted together by hand. A simple experiment will easily demonstrate how this can be done. Take a small bunch of cotton from a roll of absorbent cotton. Pull off a long strand and begin to twist the fibers in one direction. You will soon find that you have a rather short, coarse, but recognizable, cotton yarn. Rolling the fiber between the hand and the leg is another primitive method of spinning. Hand twisting by an experienced spinner can produce an acceptable yarn. Ancient textiles have been found in Peruvian graves that were woven from hand-twisted cotton yarns of excellent quality.

Before fibers could be twisted into yarns, some attempt had to be made to bring them into a more parallel alignment. This could be done by hand by running fingers through a bundle of fibers in order to straighten the fibers somewhat. Natural materials such as thistle heads (called teasels) were also used to straighten fibers. Other tools were designed to do the job more efficiently, and hand spinners still use an ancient device called a *carder,* a pair of wooden

Steps in the Historical Development of Spinning

paddles on which is mounted a leather piece set with bent wire hooks. The process of straightening fibers prior to spinning, whether it be done by hand or by machine, is called *carding*.

A small quantity of fiber was placed on one carder. The second carder was laid against the first, and each pulled in the opposite direction. This process was repeated several times until the fibers were roughly parallel and any extraneous material had fallen out. The carded fibers were put aside for spinning.

Fibers were made more completely parallel by a further step called *combing*. Combing was generally reserved for fibers of longer lengths, and the process, using a device shaped like a comb, pulled the fibers into alignment.

After the fiber had been carded or carded and combed, the actual twisting together of the fibers was begun. The spinner who twisted fibers together by hand needed a place to put the completed yarns. Her solution was to wind them onto a stick. In time, the stick itself became a tool for spinning. By notching the stick to hold the thread and by adding a weight (called the *whorl*) to the end of the stick, a spindle was made. With the whorl to provide momentum, the spinner could use the stick to help in twisting the yarn. She stood erect and held the mass of fiber under her left arm, leaving both hands free to work. A long, untwisted strand of fiber was fed to the spindle by the left hand. With her right hand, the spinner gave the stick a twist and let it fall, whirling, toward the ground. The momentum and weight of the falling spindle twisted the fibers into a continuous yarn. The right hand was used to control the quantity of fiber feeding onto the spindle. When the spindle reached the ground, the spinner bent over, picked up the spindle, and wrapped the newly made yarn around the stick. Pulling out a new bunch of fiber, she twisted the end of the unspun fiber to the end of the completed yarn, and began the process again.

For better control of spinning, bundles of fiber were mounted on a long staff. The staff also prevented the fibers from becoming entangled. The Old English word for a bundle of flax was *dis*, and so the staff on which the fiber was placed came to be known as the *distaff*.

So closely have women been associated with the tasks of spinning that many of these terms have taken on interesting connotations in modern language usage. The spinning was often done by the unmarried adult women, and so the term spinster has become a synonym for an unmarried woman. The distaff was used almost exclusively by women, and in time the term has come to connote women's activities or interests.

For many thousands of years this hand method of spinning was the only way in which yarn could be made. A major improvement in this technique originated in India when the action of a wheel was added to the spinning of the yarn. The Indian *Charka* or spinning wheel seems to have been invented sometime between A.D. 500 and A.D. 1000.[1] Since the production of cotton was paramount in India, this wheel was devised to spin cotton. The spinning wheel did not come into wide use in Europe until the fourteenth century, and it is thought to have been carried to Spain by way of the Arab countries that

[1] W. Born, "The Indian Hand-Spinning Wheel." *CIBA Review* (Basle, Switzerland; December, 1939), p. 988 ff.

Figure 13-1. Woman uses hand carders to card wool prior to spinning. The uncarded fiber is placed in a basket to the right of the picture, and rolls of carded fiber are seen on top of a basket to the left.

occupied Spain until the late 1400s. The original Indian wheel that had been used for cotton was small and close to the ground. A modification of this wheel that allowed the spinner to stand was made in Europe but the same basic wheel, with minor modifications, was used for spinning flax, cotton, or silk. Wool, however, required a bigger wheel and the wool spinning wheel was always made with a much enlarged wheel.

With the earliest European wheels, the spinner had to move back and forth in front of the wheel, turning it first in one direction to spin, then in the opposite direction to wind the yarn. Modifications of design produced a treadle mechanism for turning the wheel, and this made it possible for the spinner to sit at the wheel to spin. Another advance came in the sixteenth century with the invention of a "flyer and detachable bobbin" mechanism. This device allowed the simultaneous spinning and winding of yarn onto the bobbin, thus eliminating the intermittent nature of the older operation in which (1) the yarn was spun, (2) the spinning was interrupted to wind the thread, and then (3) the spinning was begun anew.

Throughout the development of all these processes, power was always supplied by the spinner, either through hand- or foot-and-hand motions.

MECHANIZATION OF SPINNING

The invention of the spinning wheel may be thought of as the first mechanization of spinning, but even with a spinning wheel, the quantity of yarn that could be produced was far short of the amount required for the expansion of the textile industry after the industrial revolution.

Figure 13-2. Hand spinning with spindle and distaff. The woman holds the distaff under her left arm, draws fibers from the bundle tied to the distaff, and spins fibers into a yarn by lowering the spindle with a spinning motion. Spun yarn is wrapped around the spindle as it is formed.

Figure 13-3. Spinning wheels. The wheel on the left is a flax wheel. On the ground under the wheel stands a device for winding skeins of yarn and one for hackling (carding) flax fibers. The wheel on the right is a wool wheel.

In 1741, John Wyatt and Lewis Paul built the first of a series of machines for spinning cotton yarn. Wyatt and Paul used a roller-drafting principle; that is, they fed a long strand of carded or combed fibers through a series of rollers. Each set of rollers moved at a different speed, thereby drawing out or elongating the strand of fibers. This strand of fibers was called the *roving*. From the roller the strand of fibers was stretched to a bobbin-and-flyer twisting mechanism, like that of a spinning wheel. Arkwright utilized this same principle in 1769 when he constructed a spinning machine called the "water frame," which was given this name because it was operated by waterpower.

A second spinning machine was invented by James Hargreaves sometime in the 1760s. Utilizing the basic principles of the spinning wheel, Hargreaves' "spinning jenny" made eight yarns at the same time. A later patent shows that the number of yarns that could be made was increased to sixteen, and eventually the jenny was modified to make as many as one hundred yarns.

Both the spinning jenny and the Arkwright machine had certain limitations. Yarns made on these machines were not as strong as handspun yarns, and were, therefore, not as suitable for use in the warp where greater tension was placed on the threads.

Samuel Crompton combined both the Arkwright machine and the spinning jenny into one basic machine that utilized both rotating rollers in drawing out the yarn and a moving carriage that provided the twist needed to make strong, fine yarns. This machine, known as the spinning mule, was the basic machine for producing cotton yarn in England until well into the twentieth century.

Although each of these methods made it possible for the quantity of yarn produced by one spinner to be enormously increased, they still required supervisory personnel to keep the machines operating. About 1830, a device was developed that could be added to the spinning mule to make its operation completely automatic.

At about the same time that the automatic spinning mule was developed, an American inventor named John Thorpe devised a ring spinning machine. This machine has been used in the United States since about 1830, and is the basic machine used for spinning cotton and other staple fibers today.

The most recent development in the spinning of yarns from staple fibers is a process known as "open-end spinning." In this method of spinning, air suction takes the fibers through a spinning tube in which twist is imparted to the fiber.

Modern Spinning

Natural fibers, except for silk, are all staple in length. Silk and all man-made filament fibers can be cut or broken into staple length, so that it is possible to spin any natural or man-made fiber into a yarn.

MAKING FILAMENTS INTO STAPLE LENGTHS

Man-made filament fibers that are intended to be converted into shorter staple fibers are known as *tow*. These fibers are grouped loosely, without twist. The fibers can be made into staple either by cutting or breaking.

156 *Understanding Textiles*

Cut Staple

One of the advantages of utilizing cut tow for spinning is that unlike cotton, wool, and other natural fibers, the tow fibers are aligned and parallel and need not be combed or carded to make them ready for spinning. The fibers can be said to go from tow to sliver (or as the industry terms the process, "tow-to-top") in one operation. Specialized machines make this conversion.

The Pacific Converter cuts the staple into the desired length. Fibers may be cut into uniform lengths or into variable lengths. The steps performed in this machine include

1. Heat stretching man-made fibers, if needed.

2. Forming a flat web of tow.

3. Cutting the web by a blade cutter.

4. Moving the cut fibers in such a way that not all cut ends fall at the same place in the web.

5. Rolling the web diagonally into a continuous sliver of staple fibers.[2]

A second method of converting tow to top is to break the fibers into staple lengths. The Perlock system performs this operation.

The Perlock system applies tension to the tow and pulls the stretched tow across a tow breaker wheel, a cog wheel with sharp, protruding edges. The filaments then break on the sharp edges of the tow breaker wheel. Stretch breaking is most effective with synthetic fibers, less useful in cutting regenerated cellulose.

A variation of this process called the Turbo-stapler process is used for producing high bulk fibers, especially acrylics. During stretch breaking, the fibers are extended and must be treated to relax the fiber, or else yarns will show a good deal of residual shrinkage. In the Perlock process, breaking is followed by adding crimp to the fiber, heat setting the crimp, and relaxing the fiber by a steam heat treatment. If a sliver of stretch-broken, crimped, relaxed, staple is blended with a sliver of stretch-broken, crimped but not relaxed staple, the bulking properties of acrylic fibers are much improved.

The yarns made in this way are woven or knitted into a garment, the garment is subjected to treatment with hot water, and the unset fibers shrink, causing the preshrunk fibers to stand up in bulky, fuzzy surface texture.

PREPARATION OF THE STAPLE FIBER FOR SPINNING

From the time staple fibers are supplied to the manufacturer until they have been made into yarns, they go through a series of steps, some of which are required for all yarns and fibers and some of which are optional.

These steps are:

[2]R. W. Moncrieff, *Man-Made Fibres* (New York: John Wiley & Sons, Inc., 1975), p. 652.

1. If fiber is supplied in bundles or bales, breaking or opening these packages is necessary.

2. Feeding the fiber into the carder.

3. Carding.

4. Combing (optional step).

5. Drawing out.

6. Twisting.

7. Spinning.

8. Winding.

(Steps 2 and 3 are not necessary if staple fibers have been made in tow-to-top operation.)

Figure 13-4. Bales are opened and cotton from several different bales is blended together in the opening room. Photograph Courtesy of the National Cotton Council of America.

Blending of Staple Fibers

It is sometimes desirable to blend two or more different fibers into one yarn. Frequently, man-made fibers are blended with natural fibers in order to take advantage of the best qualities of each fiber. In other blends the combination may be made to reduce the cost of the fabric by blending a less expensive fiber with a more expensive one or blending may be done to achieve decorative effects.

Blending may be done at one of several steps in the preparation of yarns from staple fibers: during formation of the lap, during carding, or during drawing out. No matter when blending is done, quantities of each fiber to be used are measured carefully and the proportions of one fiber to another are consistently maintained.

Breaking and Opening Bundles

Bales of fiber may be opened either by hand or by machine. Many modern textile mills have completely mechanized this process. Once the bales are opened, the lumps of fiber are loosened and separated by the *picker*, which also cleans off heavier impurities. The resulting *lap*, a flattened, fairly uniform layer of fibers, is fed directly into the carder by a machine. Blending of fibers may be done at this point by combining two or more fiber types in the lap.

Carding

The carding machine is set with hundreds of fine wires that separate the fibers and pull them into somewhat parallel form. A thin web of fiber is formed in this machine, and as the web is moved along it passes through a funnel-shaped device that forms it into a ropelike strand of roughly parallel fibers.

Blending can take place at the point of carding by joining laps of different fibers. Carding mixes the blend fibers together, distributing them evenly throughout the mass of fiber.

Carding is done to all fibers. In processing linen fiber, carding is done but is called *hackling*.

Combing

Whereas carding is a step in the production of all fibers, combing is an optional step in the preparation of some yarns. When a smoother, finer yarn is wanted, fibers are subjected to a further paralleling called *combing*. (Linen fibers that are combed are called *well-hackled* fibers). A comblike device arranges fibers into parallel form. At the same time, the short fibers fall out of the strand.

Combed yarns have smooth surfaces and finer diameters than carded yarns. Fewer short ends show on the surface of the fabric and the luster is increased. Combed yarns are more expensive to produce and fabrics made from combed yarns are, therefore, higher in price.

Table 13.1

Fiber	Yarns from Carded Fiber	Yarns from Combed Fiber
Linen	tow or hackled yarns	line or well-hackled yarns
Wool	woolen yarns	worsted yarns
Cotton and other staple fibers	carded yarns	combed yarns

A summary of the different terms used in referring to combed and carded yarns from different fibers may clarify this terminology.

Drawing Out

After carding or combing, the fiber mass is referred to as the *sliver*. Several slivers are combined before the drawing out process. Blending of fibers can be done by combining slivers of different fibers. During the drawing out, a series of rollers rotating at different rates of speed elongate or draw out the silver into a single more uniform strand that is given a small amount of twist and fed into large cans.

Figure 13-5. Cleaning and separation of individual fibers takes place in the carding machine. A web of fibers is formed into a thin ropelike strand or *sliver*. Photograph courtesy of the National Cotton Council of America.

Figure 13-6. A lap composed of slivers is passed through a comb that combs out short fibers. The output of the comb is formed again into a sliver. (Not all fibers are combed.) Photograph courtesy of the National Cotton Council of America.

Figure 13-7. In drawing, several slivers are combined into a strand and reduced to about the same diameter as the original sliver. Drawing blends fibers and arranges them in parallel order. Photograph courtesy of the National Cotton Council of America.

Figure 13-8 Slivers are fed into a roving frame where the fibers are twisted slightly and drawn into a smaller strand. Photograph courtesy of the National Cotton Council of America.

Figure 13-9. Roving is fed to spinning frame where it is drawn out to final size, twisted into yarn, and wound on bobbins. Photograph courtesy of the National Cotton Council of America.

Twisting

The sliver is fed to a machine called the *roving frame.* Here the strands of fiber are elongated still more and given additional twist. The product of the roving frame, an elongated, slightly twisted strand of fibers, is called the *roving.*

SPINNING

Most modern factories use one of two methods for spinning staple fibers: ring spinning or open-end spinning.

Ring Spinning

The ring spinner is made up of the following parts:

1. Spools on which the strand of carded fiber or roving is wound.

2. A series of rollers through which the roving passes.

3. A guiding ring or eyelet.

4. A traveler or small, U-shaped clip.

5. A stationary ring around the spindle.

6. A spindle.

7. A bobbin.

The strand of fibers or roving is fed from the spool through the rollers. The rollers elongate the roving, which passes through the eyelet, moving down and through the traveler. The traveler moves freely around the stationary ring. The spindle turns the bobbin at a constant speed. This turning of the bobbin and the movement of the traveler impart the twist to the yarn. The traveler moves around the ring at from 4,000 to 12,000 revolutions per minute. By adjusting the width of the traveler's circle and the number of revolutions it makes, yarns of finer or heavier diameter can be made. The narrower the width of the circle, the finer the diameter of the yarn will be. The yarn is twisted and wound onto a cone-shaped bobbin in one operation.

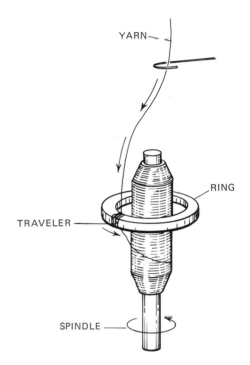

Figure 13-10. Ring spinner.

Open-End Spinning

A newer method of spinning, open-end spinning, omits the step of forming the roving. Instead, a sliver of fibers is fed into the machine by one of several methods. Single fibers or bunches of fibers are separated from the sliver, are rotated (twisted), and joined to the "open end" of the already twisted yarn which also rotates. This forms a continuing strand of twisted fibers or yarn as the continuously entering fibers join to the *open end* of the yarn being formed, hence the name "open-end spinning."[3] The end of the yarn being formed must

[3] H. Keller, "Open-End Spinning," *Modern Textiles* (February, 1968), p. 20

be kept a sufficient distance away from the entering fibers to allow adequate twist to be provided to the fiber.

A variety of different means may be used to form the yarn and to insert twist. These have been divided into the following categories; mechanical spinning, electrostatic spinning, fluid spinning, and air spinning. Neither fluid nor air spinning have had any significant commerical applications, although they have been utilized experimentally.

Mechanical spinning utilizes some mechanical surface to collect fibers for feeding into the twisting device. These fiber-collecting surfaces may be in the form of a funnel, sieve, or rotating drum. A twisting device imparts the necessary twist to the fibers. Most of the open-end spinning machines now in use are of the mechanical spinning type.

The electrostatic spinning process utilizes an electrostatic field for the movement and orientation of fibers during spinning. An electrostatic field is formed by giving the rollers that feed the sliver to the machine a negative charge and giving the twisting device a positive charge. The movement of the

Figure 13-11. Ring spinning machine in operation. Note the cones of roving at the top of the machine. The filled bobbins of spun yarn are being removed automatically at the center of the picture, and the empty spindles are in place at the bottom of the picture, ready to be moved into position for spinning. Courtesy of American Zinser Corporation.

electrostatic field is from the negative toward the positive pole, so that the fibers are arranged and moved in the same direction. Fibers are separated, made parallel, stretched, oriented, and transferred to the twisting device under the influence of the electrostatic field. Twist is, however, imparted by a specific twisting device.[4]

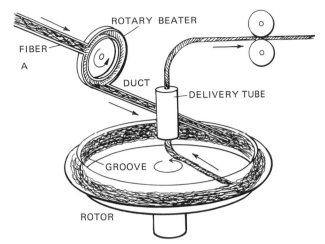

Figure 13-12. Open-end spinner. The fibers are separated into a thin stream by the rotary beater. The fibers moved by an air stream enter the rotor and through centrifugal force are carried in a V-shaped groove. The fibers are drawn off from the groove to become attached to the open end of an already formed yarn. The rotor produces the twist. Courtesy of *Scientific American.*

The advantages of open-end spinning are that it increases the speed of production, eliminating the step of drawing out the roving prior to spinning; permits finished yarns to be wound on any sized bobbin or spool; and produces yarns of more even diameter than ring spinning. On the other hand, open-end spun yarns have lower strength than ring-spun yarns and cannot be made in the finest diameters.

The quantity of yarns being produced by this method is increasing. It has been reported that the manufacturers of open-end spinning machinery have so many orders that customers may have to wait as much as four years for delivery of equipment.[5] Undoubtedly, open-end spun yarns will compete favorably with ring-spun yarns for many end uses because the process affords considerable saving in labor costs and greater potential for automation.

OTHER METHODS OF SPINNING STAPLE FIBERS

During recent years a number of new processes for spinning yarns have been introduced. The impetus for developing these processes has come largely from the fact that ring spinning has reached the limit of its development. "Any advance that is to be made [in spinning] has to be in a completely new system of yarn formation and twist insertion."[6]

[4] I. Doga, "The Fundamentals of Electrostatic Spinning," *Textile Research Journal* (July 1975), p. 521.

[5] "Open End Spinning," *American Fabrics* (Summer 1974), p. 53.

[6] D. G. H. Crawford, "Repco Spinning," *Modern Textiles* (June 1975), p. 24.

Self-twist Spinning

Self-twist spinning is used to make ply yarns, yarns made from two or more yarns twisted together. The process follows these steps:

Two rovings are utilized. Each one is passed through a pair of rollers that are both rotating and oscillating. Each set of rollers twists its roving in a direction opposite to the other. The uneven motion of the rollers forms a yarn that has both twisted and untwisted areas. Adjacent ends of the two yarns are allowed to untwist around each other. Care must be taken to space the untwisted areas of each yarn in such a way that a loosely twisted section of one yarn never coincides with a loosely twisted section of the other yarn, or a weak spot would result.

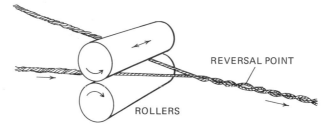

Figure 13-13. Self-twist spinning. Two separate rovings are fed between a pair of rollers that move both forward and side-to-side. The twisted rovings, each with opposite directional twist, when placed side by side, twist around each other to form a ply yarn. Courtesy of *Scientific American.*

Repco is the trademark of one commercially available self-twist spinner. Officials of the manufacturer cite the following benefits from the use of self-twist yarns: less space required for producing the same weight of yarn, reductions in annual maintenance costs and time, less waste in spinning, lower power utilization, and lower labor costs.[7]

Self-twist yarns can, of course, only be used in those fabrics that require two-ply yarns. The process also requires that fiber lengths not be too short. Wool and long man-made staple fibers are especially suitable.

Another self-twist process developed in Holland uses glue to hold the fibers together. However, this process is apparently not yet at the point where it can be commercially used for the production of yarns.[8]

Integrated Composite Spinning System

A new machine called the Bobtex Integrated Composite Spinning Machine is being used to form yarns from a composite of synthetic polymer monofilament and staple fibers. The yarn is made of three separate components. A continuous filament feeder yarn is passed through a spinneret that contains a molten synthetic polymer resin. The filament yarn and the polymer resin may be of the same or different synthetic polymers. Staple fiber slivers are fed on both sides of the feeder yarn that has been coated with polymer resin. Twist is inserted by a friction false twister. The molten resin solidifies, holding the staple fibers in place.

[7] Ibid, pp. 26, 27.

[8] J. Dulken, "New Horizons in Spinning," *Modern Textiles* (August 1971), p. 7.

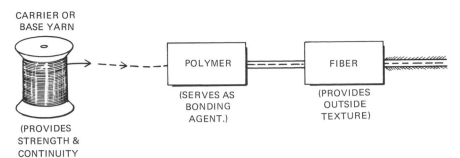

CARRIER OR
BASE YARN

POLYMER

(SERVES AS
BONDING
AGENT.)

FIBER

(PROVIDES
OUTSIDE
TEXTURE)

(PROVIDES
STRENGTH &
CONTINUITY

Figure 13-14. Bobtex integrated composite spinning system.

Variation in yarn properties can be achieved by varying the three components used. These yarns possess the properties of both filament and spun yarns. and have great potential for the creation of a wide variety of interesting yarns.

Bonded Sliver Techniques

Reiter Machine Works, Ltd., has developed a yarn manufacturing process that is said to produce colored yarns of high breaking strength and increased bulk. Fibers are handled in such a way as to eliminate several steps in the conventional spinning process. One system is referred to as the Pavena-Pavil system, the other the Pavena-Paset system. The former produces a twisted colored yarn, the latter an untwisted colored yarn. Table 13.2 compares the steps followed in the Pavena systems with conventional spinning of carded cotton, synthetics, or blends.[9]

Table 13.2
Comparison of Conventional and Bonded Sliver Spinning

Conventional System	Pavena-Pavil System	Pavena-Paset System
1. Opening and cleaning	1. Opening and cleaning	1. Opening and cleaning
2. Carding	2. Carding	2. Carding
3. Breaker drawing	3. Bonding together and coloring of fibers in a sliver.	3. Bonding together and coloring of fibers in a sliver.
4. Finisher drawing	4. Ring spinning of colored fibers.	4. Doubling, drafting and rebonding colored fiber.
5. Roving		
6. Ring spinning of un colored fibers		
7. Rewinding of dyeing tubes		
8. Dyeing		
9. Drying		

Fasciated Yarns

For a time du Pont marketed a yarn under the trademark Nandel. This particular yarn has been withdrawn from production, but should be mentioned briefly because of the different type of spinning it represents.

Fasciated yarns are made from a bundle of parallel fibers wrapped around by

[9]J. F. Dulken, "New Horizons in Spinning," *Modern Textiles* (August 1971) p. 25.

Figure 13-15. Diagram of the structure of a fasciated yarn.

surface wrapping of other fibers. The term derives from the Latin word *fasces* meaning "a bundle of rods wrapped with ribbons."[10]

Untwisted, relatively long parallel fibers (averaging five to six inches in length) predominate in these yarns. The fiber ends and wrappings also appear on the surface. As a result, these yarns have something of the qualities of both filament and staple yarns. Fasciated yarns are less fuzzy, more lustrous, and cleaner in appearance than conventionally spun yarns.

Direct Spinning

It is possible to take tow fibers and make them directly into yarns on a machine called a *direct spinner*. Tow is stretched and broken. Fibers are broken at their weakest point, which yields fibers of differing lengths. Fibers are then drawn into a sliver, twisted, and wound. The resulting yarns exhibit a high degree of shrinkage, as fibers are not given a chance to recover after stretching. The yarns are often woven into novelty fabrics where this quality can be used to advantage, as, for example, in alternating high shrinkage yarns with low shrinkage yarns to produce a puckered effect. Direct spun yarns are especially strong, but uneven in surface appearance.

NETWORK AND FILM YARNS

Recently a variety of new techniques have come into existence that allow the formation of yarns directly from synthetic polymers without the formation of fibers or the twisting of fibers into yarns. These processes include the formation of yarns by the split film process, or the slit film process, or by the creation of network yarns from foam.

Split Films

In the creation of yarns by the split film technique, a sheet of polymer is formed. The formed sheet is drawn in the lengthwise direction. Through drawing, the molecules in the polymer are oriented in the direction of the draw, causing the film to be strengthened in the lengthwise direction and weakened in the crosswise direction. This causes a breakdown of the film into a mass of interconnected fibers, most of which are aligned in the direction of the drawing, but some of which also connect in the crosswise direction.

The process is known as *fibrillation*. These materials can be twisted into

[10]O. Heuberger, S. Ibrahim, and F. Field, Jr., "The Technology of Fasciated Yarns," *Textile Research Journal* (September 1971), p. 768.

strings or twines or other coarse, yarnlike materials. The usefulness of split film yarns is limited because the yarns created are coarse. Olefins are made into split film yarns for use in making bags, sacks, ropes, and other industrial products.

Slit Films

Slit films are made by cutting film into narrow, ribbonlike sections. Depending upon the process used for cutting and drawing the film, the tapes may display some degree of fibrillation, like that described for split films. When tapes are made that do not fibrillate, they are flatter and are more suitable for certain uses. Flat tapes are used as warp yarns in weaving, and can be made into carpet backings that will be more stable, remaining flat and even. All types of tape yarns are used in making wall coverings, packaging materials, carpet backing, and as a replacement for jute in bags and sacks.

Network Yarns

A third type of yarn is created from foamed polymers in a three-stage process. A polymer is formed in which air is added to create a foam structure. The foamed polymer is fed into a buffer zone or area where the quantity of material can be regulated. Material from the buffer zone is fed into a draw chamber in which the foamed polymer is stretched.

The foaming of the polymer has created small cells or bubbles of polymer. As the material is drawn, the cell walls crack, forming individual fibers that are interconnected. The resultant yarn is made up of a network of small, interconnected fibers.

Network yarns resemble staple yarns but lack the hairiness of staple yarns because there are no free ends. They have bulk. Experimental yarns formed in this way display a range of tenacities that can be increased by the addition of some twist. However, the tenacity of network yarns is lower than that of yarns made from corresponding filament fibers. Fabrics woven on an experimental basis showed good drape and handle, but poor crease recovery. Researchers

Figure 13-16. Film fibrillation.

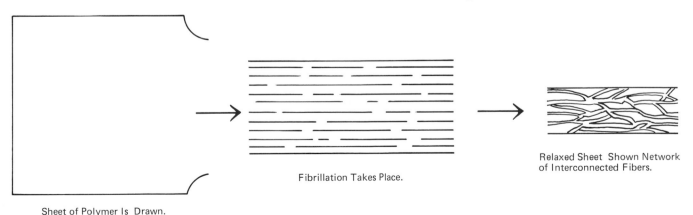

Sheet of Polymer Is Drawn.

Fibrillation Takes Place.

Relaxed Sheet Shown Network of Interconnected Fibers.

believe network yarns offer potential for a variety of uses, especially in coarse yarns, but further research and development is required before they will be commercially viable.[11]

EFFECTS OF TWIST

The degree of twist given to a yarn affects a number of aspects of its appearance, behavior, and durability. The fineness of yarns is related to twist. As a general rule, increasing twist decreases yarn size. This can be demonstrated easily by taking a strand of loose fiber, such as absorbent cotton, and twisting it. The more one twists, the smaller in diameter the "yarn" will become.

Strength increases as twist increases up to a certain point. Beyond this point, the strength of the yarn begins to decrease, and yarns with exceptionally high, tight twist may become brittle and weak.

Elasticity is increased if yarns are very tightly twisted. Very tightly twisted yarns are known as *crepe* yarns, which are generally very fine. The twist of crepe yarns is so high that they curl up unless they are held under tension, as they would be on a loom during weaving. A simple and easy test to identify crepe yarns is to unravel a yarn from the fabric and run it between the fingernails, thus removing the tension produced by sizing material. If the yarn curls up into corkscrewlike curls, it has been creped. This tendency of crepe yarns to twist makes fabrics constructed from these yarns less dimensionally stable than other fabrics, as they are more elastic.

More tightly twisted yarns shed soil more easily. Because their surface is smoother, there are fewer fiber ends to attract and hold soil. In yarns made from absorbent fibers, absorbency is lower in more tightly twisted yarns.

Abrasion resistance is increased by tighter twist. This is a logical result because in a more tightly twisted yarn many fibers are held in such a way that they appear on the surface, then into the center of the yarn, and then back to the surface again. As a result, more fibers are subject to a relatively even distribution of abrasion. Loose surface fibers in low-twist yarns also snag and pull up, creating points of wear.

The appearance of a fabric is determined to a large extent by the twist of the yarn. For example, if filament yarns of higher luster are given very low twist, they will reflect greater quantities of light, and, therefore, appear brighter than the same yarns when they are more tightly twisted. Crepe fabrics achieve a nubby, somewhat crinkled effect by using creped yarns that have a less even surface texture. Loosely twisted wool yarns may be utilized to create a fluffy, fleecy surface; tightly twisted worsted yarns produce a smooth, more even surface. The fabric designer takes advantage of these effects to create a wide variety of surface textures and designs.

Keeping these points in mind is helpful when evaluating products in relation to performance. For example, abrasion resistance is an important factor to consider in selecting an upholstery fabric, as abrasion is related to the durabil-

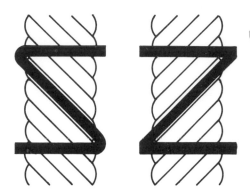

Figure 13-17. S and Z twist.

[11] P. R. Lord, *"Spinning in the 70's,"* Watford, England: Merrow Publishing Company, Ltd., pp. 73 ff.

ity of a product on which people will sit. Not only can the consumer look for a fiber that has reasonably good abrasion resistance but also for a yarn that has reasonably high twist. Low twist yarns abrade and snag more easily than those with higher twist. Also, tighter twist yarns shed soil more readily.

Direction of Twist

In twisting fibers together to form yarns, the fibers can be twisted either to the right or to the left. In textile industry terminology, this twist is called S or Z *twist*. Z twisted yarns are twisted so that the direction of the twist follows the center bar of the letter "Z." Z twist is also known as "right" twist. In S twist yarn, the twist direction follows the center bar of the letter "S." S twist is also known as "left" twist. This concept will be more easily understood if the reader takes a small bunch of absorbent cotton and makes a vertical line on the fibers with a pen. Then, suspending the fibers from the thumb and forefinger of the left hand to that of the right, rotate the fibers to the right with the upper, lefthand fingers. The line you have made will take a diagonal direction similar to that of the bar in a Z. If the upper fingers are twisted to the left, the line will follow the bar of the S.

Most yarns are made with a Z twist. However, in certain fabric constructions special effects can be achieved by combining yarns in which the fibers have been twisted in either the same or opposite direction.

SIZE OF YARNS

Since the textile industry requires some means for distinguishing between yarns of different sizes, standards of measurement have been established. There are different systems of measurement for cotton and wool, and different systems for staple and filament yarns.

Cotton yarns are measured as follows. A standard base measurement has been established. When one 840-yard hank of cotton yarn weighs one pound, the count of that yarn is established as #1. If twice as much or 1,680 yards (or 2 hanks) of cotton yarns weigh one pound, the count is #2, 4,200 yards (or 5 hanks) equal one pound, the count is #5, and so on. In low count yarns, one pound of fiber makes a smaller length of yarn. In higher count yarns, the same pound of fiber makes a greater length of yarn. Higher count yarns are, therefore, thinner than lower count yarns. Those who are familiar with sewing threads are aware that #90 thread is smaller in diameter than #60 thread.

Woolen yarns are measured by a standard that follows the same principle as that of cotton, whereby the lower the number, the coarser is the yarn. The count is determined by the number of 1,600 yard hanks per pound. Worsted yarns are measured by the number of 560 yard hanks per pound.

Linen yarn measurements are made on a different basis. The size of the yarn is determined by dividing the number of yards that weigh one pound by 300. If 300 yards of linen weigh one pound, the number would be #1; if 3,000 yards weigh one pound, the number will be #10, and so on. As with cotton and wool, the higher the number, the thinner is the yarn.

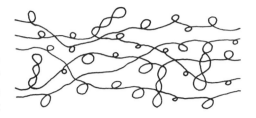
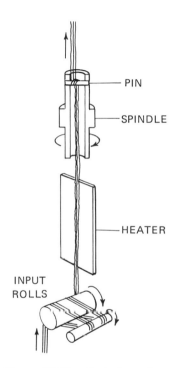

Figure 13-18. Texturing of yarns by the three-stage twist process. Courtesy of *Scientific American*.

Table 13.3

Denier (Weight in grams of 9,000 meters of yarn)	Worsted (No. of 560 yard hanks per pound)	Woolen (No. of 1600 yard hanks per pound)	Cotton (No. of 840 yard hanks per pound)	Linen (No. of 300 yard hanks per pound)	Tex (Weight in grams of 1,000 meters of yarn)
thinnest					thinnest
50	160	56	106	298	5.6
75	106	37	71	198	8.3
100	80	28	53	149	11.1
150	53	19	35	99	16.6
200	40	14	27	74	22.2
300	27	9.3	18	50	33.4
400	20	7	13	37	44.4
500	16	5.6	11	30	55.5
700	11.4	4.0	7.6	21	77.7
1000	8.0	2.8	5.3	15	111
1500	5.3	1.9	3.5	10	166
2000	4.0	1.4	2.7	7	222
coarsest					coarsest

Fabric Science. (New York: Fairchild Publications, Inc., 1974), Adapted from Pizzuto, p. 88.

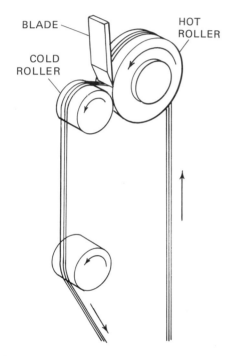

BLADE

HOT ROLLER

COLD ROLLER

Figure 13-19. Texturing of yarns through the edge crimp process. Courtesy of *Scientific American.*

Filament yarns are designated not by yarn number but by a measurement called *denier*. Denier is equal to the weight in grams of 9,000 meters of yarn. If, for example, 9,000 meters of a yarn weigh 100 grams, the denier is 100. If 9,000 meters of another yarn weigh 55 grams, the denier is 55. Unlike yarn number, a lower denier refers to a thinner yarn.

Since the textile industry has become international in scope, proposals have been made for the standardization of yarn sizing. The proposed numbering system, called the "Tex" system, expresses weight simply in terms of the weight in grams of one kilometer length of yarn. The same system would be applied to all types of yarns and fibers.

Table 13.3 presents equivalent numbers of yarns in each of the aforementioned systems. Adapted from Pizzuto, *Fabric Science* (New York: Fairchild Publications, Inc., 1974), p. 88.

FILAMENT YARNS

Yarns made from continuous filaments are divided into two groups: monofilament yarns or yarns made from one filament, and multifilament yarns made from more than one filament. For all practical purposes, filament yarns are generally multifilament. Monofilament yarns find limited use in nylon hosiery where an exceptionally sheer fabric is wanted and in saran fabric webbing used in some lightweight beach or casual furniture, as well as in a variety of industrial uses.

Monofilament yarns can be made by the conventional extrusion of large single filaments from spinnerets. The slit-film technique in which a film of synthetic polymer is cut into strips will also make single filaments, each of which can be used as a monofilament yarn.

Multifilament yarns can be given either tight or loose twist. The characteristics of each fiber, its luster, handle, and cross-sectional shape will determine the appearance and feel of the yarn into which it is made. In general, most smooth filament yarns are characterized by greater luster, have less tendency to pill, and require more yarn to cover the same area than spun yarns.

Textured Filament Yarns

Man-made filament yarns can be treated with processes that utilize heat setting or mechanical entangling of fibers to alter their texture. Yarns made from filament fibers are smooth and slippery to the touch. They lack the warmth, bulk, and comfort of yarns spun from staple fibers. Texturing of man-made filament fibers can produce softer, bulkier yarns, with increased warmth, comfort and absorbency; can decrease pilling of the fibers; or can impart stretch.

Textured yarns are commonly classified as follows:

1. *Stretch yarns.* Stretch yarns have high extensibility and good recovery from extension. The bulk of stretch yarns is, however, only moderate in comparison with other textured yarns. The major uses for stretch yarns are in stretch fabrics.

2. *Modified stretch yarns.* Stretch yarns that have been subjected to heat treatment to stabilize the yarn are known as modified stretch yarns. These yarns possess some degree of stretch, but are more stable than stretch yarns that have not been heat-set. Modified stretch yarns are produced on the same machinery as stretch yarns, but add the required heat treatment as the last step of manufacture.

3. *Bulked yarns.* Bulked yarns are used in those applications in which bulk is more important than stretch. Even so, most bulked yarns also have moderate stretch. Products in which bulked yarns are most often found include sweaters, warm hosiery, carpets, woollike knits, and upholstery.[12]

Stretch Yarns and Modified Stretch Yarns

The following processes produce stretch and modified stretch yarns:

1. *The three-stage twist process,* the first of the texturizing processes to be developed, includes the steps of (1) twisting the yarn, (2) setting the twisted yarn by the application of heat, and (3) untwisting the yarn. At this point a kinked yarn has been formed that can be stretched straight and that will return to the kinked form when stretch is removed.

For modified stretch yarn a fourth step is required. The kinked form must be stabilized. This too requires heat setting.

2. A variation of this process is known as the *false-twist process,* which is the same as the three-stage process except that it is a continuous operation that

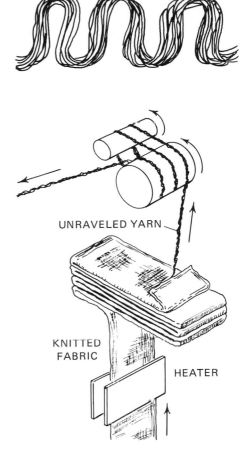

Figure 13-20. Texturing of yarns through the knit–deknit process. Courtesy of *Scientific American.*

UNRAVELED YARN

KNITTED FABRIC

HEATER

---

[12] Classification based on P. R. Lord, *Spinning in the 70's* (Watford, England: Merrow, 1970), pp. 52, 53.

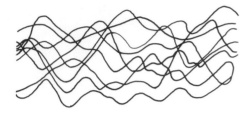

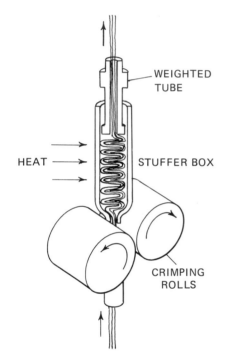

Figure 13-21. Texturing of yarns by the stuffer box method. Courtesy of *Scientific American*.

adds a second heater to stabilize the untwisted yarn. Fluflon and Superloft are examples of textured yarns made by this process.

3. *Duo twist* is another variant of the three-stage process. Two yarns are twisted together, set by passing them over the surface of a heated cone, and then untwisted and wound onto separate cones.

4. *Edge crimp* is a texturizing procedure in which heated thermoplastic filaments are drawn over a sharp knife edge. This causes certain areas of the fiber to fuse slightly, imparting a spirallike curl to the yarn. Agilon is a trademarked nylon yarn made by Deering-Milliken by this process. Agilon is used in women's hosiery, for the most part, but has also been made into socks, sweaters, and household textiles.

The stabilization of modified stretch yarns produces yarns that are bulkier, have less stretch, and exhibit lower relaxation shrinkage in steam. The trademarks under which modified stretch yarns are sold include Agilon, "stabilized type"; Helanca NT, SS and SW; Saaba; and the ARCT series of trademarks. These yarns are most often made into underwear, sweaters, and woven and knitted goods.

Bulked Yarns

The following filament yarn modifications are designed primarily to increase bulk, although some methods also produce varying degrees of stretch.

1. *Knit-deknit* produces texture by knitting the yarn into fabric tubes, heat-setting the knitted tubes, and then unraveling the knit. This creates a permanent loop form in the yarn. The process is designed so that yarns move through the process from knitting, to setting, to deknitting, and to winding in one continuous process. Fabrics made from these yarns have a crepelike texture. Trademarks of these fabrics include Bucaroni, Crinkle, and Popperoni.

2. In the *stuffer box process*, filament fibers are fed into a small chamber. The yarns are given a crimped or saw-toothed shape that is heat-set. The yarn produced is not a stretch yarn, but one with improved hand and a decreased tendency to pill. Trade names of yarns produced in this manner include Spunize, Pinlon, Type B, and Textralized. Ban-Lon is a trademark for quality, approved fabrics made primarily from Textralized yarn.

3. *Gear crimp* is imparted by passing filaments between the teeth of two heated gears that set the form of the gear teeth into the fiber.

4. A texturing process that does *not* impart stretch is the *air jet* method. This method is unique in that it can be applied to both thermoplastic and nonheat sensitive fibers alike. The texture is not provided through heat. Instead, yarns are fed through an air jet to rollers that move more slowly than the rollers that feed the fiber into the air jet. The slack yarn is formed into loops by the air jet. These loops increase the bulk of the yarns. Taslan yarns are made by

this process. Although any of a variety of fibers may be used in making Taslan yarns, those most frequently utilized are nylon, polyester, and glass.

Stretch Yarns and Fabrics

These processes are not the only means of producing stretch yarns or fabrics. Most of the methods of producing stretch have been discussed previously, so that only a brief summary of the methods is required here.

1. *Texturing*, generally done by twisting, heat setting, and untwisting.

2. Use of *elastomeric fibers*, such as spandex.

3. Alteration of fiber structure during manufacture by *grafting* side chain molecules to the polymer. This structure can produce stretch fibers.

4. Creation of *bicomponent or biconstituent fibers*. Bicomponent fibers are made by extruding two different types of fiber of the same generic class, joined side by side. One component shrinks more than the other, thereby creating a permanent crimp in the yarn. Orlon Sayelle and Cantrece nylon are examples of fibers made in this way.
Biconstituent fibers utilize the same principle, except that the constituents are each made of a different generic class of fiber. Monvelle (made from spandex and nylon) is an example of a biconstituent stretch fiber. (However, not *all* bicomponent and biconstituent fibers are stretch fibers.)

5. Cotton can be made into stretch yarns by either of two processes. In one, cotton yarns are treated with chemicals that produce crosslinkages within the fiber. These chemical resins are also thermoplastic. The cotton yarns are twisted, the twist is set with the heat, and then the fiber is retwisted in the opposite direction. Stretch is conferred both by the twisting and the crosslinking.

6. A variation of this procedure is to treat the cotton yarns with thermoplastic materials, then to heat-set crimp into the yarn.

7. Woven cotton fabrics can be given a degree of stretch through *slack mercerization*, a treatment with sodium hydroxide that shrinks the fiber and produces limited stretch.

8. *Dubblestretch* is a patented Swedish process that produces some stretch in wool. It requires special techniques in yarn production, weaving, and finishing.

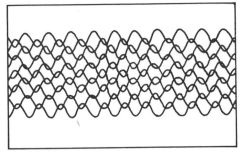

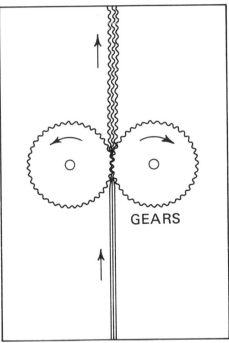

GEARS

Figure 13-22. Texturing of yarns by the gear crimp method. Courtesy of *Scientific American.*

Types of Yarns

Classification of yarns can be made on a variety of bases, and authorities often differ when they define yarn types. The following classifications are based on those included in the *Textile Handbook* of the American Home Economics Association.

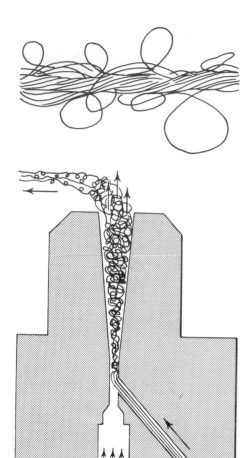

Yarns Classified by Number of Parts

Yarns that have been classified by the number of parts they possess are divided into *single*, *ply*, and *cord yarns*. A single yarn is made from a group of filament or staple fibers twisted together. If a single yarn is untwisted, it will separate into fibers.

Ply yarns are made by twisting together two or more single yarns. If ply yarns are untwisted, they will divide into two or more single yarns, which, in turn, can be untwisted into fibers. Each single yarn twisted into a ply yarn is called a *ply*.

Cord yarns are made by twisting together two or more ply yarns. Cord yarns can be identified by untwisting the yarn to form two or more ply yarns. Cord yarns are used in making ropes, sewing thread, and cordage, and are woven as decorative yarns into some heavy-weight novelty fabrics.

Yarns Classified by Similarity of Parts

Simple yarns are those yarns with uniform size and regular surface. They have varying degrees of twist, ranging from loose to moderate, tight or hard twist. Single, ply, and cord yarns can all be simple yarns if their components are uniform in size and have a regular surface. When one strand of fibers is twisted together evenly, it is classified as a simple, single yarn. Two simple, single yarns twisted together create a simple, ply yarn.

Yarns made to create interesting decorative effects in the fabrics into which they are woven are known as *novelty* yarns. Some authors also call these yarns *complex* yarns. Novelty yarns can be single, ply, or cord; staple or filament. The following is a list of the most commonly used novelty yarns and their definitions.

1. *Bouclé*. Bouclé yarns are ply yarns. An effect yarn forms irregular loops around a base yarn or yarns. Another yarn binds or ties the effect yarn to the base. Some sources use the terms *loop* or *curl* yarns interchangeably with bouclé.[13]

Ratiné yarns are similar to bouclé in construction. The loops in ratiné yarns are spaced evenly along the base yarn.

2. *Flake* or *flock yarns* are made of loosely twisted yarns that are held in place either by a base yarn as it twists, or by a third or binder yarn. These yarns are relatively weak and are used in the filling to achieve decorative surface effects.

3. *Nub yarns* are ply yarns in which an effect yarn is twisted around a base yarn a number of times in a small area to cause an enlarged bump or "nub." Sometimes a binder yarn is used to hold the nubs in place. The spacing of the nubs may be at regular or irregular intervals. Nubs are often of different colors than the base yarn. The terms *knot*, *spot*, or *knop* are also applied to this type of yarn.

Figure 13-23. Texturing of yarns by the air-jet method. Courtesy of *Scientific American*.

[13] M. D. Potter and P. B. Corbman, *Textiles, Fiber to Fabric* (New York: McGraw-Hill, Inc., 1967).

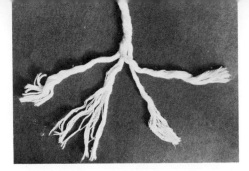

Figure 13-24. Cord yarn made from four ply yarns. Each ply can be untwisted to show many single yarns.

4. *Slub yarns* may be either ply or single yarns of staple fibers. The slub effect is created by varying the twist in the yarn, allowing areas of looser twist to be created. This produces a long, thick, soft area in the fabric called a slub. Slub yarns are irregular in diameter. The surface of fabrics woven with slub yarns shows these irregularities. Yarns made in this way have areas of varying twist, causing weaker areas in the yarn. In many fabrics, slub yarns are placed in the filling direction where fabrics receive less strain. Slubs are the same color as the rest of the yarn and cannot be pulled out of the fabric without damaging the structure of the fabric. Filament yarns can be spun with varying degrees of twist. These yarns also create a slubbed appearance in fabrics. Such filament yarns are known as *thick-and-thin yarns.*

5. *Snarl yarns* are ply yarns in which two or more yarns held at different tension are twisted together. The varying tension allows the effect yarn to form alternating unclosed loops on either side of the base yarn.

6. *Spiral* or *corkscrew yarns.* The spiral or corkscrew yarn is made of two plies, one soft and heavy, the other fine. The heavy yarn winds around the fine yarn.

7. *Chenille yarns* are made by a totally different process and require several steps in their preparation. First leno-weave fabric is woven. This fabric is cut into strips and these strips, which have a soft pile on all sides, are used as yarns. These are not yarns in the traditional sense of twisted fiber, but have been taken through a series of preliminary stages before being readied for use.

8. *Core spun yarns* are made with a central core of one fiber around which is wrapped or twisted an exterior layer of another fiber. Core-spun yarns may be made with an elastomer core, such as spandex, covered by another fiber in order to produce a stretch yarn. Other core-spun yarns include sewing thread made with polyester cores and cotton cover. *Lanese* is a core-spun and textured yarn with a polyester core and an acetate wrapping. (See Figure 11.2.)

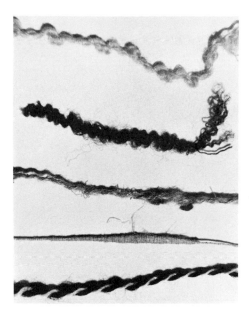

Figure 13-25. Five novelty yarns. From top to bottom: bouclé yarn, ratiné yarn, flake or flock yarn, slub yarn, and spiral or corkscrew yarn.

Recommended References

Encyclopedia of Textiles, American Fabrics. Englewood Cliffs, N.J.: Prentice-Hall, Inc., 2nd ed.

BACKER, S. "Yarn." *Scientific American,* December 1972, p. 47.

BOBKOWICZ, E., and A. J. BOBKOWICZ. "The Bob–tex Yarn-making Technology; Its Future and Implications." *Textile Research Journal,* September 1971, p. 773.

BORN, W. "Spindle and Distaff as Forerunners of the Spinning Wheel." *CIBA Review,* December 1939, p. 982 ff.

CRAWFORD, G. H. "Repco Spinning." *Modern Textiles,* June 1975, p. 24.

DOGA, I. "The Fundamentals of Electro-static Spinning." *Textile Research Journal,* July 1975, p. 21.

DULKEN, J. F. "New Horizons in Spinning." *Modern Textiles,* August 1971, p. 7.

FANNIN, A. *Hand-spinning, Art and Technique.* New York: Van Nostrand Reinhold Co., 1970.

Henshaw, D. E. *Self-twist Yarn*. Watford, England: Merrow Publishing Company, Ltd., 1971.

Ford, J. E. *Fibrillated Yarns*. Watford, England: Merrow Publishing Company, Ltd., 1975.

Hathorne, B. L. *Woven Stretch and Textured Fabrics*. New York: John Wiley & Sons, Inc., 1964.

Kluger, M. *The Joy of Spinning*. New York: Simon and Schuster, Inc., 1971.

Kotter, J., A. P. Baul, Jr., and C. L. Folk. "Single Step Spinning Arrives." *Textile World*, November 1975, p. 112.

Lord, P. R. *Spinning in the 70's*. Watford, England: Merrow Publishing Company, Ltd., 1970.

Moretz, G. "Open-end Spinning from the Spinner's Viewpoint." *Modern Textiles*, June 1974, p. 20.

"Open-End Spinning." *American Fabrics and Fashions*, Summer 1974, p. 53.

Selling, A. J. *Twistless Yarns*. Watford, England: Merrow Publishing Company, Ltd., 1971.

"Stretch Beginnings." *American Fabrics*, Winter 1971–72, p. 66.

"Textured Yarns." *American Fabrics*, Spring 1968, p. 67.

"Texturized Yarns." *CIBA Review*, 1965, #3, p. 28.

Warlick, S. J. *"A New Direction for Spinning."* *Textile Industries*, May 1976. p. 23.

Worrall, G. "Open End Spinning: A Fabricator's Viewpoint." *Modern Textiles*, June 1974, p. 25.

"Yarn and Thread." *CIBA Review*, 1965, vol. 3.

14

WOVEN FABRICS

Fabrics can be constructed in a variety of ways, ranging from the matting together of fibrous materials to the intricate interlacing of complex yarn systems. The following discussion outlines and defines the major classifications of fabric constructions. The specific techniques and processes by which these different fabrics are made are discussed in the chapters that follow.

1. *Films.* Since films are not made from fibers, they are not considered to be true textiles. They are synthetic polymers extruded in the form of sheets rather than as fibers. In some cases, these films are eventually made into fibrous form by a process called *fibrillation* or by cutting the sheet into fibers.

2. *Fiber webs.* Masses of fibers can be held together into a fabric by interlocking of fibers by mechanical action or by fusing fibers together with heat, adhesives, or chemicals. Examples of a few fabrics constructed by these means include felt, bark cloth, spunlace, and spunbonded fabrics.

3. *Woven fabrics.* Weaving of fabrics consists of interlacing of two systems of yarn at right angles. By varying the interlacing, a wide variety of different fabric constructions can be made.

4. *Looped fabrics.* Fabrics can be constructed from one continuous yarn by the formation of a series of interconnected loops. Knitting, though a complex form, is one type of looping construction. Crochet is another.

5. *Knotted fabrics.* Some fabrics are created by knotting yarns together. Lace, nets, macrame, and tatting are created by knotting.

6. *Braided fabrics.* Fabrics may be created by plaiting together yarns or strips of fabric. The components are interlaced in a diagonal pattern over and under one another to form a flat or tubular fabric of relatively narrow width.

7. *Stitch-through fabrics.* Stitch through or stitch bonding is a relatively new technique for constructing fabrics in which two sets of yarns or a mass of fibers are sewn together into a fabric structure by another set of yarns.

The Creation of Woven Fabrics

Fabrics can be woven from yarns on a simple hand loom or on a highly complex, totally automated power loom. In either case, the fabric that is produced will be made by interlacing one yarn with another. The lengthwise direction threads in a woven fabric are called the *warp yarns*. Crosswise threads are called *filling* or *weft yarns*. Warp and weft threads interlace with each other at right angles.

THE HAND LOOM

Weaving requires that the warp yarns be held under tension. Having stretched out one set of yarns, the weaver then takes a second yarn and interlaces it with the warps. The simplest interlacing is made by moving the filling over one warp and under the second, over the third and under the fourth, and so on. In the second row, the yarn goes under one, and over one, and so on. The third row repeats the pattern of the first, then the fourth row repeats the pattern of the second row. This is known as a *plain weave,* and is the simplest form of weaving.

An ancient craft, hand weaving was well known in North America, South America, and the Middle East at least 8,000 years ago. Two separate types of looms developed in different geographic areas. These looms differ in their means of providing tension to the warps. Northern Europeans utilized warp-weight looms, a vertical type of loom on which the warps were suspended from an upper bar and weighted at the bottom by small stone or clay loom weights. The force that gravity exerted on the weights provided the tension.

The second type of loom was the *two-bar loom* in which the warps stretched from one bar to another. This loom could be made either vertically or horizontally, as a frame of stakes in the ground held the two bars taut. Looms from Asia, the southern shores of the Mediterranean, and South America were of this type. South American looms often added a waist strap to the lower bars. The weaver suspended one bar from a tree or wall, and by placing the strap around her waist she could increase or decrease tension on the yarns by moving backward or forward.

The filling yarns, those running at right angles to the warps, could have been introduced by hand, but it was easier to use a needle or wrap the yarns around a stick. This latter method had the advantage of allowing the yarn to be unwound as the stick was moved across the warps. Ultimately, yarn was wound onto a bobbin and the bobbin was placed into a boatlike *shuttle.* The pointed end of the shuttle allowed the thread-carrier to move smoothly while the bobbin allowed the yarn to unwind as it was needed.

Filling yarns tended to be somewhat loose in placement, and had to be pushed into place more firmly. The earliest weavers painstakingly pushed each yarn into place with a small stick. A later, more efficient method utilized a wooden stick, shaped like a sword, which was slipped behind the filling yarns and pushed them tightly against the fabric that had already been woven. This weaver's sword or *batten* became a permanent part of the loom, although its shape was transformed gradually into a comblike device called a *reed* that was mounted on a frame. The frame retained the name batten, and a pull of the hand on the batten frame moved the reed forward, swinging the reed against the filling yarn and pushing it firmly into place.

As long as each warp yarn had to be raised by hand before the filling was interlaced with it, the process of weaving remained slow and tedious. Inventive weavers improvised a means of speeding up the procedure of raising and lowering warp yarns. Alternate rows of warps were placed over a "shed rod" or a stick that lifted them above the level of their neighboring yarns. This formation of raised and lowered yarns is called the *shed*. The bobbin could be thrust across the entire width of the cloth through the shed without stopping to raise each individual warp yarn. The alternate set of warp yarns was threaded through a series of string loops that were tied to another rod. This rod could raise the second set of yarns past those on the shed rod, and now by thrusting the bobbin under this second set of yarns that had been raised by an upward pull on the rod, the filling interlaced with an alternate set of yarns. Alternate raising and lowering of the rod made it possible to interlace warp and filling yarns quickly and efficiently. The rod that held the second set of warps was called a *harness*, the loops were called *heddles*. Heddles were used in Egypt

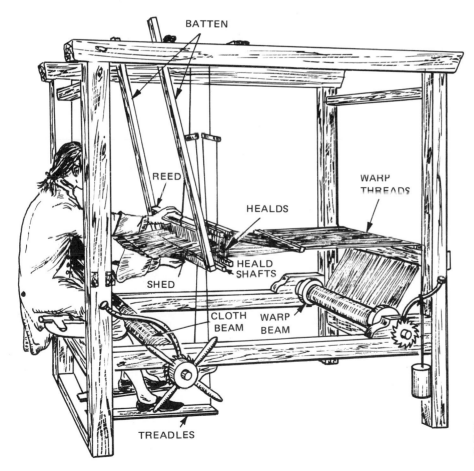

Figure 14-1. Hand loom with the parts labeled. Note that the heddles are called by the old-fashioned name of "healds."

before 2000 B.C. and in Peru at a comparable period.[1] Variety in weave could be achieved through the use of multiple harnesses, each raising a different set of warps.

The widespread use of silk probably brought about certain improvements in loom structure. Since silk fibers spin into fine yarns, these small, somewhat slippery threads made weaving more difficult. In silk weaving, the shed rod was replaced by a second heddle, as the smooth, fine yarns tended to slide against the shed rod, while the heddle held them securely.

The change from hand manipulation of harnesses to operation by foot treadle was another improvement. The loom was constructed so that pressure on a foot treadle raised and lowered the harness frame. This released the hand to operate the shuttle and the batten, and increased the speed with which the craftsman could work.

Probably the single most important invention that preceded automation of the loom was the flying shuttle. The flying shuttle, designed by John Kay, who patented it in 1733, was a device with a spring mechanism that threw the shuttle across the loom from one side to the other. In hand weaving, Kay's device was activated by a cord on either side of the loom that was pulled by the weaver. When the machine was mechanized, the flying shuttle was incorporated into the loom and operated automatically.

The above diagram, with parts labeled, depicts the basic hand loom that had developed by the time of the industrial revolution. Hand looms used by craftsmen today have the same basic structure.

AUTOMATION OF WEAVING

To transform weaving from a hand to a mechanical operation, several conditions had to be satisfied. The various motions made in hand weaving had to be automated. "The power loom of today is essentially the hand loom adapted to rotary driving."[2] The motions made in hand weaving included (1) the alternate raising and lowering of warp yarns in order to allow the shuttle to pass between them, (2) passing of the shuttle from one side of the loom to the other, (3) pressing filling yarns into place, and (4) winding up the completed cloth as it is woven.

A further requirement of power looms was that a power-operated loom had to stop automatically when a warp or filling yarn had broken. If the loom continued to function, the cloth would be flawed.

The first automatic loom was devised by Edmund Cartwright in 1784. Although it had a number of defects, this loom did work well enough to demonstrate that automatic loom weaving was feasible. Gradually, inventions by different individuals each contributed to the development of an economically viable automatic loom.

[1] Anni Albers, *On Weaving* (Middletown, Conn. Wesleyan University Press, 1957), p. 20.

[2] *Encyclopedia of Textiles, American Fabrics* (Englewood Cliffs, N.J.: Prentice-Hall, Inc., 2nd ed., 1972), p. 388.

MODERN WEAVING PROCESSES

Present-day looms can be divided between two major classifications: those that produce cloth in flat form and those that produce cloth in tubular form. Looms that produce flat woven cloth predominate. Flat looms can be further subdivided into two categories: those that use a shuttle to transport filling yarns and those that use some other means for carrying the filling from side to side. The second category, known as "shuttleless" looms, represents the most recent development in textile weaving.

Figure 14-2. Warp beam being prepared from several hundred cones of yarn. Courtesy of the National Cotton Council of America.

Figure 14-3. The wooden shuttle (into which is fitted a quill or pirn on which yarns are wound) carries yarn across the loom. Courtesy of Steel Heddle Advertising Company.

Prior to their use on the loom, warp and filling yarns must be prepared for weaving. The essential characteristics of suitable warp and filling yarns differ. Warp yarns undergo greater stress and abrasion during weaving than filling yarns; therefore, warp yarns must be strong enough to withstand these pressures. Warp yarns must be clean, free from knots, and uniform in size.

To strengthen and lubricate warp yarns, *sizing* or *slashing* is added. Size is made up of starches, resins, or gums that act as lubricants. The yarns are passed from one warp beam through a solution of sizing material. The sized yarns are dried immediately after treatment and wound onto another warp beam.

The warp beam containing the sized yarns is placed on the loom. Warp yarns must be threaded through the eyes of the heddle wires that are held in harnesses. The number of harnesses required for the loom is determined by the weave.

Once the warp yarns have been set into place, the loom goes through a series of motions: shedding, picking, beating up, and letting off. The shed is formed by raising the harnesses to form an open area between two sets of warps. The formation of the shed is known as *shedding*.

While the shed is open, the shuttle is thrown across the opening. As the shuttle traverses the cloth, the filling yarn unwinds from a *quill* or *pirn* held inside the shuttle. This lays a filling yarn across the width of the loom. The insertion of the filling is known as *picking*. Quills or pirns in the shuttle must be replaced when the yarn supply is exhausted. The frequency with which a quill has to be replaced depends upon the fineness of the filling yarn. Coarse yarns require more frequent replacement, finer yarns need to be replaced less often.

In the mechanical changer, full pirns are kept ready in a revolving case. The machine rams them into the shuttle when the shuttle comes to rest briefly after crossing the yarn. The pressure of the full pirn crowds the empty pirn out of the shuttle. It falls through a slot into a container under the loom. The new pirn is mechanically pushed into place in the shuttle, which has a self-threading device that automatically picks up the yarn when the new pirn is inserted. This allows the weaving to continue without a stop.

The rapid crossing of the shuttle leaves a layer of filling yarn. When the shed is changed, the yarn is locked into place by the change in warp positioning. However, to make the yarn lie flat and in its proper position, it must be beaten into place. *Beating up* is done by the *reed*, a comblike device that pushes the filling yarn close against the woven fabric.

As the woven fabric is formed it must be moved or *let-off* the loom in order to make room for the formation of more fabric. All of these functions are carefully synchronized so that they occur in the appropriate sequence and do not interfere with one another.

There is always the danger that a warp or filling yarn may break during weaving, causing a flaw in the cloth. Modern looms use electronic scanners that signal when a yarn is broken. A break in the electronic contact shuts off the loom, allowing the broken yarn to be repaired.

The process described is similar for most looms. The primary source of

energy for automatic looms is an electric motor that transmits the motions of the various parts of the loom through a series of mechanical devices called *cams*. Several other looms have been developed that use different devices for regulating loom motions. These are the *Jacquard* and the *dobby* looms.

Figure 14-4. Two-harness automatic loom. Note the box of full quills or pirns in the upper right-hand corner with the quill changer in front of it. Courtesy of the Belgian Linen Association.

JACQUARD LOOM

The Jacquard loom is the descendant of an oriental loom, the draw loom, which was used to weave complex patterned fabrics. Operation of the draw loom required that there be two workers; the weaver who threw the shuttle and operated the batten and a "drawboy" who raised and lowered a series of cords that controlled the pattern. The drawboy had to work from a platform above the loom while the weaver sat below.

Since the drawboy could make mistakes in the selection of cords, later modifications of the loom structure introduced a mechanical device for raising and lowering the cords. In 1805, Joseph Jacquard, a Frenchman, perfected the principle of the mechanical draw loom. To this day this same type of loom used

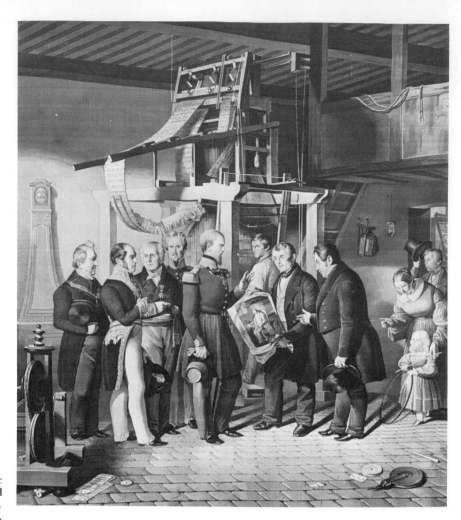

Figure 14-5. This illustration is actually a fabric woven on a Jacquard loom. In the background of the picture a Jacquard loom is depicted. Courtesy of the Metropolitan Museum of Art, Rogers Fund, 1938.

in weaving complex patterns is known as the Jacquard loom and the weave is known as the Jacquard weave.

The ability of the Jacquard loom to weave a variety of complex fabrics is a result of the ability of this machine to control each warp yarn separately. Each warp yarn is threaded through a loop in the end of a leash or cord.

Before the loom is set up, a design is worked out on graph paper and the position of each of the yarns in the design is analyzed. A punched card is prepared that corresponds to each of the filling yarns. The card contains a "code," a set of punched holes that will determine which warp yarns must be lifted for each passage of the filling. The punched cards are laced together in the correct order for the design. As the cards rotate, needles rest against the card. The needles are held under the pressure of a spring. When a needle position coincides with a hole in the card, the needle moves through the hole. The movement of the needle engages a hook, which in turn lifts the cords attached to the hook. The cords raise the yarns they hold to form the shed.

When the filling has been inserted, the needles retract, the cards rotate to the next position, and different sets of needles engage holes in the next cards. This, in turn, causes other warp yarns to be lifted to form a different shed.

The Jacquard loom installation requires a large area, and particularly a very high ceiling. The loom operates more slowly than simpler looms, so that the fabrics produced on this loom are more expensive.

DOBBY LOOM

The dobby loom might be considered as a simplified version of the Jacquard. It can be used under normal mill conditions, as it requires only the installation of a somewhat enlarged dobby "head" on a conventional loom. This machine uses wooden cross bars with metal pegs. Every cross bar determines which warp yarns will be raised to form the shed in a given row of the pattern. From twenty-four to thirty shedding combinations are controlled in this way, so that the repeats are limited to about thirty rows in size. A machine called the double cylinder dobby loom has been developed that approximately doubles the size of the repeat that can be made. The fabrics woven on this loom are less complex than Jacquard patterns and usually consist of small fancy or geometrical figures or designs.

SHUTTLELESS LOOMS

Shuttleless looms were invented to increase the speed of weaving. The modern loom with a shuttle, although much faster in operation than the earliest automatic looms, is not susceptible to further increases in speed because of the

Figure 14-6. Shuttleless rapier loom with dobby head. Rapier-holding cases can be seen extending on either side of the loom. Courtesy of Lindauer Dornier Gesellschaft Gmbh.

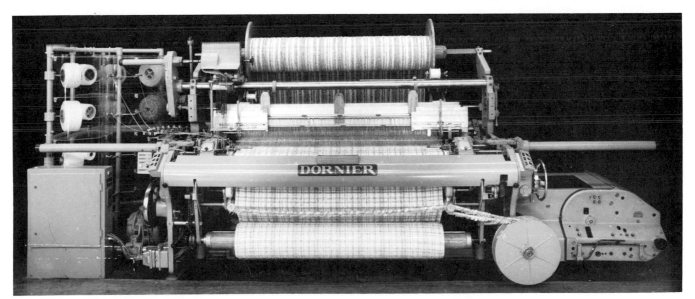

variety of operations that the machine must perform. For this reason, future loom developments are likely to be in the area of shuttleless weaving.

Shuttleless looms may be classified as to the method used in inserting the filling yarns. Four basic types have been made:

1. Looms with gripper or "dummy" shuttles.

2. Looms with mechanically operated gripper arms or rapiers.

3. Looms employing water or air jets to carry the filling.

4. Looms that mechanically propel the unsupported filling into the shed.

In hand weaving and automatic-shuttle weaving, the filling yarn is continuous and runs back and forth across the fabric, but in most shuttleless weaving, the filling yarn extends only from selvage to selvage, as it is cut off after it passes across the shed. In all shuttleless weaving the yarn for the filling is unwound from large, stationary packages of yarn that are sometimes set on one side and at other times are set on both sides of the loom.

Gripper Loom

In the gripper or dummy shuttle type of loom, a small hooklike device grips the end of the filling yarn. As the gripper is projected across the warp shed, it tows the filling behind it. The gripper can move more quickly than a conventional shuttle because of its decreased size; it can travel further more easily, thereby making possible the weaving of wider fabrics, and it does not require the step of filling the shuttle; it pulls the yarn directly from a prepared yarn package.

The gripper travels only in one direction. It is returned to the starting point by a conveyor belt. In order to maintain the speed of weaving, each loom must have several grippers, although only one is in use at any one time.

The gripper loom not only weaves fabric more quickly than the shuttle loom but it runs with less noise, making it possible for manufacturers to comply more easily with government regulations that restrict noise levels.

There is also a saving in power costs for wide-width fabrics. Narrow fabrics are not economically woven on this loom since too much time is spent in periods of acceleration of the gripper. Wide fabric widths are quite productive, as the power consumed is less than that for a conventional shuttle loom of the same size. Sheets are woven side by side on some of these looms in order to take advantage of these savings.

Rapier Loom

As in the gripper loom, a stationary package of yarn is used to supply the filling yarns to the rapier loom. One end of a *rapier,* a rod or steel tape, carries the filling. The other end of the rapier is connected to the control system. The rapier moves across the width of the fabric, carrying the filling to the opposite side. The rapier is then retracted, leaving the new filling in place.

In some versions of the loom, two rapiers are used, each half the width of the fabric in size. One rapier carries the yarn to the center of the shed, whereas the opposing rapier picks up the yarn and carries it the remainder of the way across the shed. A disadvantage of both of these techniques is the space required for the machine if a rigid rapier is used. The housing for the rapiers must take up as much space as the width of the machine. To overcome this problem, machines with flexible rapiers have been devised. The flexible rapier can be coiled as it is withdrawn, and will therefore require less space. However, if the rapier is too stiff, it will not coil; if it is too flexible, it will buckle. The double rapier is more frequently used than the single rapier.

Water Jet and Air Jet Looms

Water-soluble warp sizings are used on most staple warp yarns. Therefore, the use of water jet looms is restricted to filament yarns, yarns that are nonabsorbent, and those that do not lose strength when wet. In this technique, a water jet is shot under force and, with it, a filling yarn. The force of the water as it is propelled across the shed carries the yarn to the opposite side. This loom is quite economical in its operation. A water jet of only 0.1 centimeter is sufficient to carry a yarn across a 48-inch shed. The amount of water required for each filling yarn is less than two cubic centimeters.

Air jet looms operate in a manner similar to the water jet looms. Instead of projecting a stream of water across the shed, a jet of air is projected. High air velocity must be used to acquire enough speed to project a filling yarn across the width of the loom. Achieving such speeds increases both the sound level and the cost, and makes this type of shuttleless weaving somewhat less attractive to manufacturers than previously described shuttleless loom types.

Looms in Which the Filling Is Mechanically Propelled

In order to propel a yarn across the loom without any other support, the filling is inserted into a pair of high speed rollers that accelerate rapidly. This force is transmitted into the yarn, and the momentum projects the yarn across the width of the loom. As the front end gradually loses some momentum, the back of the yarn continues to move more rapidly than the front. This may cause some entangling of the yarns and lead to difficulties in weaving. For this reason, this is the least popular of the shuttleless loom types.

All shuttleless weaving techniques insert filling yarns from one side. In the shuttle type of loom, the carrying of the shuttle back and forth across the fabric creates a normal woven selvage, with no loose yarns to fray or ravel. In shuttleless looms, however, one of the selvages is fringed. It is necessary to reinforce this edge if the fabric is not to fray at the edges. The methods of reinforcement that are used include providing for tuck-in of the yarns at the open edge or use of a *leno* self-selvage, in which two warp yarns at the edges of the fabric twist around each filling. The tucked-in finish is the more durable.

Among the advantages of shuttleless weaving is that colors for weaving decorative fabrics can be changed more easily. Unlike shuttle looms in which

Figure 14-7. (Above) In the two-rapier type of shuttleless loom, one rapier carries the yarn to the center of the shed where a second rapier grasps the yarn (opposite) and carries it across the rest of the width of the fabric. Dornier loom. Photograph courtesy of Lindauer Dornier Gesellschaft Gmbh.

different shuttles must be provided for each different color, the shuttleless looms can be provided with a variety of colors directly from the yarn package. Other advantages include lower power requirements, lower sound levels, and smaller space requirements. However, not all fabrics can be woven on all shuttleless looms. Some recently developed shuttleless looms can weave dobby and Jacquard fabrics.

The Weaves

There are many different combinations in which warp and filling yarns can be interlaced. Some fabrics may be woven with yarns close together to form a dense fabric. Others are woven with yarns widely separated and form a fabric of open weave. The quantity of yarn in a fabric is directly related to the durability of the fabric. Those fabrics with closer, denser weaves are likely to be more durable than loosely woven, open weave fabrics.

The closeness of the weave is expressed as the thread count. With a small magnifying glass calibrated to measure an inch or fractions of an inch, it is possible to count the number of yarns in one inch of warp and in one inch of the filling. When the number of yarns in the warp is the same as the number of yarns in the filling, the weave is said to be a balanced weave. The thread count is often expressed in numerical form as 80 × 64, indicating that there are 80 warp yarns per inch by 64 fillings. When warp and filling are balanced or equal, the thread count may be stated as 80 square, meaning there are 80 yarns per inch in the warp and 80 yarns per inch in the filling. Balanced weave fabrics with the same type of yarns in warp and filling are more durable because the fabric wears evenly in both warp and filling directions.

Three types of weave structures form the basis of even the most complex weaves. Known as basic weaves, these are the plain weave, the twill weave, and the satin weave.

Visual representation of weaves is often made on graph paper. Each square of the paper represents the thread that appears on the upper side or surface of the fabric. Darkened squares represent the warp yarns.

Diagraming of weaves on graph paper is a useful exercise, but students will probably find that the concepts relating to weaves are made clearer to them if they use colored yarns or strips of colored paper to create small samples of each of the basic weaves. A small hand loom, or a child's loom, can be used for this purpose.

BASIC WEAVES

The Plain Weave

The plain weave is the simplest of the weaves. It consists of interlacing warp and filling yarns in a pattern of over one and under one. Imagine a small hand loom with the warp yarns held firmly in place. The filling yarn moves over the first warp yarn, under the second, over the third, under the fourth, and so on. In the next row, the filling yarn goes under the first warp yarn, over the second, under the third, and so on. In the third row, the filling moves over the first warp, under the second, and so on, just as it did in the first row.

The weave can be made in any type of yarn. Made with tightly twisted, single yarns that are placed close together both in the warp and filling, and with the same number of yarns in both directions, the resulting fabric will be a very durable, simple, serviceable fabric. If, however, the warp were to be made from a single yarn and the filling from a colorful bouclé yarn, a quite different, much more decorative fabric would result. Both are the product of the same, basic, plain weave.

Other patterned effects are created by varying the color of the yarns. If the warp yarns are made up of alternating colors, a two-colored lengthwise stripe can be made. If warp yarns are of one color and filling yarns are of another color, the resulting fabric (usually made of cotton or a cotton blend) is called *chambray*. Checks can be made by alternating colors not only in the warp but also in the filling direction. Plaids are made in the same way, but with greater variety in the color.

When these filling color variations are made on a shuttle loom, a special

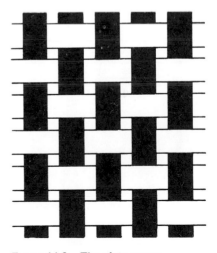

Figure 14-8. The plain weave.

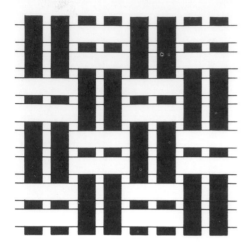

Figure 14-9. The basket weave variation of the plain weave.

Figure 14-10. Monks' cloth, a basket weave fabric with four warp and four filling yarns.

loom called a *box loom* is required in which there are as many shuttles as there are colors in the pattern. The shuttle release of each color is timed carefully so that the pattern repeat is always the same.

Plain weave fabrics are constructed from many fibers and in weights ranging from light to heavy. Weaves may be balanced or unbalanced. Decorative effects can be achieved by using novelty yarns or yarns of different colors. Together with many of these novelty fabrics, there are a number of standard fabric types made in the plain weave. In the past, these standard fabrics were always constructed from specific fibers. At present, suitable man-made fibers are also woven into many of the standard fabric constructions.

Among the best known of the plain weave, standard fabrics are the following:

Open weave, low-thread count fabrics that include *crinoline, cheesecloth, buckram,* and *gauze.* The openness of the weave and the wide spacing of the yarns in these fabrics make them limp. The durability of these fabrics is poor, and most of them have somewhat specialized uses. Cheesecloth, as the name implies, is used in producing cheese, serving as a wrapper or strainer for the curds. Cheesecloth, buckram, and crinoline can be heavily sized to serve as backing or stiffening fabrics. Gauze is often used for theatrical costumes, as well as for medical dressings. Recently, gauze fabrics from India have become popular for use in making blouses and dresses.

Sheer, soft, crisp finish plain-weave fabrics of close weave are generally made with high twist yarns. Often the yarns are combed. *Organdy,* a sheer cotton with a crisp finish, and *organza,* a similar fabric made with filament yarns, are examples of this type of construction. Organdy may be given either a temporary or permanently stiffened finish. Thread counts for organdies generally range from 72 x 64 up to 84 x 80. Other sheer, softer fabrics include *batiste,* made of mercerized cotton, linen, or cotton blended with man-made fibers. Batiste has a count of about 88 x 80. *Nainsook, longcloth,* and *voile* are other fabrics of slightly heavier weight than batiste, which were, traditionally, made of cotton. Like batiste, they are now made of man-mades and/or blends, as well. Voile has a distinctive two-ply warp, and good drapability.

Chiffon is made from fine, highly twisted yarns. Sheer evening dresses, blouses, lingerie, and other dressy garments are constructed from the fabric. Although delicate in feel and appearance, chiffon is relatively durable.

Medium-weight, plain weave fabrics include such basics as *gingham,* a woven plaid or check; *calico,* a low-count, coarse fabric, which is often printed with small designs; and *challis,* formerly made of worsted wool in a soft construction, but now made in a number of other fibers that attempt to simulate the original wool fabric. *Percale* is a closely woven, plain weave of cotton or blended fibers, made from yarns of moderate twist. Percale yard-goods are generally carded, but percale sheets are finer, more luxurious in feel, and are combed. Percale sheets have a thread count of 180 to 200 threads per inch. *Muslin* is generally woven from cotton or cotton blends. It is made in both heavily sized, bleached qualities and in better grades for sheets and pillow cases. Muslin sheets are not combed and have a lower thread count (128–140 threads per inch) than percale sheets.

Heavy or coarse plain weave fabrics include *butcher linen, crash,* and *homespun.* All of these fabrics have coarse, uneven yarns and an uneven texture.

Plain Weave Variations

Basket Weave. Using the principle of the plain weave, variations are made. The basket weave utilizes two or more warp and/or two or more filling yarns as one yarn. The resultant cloth is fairly loose in weave.

Among the more common basket weave fabrics are:

1. *Monk's cloth:* a coarse cloth of large yarns, monk's cloth uses four or more yarns as one in the weave. Its major uses are in household textiles such as curtains, spreads, and the like.

2. *Hopsacking:* made of many different fibers, this fabric simulates the fabrics used in bags for gathering hops. It has a 2-2 or 3-3 basket weave.

Sometimes a modified basket weave utilizes a double yarn in one direction, but not in the other. *Oxford cloth,* which is made in this way, is a soft fabric, often made of cotton or cotton blends, which is used for shirts. Frequently, it is made with narrow colored stripes in the warp.

Rib Variation. Ribbed or corded fabrics are created by grouping a number of yarns together in one direction before they are crossed by the yarns from the opposite direction, or by using larger yarns in one direction than in the other. If the resultant fabric shows an enlarged crosswise yarn, a crosswise *rib* is formed. If the enlarged yarn is in the lengthwise direction, a lengthwise *cord* is formed. Ribs and cords can be either relatively small or quite pronounced.

Some standard fabrics with small ribs include *broadcloth, poplin,* and *taffeta.* Broadcloth and poplin are most often woven from cotton or cotton blends, and sometimes from wool, whereas taffeta is made of filament yarns such as acetate and silk. *Faile, grosgrain,* and some *reps* have a larger rib. *Bengaline, ottoman,* and *large reps* have still larger, very pronounced ribs.

Shantung has a nubby, irregular rib in the filling. Formerly made almost exclusively of silk, shantung is now made from a variety of man-made fibers as well.

Dimity is a sheer cotton fabric that is often made with a lengthwise cord effect. Some dimity fabrics use larger yarns in both the warp and filling direction to achieve a checked or "barred" effect. *Bedford cord* is another example of a sturdy fabric constructed with a pronounced lengthwise cord.

Ribbed and corded fabrics may wear unevenly, as crossing the larger yarns exposes a greater surface area of the covering yarn to abrasion. The problem is aggravated if the crossing yarns are not closely spaced, if the rib is especially pronounced, or if the crossing yarns are loosely twisted or made from a weak fiber.

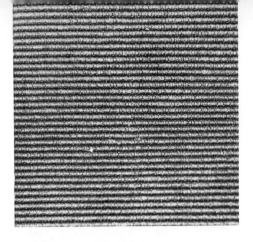

Figure 14-11. Faille fabric with pronounced crosswise rib.

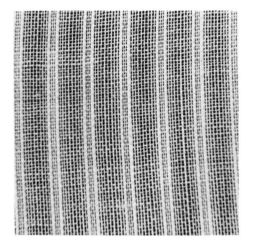

Figure 14-12. Dimity fabric with pronounced lengthwise cord.

Twill Weave

Twill weave fabrics are readily identified by the diagonal lines that the weave creates on the surface of the fabric. The yarns in twill fabrics are usually spaced closely together, packed tightly, and held firmly in place. Therefore, twill woven fabrics are usually quite strong and durable. The compact structure of twill fabrics enables them to shed soil more readily, although when soiled they may be more difficult to get clean. Depending on their construction, twill weave fabrics generally show good resistance to abrasion. Twill fabrics are often used for tailored garments, particularly when made of worsted wool yarns.

The simplest twill weave is created by the filling crossing over two warp yarns, then under one, over two, under one, and so on. In the next row, the sequence begins one yarn farther on. (See the following diagram.) The area in which one yarn crosses over several yarns in the opposite direction is called a *float*.

The lines created by this pattern are called *wales*. When the cloth is held in the position in which it was woven, the wales or diagonal lines will be seen to run either from the lower left corner to the upper right corner, or from the lower right to the upper left. If the diagonal runs from the lower left to the upper right, the twill is known as a right-hand twill. About 85 per cent of all twill woven fabrics are right-hand twills.[3] When the twill runs from the lower right to the upper left, the twill is known as a left-hand twill.

There are a number of types of twill weaves. All use the same principle of crossing more than one yarn at a regular, even progression. Descriptions of twills may be made in terms of the pattern of warp yarns crossing filling yarns. When a warp yarn crosses two filling yarns, it is written 2/1. When two warp yarns cross two filling yarns, it is written as 2/2. If the filling yarn floats and crosses three warp yarns, it is written 1/3. The first number always represents the number of times the warp yarn floats over the filling yarns.

Even-sided Twill. The even-sided twill has the same number of warp and filling yarns showing on the face of the fabric. The following diagram shows

[3] Ibid., p. 325.

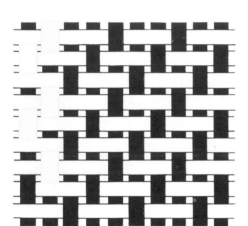

Figure 14-13. Right-handed twill weave.

Figure 14-14. Left-handed twill weave.

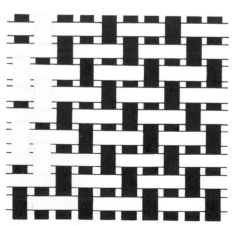

how such a weave is achieved in a 2/2 twill. Even-sided twills can also be made in 3/3 patterns.

Even-sided twill fabrics include *serge,* a popular, basic twill fabric made from any of a number of different fibers. When serge is made from wool, it is often woven from worsted yarns. Serge will take a crease well, but wool serge tends to become shiny with wear. It tailors well. *Surah* is an even-sided twill that is made of silk or other filament fibers. Often printed or woven into plaids, surah is used for neckties, scarves, blouses, and dress goods. Some twilled *flannels* are made from even-sided twill constructions.

Warp-faced Twill. Warp-faced twills have a predominance of warp yarns on the surface of the fabric with patterns of 2/1, 3/1, 3/2, and so on.

Warp-faced twills include very popular basic twill fabrics such as *denim, jean,* and *drill,* which are durable fabrics often made from cotton or cotton blends. The major uses of these fabrics include work clothes, sportswear, and mattress and pillow ticking. *Gabardine* is a warp-faced twill fabric that is durable and closely woven. It is made into a variety of weights from many different fibers such as wool, rayon, cotton, and man-made fibers.

Filling-faced Twill. Filling-faced twills have a predominance of filling yarns on the surface of the fabric. Filling yarns are generally weaker than warp yarns, so that relatively few filling-faced twills are made.

Herringbone Twill. In a herringbone twill, the direction of the twill reverses itself to form a broken diagonal that appears like a series of Vs: Herringbone patterns create a decorative effect.

Twill Angles. When the face of a twill fabric is examined, the diagonal of the wales will be seen to move at a more or less steep angle. The steepness of the angle is dependent upon two factors in the construction of the fabric: the number of warp yarns in the fabric and the number of steps between movement of yarns when they interlace.

The more warp yarns in the constructions, the steeper the angle of the wales will be. This is because the point of interlacing of the yarns will be closer together, thereby making a steep climb upward. When the steepness of the angle is the result of close spacing of warp yarns, these steeper angles are an indication of good strength.

Generally the interlacing of yarns in a twill changes with each filling yarn. There are, however, fabrics in which the interlacing of yarns changes only every two filling yarns or every three filling yarns. As can be seen by the diagram, the less often the interlacing changes the steeper the angle of the twill will be.

Satin Weave

Satin weave fabrics are made by allowing yarns to float over a number of yarns from the opposite direction. Interlacings are made at intervals such as over four, under one, over seven, under one, or over eleven, under one. Floats in satin fabrics may cross from four to twelve yarns before interlacing with another yarn. No diagonal line is formed on the surface of the fabric because the points of intersection are spaced in such a way that no regular progression is formed from one yarn to that lying next to it.

Figure 14-15. Right-handed, even-sided twill (2/2).

Figure 14-16. Right-handed, warp-faced twill weave (2/1).

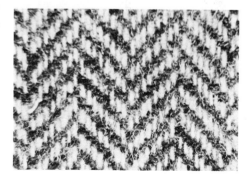

Figure 14-17. Herringbone twill fabric.

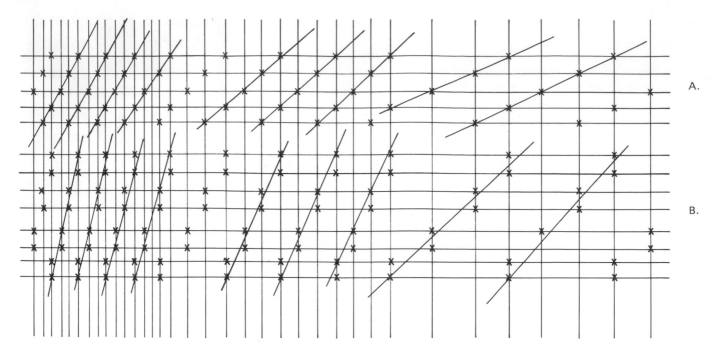

A.

B.

Figure 14-18. In A, above, the angle of the twill decreases as the yarns in the warp are spaced more widely apart. In B, the angle of the twill as compared with A becomes steeper as the frequency with which yarns change their pattern of interlacing decreases.

Figure 14-19. Satin weave. Warp yarns form floats, crossing over seven filling yarns between every interlacing.

When warp yarns form the floats, the fabric is referred to as *satin.* When filling yarns float, the fabric is called *sateen.* Sateens are most often made from cotton. Since cotton is a staple fiber, for cotton to serve as a strong warp yarn requires that it be given a fairly high twist. Much of the beauty and luster of satin weave fabrics comes from the use of more loosely twisted yarns. Therefore, in order to use staple yarns of looser twist, it is preferable that they serve as the filling, not the warp. Filament yarns, however, do not require a tight twist in order to serve as warp yarns, so that low twist filament yarns are often made to float in the lengthwise direction in constructing satin fabrics. Exceptions do exist in which cotton floats are formed in the warp, and filament floats are formed in the filling.

In *crepe-backed satin,* loosely twisted, lustrous warp yarns are combined with tightly twisted, creped filling yarns. The floats on the surface are created by the warp, so that the face of the fabric is chiefly made up of warp yarns with a satin appearance, whereas the back of the fabric is made up largely of the tightly twisted filling yarns that produce a crepe or rougher surface texture with a flat, less shiny appearance.

Satin weave fabrics are quite decorative. They are usually made from filament fibers with high luster in order to produce a shiny, lustrous surface. They are smooth and slippery in texture and tend to shed dirt easily. The long floats on the surface are, of course, subject to abrasion and to snagging. The longer the float, the greater is the likelihood of snags and pulls. Satins are often used as lining fabrics for coats and suits because they slide easily over other fabrics. The durability of satin weave fabrics is related to the density of the weave, with closely woven, high count fabrics having good durability. Satins made from stronger fibers will, of course, be more durable than those made from weaker fibers.

Some names given to satin fabrics include:

1. Antique satin—a satin made to imitate silk satin of an earlier period, often using slubbed yarns for decorative effect.

2. Double-faced satin—a satin woven from two warps and one filling to obtain satin effects on both the face and the back of the fabric.

3. Duchesse satin—a satin with a plain back and a crisp texture. The fabric is smooth and lustrous.

4. Peau de soie—soft, closely woven satin with a flat, mellow luster.

5. Slipper satin—strong, compact satin, heavy in weight. It is often used for evening shoes.

Figure 14-20. Sateen weave. Filling yarns form floats, crossing over four warp yarns between every interlacing.

FANCY WEAVES

Jacquard Weave

The operation of the Jacquard loom has been described earlier in this chapter. Jacquard patterns, when carefully analyzed, may be seen to contain combinations of plain, twill, and satin weaves, even in the same crosswise yarn. Many decorative fabrics are made by the Jacquard technique. (See Figure 18.16.) The following are some of the best known Jacquard patterns:

1. Brocade—an embossed appearance is created in brocade fabrics. Elaborate patterns, often of flowers and figures, stand out from the background. Brocades are made from a wide range of fibers and with a wide range of price and quality. Fabrics are used for upholstery, draperies, and evening and formal clothing.

2. Brocatelle—a fabric that is similar to brocade, but with figures or patterns standing in high relief. Brocatelle is used mostly for upholstery fabrics and draperies.

3. Damask—a flatter fabric than brocade, many damasks have a fine weave. Damask figures often use a satin weave to reflect light from the pattern, whereas the background is made in a plain or twill construction. Linen damasks have long been used for luxurious tablecloths. Damasks are reversible.

Dobby Weave

The dobby weave is rather like a Jacquard weave in miniature. The patterns created by the dobby weave are small, repeated patterns, usually geometric in form.

Some of the fabrics made on the dobby loom include:

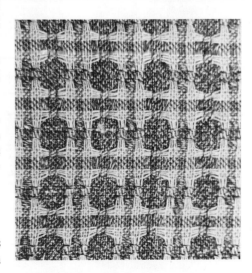

Figure 14-21. Dobby weave fabric with a small geometric pattern.

1. Bird's-eye—a cloth made with small diamond-shaped figures, the weave is said to resemble the eye of a bird. Bird's-eye is also called diaper cloth.

2. Madras cotton shirting—sometimes woven with a dobby pattern in the stripe. The figure woven may be in either a contrasting or in the same color as the background fabric.

3. Piqué—medium- to heavy-weight fabric, often of cotton, with a pronounced lengthwise cord, often combined with other small figures or patterns such as honeycomb or waffle effects.

4. White-on-white—a white dobby figure woven on a white background, often used for men's shirting.

Tapestry Weaving

Tapestry weaving differs from Jacquard weaving in that it is essentially a hand technique. Whereas Jacquard weaving utilizes repeated patterns of finite

Figure 14-22. Peruvian tapestry fabric from the ninth to the eleventh century. Courtesy of the Metropolitan Museum of Art, Fletcher Fund, 1959.

size, tapestry weaving is used to produce enormous fabrics that can be one, large picture. Tapestry weaving may be compared to painting with yarn.

Although tapestry weaving has been practiced in most cultures, the finest examples of this art are to be found in ancient Peru, in Coptic Egypt in the fifth and sixth centuries, A.D., and in northern Europe from the fourteenth to the seventeenth centuries. Since it is basically a hand technique, tapestry is made on a very elementary loom. Even after the Europeans had built large factories in which tapestries were woven, particularly in Flanders and France, the operation remained a handcraft that had been moved into a factory setting.

In the weaving of European tapestries, the loom followed the basic form of the two-bar loom. The loom was set up either vertically or horizontally, and warp yarns were measured and affixed to the loom. Filling yarns were prepared in the appropriate colors. The design of the tapestry was first worked out in a drawing or *cartoon*, as it was called. The artist who created the drawing may have been one of great stature, and painters such as Raphael and Rubens served as designers of sixteenth- and seventeenth-century tapestries. The cartoon was sometimes traced onto the warp yarns. In other instances it was mounted

Figure 14-23. Egyptian (Coptic) tapestry woven in colored wools and undyed linen during the sixth or seventh centuries A.D. Courtesy of the Metropolitan Museum of Art, Rogers Fund.

Figure 14-24. French or Flemish tapestry of
the late fifteenth century woven from wool and
silk with metal threads. Courtesy of the Metropolitan Museum of Art, the Cloisters Collec-
tion. Gift of John D. Rockefeller, Jr., 1937.

behind the loom and the tapestry weaver looked through the warp yarns to the design, following the plan of the drawing. The tapestry was woven with the wrong side facing the weaver. Sometimes a mirror was set up beneath the tapestry so that the weaver could check his progress on the right side.

The various colors of yarns were wound onto sharp, pointed bobbins that were introduced into the warp, and the weaver proceeded to fill in the area of that particular color. When the weaver reached the end of one color, a new bobbin was used for the next section. This created a problem, because as the weaver worked back and forth in a particular segment of the design, the yarns of one color did not join with the yarns of the adjacent color. This produced slits in the fabric at the place where each new color began. In some forms of tapestry weaving these holes were purposely left open, and when the tapestry was hung, the light shining through the slits added to the decorative effect of the tapestry. This practice prevails in ancient Peruvian tapestry design.

In many tapestries, however, these openings were not pleasing and a number of different techniques were used to avoid open spaces. Sections of the tapestry could be sewn shut, but this caused the fabric to be weaker at the spots where the fabric was seamed together. Two other methods were also utilized to prevent the formation of slits. Where the color of one section ended and another began, both the old and the new color could be twisted around the same warp yarns. This system worked well except that it created a slightly indistinct or shadowy line. Where clear, well-defined lines were required, the yarns of adjacent colors were fastened together by looping one yarn around the other.

In tapestry weaving all of the warp yarns are completely covered by filling yarns, so it is the filling yarns that carry the design. The warp yarns serve only as the base.

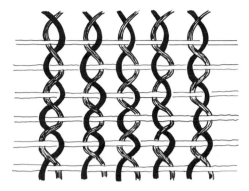

Figure 14-25. Structure of a leno weave fabric.

Leno Weave

The leno weave is the modern descendant of a technique called "twining" that was used thousands of years ago for making fabrics. In leno weave fabrics, the warp yarns are paired. A special attachment, the *doup* or *leno* attachment crosses or laps the paired warp yarns over each other, while the filling passes through the opening between the two warp yarns.

Leno weave fabrics can be made in open, gauzelike constructions. The twined (not twisted) warp yarns prevent the filling yarns of these open fabrics from slipping. Curtain fabrics are often made with leno weave. Two of the more popular leno weave fabrics are *marquisette* and *grenadine*.

Woven Pile Fabrics

Pile fabrics have been defined as "fabric(s) with cut or uncut loops which stand up densely on the surface."[4] Pile fabrics may be created by weaving or through other construction techniques, such as tufting, knitting, or stitch-

[4]M. Klapper, *Fabric Almanac* (New York: Fairchild Publications, Inc., 1967), p. 64.

through. To create the loops that appear on the surface of *woven* pile fabrics, the weaving process incorporates an extra set of yarns that form the pile. Pile fabrics, therefore, represent a complex form of weaving in which there are at least three sets of yarns.

Pile fabrics are woven by one of several methods: the wire method, the filling pile method, the double-weave method, or the terry method.

Wire Method. The wire method utilizes two sets of warp yarns and one set of filling yarns. One set of warp yarns and the filling yarn interlace in the usual manner and form the "ground" fabric. These two yarns may interlace in either a plain or a twill weave. The extra set of warp yarns forms the pile. When the pile yarns are raised by the heddles, the machine inserts a wire across the loom in the filling direction. When the warps are lowered, they loop over the wire to make a raised area. The next several filling yarns are inserted in the usual manner. The wire is then withdrawn, leaving the loop, which is held firmly in place by the other yarns. If the fabric is to have a cut pile, the wire has a knife blade at the end that cuts the yarns as the wire is withdrawn. If the fabric is to have an uncut pile, the wire has no cutting edge.

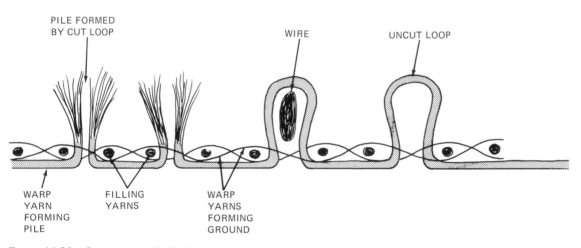

Figure 14-26. Construction of pile fabrics by the wire method.

PILE FORMED BY CUT LOOP

WIRE

UNCUT LOOP

WARP YARN FORMING PILE

FILLING YARNS

WARP YARNS FORMING GROUND

Filling Pile Method. In the filling pile method there are two sets of filling yarns and one set of warp yarns. In this technique, the extra set of filling yarns forms floats that are from four to six yarns in length. The floating yarns are cut at the center of the float and these ends are brushed up to the surface of the fabric.

In some filling pile constructions, the filling yarn that makes the pile is interlaced with the ground one time before it is cut; in others the filling pile interlaces twice. Those fabrics in which there are two interlacings are more durable than when only one interlacing has taken place. It is possible to distinguish fabrics by raveling pile loops from the fabric. Those that have been interlaced once will have the form of a small V, whereas those that were interlaced twice will look like a small W. The points of the V and W represent the places at which the yarns interlaced, and the W form is of better quality.

Corduroy floats are placed in lengthwise rows and velveteen floats are

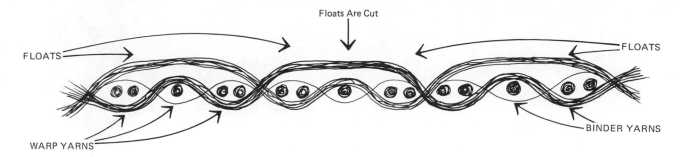

Floats Are Cut

FLOATS

FLOATS

BINDER YARNS

WARP YARNS

Cut Floats Form Pile

Cross-section of Pile Fabric (Corduroy)

Figure 14-27. Construction of corduroy by the filling pile method.

randomly spaced. The even spacing of corduroy floats produces the characteristic stripe or wale of many corduroys, whereas velveteens are characterized by a uniform, overall pile. Other decorative effects can be achieved by cutting floats selectively to vary pattern and texture.

Both wire and filling pile grounds can be made in either plain or twill weaves. Twill weave grounds will usually provide better wear.

Double-Cloth Method. The double-cloth method, like the filling pile method, is used for cut pile fabrics. Here two sets of warps and two sets of fillings simultaneously are each woven into a layer of fabric. A third set of warp yarns moves back and forth between the two layers of fabric, holding them together and being held by each fabric. The resultant fabric is cut apart by a sharp knife, thereby creating two lengths of fabric, each with a cut pile.

Velvets and plushes can be made in this way. Other nonpile fabrics can be made by the double-cloth method. These are discussed separately.

Terry Weave. Terry cloth is made by the slack tension method. Terry cloth is made with uncut loops. Two warps and one filling yarn are used. The ground of the fabric is made from one warp yarn and one filling yarn, the warp yarns being held under tension. The warp yarns that make up the pile are allowed to relax, their tension being released. As the filling yarns are pushed firmly into place, the looser warp yarns loop up on the surface, forming the terry pile. Terry pile may appear on one or both sides of the fabric.

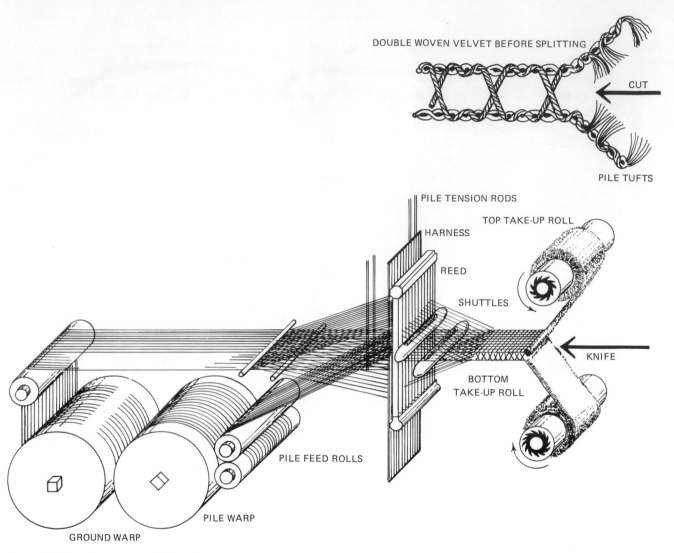

DOUBLE WOVEN VELVET BEFORE SPLITTING

CUT

PILE TUFTS

PILE TENSION RODS

TOP TAKE-UP ROLL

HARNESS

REED

SHUTTLES

KNIFE

BOTTOM TAKE-UP ROLL

PILE FEED ROLLS

PILE WARP

GROUND WARP

Figure 14-28. Construction of pile fabric by the double-cloth method. Courtesy of the Crompton Company, Inc.

OTHER THREE-DIMENSIONAL FABRICS

Chenille

Chenille fabrics have a pile that is created by the use of chenille yarns. (See Chapter 13.) The loose fiber ends that fluff up on the surface of the chenille yarn to form "caterpillars" create a soft, cut pile when woven into fabrics.

Tufted

Tufted fabrics are created by punching loops of yarn through a woven or nonwoven backing material. Handtufting is often used in "hooking" or tufting rugs. A hook is passed through the backing material, a loop is formed on the outerside of the backing, and the needle is pulled back to the wrong side, leaving the loop to form the pile on the surface of the fabric. Loops can be left uncut or cut to create a fluffy surface.

Machine-made tufted fabrics are created in much the same way as hand-tufted fabrics except that many needles punch through the fabric at the same time. A hook holds the loop in place when the needle is withdrawn. If a cut pile is being made, this hook has a small blade that cuts the loop. Tufted fabrics can be identified easily by looking at the wrong side of the fabric where parallel rows of stitches can be seen.

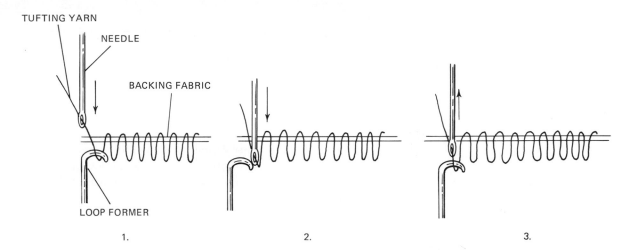

Figure 14-29. Tufting. Needle carrying tufting yarn (1) carries yarn through the backing fabric (2). A hook catches the loop, holding it in place while the needle is withdrawn (3). If a cut pile is to be made, the hook carries a blade that cuts the pile yarn.

Carpet Manufacture

Carpets are often made in pile constructions. Several major types of pile carpet construction are available to consumers. The names of the processes used for weaving carpets have become standard terminology in the carpet industry.

Wilton carpets are made on a special Wilton loom. This loom has a Jacquard attachment and can utilize up to six different colors. Patterns in Wilton carpets are woven, not printed. When yarns are not utilized in the surface design, they are carried along in the back of the carpet. This makes for a dense, strong construction. Wilton carpets of good quality are among the longest wearing machine-made domestic rugs. Piles may be cut or uncut, loops may be high or low.

Axminster carpets have the greatest versatility in machine-produced carpets in utilizing color. The loom draws pile yarns from small spools wound with yarns of various colors as they are needed for the design. The pile is a one-level, cut pile although textured effects may be attained by varying the twist or type of yarn used. Carpets made on an Axminster loom are readily identifiable because the construction produces a heavy ridge across the back of the carpet,

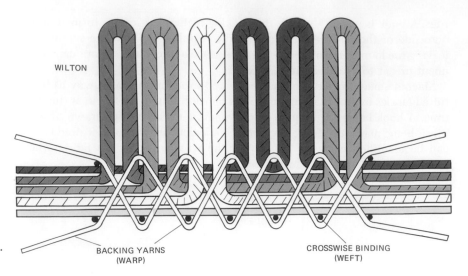

WILTON

BACKING YARNS
(WARP)

CROSSWISE BINDING
(WEFT)

Figure 14-30. Wilton carpet construction.
Courtesy of Bigelow-Sanford, Inc.

and the carpet can be rolled only in the lengthwise direction. The quality of carpets made on the Axminster loom is medium.

Velvet weave carpets should not be confused with velvet surface carpets. The term *velvet weave* refers to the construction of the carpet, the pile of which may be either cut or uncut. Simple in construction, the weave is similar to the construction of velvet fabrics. The pile is formed by wires inserted between the pile and warp yarns. The loops that are formed are held in place by the interlocking of warp yarns with the pile. The warps are, in turn, interlocked with the filling. Velvet weave carpets are usually made in solid

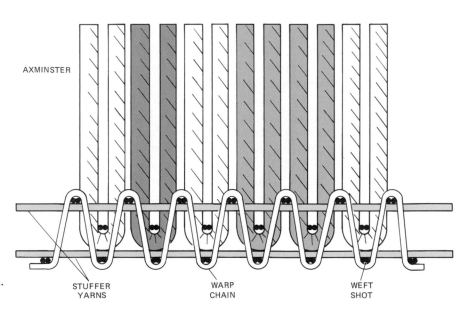

AXMINSTER

STUFFER
YARNS

WARP
CHAIN

WEFT
SHOT

Figure 14-31. Axminster carpet construction.
Courtesy of Bigelow-Sanford, Inc.

colors, but tweed effects are created by using multicolored, tweed yarns. The cost of these carpets is moderate to low.

Chenille carpets are the most expensive and the most luxurious of all machine-made carpets. They are constructed on two looms. On one loom a fabric called a chenille blanket is woven. This blanket is cut into long strips called "caterpillars," which have a fuzzy surface. A second loom weaves the strips into the carpet. These strips are used in the filling direction, and are actually sewn into place. Chenille carpet pile is cut, carpets are made in solid colors, and the pile is dense, close, and velvety in texture.

Tufted carpets are made by punching tufts of pile yarn through a woven backing of jute, heavy cotton, polypropylene, or another synthetic. The back of the carpet is given a coating of latex to hold the tufts in place. Often a second layer of backing is applied over the latex for greater stability and strength. Tufted carpets are produced rapidly, and are much less expensive to produce than woven or knitted carpets. A wide variety of effects can be created in color and textures.

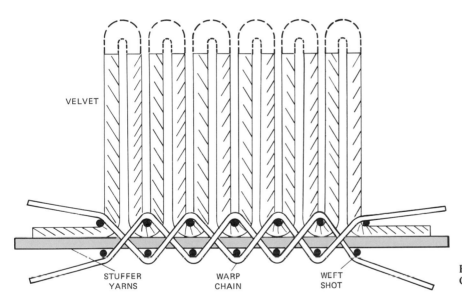

Figure 14-32. Velvet carpet construction. Courtesy of Bigelow-Sanford, Inc.

In addition to the methods of construction discussed, carpets can be made by knitting, needle punching, and flocking. These types of fabric construction are discussed in subsequent chapters.

Surface Weaves

Hand embroidery has been used for many centuries to add decoration to fabrics. With the invention of the automatic loom came the invention of looms that would create ornamental effects similar to that of embroidery.

Figure 14-33. Clipped spot design.

Figure 14-34. Closeup of dotted swiss made by the clipped spot method.

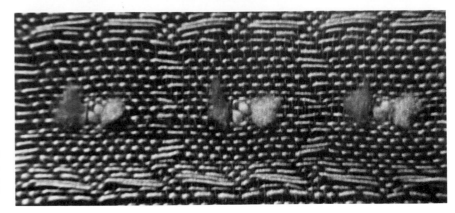

Figure 14-35. Closeup of dotted swiss made by the swivel weave. Note that in Figure 14-34, the fibers only interlace under one warp yarn, whereas in this figure the yarns appear to wrap around the warp yarns.

CLIP SPOT WEAVE

Embroiderylike designs may be achieved through the use of extra warp and extra filling yarns. In the clip spot weave, either an extra shuttle or an extra set of warp yarns interlace to create a simple woven design. The extra yarns are carried along as a float on the wrong side of the fabric when they do not appear in the design. After the cloth is completed, the long floats are generally cut away. The clipped yarns form a characteristic "eyelash" effect. Sometimes these fabrics are used inside out for design interest.

The durability of the design depends upon the closeness of the weave of the fabric into which they are woven. Domestic dotted swiss fabric is constructed by the clip spot weave. This sheer cotton fabric uses small clip spot yarns in contrasting color to create a dotted surface design.

SWIVEL WEAVE

Similar fabrics can be made in the swivel weave, which is now relatively rare. The design is made by supplying an extra filling yarn on a small shuttle or swivel. The filling design yarns are carried several times around a group of warps by the motion of the swivel to prevent the yarn from pulling out of the background fabric. The long floats between designs are knotted and clipped off. Occasionally some imported dotted swiss fabrics are found that use a swivel weave rather than a clipped spot weave. The swivel weave is more durable than the clip spot weave because the design yarns are woven in and cannot pull out of the fabric as easily as in the latter method.

LAPPET WEAVE

Lappet weave utilizes an extra warp yarn that may interlace in both the warp and filling direction with the ground fabric. The extra set of warps is threaded through needles set in front of the reed. The yarns are carried in a zigzag direction, back and forth to form an embroiderylike design. The design is created on the right side of the fabric, the excess yarn being carried along on the wrong side. Extra yarn is not clipped away from the back of the fabric, but can be seen as it is carried from one design area to another. Imported Swiss braids often utilize the lappet weave, but it is seldom found on merchandise in the United States.

Embroidery

Embroidery is not a method of constructing fabrics, but a method of decorating them. It is mentioned at this point because the effects it produces are similar to those achieved by the surface weaves discussed in the preceding section. Embroidery is often used in conjunction with appliqué.

Appliqué is the cutting of small pieces of cloth or other materials, which are then attached to the surface of a larger textile. The decoration of fabrics by appliqué is an old technique. Archeologists have identified appliqués from as early as the fifth century B.C. These very early forms were wall hangings or carpets in which the base material was felt and the designs were achieved by cutting other, smaller pieces of multicolored felt into designs that were sewn onto the larger piece of fabric.

Since appliqués are most often attached to the base fabric by hand stitches, they are often combined with embroidery. Embroidery is the use of yarns applied with a needle in a variety of stitches to form a decorative pattern. Embroidery is a skill that has been practiced by women for many centuries. The translation of writings from classical Greece includes many references to fine embroideries. The ancient Greeks considered weaving and embroidery to be fitting occupations for goddesses and noblewomen. One interesting Greek textile showing evidence of embroidery has been dated at 500 B.C., and provides some of the earliest evidence of the development of embroidery skills.

It is believed, however, that embroidery was practiced long before this date.[5]

A wide variety of different types of embroidery and embroidery stitches have been developed in all parts of the world. Each area originated a style with a distinctive repertory of stitches and decorative motifs.

One of the most famous decorated textiles ever made was created by embroidery. Called the Bayeux tapestry, this representation of the conquest of Britain by the Normans is actually a large embroidery, not a tapestry. On its 231-foot length and 20-inch width, 72 embroidered pictures show the sequence of events that led to the Battle of Hastings and the conquest of England by William the Conqueror in 1066. The embroidery, made almost 900 years ago and now discolored with age, is still displayed in the Cathedral at Bayeux, France.[6]

American embroidery forms originated in Europe, especially in England. From the general category of embroidery, a number of specialized forms have broken off to become separate art crafts. These include crewel embroidery, cross-stitch embroidery, and needlepoint.

In embroidery, a wide variety of stitches are used to outline and fill in the design. The choice of stitch is usually related to the effect the sewer wants to achieve. The yarns may be made of any fiber.

Crewel embroidery is done with crewel wool, a loosely twisted fine yarn that probably was named after the English town of Crewel. Traditional crewel embroidery uses stylized forms and a repertory of specific basic stitches.

Made of two stitches that crossed in the center to form an X, the cross-stitch is one of the simplest of the embroidery forms. In Early American times it was the first embroidery technique taught to little girls. Combinations of the X-shaped stitches were used to make samplers or to decorate all kinds of household articles.

Needlepoint embroidery covers a canvas base with thousands of tiny stitches. Queen Elizabeth I of England was said to have preferred it to all other embroideries, and in the 1920s, Alice B. Toklas, companion to the writer Gertrude Stein, made a number of needlepoint chair covers after designs created for her by Picasso. Needlepoint has its own repertory of specialized stitches that are selected according to the pattern they will make in the often complex needlepoint design.

SCHIFFLI EMBROIDERY

Schiffli embroidery machines mechanically apply embroidery to woven fabric. The embroidery is not accomplished as an integral part of the weaving process, but utilizes hundreds of needles to embroider patterns onto cloth after it is woven. Schiffli designs are often used by manufacturers in the United States and are successfully applied to a variety of fabrics of various fiber content and weave construction.

[5] A. T. B. Wace, "Weaving or Embroidery? Homeric References to Textiles," *American Journal of Archeology* (January 1948), p. 51.

[6] R. W. Lane, *Book of American Needlework* (New York: Simon and Schuster, Inc., 1963), p. 19.

Figure 14-36. Appliquéd quilt made in the United States in the mid-nineteenth century. The Metropolitan Museum of Art. Posthumous gift of Miss Eliza Polhemus Cobb (through Mrs. Arthur Bunker), 1952.

Figure 14-37. Machine-made Schiffli embroidery.

Multicomponent Fabrics

A number of fabric types are made up of several sections or segments. Only one of the processes for making multicomponent fabrics involves weaving. These fabrics may be classified as

1. interwoven fabrics.

2. quilted fabrics.

3. laminated or bonded fabrics.

INTERWOVEN FABRICS

Interwoven fabrics are also called double-cloth fabrics. They are made with either three, four, or five sets of yarns.

Double-faced fabrics are made with *three sets of yarns*. Woven either from two sets of warp yarns and one filling yarn or from two sets of filling yarns and one warp yarn, the effect of the weave is to produce the same appearance on both sides of the fabric. Some blankets and double-faced satins are examples of fabrics that are woven in this way.

Fabrics made with *four sets of yarns* use two sets of warp yarns and two sets of filling yarns. Yarns from both layers move back and forth from one layer to another, as required by the design. In some areas, the two fabrics are totally separated; in others, all four sets of yarns are interwoven. Matelasse is one fabric made by this process. The two layers of these fabrics cannot be separated without destroying the fabric. The cut edge of the fabric will show small "pockets" where fabric layers are separate. The pocket boundaries are the point at which yarn sets interchange from one side of the fabric to the other.

Fabrics with *five sets of yarns* are produced in the same way as double-woven pile fabrics. Two separate fabric layers are constructed. Extra yarns travel back and forth between the two layers to hold them together. These fabrics are often reversible, with one side being of one color and one side of another color. If the connecting yarn is cut, the two segments of the fabric can be separated into two individual pieces of cloth.

QUILTED FABRICS

Quilted fabrics have been made for centuries. A filling material (usually cotton batting, wool, or down) is sandwiched between two layers of decorative outer fabric. These layers are sewn together with strong thread in selected areas to keep the filling material from shifting about. The location of the stitches forms a padded design that might take geometric, floral, or other shapes. (See Figure 14.36.)

Many quilted fabrics are produced commercially for apparel or household use. Synthetic fiberfill has, to a large extent, replaced the natural fillers because of its easy-care aspects.

The performance of quilted fabrics is related to the closeness of the quilting stitches, the size of the stitches, the type of thread used for stitching, and the durability of the outer fabric. If stitches are spaced too far apart, the filling will shift about and become uneven. If quilting stitches are too large, stretching of the cloth will tend to break the thread. The outer fabric layer should have a firm, close, well-balanced weave. Well-balanced fabrics will have better abrasion resistance and durability. A close weave is also important if the filling is not to work its way out through the covering fabric. Down-filled comforters or quilts require the use of an inner layer of down-proof ticking, a dense, closely woven ticking fabric that prevents the escape of small bits of down.

New Techniques for Quilting

Furthermore, changes have taken place in the methods by which some quilted fabrics are produced. Instead of sewing quilted fabrics with thread, sewing may be done with heat or adhesives. Thermal or heat stitching requires that all components be thermoplastic. The heat application causes the components to fuse together in the heat-stitched areas.

Another technique used to produce raised surface patterns with layered fabrics places a layer of fabric that is not heat sensitive over fabric, foam, or fiberfill that is heat sensitive. A design is printed on the fabric with a special chemical, which holds the layers together in the printed area. The fabric is subjected to heat that causes the backing fabric to shrink, thereby producing a raised pattern on the face fabric.

LAMINATED OR BONDED FABRICS

The terms *laminated* and *bonded* have been defined by the American Society for Testing Materials as follows:

1. "bonded fabric—a layered fabric structure wherein a face or shell fabric is joined to a backing fabric, such as tricot (a knit fabric), with an adhesive that does not significantly add to the thickness of the combined fabrics."

2. "laminated fabric—a layered fabric structure wherein a face or outer fabric is joined to a continuous sheet material, such as polyurethane foam, in such a way that the identity of the continuous sheet material is retained, either by the flame method or by an adhesive, and this in turn normally, but not always, is joined on the back with a backing fabric such as tricot."

Several different methods can be used to join fabric to fabric, fabric to foam, or fabric to foam to fabric.

Fabric-to-Fabric Bonding

When two layers of fabric are joined, the purpose is to provide greater stability and body to the face fabric, or to create a self-lined fabric. The underlayer in laminated fabrics is often tricot or jersey. Knits are used because they have good flexibility and are relatively inexpensive. For the most part, fabrics used in laminating are less expensive and lower quality fabrics that can be upgraded by this process.

Two methods can be used for laminating fabric to fabric. The *wet adhesive* method places an adhesive material on the back of the face fabric and together they are passed between heated rollers that activate and set the adhesive.

The second method is known as the *foam-flame* process. A thin layer of polyurethane foam is melted slightly by passing it over a flame. The two layers of fabric are sandwiched around the foam, which then dries, forming the bond between the two layers of fabric. Ideally, the layer of foam that is used should be so thin that it virtually disappears. (The foam in the finished fabric is about 1/100th of an inch thick.) The foam does, however, add body to the fabric and produces a somewhat stiffer fabric than the wet adhesive method. It is preferable that the foam method not be used with open-weave fabrics because of the possibility that some of the foam may appear on the surface of the fabric.

Fabric-to-Foam Lamination

Fabrics are laminated to polyurethane foam when it is desirable to provide some degree of insulation. Winter coats and sportswear, for example, are made from these fabrics. The foam-flame process can be used to manufacture such fabrics. A thick layer of foam is utilized. Only one side of the foam, that to which the fabric attaches, must be heated. Still another foam process flows the sticky foam onto the fabric, cures the fabric, and causes the foam to solidify and adhere to the fabric at the same time.

When laminates first entered the retail market, customers found wide

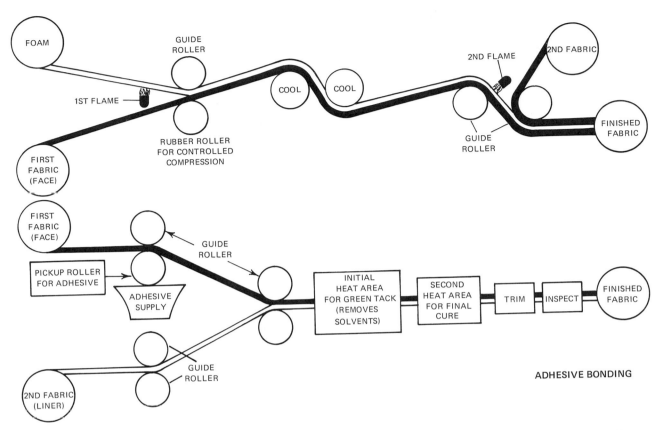

FLAME-FOAM BONDING

ADHESIVE BONDING

Figure 14-38. Flame foam and adhesive bonding. Courtesy of Celanese Corporation.

variation in the permanence of the binding. Some fabrics separated during laundering, others separated during dry cleaning, and still others separated during use. Often the backing and face fabrics shrunk unevenly, causing wrinkling and puckering. Today many of these problems have been overcome. Although laminated fabrics of varying quality are still sold, many of these fabrics are labeled with guarantees of serviceability. The label term Certifab guarantees bonding and dimensional stability in dry cleaning or laundering for one year. Celabond is the same guarantee, but is applied to fabrics laminated with certain acetates.

Although most of the fabrics used for clothing, for the home, and for industry are made either by traditional weaving, tufting, or knitting methods, research into, and development of, new methods for constructing fabrics is constantly in progress. Several recent methods of fabric construction that are related to knitting are discussed in Chapter 15. There is, however, another method of constructing fabrics that is closely related to traditional weaving and it is known as triaxial weaving. The term is derived from *tri-* meaning "three" and

Triaxially Woven Fabrics

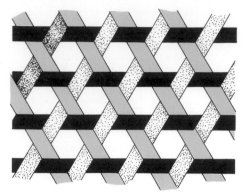

Figure 14-39. Triaxial fabric structure.

axial, meaning "of or pertaining to the axis or center line." In other words, triaxial fabrics have three axes or center lines. Traditionally woven fabrics have a biaxial form, or two axes, the lengthwise and cross wise axes.[7]

Triaxial fabrics can be woven by modifying the standard weaving procedure in one of two ways: one set of lengthwise yarns can be interlaced with two sets of crosswise yarns or two sets of lengthwise yarns interlace with one set of crosswise yarns. The latter method, two warp yarns with one filling yarn, is most often used.

Special cams in the loom manipulate the yarns so that the double set of yarns (either warp or filling) is carried in a diagonal direction. All three sets of yarns interlace.

Triaxial weaves are not entirely new. The construction of snowshoes and some forms of basket work sometimes utilize a triaxial construction. Mass-produced fabrics have not, however, been made in a triaxial weave. The trademark Doweave has been registered to refer to such constructions. The major advantage of triaxial weaving is in its stability not only in the length and crosswise directions but also in the bias. Biaxially woven fabrics have no stability in the bias direction. The research and development of triaxial fabrics was initiated in an attempt to produce fabrics of increased stability for use in the aerospace industry.

Recommended References

ALBERS, A. *On Weaving.* Middletown, Conn.: Wesleyan University Press, 1965.

BUHLER, K. "Basic Textile Techniques." *CIBA Review.* January 1948, p. 2297 ff.

DONEGAN, J. H., Jr. "Which Weaving Machine?" *Textile World.* August 1973, p. 9.

D'HARCOURT, R. *Textiles of Ancient Peru and Their Techniques.* Seattle: University of Washington Press, 1962.

EMERY, I. *The Primary Structure of Fabrics.* Washington, D.C.: The Textile Museum, 1966.

Encyclopedia of Textiles, American Fabrics. Englewood Cliffs, N.J.: Prentice-Hall, Inc., 2nd Ed., 1972.

"Evolution of Mills and Factories." *CIBA Review.* 1968, vol. 1.

Handbook on Bonded and Laminated Fabrics. American Association of Textile Chemists and Colorists, Triangle Park, North Carolina, 1974.

KELLER, A. "New and Further Developments in Shuttleless Weaving Machinery." *International Textile Bulletin,* #2, 1975, p. 105.

LORD, P. R., and M. H. Mohamed. *Weaving: Conversion of Yarn to Fabric.* Watford, England: Merrow Publishing Company, Ltd., 1973.

McNEIRNEY, F. "Advances in Weaving." *Modern Textiles,* February 1976, p. 10.

REGENSTEINER, E. *The Art of Weaving.* New York: Van Nostrand-Reinhold Co., 1970.

ROBINSON, A. T. C., and R. MARKS. *Woven Cloth Construction.* London: Butterworth & Co., 1967.

SKELTON, J. "Triaxially Woven Fabrics: Their Structure and Properties." *Textile Research Journal,* August 1971, p. 637.

"Shuttle-less Keys Weaving Comback." *Textile World,* February 1974, p. 51.

"The Woven Story, U.S.A." *American Fabrics & Fashions.* Fall 1973, p. 39 ff.

[7] J. Skelton, "Triaxially Woven Fabrics," *Textile Research Journal* (August 1971), p. 637 ff.

15
KNITTED FABRICS

Few segments of the textile industry have grown so rapidly in recent years as has the knitting industry. Advances in knitting production techniques along with the use of synthetic fibers, such as acrylics and polyesters, for knit goods have led to the manufacture of knitted items ranging from men's tailored suits to upholstery.

The knitting industry may be divided into four branches: knitted outerwear, knitted yard goods, knitted hosiery, and knitted underwear. Knitted yard goods mills produce a wide variety of fabrics in either flat or circular form that can be cut and sewn into apparel and other items. Those mills that produce outerwear, hosiery, or underwear may knit the item directly or may knit sections of a garment (such as sleeves, body sections, and the like) that are sewn, or cut and sewn, together. These mills complete the garment from knitting right through to construction in the same mill.

Historical Development of Knits

Although the earliest known fragment of knitted cloth dates from the fourth century A.D., hand knitting apparently came to Europe from the Middle East during the medieval period. Apparently the Arab conquerors of Spain imported the technique of knitting from their homeland sometime after A.D. 1000. Knitting spread gradually to the rest of Europe. Because knits were more elastic than woven goods, they quickly gained popularity, especially for making stockings and gloves.

Today one thinks of hand knitting as a process that uses two or more knitting needles, but the earliest hand knitting was done not on needles but on a frame into which a series of pegs had been set. Yarn was looped around each peg. To make the stitches, the knitter pulled a new loop of yarn through the old loop encircling the peg, slipped the old loop off the peg, and placed the new loop around the peg. This was done with a hooked needle. Eventually, a long, pointed knitting needle, such as those used today, replaced the pegs for holding the loops and a second needle replaced the hook for adding and subtracting loops.

The use of two needles or of the knitting frame made a flat fabric. A round tube of fabric could be made by using a circular needle, a round frame, or a set of four needles.

Figure 15-1. Knitted cap made in Italy in the seventeenth century. Courtesy of the Metropolitan Museum of Art, Rogers Fund, 1927.

Since the knitting process was relatively simple, it lent itself to mechanization somewhat more easily than weaving. By the late 1500s a knitting frame machine had been invented by William Lee. This machine made mechanically all of the kinds of knits that had previously been made by hand. Lee's machine continued in use until further refinements of machine knitting were made during the industrial revolution.

Machines for Knitting

"Knitting is the process of making cloth with a single yarn or set of yarns moving in only one direction. Instead of two sets of yarns crossing each other as in weaving, the single knitting yarn is looped through itself to make a chain of stitches. These chains or rows are connected side by side to produce the knit cloth."[1] The interlocking of these loops in knitting can be done by either vertical or horizontal movement. When yarns run or interlock across the fabric, the knit is known as a *filling knit*. When yarns run lengthwise or up and down the fabric, the knit is known as a *warp knit*.

Both warp and filling knits are made by machine. There are two basic types of knitting machines: the flat type and the circular type. The flat type knitting machine has needles arranged in a straight line and held on a flat needle bed. The cloth is made by forming stitches on these needles. The resulting fabric is flat. Machines with flat beds are used to make both warp and filling knits.

[1]*Encyclopedia of Textiles, American Fabrics* (Englewood Cliffs, N.J.: Prentice-Hall, Inc., 1972), p. 415.

The circular knitting machine has needles arranged in a circle on a rotating cylinder. The resulting fabric is formed into a tube. Circular knitting machines produce filling knits almost exclusively.

For nearly 200 years after its invention in 1589, Lee's machine was used without further improvement. Using a "spring beard needle," Lee's machine produced flat knitted fabrics by mechanically passing one loop of yarn through another.

LOOP FORMATION

The spring beard needle is formed from one piece of thin wire. (See diagram.) One end of the needle is drawn into thinner dimensions and curved to form a

Figure 15-2. Circular Morat knitting machine. The yarn is held on the spools at the top of the machine. The completed fabric can be seen emerging in tubular form at the bottom of the machine. Courtesy of Sultzer Brothers, Inc.

hook. The flexible outer side of the hook can be pressed against the stem of the needle to close the hook. The loops are formed as follows:

1. The old loop is held on the stem of the needle below the hook. (A)

2. A new loop is formed around the outside of the hooked section of the needle. (B)

3. The needle rises, dropping the new thread to the stem. (C)

4. The needle falls again to bring the new thread into the hook. (D)

5. At the same time a presser comes in, closing the hook so that the old thread is held outside the hook. (D)

6. The needle falls further, sliding the old loop off the needle. The new loop is now held inside the hook. (E)

7. The needle is now ready to repeat the cycle. (F)

In 1847, Matthew Townshend invented a different type of hook known as the *latch needle.* Its operation is similar to that of the spring beard needle, except that instead of having to mechanically press the flexible wire of the needle

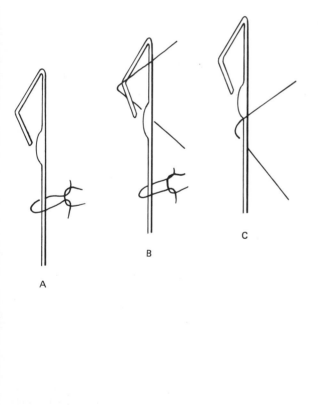

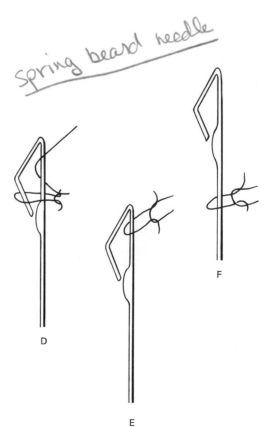

spring beard needle

Figure 15-3. Formation of a loop by a spring beard needle.

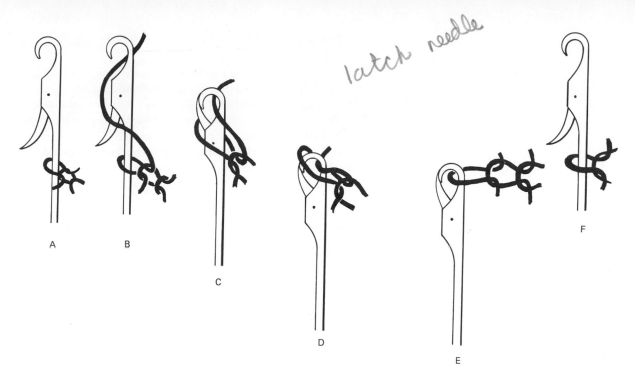

latch needle

Figure 15-4. Formation of a loop by a latch needle.

closed so that the new yarn loop will not slide off, a latch closes to hold the yarn in place. The steps in the cycle of the latch needle are

1. The old loop is held on the stem of the needle. The latch is open. (A)

2. A new loop is formed around the hook of the needle. (B)

3. The needle falls, the old loop rises, closing the latch of the needle. (C)

4. The old loop is cast off, (D and E), the latch opens, the needle rises, and the new loop slides down to the stem of the needle. (F)

The needle is now ready to repeat the cycle.

In knitting terminology the rows of stitches that run in vertical columns along the lengthwise direction of the fabric are known as *wales.* This corresponds to the warp direction of woven fabrics. Crosswise rows of stitches or loops are called *courses*. The direction of the courses corresponds to the filling of woven goods.

The size of the needle and the spacing of the needles on knitting machines determine the size of the knit stitches and their closeness. The closeness of the stitches determines whether a knit fabric will be lightweight and open or heavier and more dense. The term *gauge* is used to describe the closeness of knit stitches. Gauge is the number of needles in a measured space on the knitting machine. Higher gauge fabrics (those with more stitches) are made with finer needles; lower gauge fabrics are made with coarser or larger needles.

The term *cut* is also used to designate the number of needles per inch in the needle bed of a circular filling knitting machine. To describe the stitch density of a single- or double-knit fabric, the fabric may be designated as an 18-, 20-,

KNOW THIS

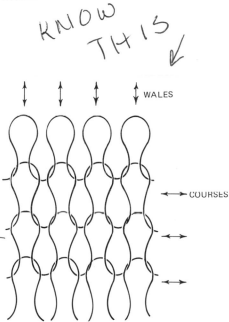

Figure 15-5. Rows of stitches that run in a vertical column along the lengthwise direction of the fabric are called wales; crosswise rows of stitches or loops are called courses.

22-, or 24-cut material. The higher the cut, the closer are the stitches; the lower the cut, the coarser is the fabric.

Varying types of knitting machines measure gauge over different distances on the machine. For example, circular knit hosiery measures the number of needles in 1 inch, full-fashioned knitting in 1.5 inches, and raschel knits in two inches. Because of these differences it is best to keep in mind the generalized principle that the higher the gauge, the closer are the stitches.

The quality of needles used in manufacturing knit goods is directly related to the quality of the fabric produced. Needles of uneven size and quality will produce knit fabrics with uneven-sized stitches and imperfect surface appearance.

In *warp knits*, those knits in which the yarns interlace vertically, one or more yarns are allotted to each needle on the machine, and those yarns follow the vertical direction of the fabric. For filling or *weft knits*, those in which the yarns interlace horizontally, one or more yarns are utilized for each course and these yarns move horizontally across the fabric. In weft knits, one yarn may have from twenty to several hundred needles associated with it.

Filling or Weft Knits

Filling or weft knits are created on any of the following basic knit machines:

1. Flat or circular jersey or single knit machine.
2. Flat or circular rib machine.
3. Flat or circular purl or links-links machine.

JERSEY OR SINGLE KNIT MACHINE

Jersey or single knit machines produce a smooth fabric with wales on the right side of the fabric and courses on the wrong side. The loops formed by the jersey machine are formed in one direction only (see diagram), which gives a different appearance to each side of the fabric. The basic fabric produced by this machine is known as a *plain*, *single knit*, or *jersey*.

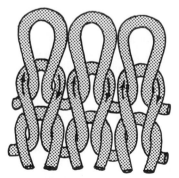

TECHNICAL FACE

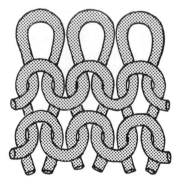

TECHNICAL BACK

Figure 15-6. Plain or jersey knit stitch. Courtesy of the National Knitwear Manufacturers Association.

Plain, single knit, or jersey stretches equally in both the lengthwise and crosswise directions. If one stitch breaks, the fabric may ladder or "run." A great many items of hosiery, sweaters, and other wearing apparel are made in the plain knit. Jersey fabrics tend to curl at the edges and are less stable than some other types of knits. This is the result of the pressures exerted during knitting. Special finishing techniques are used to overcome these tendencies and maintain fiber stability; the principal ones use starches, gum mixtures, polyvinyl acetate emulsions, and resins.

In addition to knitting plain or jersey fabrics, jersey machines can be used to make a number of variations of the jersey construction. These include pile fabrics, knitted terry and velour, full-fashioned, and plated fabrics.

High Pile Fabric

High pile fabrics, such as imitation furs and plushes, are usually knitted, utilizing a jersey machine. While the knitting is taking place, a sliver of staple fiber is fed into the machine. These fibers are caught in the tight knit and held firmly in place. Although any staple fiber can be used for the pile, the greatest quantity of these fabrics are made with acrylic and modacrylic fibers in the pile.

By using staple fabrics of varying lengths, adding color through fiber dyeing or printing on the surface of the pile, and by shearing or brushing the pile, an enormous variety of effects can be achieved. The use of knitted pile fabric ranges from excellent imitations of furs, such as leopard, tiger, mink or mouton, to colorful pile outerwear, coat linings, or pile carpet fabrics.

Knitted Terry and Velour

Jersey knits can also be utilized in the production of knitted terry fabrics and knitted velours. Two yarns are fed into the machine simultaneously, picked up by the same needle, and knitted in such a way that one of the yarns appears on the face of the fabric, the other on the back. The yarn that forms the terry is pulled up to the surface of the fabric. If the pile remains uncut, the resulting cloth is like a one-sided terry cloth. If the pile is cut, the fabric is called *velour*.

Terry fabrics made by this process are not as durable as woven terry cloth, nor do they hold their shape as well. On the other hand, they have softer draping qualities. The knitted velours are softer and more flexible than woven pile fabrics, such as velveteen. Major uses for both fabrics are for sports and loungewear, for infants' and children's clothing, and for household items such as towels and slipcovers.

Full-fashioned Knits

Weft knits can be made on either flat or circular knitting machines. In hosiery and sweaters the item itself or sections of the item are made on specialized knitting machines. When sweaters or stockings are knitted, the shape may be incorporated by increasing or decreasing the number of stitches.

Knitting is the generic name given to the many systems of fabrication characterized by looping of threads. in contrast to other systems such as weaving on felt. Also may be completing whole complet garment.

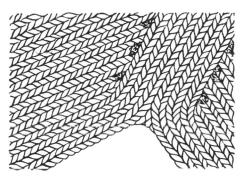

FASHION MARKS

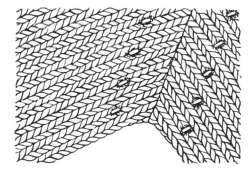

MOCK FASHION MARKS

Figure 15-7. Fashion marks contrasted with mock fashion marks. Courtesy of E. I. du Pont de Nemours & Company.

Where stitches have been dropped or added, *fashion marks* appear. Fashion marks—small alterations in the surface caused by the shifting of the needles and the change in position of the yarns—are an indication of better quality in that the consumer can be sure that the shaping of the garment is permanent. Items made in this way are referred to as "full-fashioned." Some manufacturers will create mock fashion marks to give the appearance of better quality. A careful examination of the area will show that in a true full-fashioned item the number and direction of stitches change. In mock fashion marks, this does not occur. Mock fashion marks are usually produced by embroidery and have a long yarn float on the wrong side between "marks." (See Figure 15.7.)

Plated Fabrics

In creating plated fabrics, the knitting machine feeds two separate yarns at the same time. By varying the color, texture, or type of yarn, interesting decorative effects can be achieved. It is also possible to utilize one yarn as the face yarn, and another as a backing yarn. Using an expensive face yarn with an inexpensive backing yarn can help to keep the cost of the fabric at a lower level. Plating varies from relatively simple construction to very intricate pattern designs.

RIB KNIT MACHINES

The machine used to produce rib knits is different from the machine used for plain knits in that it has two needle-holding beds located opposite each other. The fabric is actually created between the two sets of needles.

"A rib knit fabric is characterized by lengthwise ribs formed by wales alternating on the face and back of the cloth. If every other wale alternates from front to back, it is called a 1 x 1 rib. If every two wales alternate, it is called a 2 x 2 rib."[2] The larger the number of wales that alternate, the more pronounced the rib will be. A 1 x 1 rib made in a fine gauge may hardly be visible to the eye. Fabrics may appear to be a jersey on both sides.

Rib knits have greater elasticity in the width than in the length. They are stable, and do not curl or stretch out of shape as do the jersey knits.

Double Knits

Double knit is not a standard technical term, but has come into wide use to describe "any of the numerous fine rib knits that appear to have been knitted twice. The effect is produced by two-needle construction."[3] Wales show clearly on both sides of the fabric, giving fabrics a similar appearance on both sides.

Double knits are made on a rib knitting machine and on a variant of the rib knitting machine, the interlock machine, that utilizes one long and one short

[2] Ibid., p. 354.
[3] Ibid., p. 369.

1 X 1 RIB FABRIC

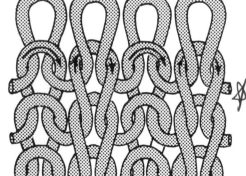

Figure 15-8. 1 x 1 rib fabric structure. Courtesy of National Knitwear Manufacturers Association.

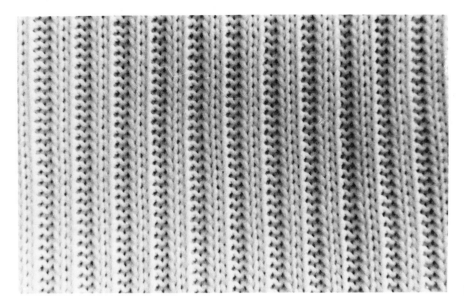

needle to make one knit stitch behind another. The resulting fabric is firmer and thicker than the usual rib knit. It is also more stable in the width direction.

Twice as much yarn is incorporated into the double knit fabric as into comparable single knits. The resulting fabrics are more stable than plain knits, have excellent draping qualities, and are easier for the home sewer to handle. Large quantities of double knits have been made in textured synthetic yarns, and double knits are widely used for easy-care clothing for men, women, and children. The home furnishings industry is beginning to utilize substantial amounts of double knit fabrics for upholstery, as well.

PURL OR LINKS-LINKS MACHINE

The purl or links-links machine draws every other course to the opposite side of the fabric, thereby producing a fabric with the same appearance on both sides. The raised courses produce a somewhat uneven surface texture.

The name *links-links* is given to the machine because the machine moves only to the left. *Links* is the German word for "left."

The links-links machine operates somewhat more slowly than other knitting machines, causing the price of purl fabrics to be higher than those of other knits. The machine has a latch-type knitting needle with a hook on either end. This makes possible the construction of stitches on alternate sides of the fabric. The double needle arrangement makes this the most versatile of the weft knitting machines, as it can make plain, purl, or rib knits.

Purl knit fabrics are often made into a wide variety of decorative sweaters. Interesting textures can be achieved by the use of fluffy, soft yarns. The versatility of the machine makes possible the creation of a variety of patterns in these knits.

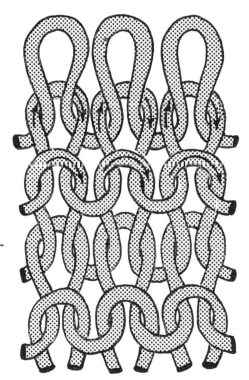

Figure 15-10. Purl knit structure. Courtesy of the National Knitwear Manufacturers Association.

WEFT KNIT STITCH VARIATION

Variations in surface texture of weft knits can be achieved through the use of special stitches such as the *tuck stitch* or the *lace stitch*.

The tuck stitch is made by programming certain needles to hold both an old loop and a new yarn without looping off the old stitch. This creates an elongated stitch, which appears in the fabric as a variation in the surface pattern. In the miss stitch, some needles are immobilized, and instead of catching the stitch they allow the yarn to be carried across the back of the fabric. Lace stitches drop or remove loops in certain areas of the fabric in order to create an open pattern. Combinations of the tuck, miss, and lace stitches with basic rib, plain, or purl knit stitches can create such varied effects as raised cables, open work alternating with plain knit, and a wide range of other decorative fabrics.

Warp Knits

warp insersion
`improve stability

In warp knitting each yarn is knitted by one needle. The needle bar that carries the needles moves sideways as well as up and down so that the yarns are carried both vertically and, to a limited extent, diagonally. This diagonal motion is needed to assure that the yarns interlace not only with the stitch directly below but also with stitches to the side. If the yarn interlaced only vertically, there would be no point at which each individual chain of stitches was attached to its neighboring chain.

This construction provides resistance to laddering or running, since each stitch is most directly connected not with the stitch beneath but also with a stitch placed diagonally and lower. In forming the stitch, diagonal underlay moves the yarn from loop to loop. (See Figure 15.11.)

Several types of warp knits are made on a number of different warp knitting machines.

TRICOT

Tricot machines account for the largest quantity of warp knits. Tricot fabric is knit flat. On the right side the wales create the appearance of a fine, lengthwise line. On the wrong side, crosswise ribs appear in a horizontal position.

In the manufacture of tricot, a guide bar moves the yarns from side to side. The tricot machines may have from one to four guide bars. The greater the number of bars, the greater is the distance the yarn moves between stitches. In moving from one placement to the next, underlay yarns are carried across the back of the fabric. This extra yarn creates heavier weight fabrics.

Tricot fabrics are identified as one-bar, two-bar, three-bar, or four-bar, depending on the number of guide bars used in their manufacture. One-bar or single-bar tricot is relatively unstable and is seldom used for garments. It is, however, used as backing for some bonded fabrics. It will run, because the loops interlace close together. Two-bar tricot is stable and fairly light in weight, and is used extensively in lingerie, blouses, and the like. Three and

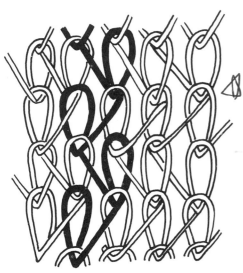

Figure 15-11. Construction of the simplest single guide bar tricot fabric. Darker area shows how one yarn is carried through the fabric.

four-bar tricots are used for dresses and menswear, and are heavier than two-bar tricot.

In addition to the basic tricot fabric, a number of variations can be made. A tricot satin is produced by allowing yarns to float further across the surface of the fabric before they interlace. Other textured tricots known as "brushed tricots" are made with a raised, napped surface or with a small loop. The fabric as knitted is smooth on both sides. The surface effects are achieved during finishing when the fabric is passed through a special machine equipped with wire rollers that either pull loops to the surface of the fabric or break some of the filaments to give a "brushed" or soft, napped surface. Brushed or looped tricot fabrics are made with long underlaps that form the pile or loops.

Three- and four-bar tricot constructions permit the carrying of hidden yarns through the fabric. Monofilaments that stabilize the fabric or spandex filaments for stretch may be concealed in the complex structure of the tricot fabric.

Tricot fabrics can be made with a variety of open weave effects to create interesting lacelike patterns, as well.

RASCHEL KNITS

Raschel knitting machines are capable of enormous variation in construction. Raschel machines may have from two to forty-eight guide bars. The knits made on this machine range from fine, knitted laces to heavy-duty fabrics. Elaborately patterned surface effects can also be achieved with the Raschel loom. Raschel fabrics may be knitted flat or tubular, although most are knitted flat. The versatility of this knitting machine makes it possible to knit fabrics that, to the eye, have the appearance of woven goods or lace.

Among the most popular types of Raschel fabrics are powernet or elastomeric yarns for foundation garments and swimsuits; thermal cloth for cold-weather underwear; lace; netting; carpet; and tailored menswear fabrics. One of the parts of the Raschel machine that makes these variations possible is a special mechanism called a *fall plate*. In the normal knit-stitch formation, the needle moves up and down, looping yarns on and off the needle to form a continuous chain. In the Raschel fall plate mechanism, a plate is lowered between two guide bars. This plate prevents the yarn that is held behind it from forming a normal loop. Instead, the yarn is carried along in the fabric in a horizontal or diagonal direction. In some fabrics this technique is used to simulate the effect of embroidery, in others it gives a woven appearance to the fabrics.

SIMPLEX KNITS

Simplex knitting machines create warp knits similar to tricot, but with a more dense, thicker texture; a sort of double-knit tricot. Simplex knits are used in products requiring heavier fabrics, such as women's gloves, handbags, and simulated suede-textured apparel fabrics.

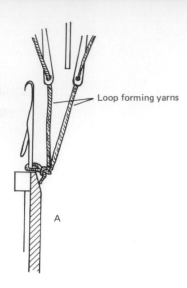

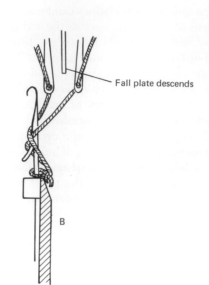

Loop forming yarns

Fall plate descends

A

B

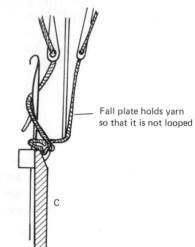

Fall plate holds yarn
so that it is not looped

C

Figure 15-12. Raschel fall plate and knitted structures made with fall plate. Reprinted by permission National Knitted Outerwear Association.

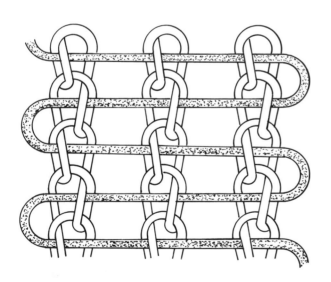

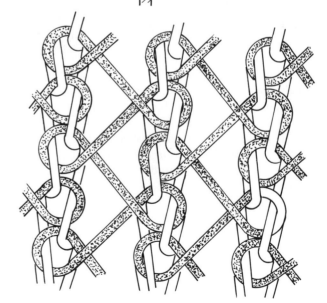

Fall plate fabrics, shown in stippled rendition

MILANESE KNITS

Milanese knitting machines knit fabrics that are used for many of the same items as tricots, but at higher price ranges. Milanese fabrics have a fine, riblike structure on the face and a diagonal rib on the back. They are similar in weight to a two-bar tricot, and are run-proof. Milanese knits are knit flat, but tubular variations of this construction can be made on a special machine, the *Marriati* knitting machine.

CIDEGA KNITS

Cidega knitting machines produce curtain fabrics in open work patterns. They are also used to produce rug-type fabrics.

CREATING PATTERN AND DESIGN IN KNITTED GOODS

Like woven fabrics, plain-colored knits can be made from fibers or yarns that have been colored, or the finished goods can be dyed. Patterns can be created by printing on the fabric. Other designs can be achieved through the manipulation of multicolored yarns.

Weft knits are easily knitted into stripes. These stripes always run across the fabric, since the pattern is achieved through varying the colors of the yarns in the different courses. Since the yarns interlace horizontally, it is not possible to knit a vertical stripe in weft single knits.

A Jacquard attachment for filling knit machines makes possible the knitting of a wide variety of patterned fabrics. Like woven Jacquard patterns, Jacquard knit designs are plotted on paper, and then transferred to the Jacquard mechanism where the machine automatically activates the appropriate needles and colored yarns.

The structure of patterns in warp knitting is determined by a system known as the *link-chain* system. Chains with links of variable heights control the movement of the guide bars. The height of the link transfers a motion to the guide bars. The guide bars set the yarn in position over a group of needles in order to form the pattern.

PERFORMANCE AND CARE OF KNITTED FABRICS

Although there is a great variety in the quality of knitted goods sold, and the performance of any individual knit may differ markedly from that of other knits, some general guidelines for the care of knitted goods can be observed. The problems that consumers seem to encounter most often in the performance of knitted fabrics are in the areas of dimensional stability, pilling, and snagging.

Dimensional Stability

One of the reasons that knits are popular for wearing apparel is their comfort. The looped construction of knit fabrics permits the fabric to give with the body as it moves. But the stretchiness of knits also results in lessened dimensional stability. Consumers have complained about shrinkage, stretching, and distortion of knits.

Shrinkage-control treatments, heat setting of synthetics, and special resin finishes can provide good dimensional stability for knits. Unfortunately not all manufacturers provide such treatment for their products. Consumers should check labels for percentage of shrinkage or for other special treatments in order to judge potential dimensional stability. (About 3 per cent shrinkage is a garment size.) If products fail to live up to specified performance standards, items should be returned to the retailer or the manufacturer.

Knits are considered to be easy-care fabrics, and many care labels recommend machine washing. Some labels will also specify that the fabric can be dried in an automatic dryer. In general, however, knits will shrink more in the dryer than if air dried. Knits maintain their shape best if they are dried flat. The weight of a wet knit, hung on a line, may cause the fabric to stretch out of shape.

The dimensions of knits usually will be retained best by professional dry cleaning. Coin-operated dry cleaning appears to offer no particular advantage over home laundering for double knit items that could be either washed or dry-cleaned, as one research study has shown that double knits cleaned in a coin-operated dry-cleaning machine also shrink more than 3 per cent with repeated cleaning. Depending on fiber content, both methods produced substantial shrinkage.[4] Shrinkage in coin-operated dry cleaning is a result of the tumbling action of the machine.

Hand knits, sweaters of wool or animal hair fiber, and other knits with a very open construction may require special hand laundering and blocking (stretching back into shape). Such items should be laid on a sheet of wrapping paper prior to washing, and the outlines traced. After washing, the garment should be stretched out on the paper to dry. While still damp, the garment should be gently stretched to fit the outline of the original dimensions.

In general, knits made of synthetics will have better resistance to stretching out of shape than will cotton, acetates, and rayons. Blending of synthetics with cottons, acetates, and rayons will improve the resiliency and dimensional stability of knitted fabrics made from these fibers. Price is a good guide—especially for children's knits.

Mechanical Damage

The loop structure of knitted fabrics makes them especially susceptible to snagging. If a loop catches on another object, it may be pulled up from the fabric surface and a long snag or pull of yarn may be formed. If the yarn that

---

[4] *Today's Knitwear*, Technical Bulletin, Textile Research Laboratory, Ohio State University, Columbus, Ohio, August 1972.

has been snagged is not broken, it can be pulled to the back of the fabric. It may be possible to gently stretch the fabric and work the pulled yarn back into place. This is difficult to do with very tightly knitted fabric structures.

If the yarn has been broken, the snag may produce a hole in the fabric. A few hand stitches with needle and matching thread should be made to secure the yarns so that the hole does not become enlarged during wearing or laundering.

Synthetic double knits or knits made from loosely twisted yarns may be subject to pilling. As the fabric is subjected to abrasion during wear, the short fiber ends that work their way to the fabric surface are rubbed into a small ball that hangs onto the fabric surface. When fibers are weak, as in cotton, rayon, acetates, wools, and the like, these fibers generally break off the fabric. But the stronger synthetic fibers cling to the fabric, making an unsightly area on the fabric surface. The use of textured yarns for knitting synthetics decreases the likelihood of pilling.

Knits may be damaged by sharp objects puncturing the fabric. If yarns are cut, a hole will result and further pressure and strain on the fabric may enlarge the open area.

Combination Knit and Weave Constructions

The combination of knitting and weaving techniques in the construction of fabrics has been used to create fabrics with greater dimension stability than conventional knits, but with some of the economy of manufacture and aesthetics of knitted goods.

CO-WE-NIT

Raschel knit construction allows the carrying of yarns across the fabric for some distance. A further modification of this process has been devised. Called Co-We-Nit (from *combined weaving and knitting*), the process inserts both warp and filling yarns into a knit structure. The knitted stitch holds the fabric together. Knitted chains move vertically up the fabric. Between the chains of knit stitches, warp yarns are laid in. A third set of yarns crosses from knit chain to knit chain, interweaving with the warps. These yarns simulate the filling of a woven fabric, although they do not actually cross the entire fabric.[5]

WEFT INSERTION

A second knit-weave process is that of weft-insertion. Here the weft yarn crosses the entire width of the fabric being woven on a warp knitting machine. When the fabric is viewed from the back side, one can see that the weft always passes under the underlap of the knit stitch and over the loops.

Weft yarns can be inserted in a Raschel machine by using a single yarn

see diagram on next page

[5] C. Reichman, ed., *Knitting Encyclopedia* (New York: National Knitted Outerwear Association, 1972), p. 83.

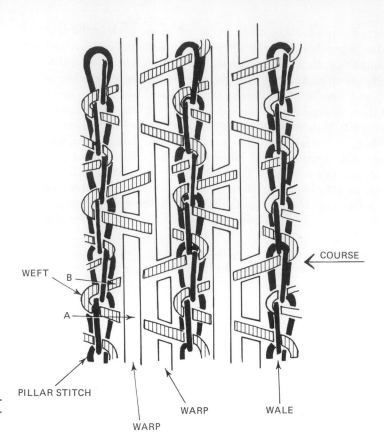

Figure 15-13. Co-We-Nit fabric structure. Reprinted by permission of National Knitted Outerwear Association.

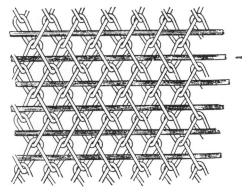

Figure 15-14. Structure of weft insertion fabric. Reprinted by permission National Knitted Outerwear Association.

carried back and forth across the fabric. This is a relatively slow process. High-speed machinery is also available in which multiple yarns are fed to the knitting elements of the machine.

Weft-insertion fabrics have the advantage of increased stability in the filling direction. When large diameter yarns are inserted, they provide increased cover and a fuller, bulkier texture than ordinary knitted goods.

WARP INSERTION

Filling knits may utilize a similar principle by laying lengthwise or warp yarns into the fabric construction. Warp yarns are fed into the machine along with the knitting yarns. Interlacing takes place in alternate rows, as filling loops cross over and under the laid-in warp yarns.

The term *laying in* is often used in knitting industries to refer to warp-insertion fabrics. Single knit (jersey) machines can accomplish this procedure fairly easily by laying-in yarns that are either too large for the needles to manipulate or by placing yarns in positions whereby they cannot be worked into the knit stitch by normal yarn paths or channels.

Such fabrics are more stable in the vertical direction but have the horizontal stretch of conventional knits. Yarns may also be laid-in to change the texture or pattern of the fabric. The Veev machine is a warp-insertion knitting machine.

Recommended References

"Computer Design: Rembrandt with a Spray Gun." *American Fabrics and Fashions,* Winter 1973, p. 64.

Encyclopedia of Textiles, American Fabrics. Englewood Cliffs, N.J.: Prentice-Hall, Inc., 1972.

"Knits: A Revolution That Succeeded." *American Fabrics and Fashions.* Fall 1971, p. 35. ff.

"New Fabric Combines Knitting and Weaving." *Modern Knitting Management,* May, 1970.

"A Primer on Knits for Tailored Menswear." *American Fabrics and Fashions.* Summer 1971, p. 63.

C. REICHMAN, ed., *Knitting Encyclopedia.* New York: National Knitted Outerwear Association, 1972.

PIZZUTO, J. *Fabric Science.* New York: Fairchild Publications, Inc., 1974.

SINGER et al., ed., *A History of Technology,* vol. III. Oxford: Clarendon Press, 1957, 181 ff.

THOMAS, D. G. B. *An Introduction to Warp Knitting.* Watford, Herts, England: Merrow Publishing Company, Ltd., 1971.

Today's Knitwear. Technical Bulletin, Textile Research Laboratory, Ohio State University, Columbus, Ohio. August 1972.

TURTON, W. "Weft Insertion: Its Place in Today's Manufacture of Fabric." *Modern Textiles,* June 1975, p. 35.

"Warp Knit Boom." *American Fabrics and Fashions,* Spring 1972, p. 35.

"Weft Insertion: The Best of Both Worlds." *American Fabrics and Fashions,* Winter 1973, p. 65.

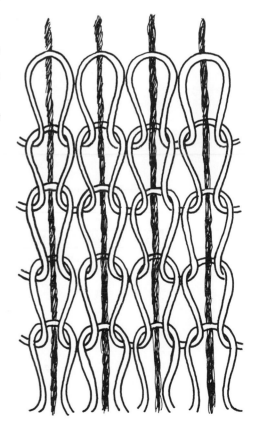

Figure 15-15. Structure of a warp insertion knit fabric.

16

OTHER METHODS OF FABRIC CONSTRUCTION

Although woven and knitted goods make up the largest quantity of fabrics produced, a variety of other construction methods are also used for the fabrication of textiles. Many of these techniques derive from processes utilized since prehistoric times, others have been developed more recently, still others are the result of new technology within the textile industry.

The fabrication methods discussed in this chapter may be divided into several broad classifications: fabrics made by knotting, by looping, by stitching yarns or fibers together, and by bonding together a web of fibers. Netting, macramé, and lace are created by knotting, either by hand or by machine. Crochet, essentially a hand technique, is made from a series of loops in a process that is somewhat similar to knitting. A new fabric construction technique, known either as stitch bonding or stitch knitting, combines yarns and/or fibers by sewing them together. Ancient techniques such as felt making or bark-cloth construction are similar in principle to the manufacture of modern nonwovens, fibers held together in a flexible web.

Nets, Macramé and Lace

NETS

Nets are created by looping and knotting a continuous strand of yarn into an open mesh. In use since prehistoric times for trapping fish, birds, and other small animals, nets also have a long history as a decorative fabric. Egyptian burial chambers, for example, contained fabric made from open work net with embroideries of pearls and precious stones.

Most netted fabrics are made with either a square or diamond-shaped mesh. The hand process is a fairly simple one of looping and knotting to form an open work fabric. The decorativeness of the net can be increased by embroidering designs on the open mesh. The terms *filet* work or *lacis* are applied to decorated nets and they are often classified as a type of lace.

Machine-made nets are manufactured on a bobbinet lace machine, or on Raschel or compound needle tricot knitting machines. Net fabrics range from lightweight tulles to heavy fishing nets.

Figure 16-1. Examples of lacis or embroidered net fabrics from the sixteenth century. Courtesy of the Metropolitan Museum of Art. Gift of Mrs. Magdalena Nuttall.

MACRAMÉ

Macramé might be considered as a variation of the principle used in making nets. Like netting, macramé uses the techniques of looping and knotting yarns. Unlike netting, however, the decorative qualities of macramé are determined by the selection and use of a variety of ornamental knots. In netting it is the open area that is important. In macramé the closed or knotted areas are emphasized.

Figure 16-2. Macramé fabric, knotted from ivory cotton in the late nineteenth century. Courtesy of the Philadelphia Museum of Art. Given by Mrs. Edward F. Bailey, 1955.

The word *macramé* seems to be Arabic in origin, and the process itself probably was brought to Europe from the Arab world. Like *filet* or *lacis*, macramé may be classified as a lace. Its first use was in finishing off the unwoven yarns at the end of a fabric. In time, macramé was constructed separately and attached to linens or garments in the same way that other trimmings were sewn into place.

The first major surge of interest in macramé came during the seventeenth century during a period of emphasis on lace making in general. Since that time macramé has experienced periods of great favor and periods of relative obscurity. During the nineteenth century it was an important decoration for clothes and household items, and fashion magazines of the 1800s are filled with instructions for macramé work. Macramé was not used widely during the early 1900s, but since the late 1960s there has been a resurgence of interest in the technique.

Since macramé does not require specialized tools, it can be made with a minimum of equipment. During the eighteenth and nineteenth centuries sailors on whaling ships often occupied their spare time in making macramé items that they bartered when they reached port.

The yarns or cords that are to be used in macramé are fastened to a holding cord, which in turn is clamped or pinned securely so that the cords will not slip. For complex work, the yarns are wound onto bobbins so that they do not become entangled. The work is done by creating a variety of knots that join the cords at different intervals. Placement of the knots and judicious selection of the type of knots make possible the creation of a variety of textures and decorative effects. Macramé is essentially a hand craft technique.

LACE

Because of its delicate beauty, lace has been one of the most sought after of fabrics. The precise origins of lace making are unknown, but its development was related not only to knotting and netting but also to embroidery. Among the earliest lacelike fabrics were those that were called *drawn work*. In drawn work, individual yarns were unraveled from a woven fabric, and embroidery stitches were used to fasten groups of these yarns together into a decorative pattern. *Cut work* was also a forerunner of lace. In cut work, areas of fabric are cut out to form a pattern and the raw edges around the open areas were embroidered both to prevent them from fraying and to add decoration. The ornamentation could be increased by throwing threads across the open area to form geometric patterns by weaving in and out, or embroidering over the threads that bridged the gap.

Although fabrics decorated by each of these techniques bear certain similarities to lace, true lace making dispensed with the base fabric and created the design from the threads alone. Laces are generally divided into two categories, according to their construction. One is called *needlepoint lace*, the other *bobbin lace*.

Needlepoint lace, which is slightly older than bobbin lace, probably originated in Venice sometime prior to the sixteenth century.[1] In making needlepoint laces, the design for the lace was first drawn on parchment or heavy paper. A piece of heavy linen was sewn to the back of the parchment to hold it straight. Threads were then laid along the lines of the pattern and basted lightly onto the parchment and linen. None of these threads was attached to any other. The lace was created by embroidering over the base threads with decorative stitches. These embroideries connected the base threads. The areas between the threads could also be filled in with fancy needlework, according to the requirements of the pattern. When the embroidery was complete, the

[1]S. L. Goldenberg, *Lace, Its Origin and History* (New York: Brentano's, 1904), p. 2.

basting threads that held the lace to the paper were clipped and the finished lace was released.

Bobbin lace or, as it is also termed, *pillow lace* uses twisted and plaited threads. It is more closely related to netting and to knotting, whereas needlepoint lace stems more from embroidery. Again the design is drawn on stiff paper. Holes are pricked into the paper in the area of the pattern. This pattern is then stretched over a pillow and small pins are placed at close intervals through the holes in the paper. The pins go through the paper and into the pillow. The thread is wound onto bobbins, and the threads are worked around the pins to form meshes, openings, and closed areas. Bobbin lace seems to have originated in Flanders or Belgium.

The techniques for making both bobbin lace and needlepoint lace quickly spread throughout Europe. Each town developed its own style of lace, which had its traditional patterns and construction features. It is this localization of design that has given us the names for most laces. Chantilly lace, for example, was first made in the French city of Chantilly; Venice point lace originated in Venice, and Val lace was first made in Valenciennes, France.

In describing the construction of laces, certain basic terms are employed. It may be helpful to define several of the most important words from this

Figure 16-3. Lace pillow with bobbins attached. The lace is made by knotting together yarn from the different bobbins around the pins. Courtesy of the Metropolitan Museum of Art. Gift of Frau Kubasek, 1907.

vocabulary. Definitions are adapted from *Encyclopedia of Textiles, American Fabrics* (Englewood Cliffs, N.J.: Prentice-Hall, Inc., 1972), p. 558.

Allovers—Relating to the design that covers the body of net, as distinguished from motifs or borders.

Baby—A term for narrow or light laces.

Bars or *Brides*—Connecting threads ornamenting open spaces in lace.

Bead edge—A series of looped threads edging a lace.

Cordonnet—The cord outline applied to a pattern.

Fillings—Fancy stitches employed to fill in open spaces.

Ground—The net serving as a foundation for patterns or designs on lace.

Guipure—The term applied to heavy work. The word itself derives from *guipe*, a cord around which the silk is rolled.

Insertion—A strip of lace inserted as a band between other materials.

Picot—Tiny loops or knots worked on the edges of a design.

Among the best known and most widely used types of lace are the following:

Alencon, a needlepoint lace that originated in France. The lace has a sheer net background with a solid design outlined in cord.

Binche, bobbin lace from Belgium. The ground has a six-pointed star shaped ground net that is sprinkled with snowflake-like figures.

Carrickmacross, an Irish lace, the ground of which is knotted hexagonals with appliqued lawn pieces. The edges of the applique are covered by buttonhole embroidery stitches.

Chantilly, French lace with a fine ground in which designs are outlined in heavy thread. At one time the lace was made of silk, but now is made in rayon, nylon, and mercerized cotton as well.

Cluny, medium to heavy-weight bobbin lace that originated in France. The designs are often of a wheel, wheat ear, bat wing, or poinsettia design.

Milanese, bobbin lace originating in Italy with a strong pattern that is made with tapes joined into patterns by fine mesh and with picot edging.

Rose point, a Venetian type needlepoint lace with strong relief cordonnet.

Venetian point, needlepoint lace not connected by mesh. The edge of the lace has an irregularly-placed picot finish.

Valenciennes, flat bobbin lace that originated in France. Popular for edgings, the lace has a mesh ground often with a scroll or floral design.

The production of lace by machine began soon after 1800. Although an earlier machine had had good success in producing manufactured nets, ma-

Figure 16-4. Hand-crocheted shawl.

chine-made laces were not perfected until John Leavers invented a machine that could make as much lace in one day as a skilled handworker could produce in six months.[2] Only an expert can tell the difference between machine- and hand-made lace. Most modern laces are produced by machine, on the Leavers machine. Knitted laces may be made on the Raschel machine and some lacelike embroidered fabrics are produced by the Schiffli machine. Schiffli fabrics, however, are not true laces but are embroidered, woven fabrics.

CROCHET

The origins of crochet are obscure. The technique of creating fabric by pulling one loop of yarn through another with a hook was brought to the United States by Irish immigrants of the nineteenth century. The craft was evidently practiced in Irish convents as an efficient means of copying lace fabrics. During the potato famine of the 1840s, the nuns taught many poor Irish women to crochet so that they could supplement the family income. When these families came to America, they brought Irish crochet with them, and soon women throughout the United States had learned to crochet.

Crocheting is closely related to knitting. Both join together a series of interlocked yarn loops into a variety of open and/or closed patterns. Crochet is made with a single needle or hook, whereas knitting uses several needles.

Stitch Through

A process known variously as *stitch through, stitch bonding, stitch knitting*, or *mali* (from one machine used in its manufacture) produces fabrics for apparel, household, and industrial uses. First developed in East Germany, stitch-through machines work at speeds ten times faster than the fastest knitting or weaving machines.[3] Such fabrics have the advantage of being less expensive to produce, not only because of the increased volume of cloth produced by each machine but also because less yarn is required for stitch-through fabrics than for woven fabrics. Some stitch-through fabrics may also have greater bursting strength and tear strength than conventionally woven fabrics of comparable yarn size and fiber type.

Three basic types of stitch-through fabrics are produced: a flat fabric of stitched yarns that is most similar to conventional fabrics, a pile fabric, and batting.

Heinrich Mauersberger, an East German inventor, developed the stitch-bonding concept after having observed his wife mending a fabric in which the filling threads had been worn away. Mauersberger called his process and the fabric it produced *Malimo*.

Malimo fabrics are made with three sets of yarns. Warp yarns are fed from a

[2] D. E. Schwab, *The Story of Lace and Embroidery* (New York: Fairchild Publications, Inc., 1951), p. 10.

[3] M. Klapper, *Fabric Almanac* (New York: Fairchild Publications, Inc., 1967), p. 7.

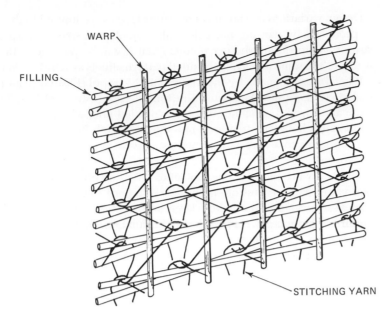

Figure 16.5 Structure of Malimo stitch-through fabric. Courtesy of Bahlo Textile Corporation.

warp beam. Filling yarns, held in creel magazines on either side of the machine, are laid across the top of the warp yarns, and a third set of yarns sews, stitches, or knits the warps and fillings together. The Malimo machine has been described as looking like a modified warp knitting machine.[4] Another machine developed in Czechoslovakia that operates on the same principle is called the *Arutex* machine.

[4]P. R. Libbey, "Stitch Through Fabric Technology," *Modern Textiles* (June 1974), p. 34.

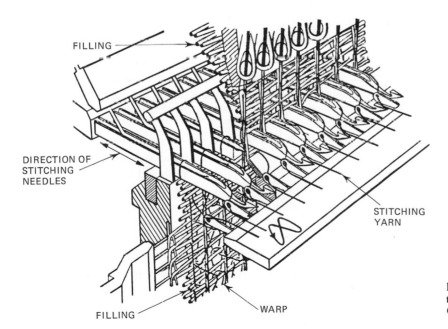

Figure 16-6. Construction of Malimo stitch-through fabrics. Courtesy of Bahlo Textile Corporation.

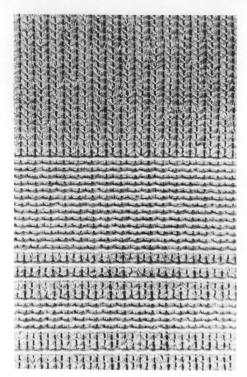

Figure 16-7. Fabric constructed by the stitch-through technique.

Design variations in Malimo and Arutex fabrics are limited to those that can be produced by varying the color, placement, and size of warp and filling yarns. Inventor Mauersberger predicts that it will be possible in the future to produce "the same mechanical guided pattern effects as achieved in knitting."[5]

Pile fabrics are made by the Malipol and Liropol (East German processes), Araloop (Czechoslovakian), and Kraftomatic (English) machines. The Kraftomatic and Liropol machines make a two-sided pile, whereas the Malipol and Araloop machines create pile on one side of the fabric. These processes attach the pile loops to a base fabric such as conventionally woven cloth, knits, or nonwovens.

The Maliwatt and Arachne machines stitch together a batt of fiber, rather than yarns. The process offers the advantage of low production costs, since fabrics can be made directly from fibers and the step of spinning fibers into yarns is omitted. Manufacturers find that the insulation qualities of fabrics made in this way are excellent.

In the Arabeva, Malivlies, and Voltex processes a web of fibers is stitched together by using fibers from the web itself. Fibers from one side of the batt or web are looped across to the other side. The resultant fabric is not as strong as Malimo or Maliwatt fabrics, but is suitable for use in garment linings or industrial cloths in which strength is not a major requirement.

The end uses of stitch-through fabrics include apparel, draperies, blankets, towels, table linens, and industrial fabrics. Although stitch-bonded fabrics will never totally replace woven goods, predictions have been made that the production of Malimo and related fabrics will increase to the point where it will have "profound effects on traditional textile economics."[6]

Fabric Webs

FELT

Although the evidence is scanty, it is believed that the first means of making fibers into cloth was through felting. Prehistoric remains of felt materials have been found in such diverse parts of the world as Anatolia, Siberia, Europe, Southeast Asia, and South America. To understand the process by which felt is formed, it is necessary to review the structure of the wool fiber from which it is made.

The surface of the wool fiber is covered with a fine network of small scales. This scaly structure causes wool fibers to cling closely together, as the scales from one fiber interlock with the scales of another. Furthermore, the natural crimp of wool assists in felting. When masses of wool fiber are placed together, the crimped fibers become entangled. Friction increases this tangling. If the wool is subjected to conditions of heat and moisture, the scales open wider, interlocking with still more scales from neighboring fibers. At the same time, the moisture causes the fibers to shrink together such that the mass holds

[5]H. Mauersberger, "What's Ahead for Malimo Technology?", *Modern Textiles* (August 1973), p. 13.

[6]M. Klapper, op. cit., p. 7.

together more tightly. When pressure is added, the mass is flattened, producing a web of tightly joined fibers or felt. The factors essential for producing natural felt from wool are heat, moisture, and pressure.

It is not too difficult to imagine a situation in which felt might have been produced accidentally. Suppose a horseman placed a sheep fleece on the back of his horse as cushioning material. The body of the horse is both warm and moist; the rider provides the pressure and the friction. Over time, the fleece becomes matted, producing a primitive form of felt. Frequent repetition of the procedure could lead to the recognition that this material had potential for some of the same uses as the fleece from which it was made.

Eventually the natural process was reduced to a series of steps that included applying heat and moisture to a mass of wool fiber, placing the batt (or mass) of fibers on flat stones, and pounding the fibers with hammers or beaters. To vary the texture and quality of the material, fur fibers might be added, but it was the wool that served to hold the substance together.

In the commercial production of felt, a batt of cleaned wool fiber is fed into a carding machine that lays down a web of fairly even thickness. In order to improve strength and dimensional stability, two webs of carded fiber are laid across each other with the fibers of one web at right angles to the fibers of the other web.

Steam is forced through the mass of fiber, after which a heavy, heated plate or rollers are lowered onto the fibers. The plate or rollers are moved about in order to produce friction. The moisture, heat, and friction effectively interlock the fibers.

Following this operation, the fabric is passed through a solution of soap or acid that causes the fabric to shrink still further. From this stage the fabric goes to a "fulling mill" in which the fabric is subjected to further agitation, pounding, and shrinkage. After felting is complete, the fabric can be dyed or given any of the traditional finishes used on wool.

Felt has the advantage of being easily cut, and because it has no yarns, it will not fray at the edges. Felt can be molded into shape, and so has wide use in making hats. Because of its densely packed fibers felt provides a good deal of warmth, and it is not easily penetrated by water. On the other hand, felt is a relatively weak fabric, may tear under pressure, and is subject to pilling. Being rather stiff, felt does not fall into graceful folds. Its use, therefore, is somewhat limited. Modern manufacturers of wool felt supply material not only for hats and fashion accessories but also for a wide range of industrial uses.

BARK CLOTH

A process similar to that used for felt produces bark cloth, or as it is called in the Polynesian Islands, *tapa*. This nonwoven fabric was also known during prehistoric times in areas as widespread as Asia, Africa, Europe, South and Central America, and the South Pacific.

Made from certain trees, among them the paper mulberry, breadfruit, fig, or related species, bark cloth is produced by first removing strips of the inner layer of bark from the tree. This substance is softened by soaking it in water. The softened bark is placed on an anvil or flat surface and special beaters are then used to pound the bark strips in order to interlace the fibers. When the mass is sufficiently integrated, the material is dried, producing a sheet of fabric. Special texture or surface markings are achieved by pounding the material with incised hammers or embossing the flat surface on which the fibrous materials are spread to be beaten and to dry.

The process is similar to that used in making paper, and the resulting fabric is somewhat like a soft, supple paper. Printed designs are added to the surface. Although woven cotton goods replaced native bark cloth in the South Pacific in the nineteenth century, small quantities are still made for native religious garb, and as an example of native handicrafts.

Like felt, *tapa* has limited usefulness. In medium to heavy weights it does not drape or sew particularly well, and so is used chiefly for simple unsewn garments such as ponchos, sarongs, loincloths, or turbans. On the other hand, because pieces of tapa can be joined without sewing, simply by wetting the edge of two pieces and pounding them together, large pieces of fabric can be made without seams.

OTHER FIBER WEBS

Techniques by which fabrics are made directly from fibers, bypassing both spinning and weaving, have been utilized for centuries in the production of felt and bark cloth. With the development of man-made fibers, and, in particular, the synthesis of thermoplastic fibers, technologies have evolved that have made possible the large-scale production of nonwoven fabrics. Marketed extensively for both durable and disposable items, nonwoven fiber webs range from throwaway diapers to blankets, from industrial filters to tea-bag covers.

The American Society for Testing Materials defines nonwoven textile fabrics as textile structures "produced by bonding or interlocking of fiber, or both, accomplished by mechanical, chemical or solvent means and combinations thereof."[7] Excluded from this class are paper, fabrics that have been woven, knitted, or tufted, or those made by wool or other felting processes.

American Fabrics Magazine recommends that nonwoven fabrics be classified as durable products or disposable products. They define a durable product as "one which is multi-use. It is not manufactured to be thrown away after a single application."[8] Examples of this type of product are blankets, carpet-backings, and furniture padding.

Disposable products were defined as ". . . made to be disposed of after a single or limited number of uses." These are exemplified in disposable diapers, towels, or tea-bag covers. Some items, *American Fabrics* points out, are disposable not because of their durability but because of their purpose. Medical

[7] *1974 Annual Book of ASTM Standards. Textiles, Yarns, Fabrics, General Methods* (Philadelphia, Penna.: American Society for Testing Materials, 1974), p. 24.

[8] *American Fabrics* (Summer 1974), p. 40.

gowns, for example, or airplane and train headrests, might withstand multiple use, but for sanitary reasons they have limited use periods.[9]

Nonwoven fabrics are made from both staple and filament fibers. Filament fibers are made into fabrics by spun bonding, which is discussed later. Staple fibers may be made into fabrics by several different processes.

Staple Fiber Web Formation

Both durable and disposable staple fiber nonwovens are manufactured in several stages. The first step, the forming of the web of fibers, is done by either *dry forming* or *wet forming*.

Dry Forming. The earliest nonwovens were prepared by a dry-forming process based on the carding of textile fibers. Staple lengths of fiber were mechanically carded (or garnetted) into a web in which all of the fibers ran in the same general direction.

A second method of dry forming developed later. In this process, called *air laying*, a batt of fibers is fed into a stream of air. The fibers are carried in the air, the airstream is filtered, and the fibers are deposited into an evenly distributed layer of fibers in a random arrangement. Random arrangement of fibers produces a stronger fabric, one that may be better for some uses than carded webs. Also, because air-laid fibers are not subjected to the mechanical action of the carder, fibers are not so likely to be damaged during manufacture.

Wet Forming. Wet forming is similar in principle to air laying. However, a stream of water carries the fibers instead of a jet of air. The stream of water is flowed onto a forming screen that filters the fibers from the water. The direction of the fibers is random, and the fibers are not damaged in processing.

Binding the Fibers Together

Once a web has been formed, some treatment must be given to bind the fibers together. This can be done by using a bonding or adhesive material or by entangling fibers.

Bonding. Bonding may be achieved by *applying an adhesive material* to the web, then setting the adhesive. This, in essence, "glues" the fibers together. When adhesive is applied to the surface of the fiber web, it tends to make the fabric stiff and more rigid. Also, fabrics exhibit the characteristics of the adhesive material on the surface rather than the characteristics of the original fiber. To overcome this disadvantage, adhesives may be imprinted onto the surface in selected areas. The printing patterns are developed carefully to assure that adequate bonding takes place among fibers to maintain fabric strength. Such fabrics are less rigid and have better drapability and a more pleasant surface texture than those that have been completely coated by an adhesive.

Thermoplastic fibers may be bonded by heat. The application of heat causes the fusing together of heat-sensitive fibers, which effectively fastens them

[9] Ibid.

together. As in bonding with adhesives, heat may be applied in a pattern to provide sufficient bonding for durability and to allow greater flexibility and softness in the end product.

Entangling the Fibers. Fiber webs produced by the dry web methods may be joined by entangling the fibers in some way. One of these methods has already been discussed under the heading of stitch-bonded fabrics. It is the technique (made by the Maliwatt and the Arachne machines) of *chain stitching* or knitting through a batt of fibers.

Another method, known as *needle punching*, has wide use in the home furnishings industry. The web of fibers is fed through a series of barbed needles. These needles mechanically entangle the fibers together, causing them to form into a coherent and uniform mass. Needle-punched fabrics are generally more flexible than bonded fabrics. They are most frequently used in durable products such as carpet backings, indoor-outdoor carpet face, blankets, and insulation materials.

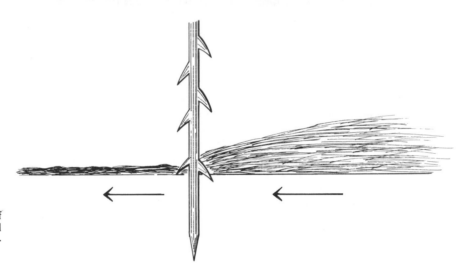

Figure 16-8. Needle punching. The batt of loose fiber at the right passes under hooked needles that punch through the fibers, entangling them into a cohesive sheet.

Spunlace goods are sheets of fibers made by air entanglement. No adhesive or binder is used. As in the needlepunch process, the entanglement of the fibers holds the fabric together. The drapability of spunlace fabrics is similar to that of woven fabrics. Nexus is the trademark of a spunlace polyester fabric produced in cooperation by du Pont and Burlington Industries. Du Pont produces the roll goods whereas Burlington dyes, prints, embosses, or otherwise completes the fabrication. So far Nexus has only been used for home furnishings and apparel fabrics. It is, however, being studied for a variety of industrial applications.

Spun Bonding

Spun-bonded fabrics are manufactured from synthetic filament fibers in a process that has the economic advantage of taking the fiber directly from the

Figure 16-9. Sleepwear made from Nexus spunlace fabric. Courtesy of Burlington Industries.

Figure 16-10. Closeup photograph of spun-bonded fiber web.

spinning stage to the fabric forming stage without costly intermediate processing. A web of continuous filaments is laid down in random arrangement. The application of heat, chemicals, or adhesives at points of crossing of the fibers effectively bonds them together.

Du Pont uses the process on polyester to produce Reemay, Typar, and Tyvek. Reemay is a polyester fabric used for apparel interlinings, backing layers for carpets, and furniture and bedding uses. Typar, a spun-bonded polypropylene, is used in bagging, packaging, furniture construction, filtration, and carpet backing. Tyvek is an olefin sheet that is tough and durable. A kind of cross between paper, fabric, and film, Tyvek is extensively used for wall coverings, tags, packaging materials, charts, maps, and the like.

Cerex is a nylon spun-bonded fabric produced by Monsanto and used as carpet backing, in furniture manufacture, and for industrial fabrics. Mirafi, a porous heat-bonded fabric made from biconstituent fibers by Celanese, is used by engineers for roadbuilding, in combating soil erosion, and in other forms of construction.

ECONOMIC IMPORTANCE OF NONWOVEN FABRICS

With $1.2 billion having been spent on nonwovens in 1974, and with an annual growth rate of 12 to 14 per cent for the nonwoven industry, it is certain that consumers will select and use increasing numbers of products made from such fabrics.

At the present time, major marketing areas for nonwovens include durables such as interfacings, interlinings, carpet backings, furniture and bedding, automotive and furniture padding, indoor-outdoor carpet, blankets, and the construction industry. Disposable nonwovens are used in diapers, medical-surgical products, wipes, packaging, and filters.

Fibers used for durables include synthetics such as polyester, polypropylene, polyethylene, nylon, and modacrylic. Rayon is also used in large quantities for disposables. As much as 85 per cent of the fiber used in disposables is rayon.[10] Smaller percentages of polyester, cotton, acetate vinyon, and modacrylic are also utilized in disposables.

Future Directions for Nonwovens

Although not all in general commercial use, several new processes allow the manufacturer to create fabrics directly from synthetic solutions, avoiding even the steps of fiber spinning and drawing. These processes have obvious economic advantages in that when steps are eliminated in manufacturing, costs are decreased.

Hercules manufactures a plastic netting material from high-density polyester or polypropylene. A film is extruded, embossed, and then stretched. During stretching, the fabric breaks into an open-work pattern of interconnected, thin bars. A variation of the embossing pattern is used to create a wide variety of patterns. Delnet is the trademark for these fabrics.

In another of these processes, known as *melt blowing*, a molten polymer is extruded through a row of spinneret holes. Hot air streams are directed in such a way that they cause the polymer to form into filaments and, at the same time, deposit them in a random web that can be bonded together at once, or later, as the manufacturer chooses.

Another process uses polyamide film that is programmed to break into continuous filaments or into an interconnecting filament network after drawing and heat-treating the film.

At the present time, the manufacture of nonwovens utilizes existing man-made fibers. The future development of this industry is likely to lead to the synthesis of fibers that are engineered specifically for nonwovens. This will improve the quality of nonwoven goods. Although no one anticipates that nonwovens will ever totally replace woven goods, consumers will find an increasing quantity and variety of nonwoven goods from which to select in both disposable and durable items.

"A. F. F. Appraises the Non-wovens." *American Fashions and Fabrics.* Summer 1974, p. 39.

ALLEN, G. G., J. R. FOX, C. W. INGALLS, and W. J. MCCONNELL. "Frontiers in Non-woven Technology." *Textile Industries,* April 1976, p. 43.

"Bark Fabrics." *CIBA Review.* May 1940.

Encyclopedia of Textiles, American Fabrics. Englewood Cliffs, N.J.: Prentice-Hall, Inc., 1972.

Recommended References

[10] *American Fabrics* (Summer 1974), p. 40.

"Felt" *CIBA Review.* November 1958.

GOLDENBERG, S. L. *Lace: Its Origin and History.* New York: Brentano's, 1904.

GUENTHER, H. W. et al. "Nexus: Spun-laced Formed Fabrics." *Modern Textiles.* December 1973, p. 40.

HARVEY, V. *Macrame.* New York: Van Nostrand Reinhold Co., 1967.

"Lace." *CIBA Review.* April 1949, p. 2670 ff.

LENNOS-KERR, P. *Non-wovens, '71.* Plainfield, N.J.: Textile Book Service.

McDONALD, M. *Non-woven Fabric Technology.* Plainfield, N.J.: Textile Book Service, 1971.

MELEN, L. *Knotting and Netting.* New York: Van Nostrand Reinhold Co., 1971.

MOREMAN, L. J. "Nonwovens: An Industry Overview." *Modern Textiles,* April 1976, p. 29.

"Non-wovens." *CIBA Review.* 1965, vol. 1.

POLLEN, M. *Seven Centuries of Lace.* New York: Macmillan Publishing Co., Inc., 1908.

POWYS, M. *Lace and Lace-making.* Boston, Mass.: Charles T. Grandford Co., 1953.

SCHWAB, F. R. *The Story of Lace and Embroidery.* New York: Fairchild Publications, Inc., 1951.

"Stitch-Through Locks in the Structure." *American Fabrics.* Summer 1967. p. 70.

WARD, D. "Spunbondeds." *Modern Textiles,* April 1976, p. 29.

17

ADDING COLOR TO TEXTILES

Most objects made by human beings are decorated in some way. Textiles are no exception. The decoration of textiles may be achieved through varying the construction of the fabric, by adding color through dyeing, or by applying color in patterns by printing.

Even the earliest fabrics excavated by archeologists show evidence of ornamentation, through either the use of natural fibers of contrasting colors, or by embroidery or dyes. Cave paintings made by prehistoric peoples of at least 25,000 years ago clearly demonstrate that these people knew how to make pigment colors from natural materials. Pottery from many cultures was painted with designs. Probably the first addition of color to fabrics was made by painting designs on the cloth.

Dyeing

NATURAL DYESTUFFS

The paints used on pottery or stone were not always serviceable on fabrics but certain substances did have a particular affinity for cloth. These dyestuffs came from a wide variety of animal, vegetable, and mineral matter. The difficulty with most of the natural dyestuffs was that they lacked colorfastness. As a result, those dyes that proved to have excellent colorfastness became important items of international trade.

Few of these early dyes could be relied upon to produce strong colors on all fibers. The coloring of fibers results from the chemical reaction of the compounds within the fibers and those within the dyestuff. The varying chemical composition or structure of the natural fibers caused each to react differently with the chemicals in each of the dyestuffs. The treatment of the fabrics with certain natural acids or oxides did, however, improve their colorfastness. These substances, called *mordants,* react both with the dyestuff and with the fiber to form an insoluble compound, thereby "fixing" the color within and on the fiber. The effect of mordants probably was discovered accidentally when it was realized that washing undyed fabrics in the water of some streams (those high in certain metallic compounds) resulted in their taking and holding colors better.

Some mordants were more effective on animal fibers such as silk and wool, others were preferable for cotton and linen. Those who worked in the dyer's trades developed skill in utilizing mordants to make fabrics of fairly good colorfastness, although it was not possible to obtain consistently excellent colorfastness until after the invention of synthetic dyes in the nineteenth century.

There were many sources of natural dyes. Vegetable dyes could be made from flowers, leaves, berries, barks, roots, grasses, weeds, vines, and lichens. The most famous of the traditional dyes made from plants included woad, indigo, madder, fustic, logwood, cutch, and safflower. The woad plant was cultivated for its blue color made from the bark of the plant. A thriving European village industry in its production continued from Roman times until the end of the Middle Ages, when woad was supplanted by indigo. Indigo, a blue of superior colorfastness from India, was somewhat easier to use. Madder was a source of reds, but also had the peculiar quality of producing several different colors or color intensities when it was employed in combination with different mordants. The chemical reaction of the metallic salts in the various mordants with the chemical compound in madder resulted in colors that ranged from yellow to rose to red. Fustic for yellow, logwood and cutch for browns, and safflower for red were other widely known dyes. By combining the primary colors of red, blue, and yellow, it was possible to create additional colors in the green, purple, and orange ranges. A good, fast, dark black was exceedingly difficult to achieve.

Mineral colors were less often used, though some iron oxides were employed. Animal sources provided some of the most effective dyestuffs. The bodies of small insects that are native to South America had been used by the Indians as a dyestuff for many centuries. This cochineal bug, which became a major item of trade between the New and Old Worlds, produced a vivid red, of excellent fastness.

The color purple has been associated with royalty for centuries. The origins of this association are based on the production of Tyrean purple, a color made from the juice secreted by a small shellfish. The technique for making the dye was known as early as 1000 B.C., and required a lengthy and complex series of steps. First the dye was "milked" from the shellfish. This white liquid, as it oxidized, turned from milky white to green, to red, to deep purple. Careful control of the color range could be used to produce a wide range of red-purple colors, the most desirable being a deep, rich red-purple. Because the process was time consuming and difficult and the supply of the dye limited, fabrics dyed with Tyrean purple were very costly and therefore available only to the rich and, in particular, to the nobility. Royalty eventually gained a monopoly on the color, and so it has come to be known as "royal purple."[1]

[1] P. Gerhard, "Emperor's Dyes of the Mixtects," *Natural History Journal* (January 1964), p. 26 ff.

SYNTHETIC DYES

William Perkin, an English chemist, discovered that a coal-tar derivative, *aniline,* colored white silk. After further experimentation, Perkin was able to make a dyestuff that had potential commercial application. It was a reddish-purple in color, called mauve.

Perkin's discoveries in the 1860s stimulated additional research with other coal-tar derivatives and related compounds, and the synthesis of a wide range of artificial dyestuffs resulted from these researches. Gradually an enormous range of synthetic dyes made from many chemical substances were developed.

The selection of dyestuffs for coloring fabrics is a decision requiring the attention not only of the highly trained dye technician but also of designers, stylists, and business managers who are knowledgeable about current fashion trends. Although some types of dyed fabrics can be bleached and redyed another color, or designs printed over plain colored fabrics, dyeing a fabric to an unpopular color may spell financial disaster for a manufacturer of piece goods.

In addition, the choice of hue is only the first of many decisions about adding color to fabrics. It must be decided at what point the color will be added and the type of dyestuff that will be used.

Since each fiber reacts differently to dyestuffs, the use of an appropriate dye is crucial to colorfastness. Since loss of color in use is a major source of consumer dissatisfaction, reputable manufacturers must choose dyes carefully.

Color is one of those areas in which the chemistry of textiles is most important. Although this text does not explore the complex chemical reactions that take place in dyeing, it is important to think of both the fiber and the dyestuff as chemical substances. The combination of fiber with dyestuff is a chemical as well as a physical reaction.

TYPES OF DYEING

Color may be added to fabric at any one of four steps in its processing. Color can be added to man-made fibers before the fiber is extruded, or dyes can be applied to fibers, yarns, or to constructed fabrics or finished products.

Solution Dyeing

When color is added to man-made fibers before they are spun, the fibers are known as *solution-dyed* or *dope-dyed* fibers. Pigment is dispersed throughout the liquid fiber solution. When the fiber is extruded, it carries the coloring material as an integral part of the fiber.

This "locked-in" color is extremely fast (that is, it will not fade). The range of colors in which solution dyeing is done is rather limited for economic reasons. The fiber manufacturer must produce substantial quantities of fiber in order to justify the expense of adding an extra step during the manufacturing process.

Figure 17-1. Multicolored spots of fiber-dyed fibers are used in this tweed fabric.

Furthermore, fiber production takes place well in advance of the time when fabrics reach the market. Fashion color trends may change fairly rapidly, so that by the time a solution-dyed fabric reaches the market, the color may be out of fashion, and not salable. For this reason, solution-dyed fabrics are generally produced in basic colors.

Solution dyeing is used on acetate to prevent gas fading. Gas fumes in the air may turn some blue or green dyes used for acetate to pink or brown.

The following is a list of some of the registered trademarks of some fibers that are solution-dyed and the companies that manufacture them.

Acrilan 2000—acrylic	Monsanto Textiles Company
Camalon—nylon	Sunshine Cordage Corporation
Chromespun—acetate	Eastman Kodak Company
Coloray—rayon	Courtaulds North America, Inc.
Jetspun—rayon (filament)	American Enka Company
Kolorbon—rayon (staple)	American Enka Company
Marvess CG—olefin	Phillips Fibers Corp.

Fiber Dyeing

Fibers may be colored in the fiber state. When color is added at this point, the process is known as *fiber dyeing* or *stock dyeing*.

Loose (usually staple) fibers are immersed in a dyebath, dyeing takes place, and the fibers are dried. This is a relatively expensive type of dyeing because it takes longer to dye the fibers than it would to dye a comparable quantity of yarns or fabrics. It does achieve a high level of dye penetration into the fiber, and fibers tend to take up the dye evenly.

Stock-dyed fibers are most often used in tweed or heather materials to create delicate shadings of color. Fiber-dyed fabrics can be identified by untwisting the yarns in order to see whether the yarn is made up of a variety of different colored fibers. In solid color yarns, untwisted stock-dyed fibers will be uniform in color, with no darker or lighter areas.

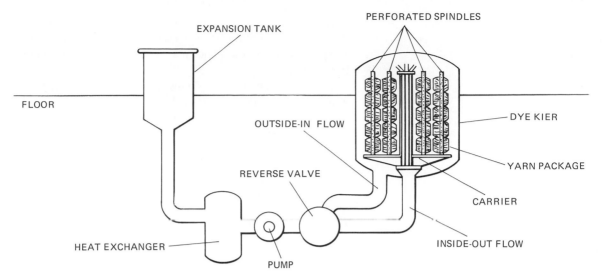

EXPANSION TANK

PERFORATED SPINDLES

FLOOR

OUTSIDE-IN FLOW

DYE KIER

YARN PACKAGE

REVERSE VALVE

CARRIER

HEAT EXCHANGER

INSIDE-OUT FLOW

PUMP

Figure 17-2. Package dyeing of yarns. Courtesy of Dow Badische Company.

Fibers for worsted fabrics are sometimes made into a sliver before they are dyed. This variation of fiber dyeing is known as *top dyeing*. By dyeing the fibers after they have been combed, the manufacturer avoids the wasteful step of coloring the short yarns that would be removed in the combing process.

Yarn Dyeing

If color has not been added either to the solution or the fiber, it can be applied to the yarns before they are made into fabrics.

Many types of fabrics utilize yarns of differing colors in order to achieve a particular design. Stripes in which contrasting sections of color alternate in the

Figure 17-3. Gingham fabric in which the design is achieved by alternating rows of yarn-dyed yarns in the warp and filling directions.

length or crosswise direction, chambrays in which one color is used in one direction and another color is used in the other direction, complex dobby or Jacquard weaves, and plaids may all require yarns to which color has already been added.

Yarns may be dyed in skeins, in packages, or on beams. Special dyeing equipment is required for each of these processes. In skein dyeing, large, loosely wound skeins of yarn are placed in a vat for dyeing. Package dyeing utilizes a number of tubes with holes into which the yarn is wound. The dye is circulated around and through the tubes in order to assure that the yarns have maximum contact with the dyestuff. Beam dyeing is a variation of package dyeing, which uses a larger cylinder onto which the yarn is wound.

Yarn-dyed fabrics may be identified by unraveling several warp and several filling yarns from the pattern area in order to see whether they differ in color. Not only will each yarn be a different color but the yarns will have no darker or lighter areas where they have crossed other yarns.

Piece Dyeing

Fabrics that are to be a solid color are usually piece-dyed. In piece dyeing, the finished fabric is passed through a dye bath in which the fabric absorbs the dyestuff. A number of different methods are used for piece dyeing, each of which has some slight differences in the way in which the fabric is handled. Some of these methods are especially suitable to certain types of fabrics, and unsuitable for others.

Beck, box, or *winch dyeing* is frequently used in dyeing wool fabrics and knits, as it places relatively little tension on the fabric during dyeing. (See Figure 17.4.)

Jet dyeing is a relatively new method of dyeing that utilizes jet propulsion to improve dye penetration. Dyeing takes place in a closed system that carries a fast-moving stream of pressurized dye liquor.

A fluid jet of dye penetrates and dyes the fabric. After it passes through this jet, the fabric is floated through an enclosed tube in which the fluid moves faster than the fabric. This prevents the fabric from touching the walls, keeping it constantly immersed in the dyebath. Turbulence is created by locating elbows in the tube. The turbulence aids in diffusing dyes and other chemicals. Since no pressure is put on the fabric, even very delicate fabrics can be dyed by this process. Jet dyeing has the advantage of being economical in operation and at the same time allowing a high degree of quality control.

Jig dyeing is a process that places greater tension on the fabric than either of the aforementioned processes. Fabrics are stretched across two rollers that are placed above a stationary dyebath. At regular intervals, the fabric is passed through the dyebath. The tension created by placing the fabric on the rollers means that this process must be reserved for fabrics with a fairly close weave that will not lose their shape under tension.

Beam dyeing, which is used for lightweight, fairly open weave fabrics, utilizes the same principle as beam dyeing of yarns. The fabric is wrapped around a beam and immersed in the dyebath. Tightly woven fabrics would not

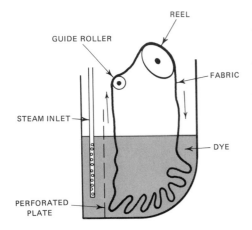

Figure 17-4. Side-view diagram of a typical dye beck showing movement of fabric through the dyebath. Courtesy of Dow Badische Company.

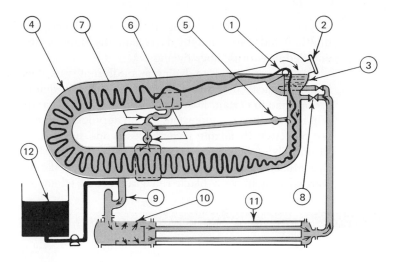

1. Fabric guide roll
2. Loading and unloading port
3. Header tank
4. "U" tube
5. Suction control
6. Suction control
7. Suction control
8. Delivery control
9. Main Pump
10. Filter
11. Heat exchanger
12. Service tank

Figure 17-5. Hiska jet-dyeing machine. Reprinted by permission of National Knitted Outerwear Association.

allow sufficient dye penetration; hence the need to apply this method to loosely woven cloth. It has the added advantage of not putting tension or pressure on the goods as they are processed.

Pad dyeing is a process used in producing large quantities of piece-dyed goods that can withstand tension and pressure. Fabrics pass through a dyebath, then through pads or rollers that squeeze out the excess dye, and then into a steam or heated chamber in which the dye is fixed or set.

Vacuum impregnation is a dye system introduced to improve the dyeing of heavy-weight fabrics. Because of their thickness it has been difficult to get good dye penetration of fabrics such as corduroy, sateens, and heavy-weight ducks. Trapped air, caught in these denser fabrics, makes dyeing them difficult. In this vacuum system, the fabric comes into contact with a perforated stainless steel cylinder into which a vacuum pump draws air, while, at the same time, the dye liquor is applied to the fabric. This means that dye and fabric come into contact in a pressurized chamber, with the result that the dye penetrates the fabric more thoroughly. The vacuum system has been particularly useful in dyeing corduroy fabrics and other pile fabrics as it allows equal dye penetration of both the pile and the ground fabric.

Cross Dyeing

The increased use of blended fabrics, that is, fabrics composed of two or more different fibers, has both created problems for the dyer and presented him with new techniques to use. Dyeing of piece goods is less expensive than fiber or yarn dyeing. Cross dyeing utilizes piece-dyeing techniques to produce a multicolored fabric, thereby decreasing the higher costs of production that are entailed in yarn or fiber dyeing.

Each fiber responds to dyeing in a different way. Because of the differences in the chemical composition of fibers and different dyestuffs, there are dyes that are specific to certain fibers or fiber groups. For example, there are dyes that will be effective on nylons, but not on acrylics, or dyes that will color silk, but not polyester. By mixing several dyes in one dyebath, each of which is specific to one fiber, the manufacturer can pass a blended fabric through a single dyebath, and each fiber will pick up only its specific dye. For example, if one wanted to achieve a black/red/gray tweed effect using a blend of rayon,

Figure 17-6. Beam dyeing of fabric. Courtesy of Allied Chemical Corporation.

acrylic, and nylon fibers, it would be possible to pass the fabric through a dyebath in which there was a black dye specific to rayon, a red specific to acrylics, and a gray specific to nylon. The resulting fabric would be made up of black rayon, red acrylic, and gray nylon fibers. Plaids or stripes can be created by alternating yarns of different fibers, so that, for instance, nylon yarns are dyed red and polyester yarns are dyed blue to make a blue and red stripe.

Union Dyeing

Conversely, the dyer has difficulty in piece dyeing solid-colored, blended fabrics because each fiber takes up the dye differently. It is sometimes necessary for the dyer to select several different types of dyes of the same color, mixing them together in the same dyebath, in order to achieve a uniform color in a fabric that is made of several different fibers. This type of piece dyeing is called union dyeing.

Tone-on-Tone Dyeing

A more subtle method of creating pattern with color is utilized in tone-on-tone fabrics. Here two different types of the same generic fiber might be used. Both types respond to the same type of dye, but one may be less absorbent so that, for example, a lighter and darker shade of the same color results.

DYESTUFFS AND COLORFASTNESS

A substance that produces color is taken into the fiber, yarn, or fabric when fabrics are dyed. The way in which the fiber absorbs the dyestuff is related to both the structure of the fiber and to the chemical reactions between the dyestuff and the fiber.

Fibers are made up of both crystalline areas (areas where molecules are highly oriented) and amorphous areas (areas where molecules are not so highly oriented). The dyestuff, carried in a solvent, penetrates the fiber most easily in the amorphous areas where the fiber is weakest and where it is most chemically reactive. Fibers, like the synthetics, with a more completely crystalline structure, are less absorbent, and therefore more difficult to dye.

Most fibers tend to have a higher degree of crystalline structure around the outer portion of the fiber, and so the wall of the fiber may be difficult to penetrate. In order to allow the dye to penetrate the fiber skin, the dye must be carried in a solvent. The solvent that is most often used is water. Organic solvents are used for some dyes that are not water soluble. These solvents are relatively expensive, so that organic solvents are sometimes combined with water to decrease cost.

In addition to providing a solvent in which the dyestuff is carried, the fiber must be treated to make it more receptive to the dyestuff. This is done by swelling the fiber through the use of heat in conjunction with the liquid solvent.

Once the dye has entered the fiber, it may become fixed more or less permanently by a chemical reaction between the chemically reactive elements in the dyestuff and the reactive groups in the fiber. Sometimes a mordant is used to fix the dye or to assist in dye penetration.

Colorfastness

A fabric that retains its color during care and use is said to be *colorfast*. Fabrics may be more or less colorfast to a variety of different substances or conditions. The importance of colorfastness depends on the use of the fabric. Colorfastness to laundering is, of course, important in those garments and household textiles that must undergo frequent laundering. Some colors are not fast to laundering, but are fast to dry cleaning, or vice versa.

Perspiration may cause some color loss and many colors are not fast to light. Ascertaining the colorfastness to sunlight of curtains, draperies, carpets, or other items that have prolonged exposure to sunlight may be important in evaluating the usefulness of fabrics for these items. Some colors may be lost or diminished by heat.

Some dyes tend to "crock" or rub off on fabrics, or other materials with which they come in contact. Others will "bleed" into water during laundering and may be picked up by lighter colored fabrics. Chlorine bleaches will remove color from most dyed fabrics, but some types of dyestuff are more sensitive than others to the action of chlorine bleaches.

Even dyes that belong to the same class of dyestuffs can have differing degrees of colorfastness to the same condition, so that the consumer has no real guarantee of permanence of color unless a label specifies that a particular fabric is colorfast. Dye performance labeling is not required by any form of legislation or regulation. Some manufacturers do, however, include colorfastness information on labels. Such labels will generally describe the conditions under which the fabric is colorfast, such as "colorfast to laundering, but not to chlorine bleaching," or "colorfast to sunlight." A few terms may be found on labels that carry an assurance of colorfastness, such as trademarks that have been applied to solution-dyed synthetic fibers. The colorfastness of one class of dyes, the *vat dyes*, is so consistently good for laundering that the term "Vat Dyed" on labels has come to be accepted as an assurance of good colorfastness.

A variety of tests have been developed to determine the colorfastness of fabrics. Fabrics can be tested to determine their colorfastness to laundering, dry cleaning, light, perspiration, and crocking. These tests are discussed in detail in Chapter 23, "Textile Testing and Standards."

DYE CLASSES

Dyestuffs are divided into a number of classifications. Within each of these classifications there exists a range of colors, and each of these colors may vary somewhat in its fastness to different conditions.

The ability of the fibers to accept each of these dye classes depends upon several factors. One is the availability of appropriate chemically reactive groups in both the fiber and the dyestuff, and the other is the chemical composition of the dye liquor. Dyes that must be applied in an alkaline medium, for example, are difficult to use on protein fibers because the alkalinity of the dyebath may harm the fiber. Likewise, dyebaths that are strongly acid in nature may be harmful to cellulose fibers.

In the following discussion of specific dye classes, these classes are grouped according to the fiber types for which they are most widely (though not exclusively) used.

Dyes Most Often Used on Cellulosic Fibers

Azoic Dyes. Azoic dyes (also called Naphthol dyes) are used primarily on cotton fibers, but can also be applied to acetates, olefins, polyesters, and nylons. The reaction that produces dyeing takes place when two components, a diazonium salt and a naphthol compound, join together to form a highly colored, insoluble compound on the fabric.

These dyes are also known as "ice dyes" because the reaction takes place at lowered temperatures. Their colorfastness is good to laundering, bleaching, alkalis, and light. They do tend to crock, somewhat. The color range is broad, although somewhat deficient in blues and greens.

Direct Dyes. Direct dyes are water-soluble dyes that are primarily used for cotton and rayon, although some polyamide and protein fibers are also dyed with these compounds. These dyes have the advantage of being applied directly in a hot aqueous dye solution in the presence of common salts required to stabilize the rate of dyeing. They also possess the disadvantage of poor fastness to laundering. An aftertreatment with copper salts is sometimes used to form a more stable dye compound. This improves colorfastness by forming a chemical compound of the dye molecule, the cellulose, and the copper salts. Other special finishes have also been developed to make the dye color more stable.

Vat Dyes. Vat dyes are insoluble in water. By chemical reduction they are converted to a soluble form. The dye is applied to the fibers, then the dye, now within the fiber, is reoxidized to the insoluble form. This creates a color that is fast to both light and washing.

Because vat dyes must be applied in an alkaline solution, they are not suitable for use with protein fibers. Primarily used with cottons and rayons, vat dyes are also used on acrylics, modacrylics, and nylon. These dyes provide a wide range of colors except for reds and oranges.

Sulfur Dyes. Sulfur dyes produce mostly dark colors, such as black, brown, or navy. Applied in an alkaline solution to cottons and rayons, fabrics dyed with sulfur dyes must have carefully controlled processing or a buildup of excess chemicals on the fibers will eventually cause the fibers to be weakened. Colorfastness of sulfur dyes is good to washing and fair to light. Black and yellow sulfur dyes may accelerate light degradation of cellulosic fibers.

Acid Dyes. Applied in an acid solution, acid dyes react chemically with the basic groups in the fiber structure. Because wool has both acid and basic groups in its structure, acid dyes can be used quite successfully on wools. These dyes are utilized to a lesser extent for dyeing nylon, acrylics, some modified polyesters, polypropylene, and spandex. Acid dyes cannot be used on cellulosic fibers because these fibers are susceptible to damage from acids. Colorfastness of acid dyes varies a good deal, depending on the color and the fiber to which the dye has been applied.

Chrome or Mordant Dyes. Used on the same general group of fibers as acid dyes, chrome or mordant dyes use a metallic salt that, when added to the dye molecule, reacts to form a relatively insoluble dyestuff with improved wet and light fastness. As the name of the dye indicates, chrome salts are most often used for the process, but salts of cobalt, aluminum, nickel, and copper can also be utilized. Especially effective for dyeing wool and silk, these dyes have excellent colorfastness to dry cleaning.

Dyes Used for Both Cellulosic and Protein Fibers

Basic Dyes. Basic dyes are alkaline in reaction because they contain amino groups. Since the reactive group is basic, they combine well with acid groups within fibers. Since wool contains such groups, these dyes are effective in coloring wools. Acrylics also have "acid sites" in their structure and can be readily colored by basic dyes. With the addition of a mordant, cellulose fibers, too, can be dyed with basic dyes.

The colors that these dyes produce are exceptionally bright. Unfortunately, except when used on acrylics, basic dyes have rather poor colorfastness to light, laundering, or perspiration. However, recent basic dyes developed for use on acrylics produce excellent fastness.

Reactive Dyes. Although reactive dyes have been most widely used on cellulosic fibers, some colors are appropriate for use on protein fibers, nylon, and acrylics. In this class of dyes, the dyestuff bonds chemically with the fiber. Color fastness of these dyes is generally good to all types of use.

Dyes Used Primarily for Man-made Fibers

Dispersed Dyes. Developed for coloring acetates, disperse dyes are now used to color many other man-made fibers. The dye is insoluble in water. Particles of dye disperse in the water without dissolving, but dissolve instead in the fibers. Colors produced with these dyes cover a wide range and generally have good fastness. Blues, however, tend to be discolored by nitrous oxide gases in the atmosphere, and may gradually fade to a pinkish color. Greens may fade to brown. This is known as "fume" fading. (See Chapter 4.) Disperse dyes are used extensively on polyesters and other fibers for transfer printing. (See Chapter 18.)

Pigment Colors. Not a true dye, pigment colors are added to the solution of synthetic fibers before they are extruded to produce a permanent and very fast color; or they may be attached to the surface of the fabric by a resin. When the resin is "cured" or permanently fixed to the fabric, the dye is also fixed on the fabric surface.

Fugitive Tints

Colors that are not permanent are sometimes called *fugitive tints*. In most dyeing processes, the manufacturer wishes to produce a color that is permanent and one that will not disappear in use or in processing. An exception is found in the use of fugitive tints such as Versatint, a range of colors produced by Milliken Chemical Company.

These dyes are utilized to identify fibers or yarns during the manufacture of fabrics. By dyeing fibers or yarns of a particular generic type to a specific tint, the manufacturer has a readily identifiable color code. When the processing of the materials is complete, the manufacturer can remove the color by a simple wash, often in cold water.

"Color and Textiles." *American Fabrics and Fashions,* Winter 1972, p. 43.

Encyclopedia of Textiles, American Fabrics. Englewood Cliffs, N.J.: Prentice-Hall, Inc., 1972.

FAIRLIE, S. "Dyestuffs in the 18th Century." *Economic History Review,* April 1965, p. 488 ff.

"Jet-dyeing of Polyester Piece Goods." *CIBA Review,* #2, 1969, p. 48.

KRAMER, J. *Natural Dyes, Plants and Processes.* New York: Charles Scribner's Sons, 1972.

STEVENS, C. B. "Recent Developments in Colourants and Colouration Methods." *Textile Month,* March 1976, p. 35.

"The Magic of Fiber-mix Dyeing." *American Fabrics,* Summer 1968, p. 83.

Recommended References

18

TEXTILE PRINTING AND DESIGN

Important decisions in the creation of a textile product must be made when its design and/or its color are chosen. Although many thousands of yards of fabrics are processed in solid colors, thousands more yards of fabric have designs applied through printing.

The application of a pattern to fabric by the use of dyes, pigments, or other colored substances may be effected by a variety of hand or machine processes. Free-hand painting of designs on fabrics is probably the oldest technique for applying ornament, but hand painting is a time-consuming procedure. Furthermore, it does not always result in a uniform repeat of a motif that is to be used more than once. If a design is transferred to a flat surface that can be coated with a dye and then stamped onto the fabric, the same design can be repeated many times over simply by pressing the decorated surface against the fabric. This process is known as *printing*. Over many centuries, a variety of techniques for printing designs have evolved.

Early Forms of Printing

BLOCK PRINTING

Block printing appears to be the most ancient of these techniques. Some experts assign a date of 2000 B.C. to printed fabrics from the Caucasus in Russia. Blocks that were used in printing textiles have been recovered from Egyptian graves of the fourth century A.D.[1] This is the simplest of the printing techniques and requires only a limited technology. A block of material (usually wood) has a design drawn on one flat side. The design is carved by cutting away the spaces between the areas that form the pattern, thus placing the design in a raised position. Color is applied to the surface of the block, and the block is pressed onto the cloth. Anyone who has ever made a potato or linoleum print should recognize the technique. Sometimes during printing, the block was tapped with a mallet to assure complete contact of the block with the fabric.

[1] R. Haller, "The Technique of Early Cloth Printing," *CIBA Review*, vol. III, p. 933.

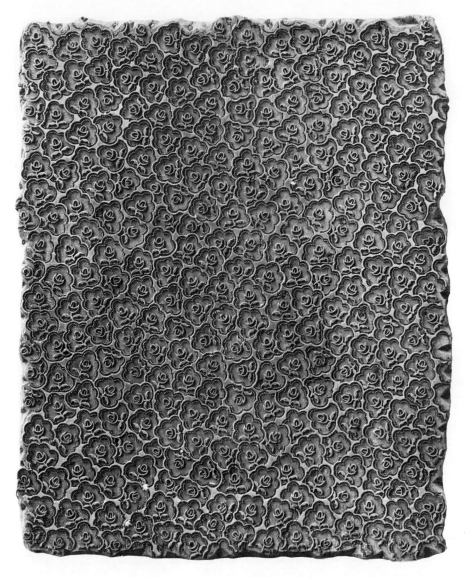

In order to make the best possible print, the dye had to be in a viscous form, otherwise the incised areas would have been filled in by the watery dye substance and the block would not have carried sufficient dye to make a clear image.

Mordant Printing

Inventive printers found another means of combining printing and dyeing to add color patterns to fabrics. Colorfastness without mordanting was very poor. The printer learned to print the mordant onto the surface of the fabric and then to pass the entire cloth into the dyebath. The mordanted areas absorbed

Figure 18-2. Indonesian woman uses tjanting for applying wax to a batik fabric. Courtesy of Exxon Corporation.

the dye permanently, the rest of the cloth picked up dye only on the surface. When the fabric was rinsed after the dyebath, the dye washed out of the unprinted areas and left a colorful design on the section that had been impregnated with the mordant.

By using different mordant materials, different colors could be produced from the same dyestuff. Madder was especially useful in this respect. When the dyer printed the surface with several different mordants, immersed the fabric in the dyebath, and rinsed away the excess dye, he produced a fabric printed with two or three different colors. This process was evidently used in Egypt during Roman times. The Roman writer Pliny describes a mysterious process in which an "invisible ink" (the mordant) was painted onto fabric and the fabric passed through another solution (the dye). After rinsing, a multicolored fabric "magically" appeared.[2]

RESIST PRINTING

In resist printing, a substance coats the fabric in preselected areas, thus preventing the fabric from absorbing dye in these areas. Resist materials have included starch, clay, and wax. The technique has been used to produce designs on textiles in many different cultures, including Persia, India, South America, Egypt, and the Far East. Although the pattern of the resist material can be said to be "printed" onto the fabric, the application of color takes place by dyeing, just as in mordant printing.

Batik

Today the best known wax-resist process is that used for the making of *batik*. The name batik originates in the Indonesian Archipelago where resist printing has become an important art form. An analysis of the batik method will show clearly how resist printing is done. Wax is applied to the areas that the printer does not want to dye. In Indonesia a small, spouted cup with a handle is used to apply the wax. As the wax is heated, it melts and the liquid wax is poured from the cup or *tjanting* onto the cloth. When it hardens, the wax coats the fabric so that the dye cannot reach the fibers.

If several colors are to be used, the process becomes somewhat more complex. For example, if a fabric is to be colored white, red, and blue, the artisan begins with a creamy-white cotton cloth. Those areas that are to remain white are coated with wax and the areas to be red are also covered. Only the area to be colored blue remains exposed. The fabric is now subjected to a blue dyebath, and the exposed areas take on the blue tint.

Next, the wax is boiled off and reapplied to the blue and white areas. The fabric is placed in the red dyebath. Since both the blue and white areas are covered with wax, the red color penetrates only the uncovered areas of the design. After dyeing is complete, the fabric is treated with a fixative (a

[2] E. Lewis, *Romance of Textiles* (New York: Macmillan Publishing Co., Inc., 1937), p. 66.

mordant) to make the colors fast, and a final rinse in hot water removes all traces of wax.

For faster production, a technique was devised whereby the wax could be printed onto the surface of the fabric with a device called a *tjap*. As in block printing, the design is carved on the tjap block. The block is dipped in wax, the block is pressed onto the fabric, and the molten wax is thus imprinted on the cloth. Well-to-do Indonesians look upon the tjap-printed fabrics as inferior in quality, although to the untrained eye they look much the same as those made with the tjanting.

Tie-and-Dye

Resist designs can be produced by the tie-and-dye method in which parts of the fabric are tightly wound with other yarns. When the fabric is placed in a dye bath, the covered areas are protected from the dye. Careful attention to the shape of the wrapping and the placement of the tied areas can produce intricate and attractive patterns. In Indian textiles, the tie-and-dye method is known as *bandanna*.

Ikat or Warp Printing

A complex and unusual variation of resist printing has been practiced in many places. The process, called *ikat*, required the weaver to prepare the warp yarns on the loom. Selected sections of the yarns were then colored with a resist material—wax, clay, or other yarns as in tie-and-dye. The warps were dyed, and the covered area did not absorb the dye. If a more complicated pattern were required, the warp yarns might be treated several times, as in the batik procedure. When dyeing was completed, the resist material was removed, and the filling was woven into place. This produced a fabric design of blurred, indistinct patterns. Ikat fabrics often have a shimmering, soft quality that is very beautiful. The technique called *warp printing* grows out of the ancient ikat process. In warp printing, a design is printed onto the warp yarns by a roller printing device prior to the interlacing of the fillings. Warp prints have the same soft, shimmering patterns that are characteristic of ikat.

Block printing, batik, stenciling, and tie-dyeing are methods of color application used largely by either native craftsmen from Africa, South America, and the Orient or by persons using these techniques as hobbies or art forms. Such fabrics are sometimes produced commercially in small quantities, usually at very high prices.

MECHANIZED PRINTING PROCESSES

Silk Screen Printing

Silk screen or screen printing is a method of applying colored design that is done either by hand or by an automated process. The fabric to be printed is

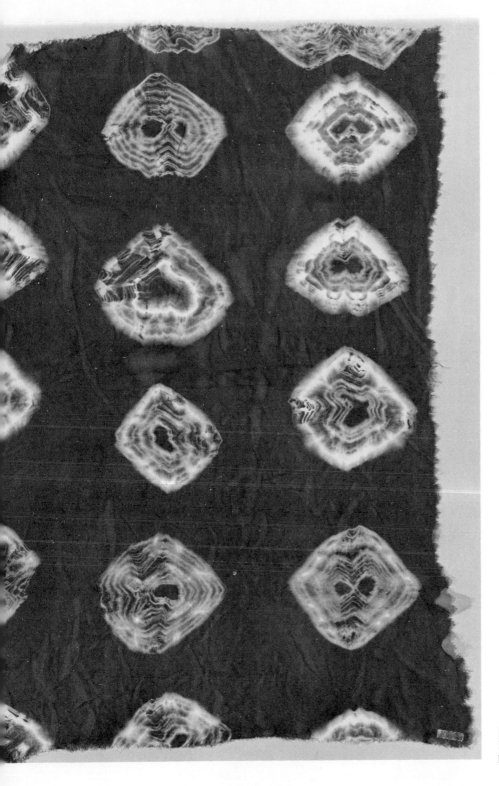

Figure 18-3. A tie-dyed fabric. Courtesy of the Metropolitan Museum of Art. Gift of Fay Halpern, 1972.

Figure 18-4. Ikat fabric from the Dutch East Indies. The central portion of the fabric had the design applied to the warp yarns before the filling was inserted. Courtesy of the Metropolitan Museum of Art. Gift of Mrs. Delia Tyrwhitt, 1965.

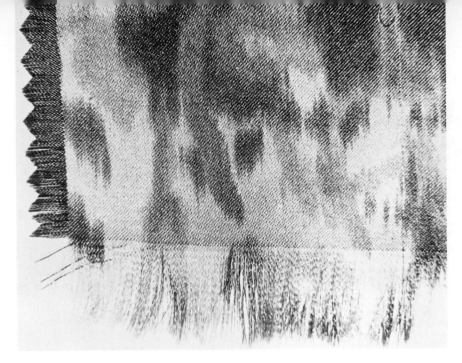

Figure 18-5. Warp-printed silk fabric.

spread out on a long table. A screen is prepared for each color of the design. At the time this procedure was developed, fine screens of silk were used, hence the name "silk screen printing." Today screens of synthetic fibers or metal mesh are more likely to be used.

A lacquer coating closes off all areas of the screen except the area in which one of the colors of the design is to be printed. For example, if a red rose with green leaves is to be printed, one screen is made that closes off all but the red rose area, and another is made that closes off all but the green leaves.

The design is transferred to the screen, often by a photochemical process in which the design for each color is photographed separately. The screen is coated with a photosensitive material that will serve to opaque or close out the sections of the screen that will not be penetrated by the dye. The screen is held in contact with a photographic plate that corresponds to patterns to be placed on the screen. A high-intensity light is directed toward the photographic plate, behind which the screen has been placed. The exposed areas of the screen are changed chemically so that they can be washed out, and the unexposed areas remain opaque. The opaque areas are further reinforced by a layer of lacquer.

The printer takes the screen, which is mounted on a frame, and places it in the correct position above and against the fabric. Dye is coated on the back of the screen. A squeegee is run across the screen and presses the dye through the open area of the screen, onto the fabric. To color the next section of the fabric, the screen is moved further along the fabric.

Hand screen printing is a slow process. Automation has been achieved in the manufacture of flat bed screen prints by making the frames stationary and moving the fabric along on a belt from screen to screen. The squeegee action, too, is done automatically. The newest flat bed screen printing machines have a maximum speed of 1,200 yards per hour of fabric for a 36-inch repeat. Older

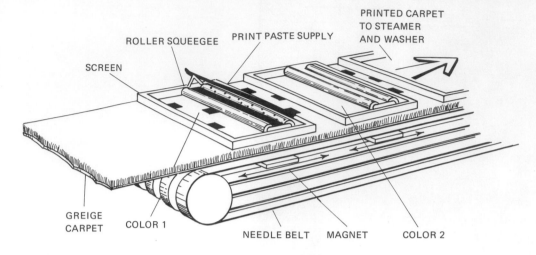

Flat-bed Zimmer carpet printing machine lays down each color separately from printing paste applied by means of two magnetic roller squeegees. Pressure is controlled by the selection of heavy or light squeegees and by varying the current going to the electromagnet. Endless belts fitted with needles assure a positive drive for good register.

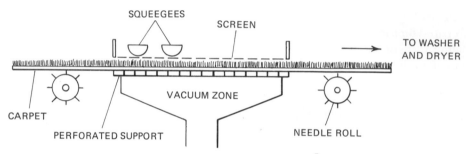

The BDA Screen printer uses a series of screens, one for each color; the basic unit is sketched above.

Figure 18-6. Silk screen printing of carpets. Courtesy of *Modern Textiles* magazine.

machines had worked at a maximum capacity of 800 yards per hour and often less.[3] This is, however, a limited production when compared with rotary screen printing and roller printing.

Rotary Screen Printing

In addition to flat bed screen printing, a rotary screen printing technique has been developed that makes possible an output of quantities of up to 3,500 yards per hour. Instead of using a flat screen, screens are shaped into rollers. As in the hand process, a screen is prepared for each color. The dye feeds through the unscreened area, pushed out from inside the roller by a squeegee. Fabrics move continuously under the rollers, and up to twelve colors may be printed on one fabric. The production of screens for rotary screen printing is less costly than the engraving of the heavy copper rollers used for roller printing, and the use of rotary screen printing techniques is increasing.

[3]L. W. C. Miles, *Textile Printing* (Watford, England: Merrow Publishing Company, Ltd., 1971), p. 13.

Figure 18-7. Rotary screen printing machine. Courtesy of Great Eastern Textile Printing Company, Inc.

Roller Printing

Like rotary screen printing, roller printing utilizes a series of rollers, each imprinting a different color on the fabric. Up to sixteen different colors can be used on one fabric.[4] The length of the repeat (the interval at which the design is repeated) is determined by the diameter of the roller. Printing speeds of 100 to 200 yards per minute are possible.[5]

The rollers are made of copper, plated with chromium for durability. The design of each color is accurately transferred to the roller by one of several processes. In photoengraving, a photographic image of the design is etched onto the roller, or a pantograph may be used to transfer the design from a flat surface to the roller. This device allows markings to be made on the roller simultaneously with the tracing of the design from a master design.

Once the rollers have been prepared, they are installed in exact position on the printing machine. The fabric to be printed moves over a rotating drum. Behind it is placed a layer of fabric that will absorb excess dye and keep it from being deposited on the drum. The design roller also rotates, moving first through a color pan. A *doctor blade* scrapes off excess dye from the roller, and the roller then rotates against the cloth and the design is imprinted. The fabric moves on to the second roller where a second color is imprinted, and so on, in a continuous printing operation.

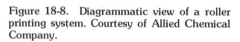

Figure 18-8. Diagrammatic view of a roller printing system. Courtesy of Allied Chemical Company.

[4] M. D. Potter and P. B. Corbman, *Textiles, Fiber to Fabric* (New York: McGraw-Hill, Inc., 1967), p. 185.

[5] Miles, op. cit. p. 31.

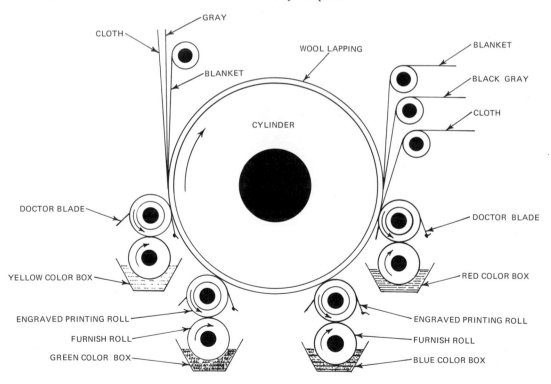

Rollers must be aligned perfectly in order to keep the print in registration. If rollers are not correctly positioned, the resulting print will have one or more colors that do not fall in quite the correct position, causing the print to be distorted. The printed cloth is dried immediately, and then passes to a chamber in which steam or heat sets the dye.

Roller printing is superior to other types of printing for fine or precise designs. However, roller printing requires skilled labor, and much heavy manual work in the changing of the color troughs and rollers. The initial investment of time and money in the preparation of rollers for roller printing and in setting up the machines is such that production of small quantities of printed cloth is not economical. Roller printing is more advantageously used for lengthy runs of the same pattern.

Variations of Roller Printing

Duplex Printing. Duplex printing is done on a special machine that imprints designs on both sides of the fabric at the same time. Most often, the same design is printed on opposite sides, although two different designs can be printed on each side. The resulting fabric looks like fabric with a woven design. This process is seldom used now, as it is almost as expensive to create duplex prints as it is to weave designs.

Blotch Prints. In blotch prints both a colored background and design motifs are printed onto the fabric. These prints should be differentiated from over-printing, or printing of a design on a fabric that has already been piece-dyed. Blotch prints can generally be distinguished from overprinting by a close examination of the fabric. Background colors of blotch-printed fabrics usually have a lighter color on the wrong side than on the right side of the fabric. Sometimes, too, minute, uncolored areas appear between the sections of background color and the design. Blotch prints can be made on either a rotary screen printing machine or on a roller printing machine. Blotch-printed fabrics made by screen printing may have better color penetration in background color areas than those made by roller printing.

Discharge Printing. Piece-dyed fabrics may be printed with a substance, known as a *discharge paste*, that removes color from specific areas of the fabric. If fabrics are not processed carefully to remove all of the discharge paste, these chemicals may eventually weaken the fabric in the areas from which color has been discharged. Discharge prints are recognizable because the color of the background design of the fabric is the same on both the front and back sides.

Flock Printing. By imprinting an adhesive material on the surface of a fabric in the desired pattern, and then sprinkling short fibers over the adhesive, a flocked print may be created. Flocking as a type of finish is discussed at length in Chapter 19.

Resist Printing. Resist printing is a combination printing and dyeing method. A substance that resists dyes is printed onto the fabric in selected areas. Later, when the fabric is passed through the dyebath, the resist material prevents the fabric from absorbing the dye, thereby creating a design. This machine process follows the principle utilized in handmade batik fabrics.

Figure 18-9. Flocked design printed on a sheer nylon fabric.

Warp Printing. Warp yarns can be printed before they are woven into the fabric. The resulting fabrics have a delicate, shimmery quality that is achieved by the indistinct patterns created in warp printing. Warp printing is applied to higher priced fabrics. (See Figure 18.5.)

Heat Transfer or Sublistatic Printing

Heat transfer or sublistatic printing is a system of printing in which dyes are applied to a paper base, and then transferred from the paper to a fabric. The transfer of colors takes place as the color sublimes through vaporization. This is achieved by rolling the paper and the fabric together under pressure and at high temperatures (424 degrees F. or 200 degrees C.)

Disperse dyes are used in this system. Since disperse dyes are effective only for some man-made fabrics, heat transfer printing has been limited to the printing of acrylics, nylons, polyesters, triacetates, and polyester-cotton blends in which the proportion of polyester is relatively high. Research is underway to determine how this type of printing can be used with other fibers.

Sublistatic printing achieves a sharpness and clarity that other types of printing cannot match. All colors are printed at the same time, thereby simplifying the operation, and requiring lower processing costs, with fewer personnel required. Production can change rapidly from one design to another, simply by changing the design paper, whereas in roller or screen printing, each separate roller or screen must be removed from the machine, and the machine set up for a new design with different rollers or screens.

Heat transfer printing has proved especially successful in printing knitted fabrics. Knitted goods are less dimensionally stable than woven fabrics. Manufacturers using conventional screen and roller printing techniques on knit fabrics experienced difficulties in making multicolor prints in which the segments of the print must fit together accurately. In sublistatic printing, all parts of the design are applied at once, eliminating the problem stretching of fabrics as they move from one roller to another.

On the other hand, heat transfer printing is slower than either roller or screen printing. Ten to fifteen yards of printed fabric are produced per minute in sublistatic printing operations, whereas roller printing can produce thirty-five yards of fabric per minute and rotary screen printing can produce forty to forty-two yards of fabric per minute.[6]

Other disadvantages of heat transfer printing that have been cited include off-grain printing. Some dyes used on nylons and acrylics have displayed variations in shade depth and, in some cases, problems with fastness to laundering. A yard of paper is required for each yard of fabric to be printed, so the disposal of paper can become a problem. On the other hand, conventional

[6]*American Fabrics* magazine (Summer 1974), p. 45.

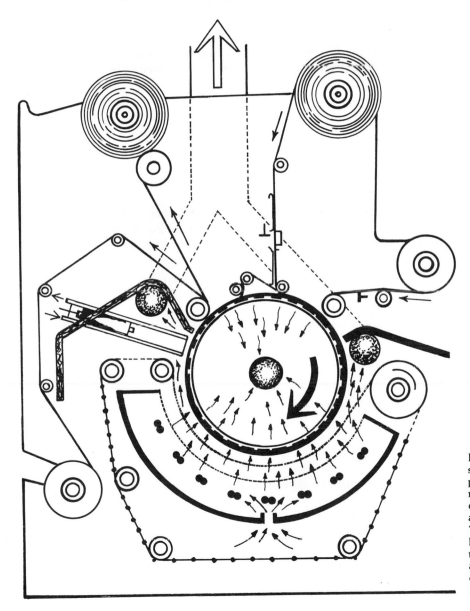

Figure 18-10. Heat transfer printing. This schematic diagram shows transfer-printing process. Unprinted fabric roll is at top to the right of the heat outlet. Gray fabric moves down to the drum where it is almost immediately joined by transfer paper from the right. The two pass through a bank of infrared heaters. Used transfer paper exits left and to the bottom, while printed fabric goes to roll at top left of the heat outlet. Schematic courtesy *Textile World* magazine. Copyright 1972 by McGraw-Hill, Inc.

dyeing and printing systems produce problems of water pollution, whereas paper can be recycled.

Photographic Printing

Photographic printing is done in a manner similar to the photochemical preparation of screens for screen printing. A photosensitive dye is coated on the fabric, a negative is placed over the fabric, light is applied, and a photographic type of printing takes place.

Other Printing Techniques

Electrostatic printing is an experimental process in which a plate with an electrostatic charge is placed behind the fabric. A stencil in the form of the pattern is placed over the fabric. Special powdered inks that can be attracted by the electrostatic charge are passed over the surface fabric, and the inks are attracted into and color the fabric in the open areas of the stencil.

Ombre printing is the printing of a rainbow or varying tone effect. The tone may change from light to dark shades of one color or vice versa, or the effect may be of a shading from one color into another. Ombre effects can also be obtained by weaving fabrics from yarns that have been yarn-dyed into shaded colors.

Polychromatic printing or dyeing is actually a dyeing method that achieves a printed effect. Several different streams of dye liquor of different colors are utilized. The dye liquor is run over the surface of the fabric. By controlling the direction and flow of the dye, a variety of different effects can be achieved. Polychromatic is a trademark of the ICI Company.

Types of Textile Designs

Textile fabrics utilize the same types of designs and design motifs that are used in a wide variety of other decorated items. These designs are often classified as being either realistic, stylized, geometric, or abstract in nature. Furthermore, certain traditional patterns in some of these categories have become classic designs used for either home furnishings or wearing apparel, or both.

REALISTIC DESIGNS

Realistic or naturalistic designs depict real objects in a natural manner. Human, animal, plant forms, or any other object may be selected for representation.

Certain traditional patterns in textile fabrics fall into this classification. *Toile de jouy*, for example, is a fine line representation of a pastoral or historic scene printed in one color on a white or off-white fabric. Most often the fabric is cotton, a cotton blend, or linen. Many floral patterns realistically depict flower and plant forms.

Figure 18-11. Toile de juoy fabric depicting the steps in the manufacture of this fabric. Courtesy of the Metropolitan Museum of Art, Rogers Fund, 1927.

STYLIZED DESIGNS

Stylized designs distort real objects. The original source of inspiration for a stylized design is generally recognizable, but the object is exaggerated or simplified in such a way as to give it an unnatural form. Paisley prints are an example of a traditional design that is a stylized leaf form from India. In addition to distorting the real form of an object, stylized designs frequently use colors and proportions that are not natural. (See Figures 18.14 and 18.15.)

GEOMETRIC DESIGNS

Geometric patterns utilize geometric forms such as circles, squares, ovals, rectangles, triangles, ellipses, and so on. Polka dots are geometric patterns, as are plaids and stripes.

ABSTRACT DESIGNS

Abstract patterns have little or no reference to real objects. Although often somewhat geometric in form, they are less rigid than geometric designs. It is sometimes difficult to place certain designs clearly into one specific design category. The distinctions among stylized, geometric, and abstract patterns may sometimes become blurred.

SUMMARY

These patterns may be created in small or large scale. The effect of the pattern may be altered by variations in scale, closeness of the design, or the colors in which it it printed. Except for hand-painted textiles, patterns must be repeated in order to cover the full length of a piece of fabric that may range from a few feet to many thousands of yards in length. The single pattern unit that is to be reproduced is called the *repeat*. The length of the repeat may range from a fraction of an inch to several feet.

A realistic pattern created in very small scale and repeated often may, from a distance, give the effect of a geometric or abstract pattern. Placing a large-scale realistic pattern against a sharply contrasting background color may emphasize its realism, whereas placing the same pattern against a low contrast background may make it seem abstract. An enormous variety of design possibilities are open to the textile designer through manipulation of scale and proportion, placement of design, and selection of color.

CROSS-CULTURAL OR HISTORIC INFLUENCES ON DESIGN

Each historic period of Western civilization and each of the non-Western cultures has developed a wide variety of traditional patterns in textile fabrics. Modern designers frequently utilize these as sources of inspiration or may copy them directly.

Reproductions of, or designs inspired by, historic textiles are more often used in fabrics for interior design than in apparel fabrics. Particular historic designs may be chosen because they are associated with certain furniture styles. Historic textiles that are most often used as a source of design include Oriental textiles, especially those of China, Japan, and India; Middle Eastern textiles, especially those of Persia and the Byzantine Empire; Renaissance; Baroque; and Early American.

Oriental Textile Designs

The early invention in China of complex looms for weaving silk led to the development of elaborately woven patterned brocades and damasks. Embroidery was another important form of textile decoration, as were hand-blocked

Figure 18-12. Embroidered Chinese fabric of the eighteenth century. Courtesy of the Metropolitan Museum of Art, bequest of William Christian Paul, 1930.

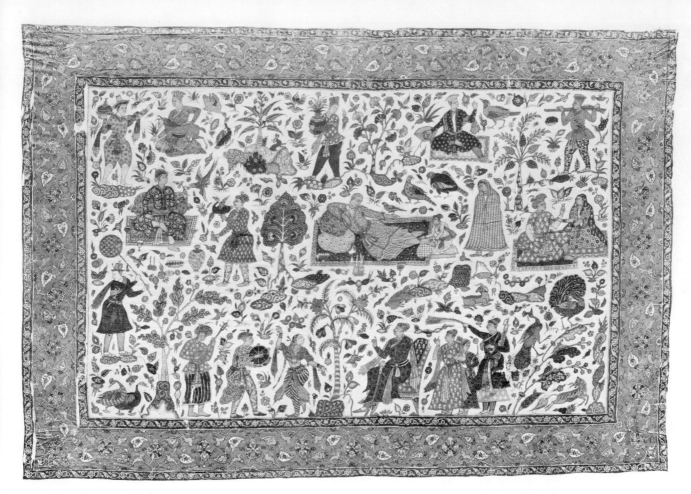

Figure 18-13. Printed and painted cotton cushion cover made in India between 1615–1640. Courtesy of the Metropolitan Museum of Art, Rogers Fund, 1928.

prints. Chinese designs lay heavy emphasis on religious symbols. Among the more widely used motifs are dragons, peacocks, chrysanthemums, peonies, and other flowers, and stylized wave and cloud motifs.

Japanese patterned fabrics are often reproduced. These fabrics are likely to emphasize human figures, blossoms, or Japanese scenes.

The influence of India in textile design is dramatically illustrated by the wide variety of fabric names that derive from Indian place names: Madras, Calico (from Calicut), and Bengaline (from Bengali), are examples. In the seventeenth and eighteenth centuries vast quantities of Indian printed cotton were imported by European countries and Colonial Americans. Paisley prints, madras, and calicos with small, often stylized design motifs are among the important Indian patterns.

Middle Eastern Textiles

Persia, like China, developed elaborate looms for weaving textiles. Brocades, damasks, and similar fabrics were especially important Persian contributions to

Figure 18-14. Persian carpet of the seventeenth century. Courtesy of the Metropolitan Museum of Art, Rogers Fund, 1931.

the history of textiles. Pattern motifs were many and varied, and included floral forms, especially poppies, roses, and flowering trees, cypresses, and the pomegranate, as well as animal forms, landscapes, hunting scenes, and birds.

The textiles woven during the Byzantine Empire were rich and colorful. Brocades, damasks, and velvets predominated. Many ecclesiastical fabrics survive, and these place heavy emphasis on Christian symbolism. Secular fabrics utilize formal motifs, including fantastic birds and animals placed inside geometric forms. Byzantine textile design formed a bridge between East and West, and melded Oriental and Roman designs.

Renaissance Textiles

The earliest designs woven in Western Europe were made in Italy. Silk cultivation spread to Italy from Byzantium, and eleventh- to thirteenth-century Italian textiles showed strong Byzantine influence. After the fifteenth century, Italian and French Renaissance styles emphasized the use of velvets, brocades, and heavy satins in a variety of rich colors.

Design motifs took stylized shapes, especially flower and plant forms, the artichoke being a particular favorite. S-shaped scrolls, acanthus leaves, and geometric patterns in small to medium sized repeats were seen.

Baroque Styles

The styles of the seventeenth century, known as *baroque* styles, were large in scale, with full, flowing, curved lines. Leafy plants, foliage, flowers, and fruit motifs predominated. Often somewhat stylized in form, they were generally made in clear, dark colors.

Rococo Designs

The rococo designs of the eighteenth century by contrast, are more delicate in scale, more realistic in representation. Oriental design motifs may be incorporated, and it is not unusual to see representations of pastoral scenes. Colors are more pastel, and there is a greater use of printed cottons and fabrics with woven stripes.

Early American Textiles

Many of the fabrics used in Colonial America were imported from Britain, the European continent, or India. Furthermore, American furniture styles were also copies of, or modifications of, other Western European furniture styles. For these reasons, many of the fabrics that are traditionally associated with Early American textiles are similar to English and French styles of the same time period, with special emphasis on the use of printed cottons and linens. American textiles in rural areas tended to be homespun. Often hand-embroidery in crewel yarns was applied.

Many museums and historic sites have extensive collections of Early American fabrics. Sometimes textile companies will reproduce one of these fabrics. When a modern reproduction of an authentic historic printed textile is made, the fabric is called a *documentary print*.

Figure 18-15. Sixteenth-century Italian velvet with cut and uncut pile areas. Courtesy of the Metropolitan Museum of Art. Gift of Mrs. Valentine A. Blacque, 1933, in memory of Valentine A. Blacque.

Textile Designs from Other Cultures

Textile designs from many non-Western cultures have become important influences in American textile fashions. African textiles have inspired many contemporary prints. Tie-dyed fabrics, block-printed fabrics, and resist prints

Figure 18-16. French brocade of the Louis XVI period with rococo floral pattern. Courtesy of the Metropolitan Museum of Art, Rogers Fund, 1920.

by African craftsmen served as the basis for many copies and adaptations. Javanese batik fabrics have long been known and imitated. Both prehistoric textile designs and modern fabrics made by the Indians of South and North America also served to inspire contemporary designers.

AATCC Glossary of Printing Terms. Research Triangle Park, N.C.: American Association of Textile Chemists and Colorists, 1973.

"Batik: Design & Colors." *American Fabrics & Fashions,* Fall 1972, p. 34.

Book of Papers. 1974 Technical Conference. Research Triangle Park, N.C.: American Association of Textile Chemists and Colorists, 1974.

Encyclopedia of Textiles, American Fabrics. Englewood Cliffs, N.J.: Prentice-Hall, Inc., 2nd ed.

FENOGLIO, R. A., and J. J. GORONDY. "Heat Transfer Printing." *Textile Chemist and Colorist,* May 1975, p. 24.

HALLER, R. "Techniques of Early Cloth Printing." *CIBA Review,* vol. III, p. 933.

"Heat Transfer Printing." *American Fabrics and Fashions,* Summer 1974, p. 45.

"Ikat." *American Fabrics and Fashions,* Fall 1975, p. 59., Summer 1975, p. 39.

KELLER, I. *Batik, The Art and Craft.* Rutland, Vt.: Charles Tuttle Co., 1966.

LEWIS, E. *Romance of Textiles.* New York: Macmillan Publishing Co., Inc., 1937.

MILES, L. W. C. *Textile Printing.* Watford, England: Merrow Publishing Company, Ltd., Monographs, 1971.

SCHAEFER, G. "The Earliest Specimens of Cloth Printing." *CIBA Review,* October 1939, p. 914 ff.

Textile Printing: An Ancient Art and Yet So New. Research Triangle Park, N.C.: American Association of Textile Chemists and Colorists, 1975.

"Transfer Printing." *Textile Month,* January 1976, p. 46.

Recommended References

19

FINISHES THAT AFFECT THE AESTHETIC PROPERTIES OF TEXTILES

The finishing of woven, knitted, and nonwoven textiles consists of the application of a wide variety of treatments and special processes that give to the fabric some quality that is needed to enhance its aesthetic or performance properties. Some finishes modify appearance, some modify behavior, and some modify both appearance and behavior.

Classification of Finishes

Finishes may be classified on several bases. For purposes of this text, finishes are divided into those that produce a change in aesthetics (that is, appearance or hand) and those that produce a change in inherent fiber characteristics.

Finishes are also separated into those that are permanent, those that are durable, or those that are temporary. Permanent finishes will last for the lifetime of the product. Durable finishes can be expected to function reasonably well for most of the lifetime of the fabric, and temporary finishes are removed after one or more launderings or dry cleanings. Renewable finishes can be added to fabrics when through use or care processes the original finish has been diminished or destroyed.

Some writers separate finishes into those that are achieved by mechanical manipulation of the fabric and those that use chemical treatments to produce the change. A finish such as calendering that simply "irons" the fabric is a mechanical finish, whereas mercerization, in which cotton is treated with sodium hydroxide, is an example of a chemical finish.

Some finishes are made permanent by utilizing the thermoplastic characteristics of synthetic fabrics. When heat-sensitive fibers are subjected to finishes involving heat treatment, the fabric may be permanently "set" in such a way that new characteristics are established. For example, in many finishes patterns are heat-set into thermoplastic fabrics by the use of heated, patterned rollers.

Chemical resins are frequently used in the treatment of fabrics to produce durable finishes. Many of these resins are also heat sensitive and can be used to achieve finishes of excellent quality that are reasonably permanent.

The finishing process produces either physical or chemical changes in the fiber or fabric. Some finishes alter the physical structure of the fabric by either physical or chemical manipulation of the fabric. For example, stiffness can be added to a fabric by applying a resin or starch to the cloth. This additive coats or penetrates the fiber, causing it to become stiffer. This change is brought about by the physical combination of the fiber with the finishing material. The chemical composition of the fiber is not altered even though a physical change is made.

By contrast, some mothproofing finishes actually alter the chemical structure of wool, exchanging the chemical cross-linkages that moths find attractive for others that moths find unpalatable. In this instance, the chemical structure of the fiber is actually changed. Some finishes also produce concurrent physical and chemical alterations in fiber and/or fabric.

A single fabric can be given several finishes that are each intended to accomplish different purposes. For example, a fabric may be bleached to enhance whiteness, and then given a permanent press finish to make it resist wrinkling. Few fabrics are manufactured that do not undergo some type of finishing. The discussion in this chapter concentrates on those finishes that affect appearance and/or hand. Finishes that affect performance are discussed in Chapter 20.

REMOVING IMPURITIES FROM FABRICS

In the processing of natural fibers, impurities such as grease and vegetable matter in wool, gum in silk, or vegetable matter in cotton have been removed. Some of the residue of these substances may remain even after spinning and weaving. Also, fabrics may become soiled during weaving. Temporary starches (called *sizings*) may have been applied, or special additives such as identifying dyes may have been used. These substances must be removed before further treatment is given the fabrics.

Cotton

The general process of cleaning fabrics after weaving is called *scouring.* For cottons, or cotton blended with man-mades, this is generally done in a *kier vat*, a large iron vessel in which soap and boiling water wash the fabrics clean. Alternate procedures for scouring cottons include use of a *J box* in which a continuous scouring and bleaching of full-width fabrics takes place. Automatic machines pass fabric through the solution at the rate of 200 yards a minute.

Silk

In addition to removing the soil or additives used while weaving silk, degumming or scouring removes any gum or sericin that remains on the silk. Often a quantity of the natural gum has been allowed to remain on the silk fiber to give it additional body and to make it easier to handle in spinning and weaving. Although a few silk fabrics are manufactured in which the gum is retained purposely in order to provide body or produce a different texture, most silk fabrics are degummed as part of the finishing process. The resultant fabric has a much softer hand.

Wool

Wool fabrics that have some vegetable matter clinging to the woven or knitted yarns must be *carbonized*. Carbonizing is accomplished by the immersion of wool in sulfuric acid. Because strong acids readily attack the cellulose of the vegetable matter and do not immediately harm protein fibers like wool, the burrs, sticks, leaves, and the like that remain in the wool are destroyed. The treatment is carried out under carefully controlled conditions so that the wool is not damaged, and the fabric is given a careful scouring afterward to remove

Figure 19-1. Fabric is scoured on a continuous basis as it passes through cleansing solution. Courtesy of West Point Pepperell.

Figure 19-2. Fabric passes over gas flame that singes or burns off excess surface fiber. Courtesy of West Point Pepperell.

or neutralize all of the acid that remains. The scouring of wool is done in solutions of less concentration and at lower temperatures than scouring of other fibers because most scouring solutions are alkaline in nature and wool is damaged by alkali.

BASIC FINISHES THAT ALTER HAND OR TEXTURE

Fulling

Wool fabrics are *fulled* in order to give the fabric a more compact structure. In a type of preshrinking, fabrics are subjected to moisture, heat, soap, and pressure. This causes the yarns to shrink and to lie closer together, and gives the fabric a denser structure. Wool cloth may be given more or less fulling, depending upon the desired characteristics of the resultant fabrics. Melton cloth, for example, is one of the most heavily fulled wool fabrics, and has a dense, feltlike texture.

Singeing

To produce a smooth surface finish on fabrics made from staple fibers, fabrics are passed over a heated copper plate or above a gas flame. The fiber ends burn off. The fabric is moved very rapidly and only the fiber ends are destroyed. Immediately after passing the flame, the fabric is passed through a water bath to put out any sparks that might remain.

The burning characteristics of fibers must be taken into account when this process is applied, as heat-sensitive fibers melt, forming tiny balls on the surface of the fabric. These balls interfere with dye absorption, so that, as a general rule, heat-sensitive fibers would be singed after dyeing or printing.

Filament yarns do not require singeing, as there are no short fiber ends to project onto the surface of the fabric. The tendency of some man-made fibers to pill may be decreased by singeing.

Stiffening

Sizing. In order to add body to fabrics, some type of sizing is often applied. This may be in the form of starch, gelatin, or resin, or a combination of these with softening substances such as oils or waxes.

Starches and gelatins are temporary sizings and are removed during laundering or dry cleaning. Inexpensive cotton or rayon fabrics are often heavily starched, and after laundering may become quite limp. For fabrics sized with starch or gelatin, it is possible to determine how heavily sized a fabric is by rubbing hard at a section of the fabric. If small flakes of starch can be removed, the fabric has obviously been sized. If the same fabric is held up to the light, one can often see more light through the area in the section from which the sizing has been removed than in other areas.

Gelatins are used as sizing on rayons because they are clear in color and do not dim the luster of the fabric. The application of the sizing, plus a hard press may create a deceptively full hand and surface luster that is lost after laundering.

Various resins can also be used to add body to fabrics. These resins produce a durable finish. The resin attaches to the surface of the fiber or actually impregnates the fiber. Sometimes resins are used in combination with starches in order to produce a reasonably durable finish in which the resin serves to "bind" the starch to the fiber.

Permanently Stiffened Cottons. By a special acid treatment known as *parchmentizing*, some cottons are given a permanently stiff character. The application of a carefully controlled acid solution causes the surface of the yarn to become softened and gelatinlike. An afterwash in cold water causes the gelatinous outer surface to harden, forming a permanently stiffened exterior. Permanently finished organdy is one of the fabrics that is made by this process. Acid finishes are also used to create certain decorative effects, which are discussed later in this chapter.

Weighting of Silk. Raw silk contains from 25 to 30 per cent of its weight in sericin or gum. When the fiber is cleaned, this substance is removed. Silks may be weighted both to enable the producer to regain some of the loss in fiber weight and to add greater body to fabrics.

The silk fabric is first placed in an acid solution of stannic chloride (a chloride of tin). The fiber absorbs the substance, then is washed, placed into a solution of sodium phosphate, and then washed again. During this process, an insoluble compound (tin phosphate) is formed within the fiber, and the weight and body of the fiber is increased. A further treatment with sodium silicate solution forms another chemical compound and still greater weight.

These steps can be repeated a number of times, and with each repetition, greater weighting is achieved. The silk fiber can hold considerably more than its own weight of this added chemical weighting.

Heavily weighted silks may have very poor abrasion resistance and eventually will break from the weight of the silk. For this reason, legislation has been passed to restrict the quantity of weighting that may be added to silk without indicating on the label that the silk has been weighted. Any silk labeled Pure Dye Silk may not contain more than 10 per cent of weighting, or 15 per cent for black fabrics. If heavily weighted silks are burned, the fabric is consumed, leaving a skeleton of the metallic compound in the shape of the woven fabric. In this way, silk samples may be tested for weighting.

FINISHES THAT AFFECT APPEARANCE

Many finishes are used because of the effect they have on the appearance of the fabric. Sometimes these finishes produce a related change in texture or hand, as well.

Bleaching

Fabrics are bleached or whitened in order to prepare them for dyeing or printing or in order to produce a fabric that is of a clear white color. Bleaches are chemical substances, so that an appropriate bleach must be selected for each fiber. Most bleaches used by industry are either chlorine bleaches or peroxygen bleaches. The peroxygen bleaches, and particularly peroxide bleaches, are used most frequently in commercial bleaching of gray (or untreated) goods, although for some fabrics other types of bleaches must be used. (Home bleaching is discussed in Chapter 21.)

Fluorescent Whiteners

In addition to bleaching, many white fabrics are treated with fluorescent whiteners (also known as optical brighteners) to enhance their whiteness. Fluorescent whiteners are not bleaches, but are dyelike compounds that emit a strong bluish fluoresence. This causes the white to appear whiter (a "bluish-white" instead of a "yellow-white") and brighter. Optical brighteners are reasonably fast to laundering. They are present in many detergents and can also be purchased for use in home laundering.

Delustering

Many of the man-made fibers have a high natural luster or brightness. Some man-made fibers are treated to reduce this luster before the fiber is formed. Pigments such as titanium dioxide are added to the solution before the fiber is extruded. The tiny specks of pigment cause the fiber to reflect less light, and thereby decrease the brightness. Delustered fibers can be identified by microscopic examination. Surface and cross sections of delustered fibers show a number of small, dark flecks or spots in a random distribution. (See Figures 4.6 and 7.5.)

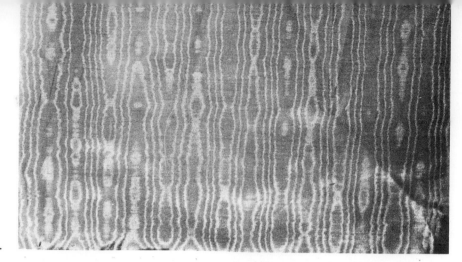

Figure 19-3.   Faille fabric with a moiré finish.

Calendering

Calendering is a broad, general term that refers to a mechanically produced finish achieved by passing fabrics between a series of two or more rollers. The object of calendering is to smooth the fabric.

Simple Calendering.   The simplest form of calendering is comparable to ironing a fabric. The calender rolls are heated and the dampened cloth is passed between the cylinders that smooth and flatten the fabric, producing a wrinkle-free, slightly glossy surface.

Glazing.   A special calender called a *friction calender* is used to produce fabrics that have a highly glazed or polished surface, such as chintz or polished cotton. Prior to passing the fabric through the calender, the cloth is saturated with either starch or resin. The fabric is dried slightly, then fed into the machine in which a rapidly moving, and a heated roller polishes the surface of the more slowly moving fabric. If starch is used to produce the glaze, the finish is temporary. If resins are used, the glaze is durable.

Schreinerizing.   The Schreiner calender produces fabrics with a soft luster, and a soft hand. One of the calenders is embossed with about 250 fine diagonal lines per inch. This roller passes over the fabric, flattening the yarns and producing a more opaque fabric with soft luster and hand. Unless the fabric is thermoplastic, the finish is a temporary one. Thermoplastic fibers are permanently set into position by the Schreiner calender's heat. If fabrics are given a resin finish before Schreinerizing, the finish will be fairly durable.

The Schreiner finish is designed to give fabrics a soft luster. Damask table linens and cotton sateens are among the fabrics given this finish routinely. Thermoplastic tricots use the finish to enhance surface luster.

Moiré.   Moiré fabrics have a watered or clouded surface appearance on the fashion side of the fabric, which is sometimes called a "grain of wood" pattern. The original technique for producing moiré fabrics is an old one, often seen in luxurious silks of the eighteenth and nineteenth centuries.

To achieve an effective moiré pattern, ribbed fabrics such as taffeta, faille, or bengaline are usually selected. The pattern is temporary, durable, or perma-

Figure 19-4. Embossed cotton fabric.

nent depending upon the fiber and/or chemicals used. In watermarked moiré, such as those used a hundred years ago, the pattern would be destroyed by laundering. Resin treatment makes the pattern reasonably durable to cleaning and laundering, and the use of heat-setting of thermoplastic fibers creates a permanent finish.

One of two methods is employed. The first, and more traditional method, places two lengths of a fabric from the same bolt face-to-face, with one layer slightly off-grain in relation to the other. Enormous pressure is put upon the fabrics by the smooth moiré rollers, and the ribs of one fabric press down on those of the other, flattening each other in some areas and causing the fabrics to reflect light differently across the surface of the fabric. The moiré produced in this manner has a random pattern with no discernible repeats.

The second method uses a roller with a moiré pattern etched into its surface. In this procedure, the roller flattens one area more than another, creating the same effect as in the first method. Here, however, the patterns are repeated at regular intervals.

Embossing. Embossed designs are produced by pressing a pattern onto fabrics. Like other calendered finishes, they may be permanent when applied to thermoplastic fibers, durable when applied to fabrics that have been resin-treated, and temporary on other fabrics.

Some embossed designs form a raised, three-dimensional pattern; others have a flat design. The flat design pattern is created by running an embossed roller with a raised pattern across the fabric. The opposite roller is made of paper and has a flat surface. Because the paper roll can "give" with the pressure, the embossed roller "prints" the colorless design by flattening some sections of the cloth.

Three-dimensional embossed designs are made with embossed rollers also. In this method the embossed roller first presses the design onto the surface of the paper roller; then when the fabric is passed between the rollers, both the engraved roller and the shaped paper roll together to mold the shape of the pattern onto the cloth.

Embossed designs provide surface texture at a lower cost than woven

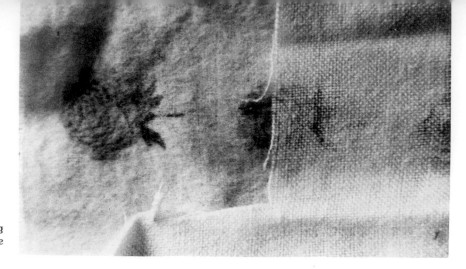

Figure 19-5. Napped cotton flannel showing the unnapped wrong side contrasted with the napped right side.

designs. If applied to nonthermoplastic fibers without special resin finishes, the embossing will be lost sooner or later. Embossed fabrics should not be ironed, since the design may be diminished by pressing.

Ciréing. Ciré fabrics are characterized by a high surface polish. A fashion term, "the wet look," has sometimes been used to describe ciré fabrics. Made by much the same process as friction calendering, ciré effects on natural fibers or rayons are produced by using waxes and thermoplastic resins. Heat-sensitive synthetics are given a permanent "wet look" by this procedure when the thermoplastic fibers fuse slightly under the heat of the rollers.

When hydrophobic fibers are given a ciré finish, some degree of water repellency is provided. This occurs as a result of the slight glazing or fusing that the fabrics undergo.

Beetling

Linens and cottons that are intended to look like linens are beetled, by pounding the fabric (in a machine equipped with hammers that strike over the surface of the fabric) to flatten the yarns and make them smoother and more lustrous. Unless a resin treatment has been given to the fabric before beetling this must be considered a temporary finish.

Napping

Napped fabrics are fabrics in which loose fiber ends are brushed up onto the surface of the fabric on either one or both sides of the cloth. Napping is applied to woven or knitted goods and should not be confused with pile fabrics in which a separate set of yarns is used to create the pile.

Napped fabrics are used for clothing and household textiles in which warmth is desired. The loose fiber ends trap air that serves as insulation. Blankets, coating fabrics, sweaters, and the like are often made from napped fabrics.

The nap is created by brushing the surface of the fabric. Napped fabrics are generally made from yarns with a fairly loose twist, so that the surface yarns will brush up easily. Long ago the brushing was done with teasels (thistle heads with many fine, hooklike, sharp projections). Today napping is more likely to be done with machines set with small, fine wires that approximate the teasel spine. These small hooklike projections catch fibers and pull them up to the surface of the fabric, creating a fuzzy, soft layer of fibers on the surface that are also caught into the yarn. Some very fine napped wools are still made by using natural teasels. The terms *gigging* and *raising* may also be used to describe the napping process. Excessive napping may tend to weaken fabrics by brushing up too many fibers, thereby weakening the basic structure of the fabric.

Brushing. Many napped fabrics are brushed in such a way that the nap runs in one direction. When this has been done, the fingers can be run across the surface of the fabric to feel that the napped fabric is smooth in one direction and rougher in the other direction. Items cut from such fabrics must be handled so that the direction of all pieces is the same. If this is not done, a fabric in which the grain runs down may reflect light differently than one in which the grain runs up. This difference in light reflection may cause pieces placed side by side to appear to be different in color.

Shearing. Napped or pile fabrics may be sheared in order to make the nap or the pile the same thickness in all parts of the fabric. The shearing is done in a machine in which sharp, rotating blades cut the pile or nap to the desired length. The machine has been compared by Potter and Corbman to a lawn-mower.[1] If some sections of the pile or nap are flattened, and other areas sheared, brushing up the uncut sections can achieve a sculptured effect.

Flocking

A surface effect that is similar to a nap or pile may be created by flocking in which short fibers are "glued" onto the surface of fabrics by an adhesive material. If the adhesive coats the entire surface of the fabric, the flocking will cover the entire surface of the fabric, but if the adhesive is printed onto the fabric in a pattern of some sort, the flock will adhere only in the printed areas.

Short lengths of fiber flocking can be made from any generic fiber type. Rayon is most often used for flocking because of its relatively low cost. Nylon may be selected for situations in which good abrasion resistance is required.

Fibers for flocking are made from bundles of tow fiber (continuous filament fibers without twist). The tow is fed through a finish removal bath, then into a bank of cutters that cut flock of the desired length. The fibers may be dyed before they are attached to the fabric, or the completed fabric may be dyed.

The attachment of the flock to the fabric is done by either of two methods. The mechanical flocking process sifts loose flock onto the surface of the fabric to be coated. A series of beaters agitate the fabric causing most of the fibers to be set in an upright position, with one end of the fiber "locked" into the adhesive.

The second method causes the fibers to be attached in an upright position by

[1] M. D. Potter, and B. P. Corbman, *Textiles, Fiber to Fabric* (New York: McGraw-Hill, Inc., 1967), p. 142.

passing them through an electrostatic field. The fibers pick up the electric charge and align themselves vertically. One end penetrates into the adhesive, and the flock is formed. Electrostatic flocking assures more complete vertical positioning, and the resultant fabrics are of better quality. It is a more costly process. There is no way for a consumer to tell which process was used when buying fabrics.

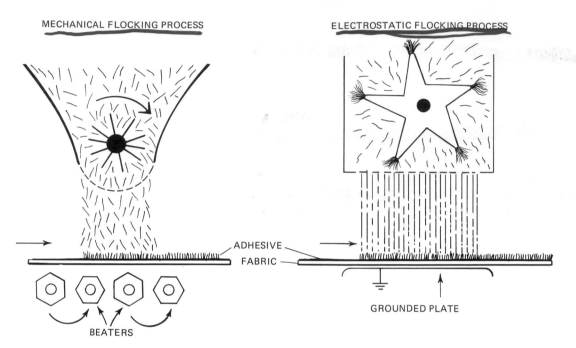

MECHANICAL FLOCKING PROCESS

ELECTROSTATIC FLOCKING PROCESS

ADHESIVE
FABRIC

BEATERS

GROUNDED PLATE

Figure 19-6. Application of flock to fabrics.

The durability of flocked fabrics is largely dependent upon the adhesives that hold the flock firmly during either laundering or dry cleaning. In some cases, flock may be removed by dry-cleaning solvents. Permanent care labels should tell the consumer how flocked fabrics ought to be handled. A second factor in the durability of flocked fabrics has to do with the fiber from which the flock has been made. For example, rayon flocking tends to wear more readily than nylon.

Burnt-out Designs

Chemicals that will dissolve some fibers can be used to produce alterations in fabric appearance. It is possible, for example, to create open areas in fabrics by imprinting a cellulosic fabric with a sulfuric acid paste that dissolves the printed area. Such fabrics are likely to fray around the edges of the dissolved area, and are not especially durable.

In blended fabrics, this technique can be used to create a number of interesting effects. Two different fibers are used. When the dissolving material is imprinted on the fabric, one of the fibers is dissolved while the other is

Figure 19-7. Dark areas of this fabric have been dissolved out by chemicals to produce a "burnt-out" design.

unharmed. Those areas that have not had chemical imprinted upon them remain intact, and create the design. By contrasting texture, luster, or color of the fiber to be burnt-out with that of the second fiber, a number of attractive decorative effects can be achieved.

Plissé Designs

A puckered or plissé effect is achieved in some fabrics by imprinting them with chemicals that cause the fabric to shrink. When these chemicals are printed in a design, some areas of the fabric shrink while others do not. This causes untreated areas to pucker or puff up between the treated areas. Cottons and rayons react in this way when treated with sodium hydroxide, an alkali, as do nylons that have been printed with phenol, an acid substance. (Plissé fabrics should not be ironed because the pressing of the plissé flattens the surface.)

Acid Design

In addition to stiffening the fabric, the acid treatment of cotton fabric causes it to become more transparent. This action can be utilized to create fabrics with a "frosted" design. Areas of the fabric are coated with acid-resistant materials. When the finish is applied, these areas remain opaque, while the acid-treated areas become quite transparent.

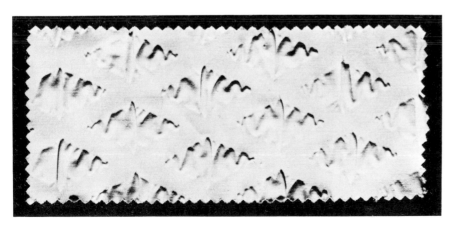

Figure 19-8. Cotton plissé puckered design created by printing with sodium hydroxide on the background to shrink the fabric, leaving puffed, untreated areas between.

Tentering

In the application of many finishes, the fabric must be immersed in a liquid. To dry the fabric without wrinkles, fabrics are stretched between two parallel chains of correct width. The fabric is held in place on the tenter frame by pins and clips. Examination of the selvage of fabrics will usually reveal either small pinholes or marks from the clips.

The tenter frame carries the fabric into a drying apparatus where the fabric is dried under tension, and made wrinkle-free. Fabrics that have not been set on the tenter frame straight will be off-grain. That is, the warp and filling yarns will not cross at right angles. Some fabrics that are off-grain can be straightened by pulling the yarns into the correct or straight position. However, fabrics that have had heat-setting or resin treatments cannot be straightened and will always be off-grain. The serviceability and aesthetic qualities of fabrics are, therefore, adversely affected by poor tentering.

Figure 19-9. Fabric entering tenter frame. Courtesy of West Point Pepperell.

Figure 19-10. Workers inspect and burl fabrics. Courtesy of West Point Pepperell.

A Few Other Finishing Steps

Before a fabric is ready to leave the factory, a visual inspection of the goods is made by running it over a roller. The process is called *perching,* and the machine used is known as a perch. The perch resembles the uprights on a football goal.

For woolens and worsteds, both *burling* and *specking* may have to be done. Specking is the removal from woolens and worsteds of burrs, specks, or other small objects that might detract from the final appearance of the fabric. It is usually done with a tweezers or a burling iron.

Burling is the removal of loose threads and knots from woolens and worsteds by means of a burling iron, a type of tweezer. Many knots must be pulled or worked to the back of the fabric because pulling them out might leave a small hole in the fabric.

The finishes described in this chapter might be summed up as ". . . the application of a pleasing or appealing effect to the fabric, comparable with the application of cosmetics to improve the facial effects of those who use them."[2]

[2] *A Dictionary of Textile Terms* (Danville, Va.: Dan River Mills, 1967), p. 41.

Recommended References

HALL, A. J. *Textile Finishing*. New York: American Elsevier Publishing Co., Inc., 1966.

HOLLEN, N. , and J. SADDLER, *Textiles*. New York: Macmillan Publishing Company, Inc., 1973.

JOSEPH, M. *Introductory Textile Science*. New York: Holt, Rinehart, and Winston, Inc., 1972.

LaBARTHE, J. *Elements of Textiles*. New York: Macmillan Publishing Company, 1975.

MARSH, J. T. *Introduction to Textile Finishing*. Plainfield, N.J.: Textile Book Service, 1966.

POTTER, M. D., and B. P. CORBMAN. *Textiles, Fiber to Fabric*. New York: McGraw-Hill Book Co., 1967.

20

FINISHES THAT AFFECT THE PERFORMANCE OF TEXTILES

The preceding chapter described finishes that have as their primary purpose the alteration of some of the aesthetic properties of fabrics. This chapter concentrates on those finishes that serve to change the behavior of textiles.

For purposes of discussion, these finishes are divided into those that improve upon innate fiber qualities in order to make them more serviceable, those that minimize fabric care, and those that affect the safety or health of the consumer.

SHRINKAGE CONTROL

A reduction in the length or width of a fiber, yarn, or fabric is known as *shrinkage*. If fabrics shrink after they have been made into garments or household items, they may decrease in size to such an extent that the item is no longer serviceable. For example, a garment with a twenty-five-inch waist size will decrease by one and one-fourth inches if it shrinks 5 per cent.

Some fibers shrink naturally. Wool, animal hair fibers, and rayon are examples of such fibers. Most fibers, however, do not shrink because of inherent fiber qualities, but because they have been stretched during the processing of yarns and fabrics. When tension is removed from these fabrics, the fabric relaxes and returns to its original unstretched size and shape.

The wetting of a fabric causes the tension that has been applied during the manufacture of the fabric to be relaxed, so that fabrics generally shrink after the first and up to the fifth laundering. This type of shrinkage is known as *relaxation shrinkage*. Procedures and solvents used in commercial dry cleaning, as a rule do not permit fabrics to relax, as washing does, so that items that are dry cleaned may not shrink so readily. Shrinkage in dry cleaning is generally the result of the high moisture content in the solvent, or steaming during pressing.

Finishes That Improve Serviceability

The warp yarns of woven fabrics are subject to greater tension than filling yarns, so that fabrics generally shrink more in the warp than in the filling direction. Knit goods tend to stretch more during manufacture than do woven goods, and therefore knit goods are likely to shrink and change shape even more than woven goods. A number of finishes have been developed to improve the performance of fabrics in regard to shrinkage.

Compressive Shrinkage Control

For fabrics that are subject to relaxation shrinkage, such as cotton, linen, and rayons, it would seem logical to "wash" or wet the fabrics in order to allow them to return to their true dimensions. This is not, however, practical for the manufacturer, not only because the process would be time consuming but also because the required equipment would take up a great deal of space. Instead, a method has been devised in which the fabric is "mechanically" reduced to its correct dimensions.

A sample of fabric is measured, the measurements are recorded, and the fabric is laundered in such a way as to produce maximum shrinkage. The shrunken fabric is measured, and the percentages of warp and filling shrinkage are calculated. This tells the processor how much to compress the fabric.

Compression of the fabric requires that these steps be followed: The fabric is dampened, and is then placed on a machine that is equipped either with a continuous woolen or felt blanket or a rubber pad. These pads are constructed so that they can be both stretched and compressed. The fabric is carried on top of the blanket (or pad). The fabric meets the carrier at a point where the carrier is stretched around a curve. As the carrier moves from the curve to a straight area, it squeezes or compresses into a smaller, flat area. When the carrier compresses, the fabric it carries is also compressed. The fabric is then set into this compressed position. The machines used are engineered to provide the degree of compression needed for each type of fabric. The trademarks for the various patented processes of the compressive shrinkage type include Rigmel, Sanforization, and Spring-shrunk. These processes guarantee residual (or remaining) shrinkage of less than 1 per cent unless the fabric is dryer-dried.

Tumble drying or cleaning in a coin-operated dry-cleaning machine may produce yet another type of shrinkage. Consolidation shrinkage results from the return of a distorted fiber to its natural shape. Often the fiber becomes shorter and wider. The bulk of the fabric may actually increase, whereas the length and/or width decrease. Consolidation shrinkage requires the presence of mechanical action.

The Sanforized Company has developed a number of different shrinkage control processes for different types of fabrics. All provide for shrinkage of less than 1 per cent. The trademark Sanforized is used on fabrics that are meant to be ironed. Sanforized-Plus-2 is used on durable press blends, and Sanfor-Set is used on 100 per cent cotton garments that will be tumble-dried.

Knit Fabrics. During knitting and finishing, knit fabrics are subject to tension and stretching, especially in the warp direction. The construction of knits allows for greater stretch. They often shrink far more than comparable woven goods. Shrinkage may be particularly pronounced in the warp direction. Processes similar to that described in the preceding section on compressive shrinkage control have been developed recently for the treatment of knits made from natural fibers and rayon.

Although different methods are utilized to return fabrics to their relaxed position, the principle remains that of compression of the fabric. One such process developed and patented by the Compax Corporation and marketed under the name of Pak-nit feeds fabric through a machine in which a series of rollers operating at different rates of speed cause the fabric to become compressed. Pak-nit treatment guarantees less than 1 per cent residual shrinkage.

Redmanized knits (patented process by F. R. Redman Company) are stretched in the crosswise direction. This shortens the lengthwise direction where most knit shrinkage occurs. Other trade names for compressive shrinkage treatment of knits include Perma-size and Shrink-No-Mor.

Sanfor-Knit, another shrinkage control process of the Sanforized Company, addresses the problem of knit shrinkage in both length and width. In this process, test garments that have had compressive shrinkage control treatment are made up in the desired size, are washed, tumble-dried, and checked by a testing instrument called the "Knitpicker." The test instrument determines whether the garments have held both the length dimension and the elasticity in girth that will provide comfortable wear. If the garment does not meet the established standard, the knitter is advised as to changes that should be made in construction, yarn characteristics, or production techniques. Sanfor-Knit garments are available in men's T-shirts, athletic shirts, polo shirts, briefs, and sports knits.

Still another technique for controlling shrinkage in knits is known as Micrex shrinkage control. Fabrics are moved between two conveyers, each six inches apart. The cloth is kept in constant motion, both vertically and horizontally, by hot air from a high-energy nozzle system. This action allows the relaxation of the tensions that were imposed in previous operations, thereby allowing the fabric to relax to its original dimensions.

Synthetic knits are stabilized by heat setting. If heat setting has not been carefully done, the fabrics will shrink. Low-priced double knits, for example, may display shrinkage as a result of inadequate heat setting.

Shrinkage Control for Rayon Fabrics

Viscose rayon fabrics have a tendency to continue to shrink more with each successive laundering or cleaning (this is known as *progressive shrinkage*). Shrinkage control for rayons is most effective when compressive shrinkage control treatments are followed by a resin finish to stabilize the fabric.

Careful control is needed in the application of chemical resins, as excessive concentrations can lower the quality and durability of the fabric. However, if correctly applied, chemical resins penetrate the fibers to prevent further shrinkage.

Shrinkage Control for Wool

Wool and animal hair fibers are among those few fibers that show progressive shrinkage. Most textile experts believe that it is the scale structure of wool that causes this continuous shrinkage, and the scale structure is also thought to be related to the felting of wool in which fibers shrink and cling closely together. In felting, fibers become increasingly entangled owing to the interlocking of the scales from different fibers.

In addition to felting shrinkage, wool fabrics display the same type of residual shrinkage from relaxation that other fibers show. Shrinkage treatments for wool are of two types: those that alleviate the problems of relaxation shrinkage and those that eliminate or ameliorate felting shrinkage.

Relaxation Shrinkage. Several methods can be utilized to eliminate relaxation shrinkage in wool. Because these processes do not protect against felting shrinkage, fabrics that have these finishes should be dry-cleaned or handled carefully during laundering.

1. DAMP RELAXING OR STEAM RELAXING. High-quality worsted fabrics are subjected to a step that permits them to relax before they are cut into garments. The fabric is dampened or steamed, and then permitted to dry in a relaxed state. The tensions applied to the fabric during processing are thereby removed. The process is sometimes called London Shrinking, although this term is British and is not often used by American textile manufacturers.

2. CYLINDER METHOD. In this method, wool fabric is passed across perforated cylinders. Jets of steam are released through the holes in the cylinders, causing the fabric to be dampened. The damp fabric, which relaxes in size, is dried without tension.

Washable Wools. Attempts to produce washable wool fabrics that will not show felting shrinkage have led to the development of processes that alter the basic fiber structure. The wool scale structure is the cause of shrinkage; thus, most of these techniques alter the scale structure in some way.

1. CHLORINIZATION. Chlorine gas or liquid chlorine compounds apparently partially dissolve the edges of the wool fiber scales, thereby decreasing their tendency to catch on each other. This chemical is, however, destructive, and unless the process is carefully controlled it can weaken or seriously damage the cortex of the fiber. The texture of the fabric tends to become rough and harsh.

Fibers that have been subjected to chlorinization are often blended with other wool or man-made fibers. When blended with other wool fibers, problems may be encountered in dyeing, as chlorinized fibers tend to accept dyes more readily than do untreated fibers, thereby causing an unevenness in color. Dylanized is a trademark applied to some fabrics that have been subjected to this process.

2. RESIN COATINGS. A second method for the creation of washable wools is the application of a thin layer of synthetic resin to the surface of the fabric. The resins coat the scales and/or "spot weld" the fibers together in order to decrease shrinkage.

Different processes utilize varying resins. Problems encountered in the use of resins include a tendency for the fabrics to become stiff or harsh to the feel when enough resin is used to make the fabrics completely shrink-proof. Also, some resins are lost after a number of launderings.

Trademarks of resin-finished washable woolens include Lanaset, Sanforlan, Bancora, Superwash, and Synthapret. Wurlan, once a very popular finish, is no longer widely used. The process was quite complex and expensive, and newer resin finishes utilize different and less costly chemicals and simpler processes. Wurset is the name of one of these finishes. Superwash is one of the newer finishes that uses chlorination followed by a resin finish. It is used especially for sweaters and knitwear. Synthapret, a process for woven fabrics, applies resin finishes from either a water or solvent bath and not only cuts down on felting shrinkage but also improves the wash-and-wear qualities of the fabrics on which it is used.

Shrinkage Control Through Heat Setting

Synthetic fabrics may be stabilized through heat setting. Synthetics can be permanently set into shape by subjecting them to heat that is close to, but not beyond, their melting temperatures. This process is used to establish permanent dimensions for these fabrics. Synthetic knits, for example, are relatively free from shrinkage problems if they are properly heat-set, because heat setting may be used to stabilize their dimensions.

MOTHPROOFING FINISHES

Wool and other animal hair fibers are attacked by the larva of the clothes moth. The moth lays its eggs on the fabric, and when the larvae (or grubs) hatch, wool becomes their source of food. Although moth grubs will not attack all fibers, they will eat their way through most fabrics to reach wool. For this reason, other fabrics stored on top of wools that have not been mothproofed may be damaged by moth larvae trying to reach the wool.

To prevent moth damage, precautions must be taken in the care and storage of wool products. Since larvae more readily eat areas of the cloth that are soiled with food stains, clothing should be stored in a clean condition. There are a wide variety of moth repellent substances that can be applied to fabrics or placed in closed storage containers to keep the insects away.

Finishes to prevent moth damage operate according to one of two basic principles. Either the finish is a substance (an insecticide) that is poisonous to the moth larvae, or the finish alters the fiber in some way that makes the wool unpalatable to moth larvae, thereby "starving" the grubs.

The insecticide finishes may be applied during manufacture or during dry cleaning. Some of these finishes are durable, whereas others must be renewed with each cleaning. Moth Snub (Arkansas Company) is durable to laundering and dry cleaning. Mitin (CIBA-Geigy) is fast to dry cleaning but not to laundering.

The second type of finish effects a change in the chemical structure of the fiber. Through chemical treatment, the disulfide cross-linkages, which are attacked by the moth larvae, are changed and replaced by larger and stronger linkages that the moths cannot digest. These finishes are permanent.

ANTIMILDEW AND ANTIROT FINISHES

Mildew, a fungus or mold, is a whitish growth that affects certain textile fibers when they are stored in a damp condition in a warm place. This growth damages the fiber and causes serious staining. Cellulosic fibers are most susceptible to mildew. Protein fibers are less likely to be attacked.

The best protection against mildew is to make certain that the fabrics are dry when stored and that they do not become damp during storage. Mildew is an especially serious problem in warm, humid climates. Mildew weakens fabrics, and home treatments to remove stains from mildew may be degrading to them as well.

Rotting is an acute problem with bast fibers, such as jute and hemp, when they are used for bags, ropes, and other materials that are exposed for long periods to water, damp soil, or wet floors. Rot and mildew-resistant fabrics can be made by treating the fabrics with antiseptic substances. Since copper has bactericidal power, copper solutions may be used to confer a rot-resistant ability to fabrics. A variety of other chemical substances (among them phenol, formaldehyde, and pentachloral phenol) that are not harmful to the fabric and inhibit the growth of micro-organisms are also used.

During experimentation with melamine-resin finishes for crease resistance, it was learned that these finishes retarded mildew and rotting. The trade names Mel-tron (Crown Chemical Corporation) and Arigal (CIBA-Geigy) are given to processes using melamine resins to confer bactericidal qualities.

Home processes can be used to guard against mildew. An afterrinse with boric acid will retard the formation of mildew.

ANTIBACTERIAL FINISHES

Chemical substances that inhibit the growth of bacteria are also used to finish goods that will be used in health care products, apparel, home furnishings, or fabrics used in the hotel/restaurant industry.

Although these finishes are classified as either renewable or durable, even so-called durable finishes are removed gradually during laundering. Trademarks for durable antibacterial (or bacteriostatic) finishes include Arigal, Germicide, Eversan, Permafab, and Steri-septic.

Renewable finishes can be replaced during laundering. Some trademarks of renewable antibacterial finishes are Sanitized, Dowicide, and Borateem.

Certain specific quarternary ammonium compounds are known to combat diaper rash. Many diaper services routinely apply this finish to the diapers that they launder.

HEAT-REFLECTANT FINISHES

An increased level of insulation can be provided in garments and draperies by the addition of heat-reflectant finishes to textile products. Most of these products are treated with a spray coating of metal and resinous substances. The heat-reflectant material is sprayed onto the surface of a closely woven fabric. The finish is designed to keep heat either close to or away from the wearer. The finish is effective only with radiated heat.

Lining fabrics are usually constructed so that the finish is applied to the inside of the fabric. The finish reflects the body heat back, toward the wearer, thus providing added warmth. In protective clothing to be worn under hot conditions, the finish is worn to the outside in order to deflect heat away *from* the body. Draperies may also be treated to provide greater insulation for homes. Treated draperies placed inside windows may serve to keep heat inside the home or to reflect heat outward, preventing it from warming the house.

Most of the processes designed to produce heat reflectance use aluminum in the finish, as it provides excellent reflectancy. Trade names for the process include Milium and Tempo-resisto.

A variant of this principle is utilized in fabrics in which a thin layer of aluminum or other metal foil is applied to fabrics. Foylon and Scotch-Shield are trade names for this process.

LIGHT DETERIORATION

Many textile fabrics are deteriorated by exposure to sunlight, so attempts have been made to protect fabrics from light damage. Of the rays in the spectrum of the sun, the ultraviolet are the most destructive of fibers. Although antilight finishes have yet to be perfected, those that are being tried either coat the fabric or impregnate the fibers with materials that absorb ultraviolet rays but are not themselves either damaged by, or removed by exposure to these rays.

Synthetics that have been delustered with titanium dioxide are especially subject to damage from sunlight. This chemical apparently accelerates damage to the fiber and fading of dyes. The addition of certain chemical salts to the melt solution prior to spinning can ameliorate this problem.

WATER REPELLENCY

Waterproof Fabrics

A fabric that is waterproof allows no water to penetrate from the surface to the underside. Waterproof fabrics generally are coated with rubber or a synthetic plastic material. These materials do not allow air to pass through. In apparel, waterproof fabrics tend to be warm and uncomfortable. For these reasons, most rainwear is not waterproof, but water repellent. The term *water repellent* should not be confused with the term *waterproof*.

Water-repellent Fabrics

Water-repellent fabrics resist penetration by water but are not completely waterproof. Such fabrics represent a practical alternative to fabrics that keep out water and air, since they resist wetting and also allow the passage of air. The passage of air is imperative if one is to have a garment that is comfortable to wear. As Hall pointed out, "Obviously to produce fabrics of this type there has to be some degree of compromise or sacrifice; one has to be satisfied with a fabric which is not absolutely waterproof but which will keep out the water for a long period or at least sufficiently long to give satisfaction when the fabric is worn as a raincoat."[1]

Water repellency is conferred through a combination of the principles of fabric construction, the application of one of the finishes that are classified as either renewable finishes or durable finishes, and appropriate selection of fiber content.

Renewable Finishes. Renewable water repellent finishes are removed during laundering and dry cleaning. These are relatively inexpensive and easily applied, so that they can be renewed after each laundering or dry cleaning.

Either wax emulsions or metallic soaps are used to secure renewable water repellency. Both of these materials are naturally water repellent, and when they are applied in such a way that they coat the yarns of the fabric, they permit the passage of air between the yarns, but prevent the passage of water. If the fabric on which they are coated has a close, compact weave, the water repellency is improved. Of course, in conditions in which the fabric is subjected to long periods of exposure and sufficient force, water will eventually penetrate any water-repellent fabric.

Durable Finishes. As in renewable finishes, the effectiveness of durable water-repellent finishes is improved if fabrics with high yarn counts and close weaves are selected. Although the first water-repellent finishes were of the renewable type, subsequent research has concentrated on effective durable finishes. A number of different materials have been developed that confer a more permanent finish.

1. WATER REPELLENCY. Many of these finishes begin with fatty or oily substances that possess natural water repellency, then treat these substances with other chemicals to form compounds that can be absorbed by the fiber, and are also insoluble in dry cleaning or soap solutions. Pyridinium compounds, methylol stearamides, and ammonium compounds are used. Zelan is a trademark for such a finish.

Silicone compounds are also effective in producing durable water repellent fabrics. Trade names for silicone finishes include Cravanette 330, Hydropruf, Ranedare-S, and Syl-mer.

2. WATER AND OIL REPELLENCY. Most of the finishes under discussion repel water, but do not repel oil. They are quite serviceable for products in which only water repellency is required. However by using fluorochemical compounds, it is possible to produce finishes that repel both water and oil. Scotchgard, Zepel, and Unisec are trade names of three such finishes.

[1] A. J. Hall, *Textile Finishing* (New York: American Elsevier Publishing Co., Inc., 1966), p. 305.

Quarpel is an oil- and water-repellent finish used by the United States Military. It combines fluorocarbon compounds with pyridinium compounds to achieve superior performance. This finish was given an especially drastic "rain" test in which Quarpel withstood eight hours of rain as compared with one hour for other types of finishes.[2]

Some of the durable finishes are durable only to laundering or only to dry cleaning. It is especially important, therefore, for the consumer to follow care instructions attached to these products.

SOIL REPELLENCY

Scotchgard, Zepel, Unisec, or other finishes that repel water and oil may also be classified as soil-resistant finishes. They are applied to fabrics used in products such as upholstery fabrics and tablecloths to prevent staining. They may be applied to the fabric at the time of manufacture in a liquid form or sprayed onto the fabric after the fabric has been applied to a piece of furniture. Aerosol spray containers of some of these finishes can be purchased for home application. The finish tends to diminish with laundering, but can be renewed by using the sprays.

WRINKLE RESISTANCE

Resistance to creasing can be imparted to fabrics by different means. First, the fiber itself may be naturally crease- or wrinkle-resistant because of its resiliency. This is true of many synthetics and of wool. Second, because of their construction, certain fabric types resist or disguise wrinkling. Terry cloth, knits, seersucker, and plissé are such fabrics. Or, special finishes may be applied to fabrics to improve their wrinkle-resistance.

Since cellulosic fibers are most prone to wrinkling, most wrinkle-resistant finishes are applied to fabrics from these fibers or their blends. Crease-resistant finishes date back to 1929 when Tootal Broadhurst Lee Ltd.[3] patented a finish that could be used on cottons and rayons. The Tootal process utilized urea formaldehyde. The theory behind this process that was accepted at the time the process was developed was that the resin penetrated into the fiber and combined chemically with itself to form a long chain compound inside the fiber. Once inside, the resin was thought to "stuff" the fiber so that it was less flexible and therefore resisted wrinkling.

Recent textile finishing processes that have been designed to secure wrinkle resistance in cellulosic fibers also utilize synthetic resins. However, researchers today believe that the wrinkle resistance and recovery are achieved by chem-

Finishes That Minimize Fiber Care

[2] Ibid., p. 338.

[3] U.S. Patent No. 1,734,516—Cotton Textile Impregnation with Resin by Foulds, assignor to Tootal Broadhurst Lee Co., 11/5/29.

ical reactions between the resins and the molecular structure of the fiber. The long-chain molecules of the fiber are "cross-linked" through the action of the chemicals, thereby providing greater stability in the position of the molecules, and preventing them from being too greatly deformed; or upon deformation, pulling them back into alignment, thereby eliminating the wrinkles.

Moreover, although resin finishes improve wrinkle resistance, finishing reduces both the absorbency and abrasion resistance of treated fibers. The blending of cellulose with resilient synthetic fibers may have the effect of improving wrinkle resistance. Blended fibers abrade less readily, but the use of synthetics does nothing to improve absorbency. Even though most of the resin finishes are classed as durable, some loss in effectiveness is generally observable over the lifetime of the item.

Wash-and-Wear

Wash-and-wear finishes were an outgrowth of crease-resistant finishes, and, historically, were the rext group of "easy care" finishes to be developed. In the

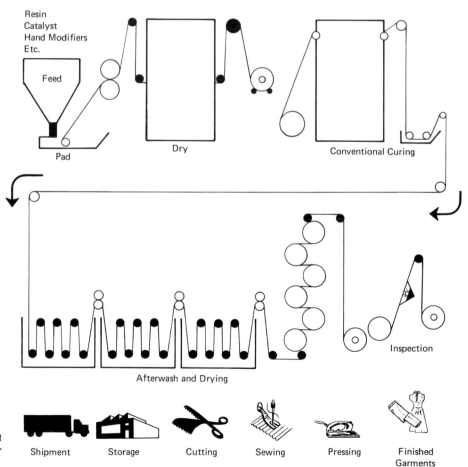

Figure 20-1. Precure durable press finishing routine. Courtesy of Monsanto Textiles Company.

312   *Understanding Textiles*

1950s, much effort was put into developing finishes that would eliminate the need for ironing after items were laundered. Many of these "wash-and-wear" finishes (as they were called) did require some touch-up pressing prior to use.

Through research, improved resin finishes were created. This research led to the development of a group of finishes known as permanent or durable press that has largely replaced wash-and-wear.

PERMANENT OR DURABLE PRESS

The terms *permanent* and *durable* press are often used interchangeably by consumers, advertisers, and the textile industry. Durable press is a more accurate term, as some of these finishes are diminished over the lifetime of the garment.

The finishes are supposed to provide durably set shaping and creases, and, if they are correctly laundered, to require no ironing. A number of commercial trademarks have been registered by different companies that produce merchandise with durable press finishes. Among these are Coneprest, Koratron, Penn-prest, Perma-prest, and Dan-Press.

Like the crease-resistant and "wash-and-wear" finishes, durable press finishes utilize the properties of fibers, fabric construction, and/or treatment with synthetic resins or other chemicals.

Utilizing Fiber Properties

Heat setting of synthetic fibers can provide durability for creases and pleats. Furthermore, synthetic fibers that are quite resilient may not require ironing after laundering. These fabrics are not given chemical finishes.

Resin Treatments

By far the largest quantity of durable press is achieved through resin treatment. The manufacturer applies the resinous material, and then follows the application of the resin with a "cure" period. The cure may be applied either before the goods are constructed into garments or other items, or after construction.

Precure or Flat-cure Durable Press. Fabrics given a "precure" treatment are finished prior to delivery to the manufacturer of textile items. The resin is impregnated into the fabric. Next, the fabrics are subjected to heat in a curing oven, which "sets" the resin. This has the effect of setting the fabric in a flat position. "Durable press" yard goods used by home sewers are made by the precure process.

When precured goods are used in manufactured items, the items are pressed with a hot-head press. The heat and pressure of the press shape the item, chiefly by heat setting the thermoplastic fibers in the blend. Precured fabrics have been made into plain dresses or blouses, curtains, table and bed linens, and draperies, all of which require relatively little shaping.

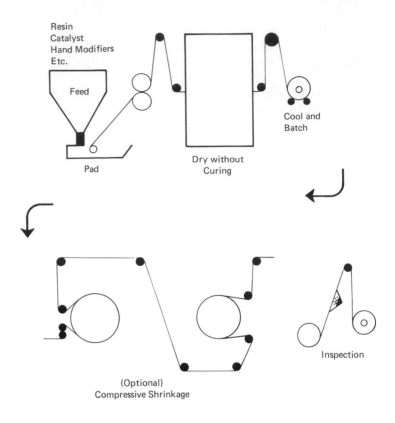

Figure 20-2. Postcuring durable press finishing routine. Courtesy of Monsanto Textiles Company.

Postcure Process. Manufacturers found that precured fabrics were difficult to handle in manufacture. Furthermore, these fabrics were difficult to press into permanent shape because they had been set as "flat." An alternative method of producing durable press items was, therefore, evolved.

In this new method, known as the *postcure* process, the fabric is impregnated with resin and dried. In this state, treated but not cured, the fabric is shipped to the manufacturer. Garments or other items are manufactured from the cloth, and then the finished item is cured in a special curing oven. Creases, pleats, hems, and the like are "permanently" set in this way. Care must be taken to be sure that the fabrics are free from wrinkles or puckers or these, too, will be permanently set.

Recure Process.   A third, and the most recent, development in curing durable press fabrics is the recure method. A special cross-linking reactant and a catalyst are used to provide a fabric that is almost completely cured at the fabric mill. Up to 85 per cent of the cross-links that will be formed in the fabric are made before the fabric reaches the manufacturer of the garment or end product. After the garments are constructed, pressing breaks some of the cross-links and reforms them, and completes the cross-linking. The *Encyclopedia of Textiles, American Fabrics,* describes the process as a system that causes "a precured fabric to be temporarily uncured, then fully recured."[4] The advantage is that both cellulose and thermoplastic components can be shape-set by heat.

Problems of Durable Press

Manufacturing.   The production of durable press items raises the cost of manufacture. The additional steps required and the cost of special equipment for finishing both contribute to this increase in price that is passed along to the consumer. Most consumers, however, appear to be willing to pay more for a product that requires less care.

In constructing items, the garment manufacturer must make changes in sewing techniques. Stitching of long seams may cause puckering unless special thread is used and unless changes in sewing machine tension, type of needle, and length of stitching, are made.

It is also important for the garment manufacturer to select findings such as interfacings, linings, hem tape, and the like that will be compatible with durable press. They must not wrinkle or shrink differently from the fashion fabric.

In Use and Care.   Durable press fabrics, like their forerunners the crease-resistant and wash-and-wear fabrics, exhibit some loss in strength, and particularly, a decrease in abrasion resistance. One hundred per cent cotton fabrics have been known to undergo loss in strength as high as 50 per cent when given durable press finishes. Areas such as collars and cuffs of men's shirts or the knees of children's pants often show the results of abrasion by fraying or "frosting." Frosting is a change in color that results from the breakage and loss of fibers because of abrasion. The soft, fuzzy ends of the fibers give abraded areas a lighter or darker shade of color, depending on the color of the synthetic fibers that have not been worn away.

Blending of cellulosic fibers with synthetics, especially with polyesters that have increased abrasion resistance, can overcome the abrasion problem to a great extent. It is therefore relatively rare to find 100 per cent cellulose durable-press items. Even with blends, however, the problem of different rates of abrasion for each fiber remains.

A variety of different blends of thermoplastic and cellulosic fibers are used for durable press. The most common of these are polyester (from 75 to 40 per

[4]*Encyclopedia of Textiles, American Fabrics* (Englewood Cliffs, N.J.: Prentice-Hall, Inc., 1972), p. 412.

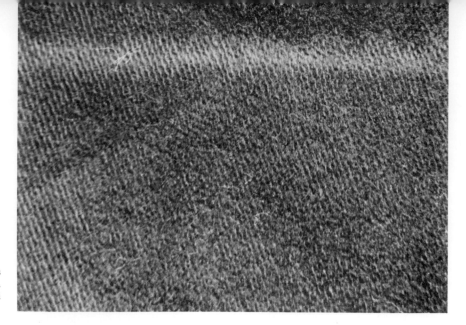

Figure 20-3. Closeup view of durable press fabric in which frosting has taken place. Darker cotton fibers have worn away, leaving a line of lighter polyester fiber.

cent) and cotton (from 25 to 60 per cent), polyester (from 65 to 50 per cent) and high-wet-modulus rayon (from 35 to 50 per cent), and varying other combinations such as rayon or cotton with nylon. Spandex is sometimes utilized for its stretch properties.

Once creases and pleats are permanently set in durable press garments, making alterations is difficult. It is easier to shorten skirts or trousers than to lengthen them, even though it may be difficult to get as crisp a press as the fabric had when it came from the manufacturer. The crease mark of the original hem will always show in a lengthened garment. For these reasons, durable press garments should be bought to fit, and should not be given extensive alterations.

Some of the synthetic fibers used in durable press allow the penetration of oil, but resist the penetration of water. This is also true of the synthetic resins used in creating durable press finishes. As a result, oilborne soils may be absorbed by durable press fabrics. Since the fabrics resist wetting, laundering (even with detergents that would normally remove oil-based soils) does not clean them effectively. When this problem became a major source of consumer complaints, special "soil-releasing" finishes were developed to overcome these difficulties. (See the following section on Soil-Releasing Finishes.)

The quantities of resins needed to produce satisfactory durable press make some of these fabrics rather stiff. They may not drape as well as fabrics without the finish. For the same reason, these fabrics may not absorb moisture readily, and may be less comfortable to wear in warm weather than untreated fabrics. Also, if fabrics are not given an adequate afterrinse, a "fishy" odor may cling to the new fabric. This odor is generally lost after one or more launderings.

Special care in home laundering is required to produce optimum durable-press performance. Washing should be done at warm rather than hot temperatures. Best results are seen when a warm wash cycle is followed by a cool rinse. Durable-press finishes are designed for use in automatic laundering equipment, especially tumble dryers. If items must be line-dried, they should be removed from the washer before the "spin" cycle in which fabrics may become creased, unless the washer is equipped with a special durable-press wash cycle.

Dry fabrics should be removed from the dryer immediately after the cycle ends to avoid having creases formed while the item lies wrinkled in the bottom of the dryer. (Dryers that have special "durable press" cycles have an initial warm drying phase, followed by a cool air phase.) If items do become wrinkled, wrinkles will be removed if they can be placed in a warm dryer for a few minutes with a damp item, and then immediately removed from the dryer.

SOIL-RELEASING FINISHES

Soil-releasing finishes were developed largely as a result of the tendency of durable-press fabrics to absorb and hold oilborne stains. The soil releasing finish should not be confused with soil-repellant finishes, although Zepel and Scotchgard are both stain resistant and soil releasing.

Soil-releasing finishes may be of two types. The first type, to which Dual Action Scotchgard belongs, prevents soil from entering the fabric by coating the surface of the fibers and yarns. Soil and stains are held on the surface of the fabric. When the fabric is laundered, the soil and stains are readily lifted away by the washing action.

The second type of soil-releasing finish makes the fibers more hydrophilic or receptive to water. These finishes do not prevent soiling or staining, but allow water and detergents to penetrate the fiber in order to remove the soil.

At the same time that soil-releasing finishes increase the receptivity of fibers to water, a second benefit is gained. Static electricity build-up is decreased as absorbency is increased. Increased absorbency also increases the comfort of the garment in warm weather. Fuzzing and pilling seem to be decreased by soil-releasing finishes, as well, since the finish almost lubricates the fabric.

Effective soil-releasing finishes should result in fabrics from which common soil is removed during home laundering with normal detergents. Oily stains, often hard to remove from durable press fabrics, should be removable in home laundering.

The disadvantage of all of these finishes is that they are gradually diminished through laundering. Trade names of soil-releasing finishes include Springs-Clean, Visa, X-it, Zip-clean, Zelcon TGF, Dual Action Scotchgard, Rhapdex SR-488, and Zepel.

ABRASION RESISTANCE

Fibers vary in their resistance to damage from abrasion (surface wear from rubbing or friction). Synthetics, generally, have better abrasion resistance than natural fibers. Abrasion resistance can also be attained by the application of certain synthetic resins to fabrics. However, these finishes apparently create

Finishes That Alter Inherent Fiber Qualities

some difficulties by causing fabrics to soil more readily. Such finishes are not widely used.

ABSORBENCY

Cellulosic fibers that are being used for diapers, towels, or other items in which absorbency is important may have ammonium compounds applied to them. These compounds increase the absorbency of the fabrics somewhat.

Some attempts have been made to increase the absorbency of synthetic fibers. Nylonizing and Nylonex are trade names of processes used for treating nylon. Hysorb is a process used to increase the absorbency of other man-made fibers. Opinions vary as to the effectiveness of these finishes.

ANTISLIP FINISHES

Smooth, filament yarns may have a tendency to slide against one another, creating flawed areas in a fabric or problems of seam slippage. This is known as yarn *slippage*. Resins coated on the surface of these fabrics will keep the yarns in place, as the resin holds yarns together at the points where the yarns interlace. Resin antislip finishes are durable.

Other antislip finishes can be created by coating silica compounds on fabrics. However, these are only temporary finishes.

ANTISTATIC FINISHES

Synthetic fibers, being poor conductors of electricity, tend to build up static electric charges. Electricity causes garments to cling or to build up charges that are dissipated through unpleasant, though mild, electric shocks when the wearer touches a conductor such as a metal door knob or another person's hand.

Some finishes have been developed that attempt to decrease static buildup. However, these finishes tend to have limited effectiveness, largely because they are gradually lost during laundering. The antistatic finishes work on either of two principles; either they coat the surface of the fiber with a more conductive substance or they attract to the fiber small amounts of moisture that increase its conductivity.

More successful cutdown in static buildup of synthetics is achieved through the modification of the fiber solution prior to extrusion. These finishes, which are permanent, incorporate compounds in the fiber structure that increase the moisture absorbency that, in turn, increases conductivity.

Antistatic sprays can be purchased for home use. Fabric softeners applied in the final rinse during laundering will also provide some reduction in static buildup.

MERCERIZATION

In 1851, John Mercer discovered that the treatment of cotton with a strong solution of caustic soda (or sodium hydroxide) altered the strength, absorbency, and appearance of the fabric. Because fabric treated in this way shrunk as much as 25 per cent of its length, the finish was not applied commercially until an English chemist, H. A. Lowe, discovered that application of the finish under tension not only minimized shrinkage but also increased luster.

Mercerization, as this finish is called, is done as follows: the cotton fabric is immersed under tension in a strong solution of sodium hydroxide for a short, controlled period of time (usually four minutes or less). The alkali is washed off and any excess alkali is neutralized.

Mercerized cotton fabrics have greatly increased luster. During mercerization the fiber swells, the natural twist of cotton is lost, and the fiber retains a fuller, rounder diameter. This smooth surface reflects more light than the untreated, flatter fiber.

The strength of the fiber is increased as much as 20 per cent. The cotton becomes more absorbent and has a greater affinity for moisture and for dyestuffs. Vat-dyed cotton fabrics that have been mercerized have excellent colorfastness, and less dye is required to produce colors. Some decorative effects can be achieved by combining mercerized yarns and unmercerized yarns in one fabric because mercerized yarns dye to darker shades than those that are untreated.

Mercerized fabrics are also more reactive. As a result, they are more easily damaged by acids and oxidizing agents. Probably for the same reason, mercerized fabrics are more receptive to resin finishes.

Mercerization can be applied to either yarns or fabrics. Most good quality cotton sewing threads are mercerized to improve their strength.

Slack mercerization, or mercerization of fabrics that are not held under tension, is used to produce stretch fabrics. During slack mercerization, yarns shrink and develop a good degree of elasticity. The finished fabric can be stretched, and when the tension is removed the goods will return to their original length. Yarns that have been slack mercerized do not have the high luster of yarns mercerized under tension; their strength is greater than yarns that are mercerized under tension.

Mercerization is both cheap and permanent, and for these reasons it is widely used on cotton goods. Linen can also be mercerized, and since it has a natural luster and good strength, the major advantage of mercerizing linen is to improve the dyeability and receptivity of linen to other finishes.

Several finishes may be said to have as their primary function an effect on either the health or safety of the consumer. Antibacterial finishes are designed to decrease the likelihood of infections, and fire-retardant finishes decrease the dangers of injury from fire.

Finishes That Improve Safety

FLAME-RETARDANT FINISHES

Finishes that make fabrics flame retardant have become especially important since the passage of a series of laws known as the Flammable Fabrics Act. The act provides for the setting of certain standards in regard to flammability that must be achieved in wearing apparel, carpets, mattresses, and children's sleepwear.

The terminology employed in a discussion of flame retardancy can be confusing. For purposes of clarifying the following discussion, a series of definitions follows.[5]

1. *Flame-resistant* material (polymer, fiber, or fabric) is one that exhibits lower flammability than other well-known materials under identical, carefully specified conditions of testing.

2. *Self-extinguishing* material (fabric or garment) is one which, when ignited at the bottom edge in a vertical position does not continue to burn after the source of ignition is removed.

3. *Flame-retardant* material is a material that decreases the flammability of a combustible polymer, fiber, or fabric to which it is added.

4. *Thermally stable* material (fiber or polymer) is one that has a high decomposition temperature, and is thus inherently flame resistant because of chemical structure (rather than through the presence of added flame retardants.)

Thermally stable materials include fibers such as asbestos, glass fiber, and certain synthetic fibers that have been developed for the aerospace industry, such as Kevlar and Nomex aramid, and Kynol novoloid fibers. These could be called fireproof substances that will not burn. At this writing, only glass fiber has had widespread commercial distribution, and it is limited to household textile products such as draperies, window shades, or lamp shades, but thermally stable synthetic fibers will undoubtedly be further developed for general use.

Some synthetic fibers are flame resistant. Modacrylics, for example, which offer adequate flame resistance at a moderate cost, are currently used in carpets and children's sleepwear. Vinyon fibers (trade names include Clevyl and Leavil) and Cordelan, a biconstituent fiber, also exhibit flame-resistant qualities. These fibers are not especially useful in carpets, as their resilience is not adequate, but they can be made into children's sleepwear.

Synthetic fibers can be modified to reduce flammability by the addition of flame-retardant materials to the solution prior to extrusion. Although modified synthetics containing flame-retardant additives have been made experimentally, relatively few have attained commercial significance.

[5]Terms adapted from "Textile Flammability," by Joseph E. Clark and Giuliana Tesoro, paper presented at the State Art Symposium on Man-made Fibers, American Chemical Society, June 1974.

Man-made cellulosic fibers with flame-retardant additives have been more successful. Flame-resistant rayon, cellulose acetate, and triacetate are available from such fiber producers as du Pont, Celanese, and FMC.

The addition of flame-retardant finishes to fabrics accounts for a good proportion of the flame-retardant fabrics now sold. Table 20.1 lists several commonly used chemical substances that produce flame retardancy on cellulose fibers, together with their trade names and the items to which they have been applied:

Chemical Substances	Trade Name	Applied to
tetrakis-hydroxy-methyl phosponium compounds and derivatives	THPC Pyroset Proban	Children's sleepwear, apparel, industrial fabrics
N-Methylol-dimethyl-phosphonopropionamide	Pyrovatex	Children's sleepwear, apparel
Chlorinated paraffins plus Sb_2O_3	FWWMR*	Industrial and military fabrics

*Fire/Water/Weather/Mildew resistant finish.

In addition to these so-called "durable fire-retardant finishes," a solution of 30 per cent boric acid and 70 per cent borax can be used as a rinse for products. This rinse will provide temporary flame retardancy, but produces a decrease in the softness and drapability of the fabric to which it is applied.

Problems with Flame Retardance

Except for thermally stable materials, flame retardancy may be lost through normal use and care of products. Laundering of fabrics treated with flame-retardant finishes must be carefully controlled. Use of chlorine bleach, soaps, or low-phosphate detergents and some fabric softeners may result in a loss of the flame-retardant finish. Laundering in hard water will also diminish the effectiveness of the finish. Since some states have banned the sale of phosphate detergents, much of the treated children's sleepwear sold in these states will gradually become combustible.

Blends of synthetic and natural fibers also create problems in relation to flame retardancy. The finishes that are effective on cellulosic fibers, for example, may not be effective when those fibers are blended with polyesters. Polyester retardants may also be rendered ineffective when the polyester is combined with cotton.

Yet other hazards result when layers of different fibers are combined. A cotton dress worn over a nylon slip will burn very differently than a cotton dress worn over a rayon slip. Often the effect of these combinations is not fully understood. These problems and others regarding flammability have yet to be overcome.

FLAMMABLE FABRICS ACT

Laws concerning the flammability of fabrics have been in effect since 1953 when the sales of *highly* flammable materials used for clothing were banned. This law was amended in 1967 to extend coverage to (excluding some types of hats, gloves, and footwear) carpets, draperies, bedding, and upholstery.

The standard for this part of the law requires that "a piece of fabric placed in holder at a 45-degree angle and exposed to a flame for one second, must not spread flame up the length of the sample in less than 3.5 seconds for smooth fabrics or 4.0 seconds for napped fabrics."[6] Five specimens measuring two inches by six inches are required for each test. The time of flame spread is taken as an average of five specimens.

Since 1967, the regulations have been modified yet further. Originally only those materials that are *highly* flammable were prohibited, but now the manufacture of all flammable carpets, mattresses, and children's sleepwear (sizes 0 to 14) is banned.

In 1972, responsibility for administering and enforcing the law was given to the Federal Consumer Product Safety Commission. Products found to be in violation of the law may be confiscated and destroyed. Persons found guilty of "manufacturing for sale, offering for sale, or selling items that do not comply with the law are subject to a fine of not more than $5,000 and/or imprisonment of not more than a year." The secretary of Commerce and the secretary of Health, Education, and Welfare are required to sponsor research concerning fire-related hazards. When, on the basis of these investigations, the secretary of Commerce determines that a new standard is needed, the Bureau of Standards is given the responsibility of conducting research analyses and developing test methods.

Standards that products must meet are established in a three-step procedure. Notice is given by the commission that there may be a need for a new standard, and individuals are invited to offer their opinions about the need. Next, a proposed standard is put forth. (A proposal has recently come from the Product Safety Commission that would combine the first two steps into one step.) Finally, the standard and test method(s) are announced. Standards and test methods become effective one year after this final notification.

Carpets

Carpet standards require that manufacturers submit samples of carpet fabric for testing prior to marketing. Eight samples are tested by the "methenamine pill" test. This pill, which simulates a source of flame such as a lighted cigarette, is placed in the center of a bone-dry sample of carpet, and is ignited. If the resulting flame does not extinguish itself before it spreads three inches in more than one of the samples, the carpet will not pass the test and must be withdrawn from manufacture.

[6]Fact Sheet, U.S. Consumer Product Safety Commission (Washington, D.C. 20207. June 1974), p. 1.

The pill test determines only surface ignition. It does not assess the contribution of carpets to the spreading of fires, the behavior of carpets in an environment created by a general fire, or the toxicity of the fumes produced.

Other test methods are used to assess the performance of carpets during fires. These test methods are controversial and are not accepted by all authorities as valid. They are not required by the Flammable Fabrics Act. The most widely used test of this type is called the "tunnel test," which uses a horizontal furnace in which the test material is mounted on the ceiling. The sample is exposed from below, at one end of the tunnel, to a gas flame of 1,400 degrees F., which is fanned by an artificial draft. Measurements are made of the volume of smoke and of the time required to spread the flames over a given distance. These figures are compared with an established smoke index and flame spread scale. The governmental agencies that regulate programs have established a level of performance on the tunnel test that carpeting installed in hospitals and facilities participating in Medicare and Medicaid programs must meet.

There are several exceptions to carpets covered under Flammable Fabrics legislation. One-of-a-kind carpets need not meet the standards. Handcraft items, oriental carpets, and the like are not covered by this law. Carpets that are six feet by six feet or smaller than 24 square feet that do not pass the pill test may be sold, provided that they are clearly labeled as being flammable.

Children's Sleepwear

Since 1972, children's sleepwear, sizes 0 to 6X, has been regulated under the Flammable Fabrics Act. For the first year that the law was in effect, sleepwear that did not meet the standards established had to be labeled as flammable. After July, 1973, flammable children's sleepwear was banned from manufacture. Already existing stocks of flammable sleepwear, however, continued to be sold after that date. Coverage under the law was extended in May, 1975, to sleepwear sizes 7 to 14.

In the established testing procedure for sleepwear, each of five samples of the fabric being tested is hung in a cabinet and exposed to a gas flame along its bottom edge for three seconds. The flame is then removed. The standard that must be met by children's sleepwear sizes 0 to 6X is slightly more stringent than that for sleepwear sizes 7 to 14. Both size groups must conform to these standards: samples cannot have an average char length of more than seven inches; no single sample may have a char length of ten inches. In the case of sleepwear in sizes 0 to 6X, no single specimen can have flaming material on the bottom of the testing cabinet ten seconds after the ignition source is removed. For sleepwear sizes 7 to 14, this part of the standard is not applied. To those who have been critical of these somewhat lesser requirements for the larger sizes of sleepwear, the Consumer Product Safety Commission justifies its regulation by contending that: "Information available to the Commission including accident data and reports of investigations indicates that the risk of injury to older children is different than the risk of injury to younger children . . . since older children are better able to protect themselves from fire.

Figure 20-4. Textile testing apparatus developed by a research associate of the American Apparel Manufacturers Association. The purpose of the apparatus is to compare the burning characteristics of seamless fabric and fabric with seams. Courtesy of the Textile Industry Product Safety Committee.

Therefore the two standards should be different because they are directed toward reduction of different levels of hazard."[7] These standards must be met not only by new fabrics but also by those that have been laundered fifty times. All sleepwear must be labeled permanently with instructions as to the care required to maintain the flame-retardant finish. Both manufactured sleepwear items and fabrics intended for use in sleepwear must meet the standard. This includes fabrics and wearing apparel such as pajamas, nightgowns, robes, and sleepers, but excludes diapers and underwear.

[7]*Federal Register,* vol. 39, no. 86, Wednesday May 1, 1974, p. 15210.

Mattresses

After December, 1973, it became illegal for manufacturers to make mattresses that are combustible. The flammability of mattresses is tested using lighted cigarettes, which were selected as a source of ignition because statistics showed that the greatest number of mattress fires were caused by smoking in bed.

This testing procedure requires that nine cigarettes be placed at various points on the mattress and another nine cigarettes between two sheets on the mattress. To pass the standard, the char length on the mattress surface may not be more than two inches in any direction from any cigarette.

The legislation applies to mattress ticking filled with "any resilient material intended or promoted for sleeping upon" and includes mattress pads. Pillows, box springs, and upholstered furniture are excluded.

Other Standards

Consideration is also given to requirements of flame retardancy for other products. The Federal Trade Commission has begun to solicit opinions as to the need for standards in upholstered furniture, blankets, and children's wearing apparel. Individual states have enacted their own flammability legislation. California, for example, has enacted legislation that forbids the sale of any combustible clothing for children, sizes 0 to 14.

More research is required to find better fire-retardant fibers and finishes, and accurate ways of evaluating the interaction of different types of fibers in fires. Furthermore, questions have been raised about potential health hazards from one of the chemical substances (TRIS) being used to provide flame retardancy. Critics claim that some of this material has not been tested adequately to determine whether it may produce dermatitis, or may in some instances be potentially carcinogenic. It is likely, however, that the Flammable Fabrics Act will eventually be extended to other product categories.

SUMMARY

Whereas the finishes discussed in Chapter 19 were compared to "cosmetics," used to enhance the physical properties of fabrics, the finishes discussed in this chapter are designed to modify the actual behavior or properties of textiles. Although finishes may change the appearance, texture, and hand of a fabric they do so for more than cosmetic reasons. Finishes that modify, or in some way improve, inherent fiber properties may result in an increase in price and/or a change in care requirements, but consumers have generally been receptive to the improvements and willing to pay for them. But the costs of some finishes cannot be measured only by an increased price tag on the product. Durable-press finishes do result in shorter wear life and may result in more frequent replacement of garments, and there are other kinds of tradeoffs involved. For example, proper laundering of fire-retardant finished products requires the use of phosphate-containing detergents. Phosphates have been cited as a cause of water pollution. The choice is between one kind of hazard and another. There are no easy answers and no simple solutions.

Recommended References

Book of Papers. 1974 Technical Conference. American Association of Textile Chemists and Colorists. Research Triangle Park, North Carolina.

"Establishing World Flammability Terms." *Textile World,* January 1975, p. 107.

"Finishing: An Overview." *Textile Industries,* May 1975, p. 99.

"Flammability." *CIBA Review,* 1969, vol. 4.

FRANKLIN, W. E., J. P. MADASCI, and S. P. ROWLAND. "Creasable Durable Press Cotton Fabrics by Polymerization and Cross-linking." *Textile Chemist and Colorist,* April 1976, p. 28.

HALL, A. J. *Textile Finishing.* New York: American Elsevier Publishing Co., Inc., 1966.

HARPER, R. J. *Durable Press Cotton Goods.* Watford, England: Merrow Publishing Company, Ltd., 1971.

HEARLE, J. W. S. (Ed.). *The Setting of Fibres and Fabrics.* Watford, England: Merrow Publishing Company, Ltd., 1971.

KERSHAW, A., and J. LEWIS. "The Role of Polymer Treatments in Shrink-Proofing of Wool." *Textile Month,* April 1976, p. 40.

LEBLANC, B. "What's Available in Fire Retardant Textiles." *Textile Industries,* February 1976.

MARSH, J. T. *Introduction to Textile Finishing.* Plainfield, N.J.: Textile Book Service, 1966.

MCPHEE, J. R. *The Moth Proofing of Wool.* Watford, England: Merrow Publishing Company, Ltd., 1971.

NAPHTA, R. "Internal Anti Stats." *American Dyestuff Reporter,* April 1975, p. 41.

PARDO, C. E. et al. "Wurset Wool Shrink Process Proves Feasible Under Plant Conditions." *American Dyestuff Reporter,* September 1975, p. 36.

REEVES, W. A. and G. L. DRAKE. *Flame Resistance.* Watford, England: Merrow Publishing Company, Ltd., 1971.

TATTERSALL, R. "Recent Progress in Textile Finishing." *Textile Month,* March 1976, p. 42.

Textile Flammability, A Handbook of Regulations, Standards, and Test Methods. American Association of Textile Chemists and Colorists. Research Triangle Park, North Carolina.

"Where Has All the Static Gone?" *American Fabrics & Fashions,* Winter 1971, p. 51.

21

THE CARE OF TEXTILE PRODUCTS

Attention to the correct procedures for cleaning and maintaining textile products will extend the useful life of the product. Improper cleaning and storage can result in either severe damage to the fabric or an increased rate of wear over a period of time.

The accumulation of soil on fabrics is one of the factors that causes fabrics to deteriorate. Spilled food, for example, can make a fabric that is normally unappetizing to insects into an attractive meal for moths and carpet beetles. The "ground-in dirt" that television commercials decry can increase the abrasion of yarns as gritty soil rubs against fibers, causing them to break. Soil removal is, therefore, one of the most important aspects of caring for fabrics if they are to be maintained in good condition.

Soil Removal

Soil can be removed from fabrics by either laundering or dry cleaning. These processes can be carried out in the home or by professional cleaners. The principles utilized are the same in both instances, but the equipment and laundry or dry-cleaning products that are used will vary.

Soil deposited on fabrics is made up of different materials. Some types of soil are soluble, whereas other types are insoluble. Soluble dirt is made up of organic acids, mineral acids, alkaline substances, blood, starches, and sugars. All of these substances dissolve in cool or warm water and though they may sometimes require special stain-removal techniques, these soluble substances present no extraordinary problems in cleaning.

Water alone will remove soluble soil, but insoluble soils may be held onto the fabric by physical attraction, or in films, greases, or oils. Such soil requires the use of detergents or other special laundry or cleaning products.[1]

[1] Cleansing agents are known as detergents. Both soaps and synthetic detergents are, technically speaking, detergents, even though the term *detergent* is often used by the general public to refer only to synthetic detergents (sometimes abbreviated "syndets"). For purposes of this discussion the term *detergent* will be used to refer to both soaps and synthetic detergents.

The process of laundering soiled fabrics consists of wetting the fabric and its soil, removing the soil from the fabric, and holding the soil in suspension so that it does not redeposit on the fabric during washing. Detergents increase the cleaning ability of water. The addition of detergent to water decreases the surface tension of water, thereby increasing its wetting power. When the wetting power of water is increased, textiles are more completely penetrated by water. A simple experiment will demonstrate this principle. Take a small piece of nylon fabric and float it on the surface of a small bowl of water. The surface tension of the water (molecular forces in the outer layer of water) enables the nylon to float for a time, until it becomes wet throughout. Drop a few drops of liquid detergent into the water. The fabric will become wet immediately and sink.

The wet fabric is agitated by the motion of the washing machine or by hand scrubbing. The soil is broken into smaller particles and surrounded (emulsified) by the detergent, then lifted off the fabric by the action of the detergent. The detergent surrounding the soil particles prevents their being redeposited on the fabric as the washing progresses. When fabrics are rinsed, the soil and detergent are rinsed away.

Soaps

Soap is made from fatty acids and alkali that react together to form the soap. Some degree of alkalinity is necessary for cleaning, and as the soap dissolves, the washing water becomes somewhat alkaline in reaction. Much soil is acid in chemical reaction and will tend to neutralize some of the alkalinity of the soap and decrease its effectiveness. Therefore, more heavily soiled items require more soap.

To assure that adequate alkalinity is present for thorough washing, extra alkali is added to increase the effectiveness of the soap. Soaps with added alkali are known as "built" or "heavy-duty" soaps and are designed for general laundering. Less alkaline soaps are also available for laundering more delicate fabrics. Because protein fibers are damaged by excessive alkali, light-duty soaps should be used for washing wool, silk, and other delicate fabrics.

Soaps do not perform well in hard water, which is water with higher concentrations of minerals such as calcium and magnesium. The minerals in the water combine with soap to form an insoluble gray curd or scum. Once the soap has combined with these minerals, less soap is available for cleaning, and larger quantities of soap must be used. Also the hard-water scum may be deposited on clothing, leaving it gray or dull looking.

Water Softeners or Conditioners

Synthetic detergents do not produce hard-water scum as soaps do, but it is necessary to use larger quantities of detergent in hard water than in soft water.

(Soft water is water free from these dissolved minerals.) Many families, therefore, find it helpful to decrease the hardness of water by some form of water conditioning. Hard water can be softened either by commercial softening systems installed in the home to soften all water used in the household or by the addition of powdered water softeners to the laundry. Powdered softeners are of two types: precipitating and nonprecipitating.

Precipitating water softeners combine with the minerals that cause water to become hard to form a compound that precipitates or settles out of solution into visible granules. These granules may be deposited on laundered items. Also, precipitating softeners must be added to wash water *before* the soap is added. They cannot dissolve soap scum once it has been formed. Washing soda and Climalene are precipitating water softeners.

Nonprecipitating water softeners keep hard water minerals tied up in chemical combination and in solution so that neither soap scum nor a precipitate is formed. Furthermore, nonprecipitating softeners can dissolve soap scum formed before the softener was added to the water and can strip scum left in clothes from previous washings in hard water.

Minerals, such as iron or manganese, in water may stain fabrics. The addition of bleach to such water may cause the formation of colored salts that, when deposited on fabrics, cause discoloration. Nonprecipitating water softeners will prevent such staining by tying up the minerals. Calgon and Spring Rain are nonprecipitating water softeners.

Synthetic Detergents

Synthetic detergents are synthetic products made from petroleum and natural fats and oils. Unlike soaps, synthetic detergents do not form hard-water scum but dissolve readily in both hard and soft water. Some detergents are made to maintain low suds levels, whereas others are made to produce more suds. Synthetic detergents are available in high-, medium-, and low-sudsing formulations. All suds levels clean equally well, but low-suds formulations are often necessary for optimum cleaning in front-loading washers, in which the laundry is carried up and around as the basket rotates. When the wet laundry reaches the top of the circle, it drops to the bottom, thereby providing the agitation necessary for releasing soil. High-suds detergents break the fall of the fabrics, thereby decreasing the washing action. Low-suds detergents provide the cleaning agent without interfering with the washing action.

Typically, synthetic detergents are formulated from the following materials: surfactants, builders, processing aids, agents to protect washer parts, antiredeposition agents, fluorescent whiteners, and perfumes.

1. _Surfactants_. Surfactants are organic chemicals, the active ingredient in synthetic detergents that alter the properties of water and soil so that dirt can be removed. The surfactant molecule might be described as having a long "water-hating" or hydrophobic body with a "water-loving" or hydrophilic head. The action of the surfactant breaks up water droplets that

surround soil particles, allowing water to penetrate. Groups of surfactant molecules (called *micelles*) surround the soil, with the hydrophobic section of the molecule attached to the soil and the water-loving head of the molecule oriented toward the water in which the particles become suspended. (See Figure 21.1.) The most commonly used surfactants are Linear Alkyl Benzene Sulfonate (or LAS), Alcohol Sulfates (AS), nonionic surfactants, and soap. Both LAS and AS surfactants are anionic, that is, they generate negative electrostatic charges in water. Similar electric charges repel each other. Most fabrics also carry negative charges, so that the negative charge of the surfactant molecules surrounding the soil particles is effective in preventing the redeposition of soil on the fabrics being washed.

SURFACTANT REMOVING AND SUSPENDING DIRT

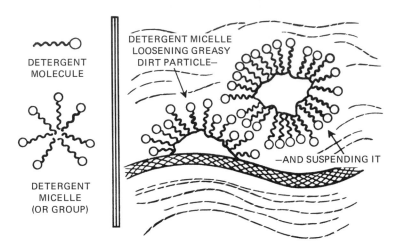

DETERGENT MOLECULE

DETERGENT MICELLE (OR GROUP)

DETERGENT MICELLE LOOSENING GREASY DIRT PARTICLE—

—AND SUSPENDING IT

Figure 21-1. Diagram showing the action of a surfactant removing and suspending dirt. Reprinted from Monograph #108, "The Technology of Home Laundering." Courtesy of the American Association for Textile Technology, Inc.

Nonionic surfactants do not carry electric charges as they dissolve. They are more effective in removing oily soil than are anionic surfactants. Soaps may also be used as a minor ingredient in detergent formulations because they help to break the foam produced by LAS-containing products. Soap is often used in controlled-suds products. Detergent manufacturers use one or more of these types of surfactants in their formulations. One of the popular detergent combinations is made up of LAS, soap, and nonionic surfactants.

2. *Builders.* Builders are substances that soften water and maintain alkalinity. Until recently, the majority of builders used in detergent formulations were phosphates, which are especially effective in counteracting water hardness. They also disperse and suspend dirt and maintain alkalinity, which is necessary to neutralize many soils that tend to be acid in chemical reaction.

Fears that phosphates may be contributing to water pollution have led some states and communities to restrict the use of phosphate-containing detergents. As a result, detergent manufacturers have developed a variety of nonphosphate or low-phosphate detergents that utilize other builders. These nonphosphate builders include sodium silicate and sodium carbonate. Research has shown, however, that detergents containing these builders are not as effective in removing soil as those with phosphates.[2]

3. *Processing Aids.* Materials are added that maintain good powder properties in powdered detergents. Commonly used materials include sodium silicate (also cited previously as a builder), sodium sulfate, and small amounts of water.

4. *Agents to protect washing machine parts.* Silicates added to detergents help to prevent corrosion of the parts of the washer that are exposed to water and detergents.

5. *Antiredeposition agents.* Although anionic surfactants help to prevent the redeposition of soil, other agents are also added to the detergent to prevent redeposition. The most common chemical used for this purpose is sodium carboxymethyl cellulose.

6. *Fluorescent Whiteners.* Fluorescent whiteners are additives that make white wash appear whiter and brighter. When light strikes a fabric on which these agents have been deposited, the agents absorb the ultraviolet wavelengths that are not visible to the human eye and re-emit them in a visible wavelength. The formulation of the fluorescent whitening agent is such that the rays of light it emits cause fabrics to reflect a whiter light, rather than light that is more yellow. Fabric, therefore, appears whiter and brighter. Fluorescent whiteners do not remove soil.

7. *Perfumes.* Many detergents contain perfumes. These products give the laundered items a more pleasant odor.

The specific formulation of each synthetic detergent varies, of course, from one product to another. In some states or localities, environmental legislation has been enacted to restrict the use of some chemicals that had been used as builders in detergents, particularly phosphates, that have been used to soften water and provide alkalinity. Detergent manufacturers have revised formulations to conform with such restrictions. Also, concern about the slow decomposition of some detergents in sewage treatment and in surface water has led to the use of biodegradable surfactants, that is, surfactants that are more readily decomposed after use.

Bleaches

Bleaches are often used along with soaps and synthetic detergents in laundering. It is important to remember that bleaches do not *clean* clothing.

[2] Carol E. Avery and Doris E. Harabin, *A Comparison of Phosphate and Non-Phosphate Detergents,* Agricultural Experiment Station, University of Rhode Island, Bulletin 415, p. 72.

Detergents and soaps do the cleaning; bleaches are used to whiten fabrics and remove stains.

Bleaches oxidize the coloring matter in fabric, and some stains are removed by the oxidation of the coloring matter in them. Two basic types of bleaches are used in the home: chlorine bleaches and perborate bleaches.

Chlorine bleaches are the stronger of the two. They utilize active chlorine to oxidize colored matter. But after the chlorine has oxidized all stains, color, and so on, it begins to oxidize susceptible fibers. For this reason, chlorine bleaches need to be used in correct concentrations and to be thoroughly dissolved before application and thoroughly rinsed out or they may damage the fibers.

The most frequent mistakes made in handling chlorine bleach are

1. Using too much bleach. Follow directions on the bleach package. Do not assume that if a little bleach is good, twice as much is better.

2. Pouring bleach directly onto clothing. Bleach should be added to a full tub of water and agitated thoroughly before any laundry is added. Adding concentrated bleach to a washer full of clothing will result in concentrated bleach being poured over some garments, which may damage them. If bleach must be added to the wash at a later point, bleach should be diluted in one or more quarts of water before it is poured into the washer.

3. Bleaching items that should not be bleached. Read care labels carefully. Some resins or fibers such as spandex will yellow on contact with chlorine bleach. Chlorine bleach damages other fibers such as silk or wool.

4. Soaking heavily stained items in concentrated bleach solutions. Exposure to concentrated bleach solutions may damage certain fibers and should be avoided. Items should not be soaked in even low concentrations of chlorine bleach for longer than fifteen minutes.

Chlorine bleaches are sold in both dry and liquid forms under a variety of trade names. Clorox, Purex, Fleecy White, and Action are a few of the trademarks of chlorine bleaches.

Commercial laundries use bleaches routinely on white cottons and linens. In order to avoid damage from chlorine bleaches, these establishments control bleaching concentrations very carefully and follow the bleaching with a "sour" treatment, in which a weak acid rinse is used. This neutralizes any excess bleach, which is alkaline in nature. It is also important to rinse bleached fabrics carefully at home or deterioration of the fibers can continue for as long as any bleach remains in the fiber.

Oxygen or perborate bleaches do not use chlorine for oxidation, but use other chemicals such as sodium perborate, hydrogen peroxide, and potassium monopersulfate. They also do not whiten as efficiently in a short period of time. These bleaches will work best if used in every laundering. Like chlorine bleaches, oxygen bleaches should be diluted before addition to the wash, as some colors may be sensitive to the bleaching action of these products. Some of the trade names of oxygen bleach include Lestare, Miracle White, Snowy, Daybrite, and All-fabric Beads-O-Bleach. Hydrogen peroxide is sold in drugstores.

Fluorescent Whiteners

Most detergent formulations contain fluorescent whiteners. It is also possible to purchase fluorescent whiteners or "optical brighteners" for use in the home. These agents do not attach themselves to different fibers to the same degree, so their effectiveness may vary from fiber to fiber. Also, chlorine bleach may destroy the active ingredients in fluorescent whiteners, so that the two products should never be added to the laundry at the same time.

Some optical brighteners for household use are called "blueing." In using blueing, which has a blue color, one must follow directions carefully. Too great a concentration of the brightener may give the white laundry a bluish tint.

Disinfectants

Chlorine bleaches not only whiten fabrics but also disinfect and deodorize. One of the purposes of laundering clothing and household items is to destroy bacteria. Ordinary laundering procedures using detergent and hot water will destroy many bacteria. When there is illness or infection in a home, however, special care may be required to sanitize items being washed.

To be suitable for sanitizing laundry, a disinfectant should kill bacteria without injuring or discoloring fabrics. Furthermore, disinfectants should not leave a residue that is harmful to the user and they must be compatible with detergents.

USDA researchers have found four types of disinfectant that satisfy these criteria that are readily available and reasonable in cost. These are

1. Liquid chlorine bleaches. (Labels should state that the bleach contains 5.25 per cent of sodium hypochlorite.)

2. Quarternary disinfectants. These disinfectants are colorless and odorless compounds that are effective in hot, warm, or cold water. Labels should carry the term *Benzalkonium chloride.* Such substances are available in drugstores, and from janitors', hospital, or dairy supply houses.

3. Pine oil disinfectants. These disinfectants are effective in hot or warm water. They have a characteristic pine oil odor that does not remain after laundering. The label should state that the product contains at least 70 per cent steam-distilled pine oil. Pine oil disinfectants are sold in supermarkets or grocery stores.

4. Phenolic disinfectants. Effective in warm or hot water, phenolic disinfectants are sold under such well-known trademarks as Pine-Sol, Lysol, and Texize 8304 Centex. The label should contain the names "orthobenzyl-parachlorophenol" or "ortho-phenyl-chlorophenol."[3] Disinfectants should be used according to the directions on the package.

[3] *Sanitation in Home Laundering,* (Washington, D.C.: U.S. Department of Agriculture, Home and Garden Bulletin, No. 97, October 1971).

Fabric Softeners

Fabric softeners deposit a waxy, lubricative substance on fibers that causes fabrics to feel softer. All fabric softeners are based on quarternary ammonium compounds. Although different compounds are used, all have a long fatty chain that imparts the soft feel to the fabric. The softening effect is especially desirable for fabrics with a napped or pile surface that may become stiffer and less soft after laundering, particularly if the fabrics are line-dried rather than dryer-dried. Towels, washable blankets, diapers, corduroy or other pile fabrics, and sweaters are often washed with fabric softeners.

In addition to making fabrics feel softer, fabric softeners cut down static electricity, make ironing easier, and improve the performance of wash-and-wear finishes, often making touch-up ironing unnecessary. At the same time, the continual use of fabric softeners causes a buildup of the softener on the fibers, thereby decreasing absorbency. On items where absorbency is an important function, such as towels or diapers, it is recommended that fabric softeners not be used in every wash, but in alternate washings or periodically.

Specific instructions for the use of fabric softeners are provided on the package. Follow these instructions carefully in order to achieve best results. Although most powder or liquid fabric softeners are added in the final rinse, rather than during the wash cycle, a few softeners have been developed that are made to be added during the wash cycle. Rain Barrel is the trademark for one of these products.

Aerosol fabric softeners are sold for use in dryers. Dryer manufacturers have expressed reservations about the use of these sprays, as they may tend to build up on the dryer drum. Removal of this residue after each use may prevent trouble, but if the residue is allowed to remain in the dryer drum, it will eventually become brown and may stain clothing. The aerosols accelerate rusting of dryer parts that then stain fabrics. They also tend to coat the electronic sensors in dryers that regulate temperature or test the humidity in the air to determine when loads are dry.

The most recent development in fabric softeners is a nonwoven fabric that is impregnated with a fabric softener. The fabrics are supplied on a roller like paper towels, and a section is torn from the roller and placed in the dryer to be tumbled with the laundry. The trade marks for such products include Bounce and Cling Free.

Starches

Starches are sizings that are added during home laundering. They help to restore body to limp fabrics. Starches also help to keep fabrics cleaner, as dirt tends to slide off the smooth finish produced by starching. Also, soil may become attached to the starching material, rather than to the fiber, making the soil easier to remove.

Since vegetable starches were originally used for this purpose, the term starch was given to these products. Today, however, "starches" may be either vegetable or resinous compounds. Sizings are added in the rinse cycle of laundering or by an aerosol spray at the time of ironing. Vegetable starches must be renewed after each washing. Resins penetrate the fiber more thoroughly and will last through several washings.

Home Laundry Equipment

Washing Machines. Except for hand-laundered items, most laundry in the home is done in washing machines. Washing machines may be of three types: automatic, semiautomatic, and wringer style. Many households use automatic dryers.

Each of these appliances differs in its construction, features, and operation. It is beyond the scope of this book to discuss the variety of types of laundry equipment that is available, but a few points ought to be made about the use of this equipment in relation to the care of fabrics.

Although some fully automatic washers have programmed cycles that require only the selection of a suitable term, such as *permanent press*, it is more likely that the user will have to select water temperature, time duration for washing, and type of agitation. Most washers offer a low, moderate, or high water temperature; washing time durations of from two to fourteen minutes; and either gentle or normal agitation. Washing machine instruction manuals will give specific directions for settings that should be used for varying types and loads of laundry. Of course, the user will have to select the detergent and other laundry additives such as bleach, water softener, fabric softener, and so on that are to be used in the wash.

Table 21.1 offers typical time, speed of agitation, and water temperature for various fiber groups:

Table 21.1

Fiber	Time	Water Temperature	Agitation and Spin Speed
Wool	1–3 min.	110–120 °F.	slow
Cotton and linen	10–12 min.	120–140 °F.	normal
Man-made and Durable press	5–7 min.	110–120 °F.	slow

The expansion of the use of wash-and-wear and durable-press finishes has led to the manufacture of washers and dryers that have "permanent press" cycles. These cycles are designed to produce optimum performance from durable-press finishes by using varying water temperatures in washing and rinsing, decreased agitator speeds in extracting water, and by ending the drying cycle with a cool temperature in order to avoid heat-setting wrinkles into dried clothing. If durable-press fabrics have been washed in a normal wash cycle rather than a durable-press cycle, the final rinse may have been made with hot water. During the extraction of the water in the spin cycle, clothes are compressed against the basket walls. If the fabric is warm, the cooling that takes place will cause the fabrics to wrinkle, whereas the cool water cycles of the special durable press cycle provide better wrinkle resistance. If the clothes are to be dried in an automatic dryer, these wrinkles will be tumbled out of the fabric. If clothes are to be line-dried, however, they should be removed from the washer before the final spin cycle.

Laundry Procedures

Although the washer and dryer do the physical work of laundering, the selection of appropriate laundry procedures is essential for efficient cleaning. Sorting, selecting washing time and water temperature, pretreating spots and stains, and carefully selecting laundry products for use all require that decisions be made by the person doing the washing.

Laundry should be sorted carefully according to color, fiber type, degree of soil, and delicacy of construction. Items should be grouped together that require the same laundry products, water temperature, length of washing, and speed of agitation.

White items should be washed together. Colorfast items may be laundered together, even if the colors are not the same, but it is advisable to separate light and dark colors. Those items that are not colorfast should be washed separately; in some cases they may have to be washed by hand. White permanent press and synthetic fabrics are most prone to discoloration if washed with items of color, and should be washed only with other whites.

Fabrics that produce lint, such as bath towels, chenille fabrics, terry items, and the like, should be washed separately from those that attract lint; that is, corduroy, synthetic fabrics, and durable press. It is especially important to separate light-colored lint-producing fabrics from dark-colored lint attractors, such as dark nylon underclothing or socks.

Heavy items such as blankets or bedspreads may have to be washed alone because of their size. When a heavy load is put into a washer, it should be arranged carefully so that the washer balance is maintained during spin cycles.

Before laundering, clothing should be checked carefully. Pockets should be emptied since coins or other items left in pockets can damage washers or dryers, and tissues left in pockets will produce lint that will be picked up by garments. Lint and dirt should be brushed out of pant cuffs. Zippers and hooks should be closed so that they do not catch onto other items and tear them. Pins, heavy ornaments, and buckles may also cause damage to fabrics, and should be removed. Tears should be mended before laundering, as the agitation of washing and drying may cause them to be enlarged.

Some items may require pretreatment for optimum cleaning. Soil lines that are formed around collars and cuffs may be difficult to remove from synthetic and durable press fabrics. The area may be pretreated by dampening the area and then rubbing liquid detergent or a paste made of powdered detergent and water over the soiled area.

Although it is better to remove stains as soon as they are made, products are available to aid in the removal of stains and other soil during laundering. Bleaches have already been discussed, and these are added during washing. Other products may be designed for use before washing. Enzyme presoak products are especially effective for protein-based stains caused by body soils, blood, eggs, and baby formula, also grass and chocolate. Fabrics are soaked for from thirty minutes to overnight, depending on instructions and the age and amount of the stain. Enzyme presoak products are not effective if they are used during laundering.

Aerosol prewash soil and stain removers that contain perchlorethylene or other petroleum—based solvents are sold for use on synthetics and durable-press fabrics. They help to remove greasy stains such as those made by lipstick, bacon fat, coffee with cream, and ballpoint pen. Instructions on the label generally recommend that they be applied to fabrics five minutes or longer before washing.

STAIN REMOVAL

Stain removal is easiest immediately after the fabrics have been subjected to staining. It is important to know the kind of material that caused the stain and the fiber of which the fabric is made. The selection of the method to use in removing the stain will be determined by the type of stain, and the type of stain remover to be used may be limited by the type of fabric.

Before any stain remover is used, the fabric should be tested to determine whether it is colorfast to the stain remover or whether it may have a finish that the stain remover will harm. Fabrics can be tested by sponging a small amount of stain remover onto a seam, hem, or other hidden part of the item. If a suitable stain remover cannot be found, it would be best to take the item to a professional dry cleaner for treatment.

The substances that cause stains generally fall into one of three categories: greasy stains, nongreasy stains, and combination stains. Combination stains are caused by materials that contain both greasy and nongreasy substances. General methods of stain removal are appropriate for each of these types of stains. The methods differ somewhat for washable and nonwashable articles.

Removing Greasy Stains[4]

To remove greasy stains from washable fabrics, the following methods may work. Some greasy stains can be removed by rubbing soap or detergent into the stain, then rinsing with warm water. More often, a grease solvent will have to be used. Grease solvents include perchloroethylene, trichloroethane, and trichloroethylene, none of which is combustible. Trichloroethylene should not be used on Arnel triacetate or Kodel polyester. Combustible grease solvents are of a chemical group called petroleum naphthas or petroleum distillates and petroleum hydrocarbons. Many stain removers are mixtures of these substances.

Care must be taken to avoid inhaling the fumes of these solvents, and the

[4] *Removing Stains from Fabrics* (Washington, D.C.: U.S. Department of Agriculture. Home and Garden Bulletin, No. 63, 1973).

rooms in which they are used must be well ventilated. Combustible removers must not be used near a source of flame or sparks.

After testing fabrics for colorfastness to the stain remover, the stained fabric is placed over a pad of absorbent, clean, white cotton fabric or paper towel; then, from the wrong side of the fabric, the stain is sponged thoroughly with the grease solvent. Fabrics with resin finishes may require several applications and more time for stain removal.

If stains have been set by heat or age, a yellow discoloration may remain after treatment. Bleaching with chlorine or perborate bleach may remove this color. Be sure fabrics are not damaged by bleaches before using either type of bleach. Nonwashable items cannot be treated with detergent or soap, but should be treated with grease solvents, as described previously.

Removing Nongreasy Stains[5]

Stains that have been set by age or heat may be very difficult to remove. Other stains, if treated when fresh, may come out quite readily. For washable items, sponge stains with cool water. Some stains may require longer soaking. If stain remains after soaking, rub soap or detergent into the stain, then rinse. If stain remains, it may be necessary to treat with bleach as described previously.

Nonwashable items can be sponged with cool water. Water may be forced through the fabric with a small syringe. Place an absorbent material under the fabric to absorb water. Stains that are not removed by this procedure can have a small amount of detergent rubbed into the fabric and rinsed out with a syringe as described. A final sponging with alcohol may help to remove the detergent and dry fabric more quickly. Fabrics should be tested to be sure they are colorfast to alcohol. Acetates should be treated only with alcohol that has been diluted. (use two parts water to one part alcohol). Stubborn stains may require bleaching.

Combination Stains[6]

Because these stains are made by substances that contain both greasy and nongreasy staining materials, the method of treatment is a combination of the methods used for greasy and nongreasy stains.

First, sponge the stain with cool water. Then, treat the stained fabric with detergent, rinse, and dry. If a greasy stain remains, treat with a grease solvent. Stubborn stains may require bleaching.

Table 21.2 lists a number of common substances that may cause staining. The methods used for removing stains are identified, and special considerations in their treatment are noted.

Other substances that cause stains may present special problems in stain removal or require special techniques to remove stains. A few of these substances are listed on page 340, along with methods for their removal.

[5] Ibid.
[6] Ibid.

Type of Stain	Greasy Stains	Nongreasy Stains	Combination Stains	Special Considerations
Alcoholic beverages		•		
Antiperspirant		•		Wash or sponge with detergent and warm water. Rinse. Some anti-perspirants may cause fabric damage or color change.
Blood		•		Stains set by heat are very difficult to remove.
Butter or margarine	•			
Candle wax or paraffin	•			Before using grease solvent, press with a warm iron between white blotters or tissues to remove as much wax as possible.
Catsup, chili sauce		•		
Chocolate, other candy			•	
Cocoa		•		
Coffee, Tea (black)		•		
Coffee, Tea (with cream)			•	
Cream			•	
Egg		•		
Mucus, vomit		•		
Food coloring		•		
Fruit, fruit juice		•		Or pour boiling water through spot from height of 1 to 3 feet, if safe for fabric.
Furniture polish	•			
Gravy			•	
Grease, lard, car grease, oil	•			
Ice cream			•	
Mayonnaise, salad dressing			•	
Milk		•		
Sauces, soups			•	
Scorch		•		
Soft drinks		•		
Tar	•			If not removed by greasy stain procedure, sponge with turpentine.
Urine		•		
Vegetables		•		
Wax (floor, furniture, etc.)	•			
Writing ink		•		

Table 21.2
Stain Removal Chart

Extensive staining by hard-to-remove substances or stains on delicate and/or nonwashable fabrics are probably best removed by a professional dry cleaner, who has a variety of spot- and stain-removing chemicals and an expert knowledge of stain removal. It is always helpful to the cleaner, however, if the customer points out the stain and identifies the staining substance.

DRYING

Automatic dryers generally provide both time and temperature settings. Temperatures for drying may range from no heat to moderate and high temperatures. The drying time is determined by the size of the load and the weight of the fabrics being dried. Some dryers have an automatic sensor that turns off the dryer when the wash is dry, whereas others will continue to tumble for the length of time set on the dial, even after the laundry is dry.

Item	Stain Removal
Carbon paper	For regular carbon paper, work soap or detergent into the stain, and rinse well. If the stain remains, try a few drops of ammonia on the stain, and then repeat the treatment with detergent. Duplicating carbon paper stains should be treated with alcohol. If necessary, rub detergent into the stain after alcohol treatment and rinse well.
Cosmetics Crayon	Apply undiluted liquid detergent, rub in well, rinse, and repeat as often as necessary. If the stained items are not washable, treat with a grease solvent.
Fingernail polish	Use nail polish remover. Test remover on scrap of fabric, as some nail polish removers will damage acetates, triacetates, and modacrylics. Amyl acetate can be used instead of acetone for these fabrics.
Grass, tobacco	If colorfast to alcohol, sponge the stained fabric with alcohol. Otherwise, work soap or detergent into the stain and rinse.
Ballpoint ink	Sponge the stain with acetone or amyl acetate fluid. Use only amyl acetate on acetate, triacetate and modacrylics. Acetone will damage these fabrics. Some ballpoint ink stains are set by washing. Test by marking a scrap of similar fabric with the same ink and washing it.
India ink	Force water through the stain until all loose pigment is removed, or this pigment will spread the stain as it is treated. Wet the spot with ammonia, work soap or detergent into the spot, rinse. Repeat as necessary. This stain is very hard to remove, once dry.
Mildew	Wash thoroughly, and dry in the sun. Bleach if necessary.
Mud	Dry and brush well. If the stain remains, treat as non-greasy stain.
Mustard	Rub in detergent and rinse. If the stain is not removed, soak the stained fabric in hot water.
Paint, varnish	If safe for color and fabric, use paint thinner recommended for this type of paint or varnish. Water-based paints may respond to treatment with detergents, oil-based paints may require treatment with grease solvents.
Pencil marks (lead) (indelible)	Rub with soft eraser. If not effective, treat as a regular carbon paper stain. Treat as for a duplicating carbon paper stain.
Rust	Treat with commercial rust remover or oxalic acid. Rust stains can be very difficult to remove.

Fabrics that have been laundered may be either line-dried or dried in an automatic dryer. Some fabrics should not be dried in dryers, because the heat and action of the dryer may cause some shrinkage in heat-sensitive fabrics. Elastics made with natural rubber may lose their elasticity over a period of time if dried in a very hot dryer. Permanent-care labels should be consulted to ascertain whether fabrics should be placed in a dryer.

Heat-sensitive fabrics should be dried at low heat or no heat settings. Durable-press and synthetic fabrics should be removed from the dryer immediately after completion of the drying cycle to prevent the setting of wrinkles.

As in washing, fabrics of similar colors should be dried together. It is possible for colors to run from one fabric to another if damp, noncolorfast fabrics are placed on top of other fabrics during drying.

PRESSING

Although many synthetic and durable-press fabrics will not require pressing, other items will need touch-up pressing before use. Linens and cottons require the highest temperature settings, synthetics the lowest. Even though irons have temperature settings for different fabric types, the iron temperature should be tested in an inconspicuous part of the item, as thermostats of irons vary in accuracy.

Fabrics are best pressed when they are slightly damp, or with steam, as wrinkles are removed more easily. Dark-colored fabrics of all fibers, silks, acetates, and rayons should be ironed from the wrong side to prevent shine. When these fabrics require pressing on the right side, press over a press cloth, not directly on the fabric.

Wool fabrics should be pressed with steam or a dampened press cloth. Silk should be pressed with a dry press cloth. Fabrics with textured surfaces should be tested carefully to see if ironing will flatten the surface. Sometimes these fabrics can be pressed lightly on the wrong side over a folded terry towel or other soft surface. Corduroy can be pressed in this way, although it is better to use a special pressing board called a needle board. Velvets, velveteens, and plushes also require the use of a needle board. These fabrics may respond better to steaming (holding a steam iron or a "wrinkle remover" steamer several inches away), then hanging to dry to allow the wrinkles to hang out. The same effect may be achieved by hanging items in a bathroom that is warm and moist from a hot shower.

COMMERCIAL LAUNDERING

Commercial laundering procedures are similar to those used in the home except that the conditions under which laundry is done commercially are more controlled and wash loads are considerably larger than in the home laundry. These large wash loads are made up of items from a number of different customers, so that identification numbers or tags must be affixed to each item for identification purposes.

The first step in the commercial laundering process is to sort the fabrics. Items are separated according to color, fiber content, and degree of soil. As many as twelve different classifications can be used.[7]

Different laundries utilize different detergent formulations and procedures, but, in general, bleachable items are subjected to several sudsings with soap or detergent and added alkali at temperatures ranging from 125 degrees F. to 160 degrees F., a chlorine bleaching at 160 degrees F. for three to five minutes, three or four rinses at different temperatures, each one lower than the last, an acid sour, and blueing. In the rinse, starch is added for those items on which customers have requested it.

[7] *Textile Handbook* (Washington, D.C.: American Home Economics Association, 1974), p. 83.

The purpose of the acid sour is to neutralize the alkalinity of the water, to remove iron stains, to kill bacteria, and to destroy excess or unused bleach. Some typical sours are acetic acid, sodium bisulfite, sodium acid flouride, and oxalic acid.

Light-colored fabrics are washed at lower temperatures than white fabrics, generally 100 degrees to 120 degrees F., and no chlorine bleach is used. Dark-colored fabrics are laundered at still lower temperatures, 90 degrees F. to 100 degrees F., as they are more likely to lose color or bleed at higher temperatures. They, too, are not bleached.

After the final rinse, fabrics are spun in an extractor to remove excess water. The extraction may be done by the same machine that washes the items or it may be done by a separate piece of equipment. This step is comparable to the spin-dry cycle on home washers.

After extraction, the fabrics are dryer-dried and, if the customer wishes, pressed. Different types of pressing equipment are used for various items. Flat pieces are ironed on a machine called a *flatwork* ironer. A smooth, heated iron plate provides the heat and pressure, while the fabrics travel across a rotating, padded roll. Special equipment is made for ironing shirts, small pieces, and oversized items such as curtains.

Silk and wool fabrics may be laundered, but are handled in special machines and without the use of chlorine bleach. Neutral soaps and detergents are used without additional alkali, and the washing machine uses a gentle agitation. Three to five rinses are needed to remove all of the soap and detergent, so that discoloration of the fabric does not take place. An acid sour is used. Extraction is done gently.

DRY CLEANING

The term *dry cleaning* derives from the use of special solvents for cleaning that dry quickly. Professional dry cleaning requires special equipment and techniques, some of which are similar to laundering. The steps in professional dry cleaning are sorting, cleaning, spotting, and finishing.

Sorting, as in laundering, is done according to fiber types, colors, degree of soil, and the like. Buttons or other trim that may be harmed by dry-cleaning solvents are removed. Cleaning takes place in a special washing cylinder comparable to the cylinder of a front-loading automatic washer. Dry-cleaning solvents are either petroleum solvents or synthetic solvents, specifically perchloroethylene or trichlorotrifluoroethane. Perchloroethylene is used by more dry-cleaning establishments than any of the other solvents.

Special soaps and detergents perform the same function in commercial dry cleaning as soaps and detergents do in home laundry. When added to solvents, these special preparations aid in soil removal.

Dry-cleaning solvents cannot be used and then discarded; instead, they are recycled and reused. Solvents are purified and accumulated soil is removed either by filtration or distillation. The continual use of dirty solvent will interfere with cleaning.

After cleaning, the garments are checked for spots or stains that have not been removed in the dry cleaning. Spotters are trained to handle different fabrics and stains as effectively as possible.

If dry cleaning and spotting have not been adequate to remove all soil, the garments may have to be wet-cleaned. Wet cleaning is not laundering, but the treatment of fabrics with water to remove soil.

Final touches are given to the clean garment in the finishing department. Buttons or trimmings that have been removed are replaced, garments are steamed or, if necessary, pressed, and minor repairs are made.

To cut corners and costs some dry-cleaning establishments may eliminate some of the steps that are usually part of the dry-cleaning process. Inferior quality dry-cleaning establishments may

1. Sort inadequately.

2. Do no cleaning of pockets, cuffs, and so on.

3. Use dirty solvent.

4. Use inferior quality solvents.

5. Fail to extract all of solvent from item, leaving an unpleasant odor.

6. Omit steps such as spotting, mending, and removal of buttons.

7. Do no wet cleaning.

8. Do no hand pressing.

Coin-Operated Dry Cleaning

Coin-operated dry cleaning is similar to the coin-operated "laundromat." The customer puts clothing to be cleaned into a machine that tumbles clothing in a nonflammable, dry cleaning solvent (either perchloroethylene or fluoro-carbon). The owner of the dry cleaning establishment supplies only the machines and the cleaning fluid. The customer must sort items, put them into the machine, and take them out at the end of the cycle.

The cost of coin-operated dry cleaning is well below that of full-scale professional dry cleaning. The services that normally come with dry cleaning, that is, spotting, mending, pressing, and so on, are, of course, lacking. Sometimes the solvents used in coin-operated dry cleaning are not cleaned adequately.

STORAGE OF TEXTILE PRODUCTS

Between uses, textile items may be put away for either short or long periods of time. Some attention to the way in which clothing is stored may help to prolong the life of textile products.

Textile products will wear longer if given a chance to "rest" between uses. Rotating items in use, either clothing or household textiles, will provide this rest period. Storage practices may encourage this rotation. For example, towels or bed linens that have been laundered may be placed at the bottom of the stack of items, and the next item to be used taken from the top of the stack.

When table linens, bed linens, or other items are pressed, care should be taken to fold these items at different places. Continuous folding of fabrics, especially where sharp creases are pressed into the material, in the same place will cause the yarns to break or wear first in those spots.

Fabrics that are to be put away for long-term storage should always be put away clean. Moths or other insects will more readily attack soiled fabrics. Furthermore, some spots or stains that are only slightly evident may be oxidized. Oxidized stains darken and are exceedingly difficult to remove. Fabrics should not be put away with pins left in them, as the pins may rust and cause stains to appear around the pinned area.

Fabrics that are subject to attack by insects and mildew should be stored carefully. Wool and animal hair fabrics can be mothproofed before storage, or stored in tightly closed containers with moth repellants.

Fabrics that are susceptible to mildew should be stored dry, in a dry place. If fabrics that are normally starched are to be stored for a long period of time, it is best to store them without starching, as silverfish find the starch especially appetizing. If starch is required later, garments can be spray starched before use. If starched garments are stored, they should be put away in a closed container that insects cannot penetrate.

FURTHER SOURCES OF INFORMATION

Many organizations publish booklets or pamphlets that offer information to the consumer about the care of textile products. Soap and detergent manufacturers, and women's magazines frequently publish materials that instruct the consumer in the appropriate care techniques for textiles of all kinds.

Consumers who wish to obtain further information about textile cleaning, storage, and maintenance can often find current information on these subjects from the Department of Agriculture and from State Home Economics Extension Offices. Lists of publications of the U.S. Department of Agriculture can be obtained from the U.S. Government Printing Office, Washington, D.C. 20402. Most of these materials are published as "Home and Garden Bulletins." Lists of state extension publications are generally available from the land-grant college in each state.

Recommended References

AVERY, C., and D. HARRABIN. *A Comparison of Phosphate and Non Phosphate Detergents*. University of Rhode Island Bulletin #415, November, 1975.

Detergents—In Depth. Proceedings of symposium sponsored by the Soap and Detergent Association, March 1974, Washington, D.C.

"Fabric Softeners." *Consumer Research Magazine*, October 1975, p. 75.

FORTRESS, F. "Problems of Cleaning Textiles." *Textile Industries*, March 1976. p. 65.

Removing Stains from Fabrics. Washington, D.C.: U.S. Dept. of Agriculture, Home and Garden Bulletin No. 63, 1973.

Rhode, R. O. "How Non-phosphate Detergents Affect Dyed Fabrics." *Textile Chemist and Colorist,* October 1974, p. 33.

Sanitation in Home Laundering. Home and Garden Bulletin No. 97, USDA, October, 1971.

Soaps and Detergents. Home and Garden Bulletin No. 139, USDA, October, 1973.

The Technology of Home Laundering. Textile Monograph #108. New York: American Association for Textile Technology, 1973.

Textile Handbook. Washington, D.C.: American Home Economics Association, 1974.

22

TEXTILES AND THE ENVIRONMENT

As the general public becomes more mindful of dangers to the natural environment from industrial production, the relationship of the production of modern textiles to ecological problems becomes an issue of public concern. Environmental problems relating to the production and processing of both natural and man-made fibers occur in four areas. The first of these concerns the health of the workers in the textile industry. Second, textile manufacture can produce pollution of the air and the water, and used textile fibers may create waste disposal problems. Third, home care of textiles requires the use of detergents or soaps, which have been cited as pollutants of the water supply. And, finally, many synthetic fibers are made from petroleum and petroleum products, which may be in shorter supply and have become increasingly expensive over the past several years.

Health Hazards to Textile Workers

LUNG DISEASE

The detrimental effect of inhaling small particles of grit or other hard inorganic matter has been recognized for many years. The constant exposure of the lungs to these irritants is harmful and will eventually produce lung disease in many of the persons exposed.

This has long been recognized as a hazard in the production of asbestos. Recently, two similar problem areas in textile processing have been given increased attention. It is thought that early forms of glass fiber did not produce problems of lung disease because the diameter of the glass fibers was sufficiently large that the body's respiratory protective screening mechanisms prevented glass fiber from entering the lungs. In recent years, however, glass fiber has been manufactured in much smaller diameters, and can now be inhaled. Like asbestos, these small, hard, glass particles do cause lung damage and disease.[1]

A third culprit has been identified: namely, cotton. It is not the cotton fiber

[1] K. Montague and P. Montague, "Fiber Glass," *Environment* (September, 1974), p. 6.

that causes lung disease, but the nonorganic, hard impurities that are part of the untreated cotton fiber that are present in the dust generated by the breaking and opening of cotton bales, which is necessary in the preparation of cotton for spinning. Cotton workers engaged in processes from the opening of the bales through to carding may, after a period of exposure, develop byssinosis, or "brown lung" as it is called by the workers.[2]

In all three cases, the solution of the problem is essentially the same. The amount of dust must be decreased to a safe level, or else the worker must be given personal protective devices to filter out the dust.

The problem is still under study. Manufacturers are experimenting with air ventilation systems that remove a significant amount of dust, and with personal safety devices, rather like gas masks, that can be worn by workers. Unfortunately, worker response to the discomfort of masks has been somewhat negative. It has also been found that the way in which workers carry out their tasks is related to the amount of irritant inhaled. Researchers have recommended that workers be trained to change their work practices if they are detrimental.

TOXICITY OF CHEMICALS

Some of the chemical substances with which textile workers come in to contact are highly toxic. For the most part, companies have been able to identify these substances and protect workers from contact with them.

From time to time, however, research findings point out new materials that are harmful which have never been identified before as presenting any serious health problems. Vinyl chloride is such a chemical. An important ingredient in the production of polyvinyl chloride plastics, vinyl chloride, is used in the production of plastic backings and coatings for fabrics. Evidence indicates that continued exposure to vinyl chloride will produce cancer of the liver in some of the persons exposed. Unfortunately, this discovery has come too late to help those who have already been affected, but steps will now have to be taken to protect those workers who must handle this material in the future.

NOISE

Noise levels in textile manufacturing plants can be very high. Governmental standards regulating the noise levels have been imposed, and manufacturers must comply with these requirements. The standards limit noise on the basis of the level of noise in relation to the length of exposure of the employee to the noise.

These standards were imposed because of the relationship between high noise levels and hearing loss. It is the responsibility of the company to lower noise levels in those cases where the standards are not met. This presents a

[2]R. S. Brown, M. Mayer, Jr., and J. Kotter, "Dust and Noise Control in Cotton Processing Machinery," *Book of Papers*, 1974, National Technical Conference, AATCC, 1974, p. 408.

more difficult problem in factories using older equipment that operates at much higher sound levels than newer textile equipment, which is engineered to satisfy these requirements. Shuttleless looms are an example of a newer type of textile machinery that has made a significant contribution to the reduction of noise levels.

Although investigations are underway as to how best to cope with the health and safety hazards of the textile industry, complete solutions to these problems do not yet exist. National safety standards have been established by the Occupational Safety and Health Act of 1970 (known as OSHA), and companies must now adapt equipment and work situations to meet the requirements of the law.

Textiles as a Source of Air and Water Pollution

THE MANUFACTURERS

Textile production has always been a source of water pollution. Not only the man-made fibers but also natural fibers have created pollutants in the scouring of wool, and in many of the dyeing and finishing operations. The recently awakened concern with the industrial pollution of air and water has focused attention on these unpleasant by-products of textile manufacture. Federally mandated standards for clean air and water have been imposed, and textile companies are required to comply with these regulations.

Problems in relation to air pollution seem to be generated during heat setting, in which the organic compounds used for finishing are vaporized and carried off in gaseous forms; in piece dyeing, where some dye materials are carried off in water vapor; and in a wide variety of processing steps that utilize chemical solvents.

Water pollution can take place at almost any step of textile production, from preparation of the fiber through to the finishing of fabrics. Not only does this water pollution pose a threat to fish and the ecological balance of streams but also recent research studies suggest a link between the presence of asbestos in the water supply and increased levels of cancer.[3] Dyeing and finishing of fabrics utilize a great deal of water, and the disposal of the chemicals used in these processes presents serious problems for the manufacturer.

The legal requirements for meeting clean water standards imposed by either local, state, or national governments have led the textile industry to look for means to dispose of wastes in ways that do not pollute streams. Recycling of water or other processing materials such as sizing, treating the water to render it safe or to remove pollutants, and using biodegradable substances are three measures that can be used by manufacturers to maintain clean water.

Disposal of solid wastes from textile firms and from chemical companies associated with the textile industry is another difficulty. Incineration and burial, which have been used to eliminate wastes, both present problems. Burial may lead to the contamination of ground water, to fires, or to the generation of noxious gases from the indiscriminate mixing of chemical sub-

---

[3] "Pollution and Public Health: Taconite Case Poses Major Threat," *Science* (October 14, 1974), p. 31.

stances. Incineration may produce air pollution or water pollution as a by-product of the incineration process. To be successful, both processes require careful monitoring and control.

The disposal of waste products of all kinds by textile manufacturers is an ongoing problem that the industry, like all other industries, is trying to solve. John Lomartine in a paper presented to the American Chemical Society in June, 1974, suggested the ways that textile companies might respond to the requirement for a cleaner environment.

1. A heavy contaminator could be replaced by a light contaminator.

2. A new processing concept could be adopted where all water is cleaned before being returned to its source and/or water recycling processes could be used.

3. Operations could be improved so that they generate less waste and not only aid in the disposal problem, but also generate more prime salable material.

4. Recycling of waste into the process will become more prevalent. An added advantage of this move will be more efficient conversion of raw materials.

5. Use of waste as fuel, feeding boilers to produce steam. At the very least, incineration of burnable waste will be done if for no other reason than to reduce the volume of material to be disposed. As energy sources become more expensive, the burning of waste becomes more attractive.[4]

THE CONSUMER

In some respects, the problems of disposal of textile items after they have been used by the ultimate consumer are even more difficult than the disposal of waste products generated in the manufacture of textiles.

Natural fibers are biodegradable and will eventually break down, but synthetics are quite resistant and are not so easily disposed of. Recycling has been recommended as a means of disposing of used textiles, but the recycling of textiles is complicated by a number of factors. (Purchases or gifts of second-hand clothing are one form of recycling clothing.)

Only 17 per cent of textile wastes are recycled, compared with 88 per cent for stainless steel, 48 per cent for aluminum, and 61 per cent for copper.[5] The reasons that textile wastes are so infrequently recycled are related to the regulations that place limitations on the sale and use of used textile fibers. Companies that reclaim textile fibers may find it economically unproductive to handle all types of materials.

[4] John Lomartine, *"Fibers and the Environment."* Paper presented at the American Chemical Society Symposium on Man-made Fibers, June 1974. p. 2ff.

[5] M. Sheftel, "Utilization of Textile Fiber Waste," Paper presented to the American Chemical Society Symposium on Man-made Fibers, June 1974, p. 1.

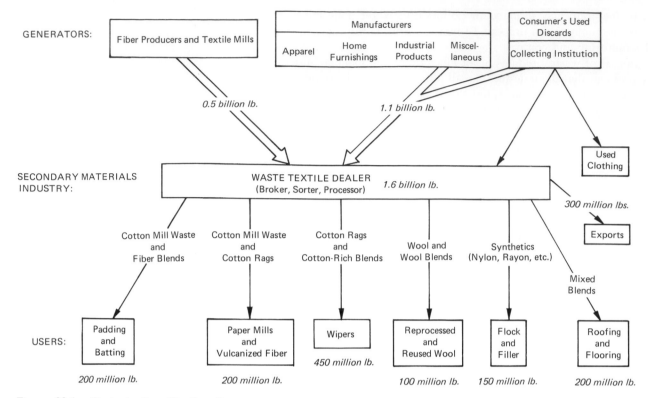

GENERATORS:

Fiber Producers and Textile Mills

Manufacturers

Apparel | Home Furnishings | Industrial Products | Miscel-laneous

Consumer's Used Discards

Collecting Institution

0.5 billion lb.

1.1 billion lb.

SECONDARY MATERIALS INDUSTRY:

WASTE TEXTILE DEALER
(Broker, Sorter, Processor)   1.6 billion lb.

Used Clothing

300 million lbs.

Exports

Cotton Mill Waste and Fiber Blends

Cotton Mill Waste and Cotton Rags

Cotton Rags and Cotton-Rich Blends

Wool and Wool Blends

Synthetics (Nylon, Rayon, etc.)

Mixed Blends

USERS:

Padding and Batting

Paper Mills and Vulcanized Fiber

Wipers

Reprocessed and Reused Wool

Flock and Filler

Roofing and Flooring

200 million lb.   200 million lb.   450 million lb.   100 million lb.   150 million lb.   200 million lb.

Figure 22-1. Waste textile utilization flow. Reprinted from *Textile Industries,* December 1972, p. 43.

Textile waste from manufacturers of garments or other textile products is relatively easy to process, since the manufacturer can identify the textile fiber. In reclamation fibers must be sorted into different generic categories and the identification of unknown man-made fibers or blends is difficult. Chemical analysis for identification purposes may be necessary. Recycling textiles used and discarded by consumers is extremely difficult. Not only is fiber content unidentified but the quality of fibers may also be quite uneven as a result of wear.

Natural fibers and rayon present relatively few problems of identification and recycling. Wool is reprocessed or reused and made into "new" fabrics. Cotton, linen, and rayon can be utilized in the production of fine rag paper or in battings, and paddings.

The separation of blends into their component parts is more difficult. Often this is achieved by identifying the components of the blend, then dissolving out one of the fibers, leaving the other intact. Man-made fibers can be reused in making flock, as industrial fillers in the manufacture of plastic or in the regeneration of synthetic fibers.

Special finishes that are applied to fabrics may create additional problems for recycling. Many of these finishes are virtually impossible to recycle, and they contaminate the fibers, making their recycling impossible too.

As the raw materials from which many textiles are made become more scarce, the importance of recycling textile products becomes increasingly important. It is imperative that intensive research into the ways to turn discarded textile products into usable raw materials be given priority.

Figure 22-2. Typical flow of textile fibers in process and the resulting generation of textile waste. Reprinted from *Textile Industries*, December 1972, p. 43.

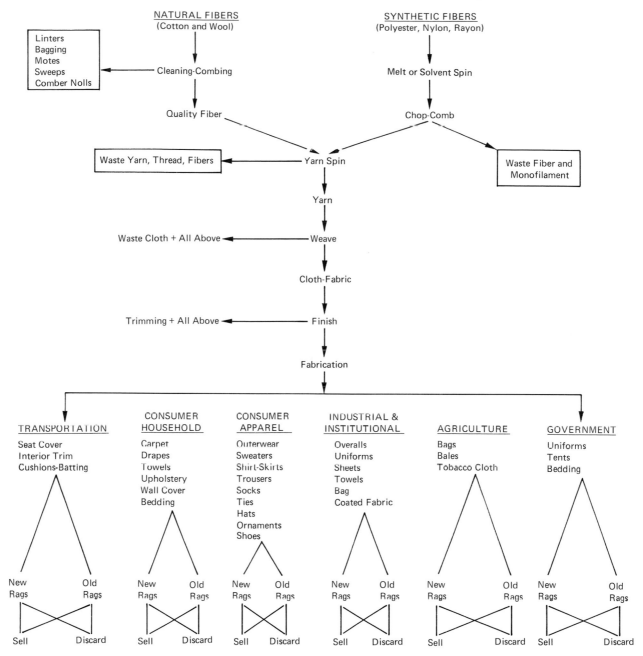

POLLUTION FROM DISPOSAL OF GLASS FIBER

Along with most other solid waste products that cannot be incinerated, used glass fiber fabrics, insulation, and building materials, are placed in land fill trash dumps. Researchers have found that levels of glass fiber in the air near these dumps can be fairly high.

With the increased concern about very fine glass fiber as a potential cause of lung cancer, environmentalists believe that the increasing levels of glass fiber present in the air may pose a serious threat to health. Because there is a lengthy delay between exposure to materials such as asbestos and glass fiber and the onset of disease, it is believed that the full consequences of such pollution may not become evident for twenty to fifty years.[6]

POLLUTION FROM HOME LAUNDERING

The fear of water pollution from household wastes that contain large quantities of phosphates has led some states and communities to restrict the sale of phosphate-containing detergents. Other communities have totally banned detergents from use. These restrictions have generally been made as a result of local conditions that have generated public support for such measures.

In some areas where the ground water level is close to the surface, detergents have been seeping into the drinking water supply. Because detergents do not biodegrade as rapidly as do soaps, they have been banned from use in localities where they have been found to contaminate the water. In these communities only soaps may be used, and stores do not sell detergents for laundering or any other cleaning.

Other local and state governments have passed regulations banning the sale of phosphate-containing detergents. Claims and counterclaims are made by the detergent manufacturers and the supporters of these laws. Environmentalists claim that phosphates simulate the growth of algae, whereas detergent manufacturers respond by claiming that phosphates from detergents contribute negligibly to these levels and blame other sources of phosphates, such as chemical fertilizers. Furthermore, the manufacturers dispute the environmentalists' claim that increased phosphate levels do increase algae growth. More research is required to prove the case for or against phosphates in detergents.

For those areas where phosphates have been outlawed, detergent companies have produced phosphate-free detergents in which other alkaline salts, such as sodium carbonate and sodium silicate, are used as substitutes for the phosphates. One of the major disadvantages of substituting other nonphosphate detergents for phosphate-bearing detergents is that residues left by these substances have a detrimental effect on flame-retardant finishes.

When more evidence has been collected as to the effectiveness of the ban of phosphate in decreasing pollution, the situation will be reassessed and a consistent public policy will probably evolve. In the meantime, the manufac-

[6]K. Montague and P. Montague, op. cit., p. 8.

turers of detergents appear to be working toward the production of a wide range of detergents that are more biodegradable, that is, substances that decompose more rapidly during sewage treatment.

Textiles and Energy

The energy crisis that developed in the United States in 1973–1974 created a ripple effect in the textile industry as it did in all areas of the national economy. Any changes in petroleum supply or increased prices will adversely affect the textile industry since petroleum and petroleum by-products are the most important single raw material used in the manufacture of most synthetics. Since many of the chemicals used to manufacture synthetics are derived from oil, the cost of these chemicals has been increased greatly by raised oil prices. The supply of these chemicals will decrease if supplies of oil should decrease. Furthermore, the cost of energy to power the plants that produce fibers, yarns, fabrics and finishes is also soaring.

The question is often asked, "Will we now abandon man-made fibers and return to the use of natural fibers?" The answer must be "no." There are not enough natural fibers to supply the demands of consumers from all over the world. And as food supplies become short, underdeveloped countries can ill afford to turn land now used for the production of food to the production of textile fibers.

The textile industry uses 1 per cent of the nation's petroleum supply.[7] In the interests of preserving jobs and supplying the needs of the country for textile products, it is unlikely that the textile industry's share of the oil supply will be drastically cut. Instead, prices have risen, especially for those fibers in which supplies are shortest.

One of the trends that will be accentuated as a result of the energy crisis is the production of blends of natural and man-made fibers, which have been well-accepted by consumers. Many of the double-knit fabrics that were formerly made of 100 per cent polyester may, in the near future, be made of blends of cotton and polyester, especially since American cotton growers are attempting to increase the levels of cotton production.[8]

The consumer must also think in terms of energy use for the care of textile products. Washing, drying, and ironing all require the expenditures of energy, energy that is not only becoming more scarce but very expensive. The selection of fabrics that require shorter drying time or can be line-dried, as well as those that can be washed in cooler water, or do not require ironing, will have the end result of costing the consumer less money because less energy will be used in their care.

An increased consumer emphasis on durability may also contribute to a reduction of energy needs. If textile items are used longer, they will have to be replaced less often, thereby reducing the amount of the raw materials needed. Longer use before disposal will also decrease the problem of disposal of used

[7] Nancy G. Harries, "Textile News: The Energy Situation," *Family Economics Review*, U.S.D.A. Summer 1974, p. 8.
[8] Ibid.

textiles. Fashion, however, is such an important aspect of the apparel industries that many items are discarded before they are outworn. Even an energy crisis is not likely to remove fashion as a factor in clothing choice. Consumers may find it useful to identify certain of their purchases as "fashion" items in which durability may not be so important as it is in "classic" or other items that do not go out of style quickly.

Summary

Both industry and the public have obligations for the protection of the environment. Whereas at first glance industry would seem to be more responsible for pollution, a deeper examination of the issues leads inexorably to the conclusion that this is a shared responsibility. In the long run, the public must be willing to pay for the improvements in pollution control that industries make. Environmentally safe manufacturing of textiles is expensive. The cost of cleaner factories and mills will be paid for by increasing prices of the items that are marketed. There is no other way that a free enterprise system that operates on the profit motive can produce its goods.

No one relishes increases in the cost of textiles, but the alternatives are unthinkable. The trade-off for lower prices would be to continue the deterioration of the environment that future generations will inherit.

Recommended References

BAJAJ, J. K. L. "Recycling Man-made Fibers." *Textile Industries.* December 1972, p. 42.

"Flame Retardant Chemicals and Ecology." *Textile Industries.* February 1976, p. 74.

HARRIES, NANCY G. "Textile News: The Energy Situation." *Family Economics Review.* U.S.D.A., Summer 1974, p. 7 ff.

HATCHER, JOHN D. "The Environmental Problem of Dust from Cotton Processing." A paper presented to the American Chemical Society Symposium on Man-made Fibers, June 1974.

LEVINKAS, GEORGE. "Fibers and the Environment." Paper presented to the American Chemical Society Symposium on Man-made Fibers, June, 1974.

LOMARTINE, JOHN. "Fibers and the Environment." Paper presented to the American Chemical Society Symposium on Man-made fibers, June, 1974.

MIKI, R. T. "Domestic & International Implications of Environmental Regulations." *Textile Chemist and Colorist.* July 1975, p. 14.

NORTHRUP, H. L., and W. F. TURNER. "Air Pollution Control in Textile Finishing." *Textile Chemist and Colorist.* April 1975, p. 22.

SHEFTEL, M. "Utilization of Textile Fiber Waste." Paper presented to the American Chemical Society Symposium on Man-made Fibers, June 1974.

"Soaps and Detergents for Home Laundering." U.S. Department of Agriculture, Home and Garden Bulletin #139. Washington, D.C. Revised October, 1973.

The Textile Industry and the Environment. 1973. Proceedings of Conference sponsored by the American Association of Textile Chemists and Colorists, May 22–24, 1973, Washington, D.C.

WARLICK, S. J. "Progress in Spinning Noise Control." *Textile Industries,* December 1972, p. 42.

23

TEXTILE TESTING AND STANDARDS

Governmental agencies, product manufacturers, retailers, and consumer groups may all become involved in the establishment of performance standards for textile products. A *standard* is a defined level of performance that a product must achieve in order to be considered as acceptable for use.

Except in the case of flammability standards, manufacturers are not required by law to conform to textile product standards. Some retailers, however, require that wholesale manufacturers from whom they buy must produce goods that meet specified standards. The Department of Defense establishes minimum standards for textiles used by the military and some federal agencies or funding regulations for federally financed construction projects require that carpets, draperies, and the like conform to stated standards. Standards also provide a basis for the comparison of results of studies of textiles by different researchers. Although the general public does benefit from the use of standards by segments of the textile industry, most consumers are unaware of their existence.

Organizations That Establish Standards

The organizations most actively involved in establishing textile standards are the American National Standards Institute (ANSI) and the Federal Government. ANSI is a nonprofit federation, whose membership is composed of trade, labor, technical, and consumer organizations and governmental agencies. ANSI does not originate standards. Proposals for standards may originate with any of the members of the federation, but all groups in the Institute must approve the final versions of proposed standards. The standards that are established are still voluntary, but they do provide the establishment of an accepted base level of quality for voluntary participants.

The federal government, through the Office of Engineering Standards Services, works with the textile industry to establish not only standards of performance but also standard sizes, grading, test methods, and the like. Although these standards are also voluntary, they are established cooperatively by government and industry, often at the request of industry, and are subsequently adopted rather widely.

The Consumer Product Safety Commission was established under the Consumer Product Safety Act of 1972. This commission has broad jurisdiction over product safety, one area of which is fabric flammability. The commission oversees the administration and revision of standards that items covered under flammability legislation must meet.

Specific federal agencies and the military establish standards that the products they buy must meet. Compliance with these standards is essential if companies wish to do business with such agencies.

TEXTILE TESTING AND TEXTILE STANDARDS

In order to determine whether textile products meet established standards, such products must be tested. Textile standards and textile testing are, therefore, closely involved. The two groups that have developed the most widely used textile testing methods are the American Association of Textile Chemists and Colorists (AATCC) and the American Society for Testing and Materials (ASTM).

The American Association of Textile Chemists and Colorists is composed of persons from the textile wet processing industry, textile chemists, others working in varying segments of the textile industry, and educators. The Association establishes testing methods, largely in the area of chemical testing, and maintains an active educational program implemented through national and regional meetings, and a monthly journal, the *Textile Chemist and Colorist*. Specific test methodologies are described fully in an annual publication, *The Technical Manual*.

Tests established by the American Society for Testing and Materials are more specifically focused on physical testing and the testing of fabric construction. ASTM test methods are published annually in a book of *ASTM Standards*. Many of the standards promulgated by ANSI have been developed by ASTM.

An examination of the catalog of the American Standards Institute reveals that textile standards are given a key letter and number for identification purposes. Standards listed under the identification L-14 are physical and chemical test methods, and have been established either by ASTM or AATCC.

Standards carrying the identification numbers L-22 are "performance requirements for textile fabrics," and the number L-24 identifies performance requirements for institutional textiles.[1] Copies of these standards can be purchased from the American National Standards Institute, 1430 Broadway, N.Y., N.Y. 10018.

Testing Established testing methods have validity, that is, they are accepted by authorities in the field as reliable. Not only do industry and the government require testing of materials in ways that are accepted as reliable and standard-

[1] Catalog, ANSI, 1975, p. 70.

ized but researchers also require a body of accepted tests for use in comparing data accumulated by different researchers working in different laboratories. Specific tests of the type established by AATCC and ASTM are too numerous to discuss here. These testing methodologies are given in detail in the technical publications of these organizations and can readily be obtained for use by interested persons.

Although most students in introductory textile courses do not become involved with extensive textile testing, it may be helpful for students to have some familiarity with testing equipment and the types of testing that can be done. There are, also, some simple forms of testing of textile products that can be carried out in the classroom or at home without specialized equipment that will provide a general evaluation of fabrics.

Laboratory testing is carried out under carefully controlled conditions. Temperature and humidity are maintained at standard levels: 70 degrees F. (21 degrees C) and 65 degrees humidity. Testing equipment must conform to specifications established in the testing methodology, and fabric samples must be of uniform size. More than one test must be run in order to determine a consistent pattern of behavior and results.

Classroom or home test methods cannot meet the same rigorous criteria for controlled conditions, but should maintain as much control as possible over conditions under which testing is done, size of samples, number of tests run, and so on.

DIMENSIONS, WEIGHT, AND THICKNESS

Certain data must often be collected about textiles prior to testing. Information about dimensions and construction is obtained in the following ways.

The length and width of the fabric or fabric sample are determined by measuring the fabric. Samples are placed flat, free from wrinkling, and un-stretched. Length is measured parallel to the selvage and width is measured perpendicular to the selvage. Measurements may have to be taken at several points and averaged, as distortions of the fabric may have taken place during handling.

Fabric weight may be expressed in one of three ways: ounces per square yard, ounces per linear yard, and linear yards per pound. For the measurement of ounces per linear yard, one linear yard of fabric is weighed. The width of the yard must also be noted. In measuring linear yards per pound, one pound of fabric is weighed out, then the fabric length is measured. Again, the width of the fabric must be noted. The same measurements may also be made in grams, rather than ounces. Ounces per square yard are calculated as follows: one square yard is equal to 1,296 square inches. Ounces or grams per square yard equal 1,296 times the weight of the sample (in grams or ounces) divided by the area of the sample (expressed in square inches). The formula might be written as follows:

$$\text{Oz. or gms. per sq. yd.} = \frac{1{,}296 \times \text{weight of sample}}{\text{area of sample}}$$

Fabric thickness is measured in thousandths of an inch by a device called an *automatic micrometer*. This may be an important measurement for pile fabrics or may be used in conjunction with tests for shrinkage or abrasion.

THREAD COUNT

Thread count is the number of yarns per inch in a fabric. The fabric is examined with a calibrated, square magnifying glass called either a *linen tester* or a *pick glass*. The glass is marked off in fractions of an inch or in centimeters and the number of warp and filling yarns beside these calibrations can be viewed in magnified form with the glass and counted. In knitted fabrics the number of wales or courses per inch is calculated.

The glass is lined up along a lengthwise yarn or crosswise yarn, the yarns in that direction are counted, and the count is expressed as a round number of warps by a round number of fillings. A yarn count of 75×50, for example, would mean that the fabric has 75 yarns in the warp direction and 50 yarns in the filling.

If the number of warps and fillings are about the same, the fabric may be said to have a balanced count, and could be written as a count of 75 square or 75 warps by 75 fillings. Sometimes, as in sheets, the thread count is written as warp plus filling yarns per inch.

STRENGTH

Fabric strength evaluations are made as breaking strength, tearing strength, or bursting strength. A variety of machines are used to measure strength, and fabric samples are prepared for testing according to ASTM test method specifications.

Breaking strength is the force required to break a woven fabric when it is pulled under tension. The measurement is made of the pounds or grams of force required to break the fabric. Half of the samples are prepared with warp yarns running in the direction of stress, and the other half with the stress in the filling direction. The figures are averaged.

The tearing strength of a fabric, expressed in pounds or grams, is the pressure required to continue a tear or rip already begun in a woven fabric. As in breaking strength, an average of values for warp and filling yarns is taken.

Bursting strength is the pounds or grams of pressure required to rupture a knitted or other nonwoven fabric. Force is applied to the fabric from below or above the fabric as it is held flat.

Strength tests are often used as a measure of the effect of different conditions on fabrics. Researchers may use these tests to make comparisons between control or untreated fabrics and experimental fabrics. For example, breaking strength tests may be used to determine whether special finishes affect the strength of a fabric.

There are no hand tests for breaking strength that have the accuracy of

Figure 23-1. Pick counter used to facilitate counting threads per inch or wales and courses of knitted goods. Courtesy of Alfred Suter Company, Inc.

testing performed on machines. Strength testing in the classroom or at home is limited to estimations of difference in strength. Yarns can be raveled from fabric samples, and comparisons made of the strength required to break them by pulling. A tear can be started at the edge of a woven fabric, and some estimate is then made of the strength required to continue the tear.

ELONGATION AND RECOVERY FROM STRETCHING

At the same time that breaking strength is being tested on a breaking strength testing machine, the degree of elongation that the fabric undergoes before breaking may be determined. The breaking strength machine is designed to record both the force required to break the sample and the inches of elongation before the sample broke. The percentage of stretch the sample underwent is calculated.

Fabrics may also be tested for recovery from elongation. Samples are stretched to a certain percentage of their length (often 2 per cent), then permitted to recover for a specified length of time. A remeasurement is made, and the percentage of elastic recovery is calculated by determining the length before stretching, length after stretching, and length after recovery. Since some fabrics recover gradually from stretching, measurements of recovery may be made after varying periods of time.

Although students in the classroom lack the sophisticated equipment required for very exact testing of elongation and recovery from stretching, fabric samples can be measured, subjected to stretching by pulling the fabric between two clamps for a period of time, and then measuring to determine whether stretching has taken place. A second measurement taken after the fabric has been permitted to recover will allow some approximate determination of recovery from stretching.

Figure 23-2. Tensile tester used for testing tensile strength of fabrics and cords. Many tensile machines can be adapted to perform tearing and bursting strength tests. Courtesy of Alfred Suter Company, Inc.

SHRINKAGE

Fabric samples can be tested for shrinkage after laundering or dry cleaning, and the percentage of shrinkage can be calculated. Such tests can be done easily in the classroom or at home, although without temperature and humidity control, the results of these tests will always be approximate.

For best results, samples should be of an adequate size to make the calculations more exact. The smaller the sample, the greater is the likelihood of error. Samples marked off in the numbers ten or twenty also make numerical calculations easier. If the sample is large enough, an area ten inches square is marked off in indelible ink following grain lines. The sample size should not be cut to ten inches, but several inches on either side of the markings should be allowed; otherwise the edges of the fabric may lose threads through raveling and the results may not be accurate.

The sample should then be laundered by hand or by machine. The sample should be laundered by the same method that would be used for a garment made from the fabric. After laundering, the fabric is spread flat, dried, and then remeasured. The percentage of shrinkage is calculated by this formula.

$$\% \text{ shrinkage} = \frac{10 \text{ inches} - \text{distance between marks after laundering}}{10 \text{ inches (marked length of original)}} \times 100$$

If only a small sample of fabric is available, it can be measured, then washed by hand, and remeasured with the shrinkage calculated as before, using the appropriate measurements:

$$\% \text{ shrinkage} = \frac{\text{length of original sample, less length after laundering}}{\text{divided by length of original sample}} \times 100$$

To prevent the fraying of small samples it is best to overcast edges by hand, or some other method of preventing the sample from raveling should be used.

An evaluation of dimensional stability to dry cleaning can be made by immersing measured samples of fabric in dry-cleaning fluid, agitating the samples, then drying. The instructions on dry-cleaning fluids should be carefully followed since many are either flammable or toxic if inhaled in a closed area.

ABRASION RESISTANCE AND PILLING

Abrasion resistance is tested on different types of abrasion-testing machines. The results of tests run on different machines cannot be compared, as each machine tests with a different motion and each holds the fabrics in different positions.

No home test will provide a completely accurate measure of abrasion resistance; however, stroking a piece of sand paper back and forth across the surface of a fabric may give a general indication of the tendency of the fabric to abrade. Machines such as the Brush Pilling Tester or Random Pilling Tester are used to evaluate the tendency of fabrics to pill.

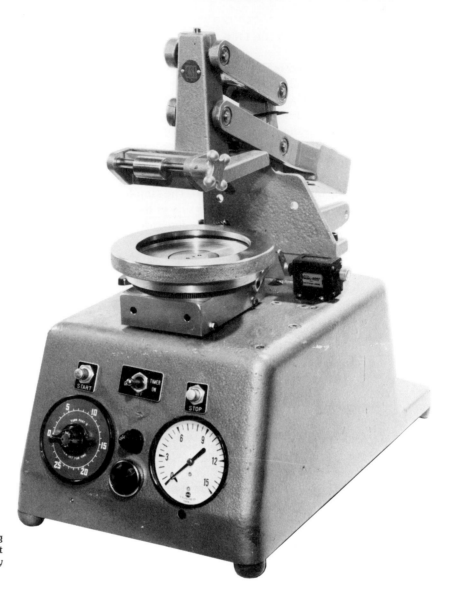

Figure 23-3. CSI Surface Abrader for testing surface abrasion. Other instruments will test for flex abrasion and edge abrasion. Courtesy of Custom Scientific Instruments, Inc.

COLORFASTNESS

The colorfastness of fabrics to a variety of substances and conditions can be measured by the use of a wide variety of specific testing methods and machinery. Atmospheric conditions may result in color loss for some fabrics. Fume fading—loss of color caused by an exposure to atmospheric gases—can be measured in a device called a *gas fading chamber*. Fabrics in this enclosed chamber are exposed to gases and their color loss is determined.

Color change is ascertained by keeping a control or untreated sample of the fabric being tested. Tested samples can then be checked against the original.

Comparisons should always be made under the same kind of lighting, as different light sources can alter the appearance of colors. For laboratory testing, color scales have been established that make it possible to determine more precisely the degree of color change that has taken place. Samples of both treated fabrics and control fabrics are compared to the standard scales, and numerical ratings are assigned.

An exposure to sunlight may cause color loss in some fabrics. A simple home method for testing for fading from exposure to the sun is to tape a sample fabric in a sunny window. The sample is exposed to the sun for a period of time, and is then compared to an unexposed sample. This method does not provide a gauge of really long-term exposure, and the hours of exposure to sunlight are dependent upon the weather and time of year.

The Fade-o-meter, a machine that duplicates the fading action of the sun, is used in laboratories to test for colorfastness to light. Samples may be exposed for varying periods of time and the loss of color is compared with a control sample.

Some fabrics lose color through crocking, or rubbing against another fabric. Some fabrics crock when dry, some when wet, and some when both dry and wet. Testing for crocking is relatively easy:

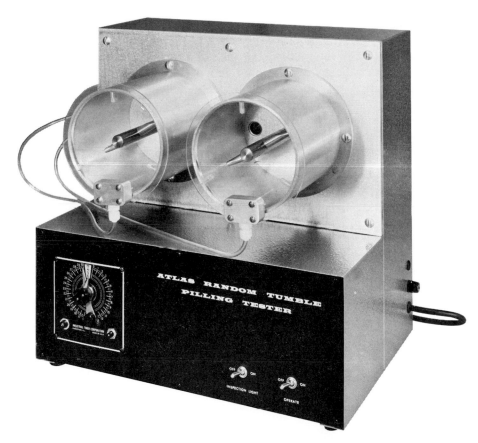

Figure 23-4. Random Tumble Pilling Tester for determining the pilling and fuzzing characteristics of all types of fabrics. Courtesy of Atlas Electric Devices Company.

Figure 23-5. Fade-o-meter for determining color fastness to sunlight. Courtesy of Atlas Electric Devices Company.

1. Dry crocking. Place a sample of the fabric to be tested on a flat surface. Fold a piece of clean, dry, white cotton fabric over the forefinger. Rub back and forth across the test fabric. Examine the white fabric to determine whether any color has rubbed off.

2. Wet crocking. Wet the clean, white fabric and rub. Determine whether any color has rubbed off.

A laboratory device called a *Crockmeter,* that can be used for testing for crocking, works on the same principle as the home test, by rubbing a white fabric sample across the fabric to be tested.

Laundering and dry cleaning may produce color loss in some fabrics. A machine known as the *Launder-Ometer* is used to perform laboratory wash fastness tests. One forty-five minute treatment in the Launder-Ometer is equivalent to five home launderings. The same device can be used to test for colorfastness to dry cleaning.

Home tests for washfastness are made as follows:

A small sample of fabric is cut. A pint jar with a screw top is filled with water of the temperature appropriate for the fabric and a half-teaspoon of detergent or soap powder. The sample is placed in the water, and the top is placed on the jar and tightened. The jar is shaken briskly for a minute, allowed to stand for five minutes, and is then shaken again for a minute. If a more severe laundry action is wanted, the water can be agitated with a spoon and the stirring repeated four times instead of two.

Pour the used wash water into a clear glass and look to see if the fabric has bled any color into the water. (It is possible for samples to lose some surface dye without undergoing noticeable color loss themselves.) Rinse the sample, dry, and then compare to the control sample.

It is possible to determine whether other fabrics are likely to pick up color lost by the test fabric during laundering. One or more samples of white fabric can be cut in half. Wash one half of the sample along with the test sample,

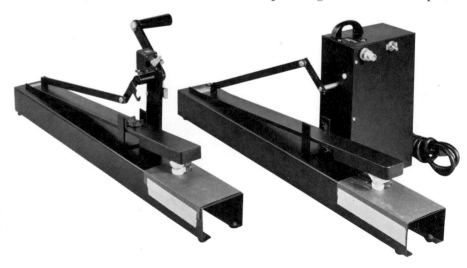

Figure 23-6. AATCC Crockmeter that provides standard motion and pressure for determining colorfastness to crocking. The model on the left is operated manually, the model on the right is motorized. Courtesy of Atlas Electric Devices Company.

rinse, dry, and then compare it with the unwashed white sample to determine whether any color has been picked up during washing. Special cloth containing a number of different fiber samples can be used for this testing in order to determine whether color pickup is general or limited to one fiber type.

Colorfastness to dry cleaning can be determined by immersing fabric in dry-cleaning fluid for five minutes. Fluid can be examined for color change, and when it is dry, the sample can be compared with the control.

AATCC has devised tests for colorfastness not only to laundering and dry cleaning but also to other conditions including perspiration, chlorine bleach, chlorinated water (as in swimming pools), sea water, water spotting, and the like. Specific tests are described in the *Technical Manual.*

WRINKLE RECOVERY

The AATCC Wrinkle Tester allows an evaluation of wrinkle recovery by first subjecting a sample of fabric to wrinkling and then allowing a period of recovery. Finally, samples are evaluated by comparing them to specified visual standards (replicas of fabric with varying degrees of wrinkling) and rating the samples.

A second method measures the angle of recovery of test samples. Samples of fabric are folded to make a crease, the creased sample is mounted on a Wrinkle Recovery Tester, and the angle of recovery after creasing is measured.

Home tests for crease recovery can be as simple as crushing a sample of fabric within a closed fist for three minutes and then removing the pressure, allowing the fabric to relax. Fabrics with good wrinkle recovery will appear less wrinkled than those with poor recovery.

A sample of fabric can be folded and placed under a one-pound box of sugar or other packaged material for a period of time. When the weight has been removed, the sample can be examined to see how sharp a crease has been formed. Allow the sample to relax for a while, then examine it again to determine whether the sharpness of the crease has diminished.

TESTS TO DETERMINE EFFECTIVENESS OF SPECIAL FINISHES

A number of tests have been devised to determine the effectiveness of special finishes. These tests cover such areas as crease resistance, durable press, wash-and-wear performance, durability of applied designs and finishes to dry cleaning, oil repellency, soil release, water resistance and repellency, and weather resistance. Specific instructions for testing in these and other areas are included in the *Technical Manual* of the American Association of Textile Chemists and Colorists and in the *Book of ASTM Standards* of the American Society for Testing Materials.

Figure 23-7. AATCC Perspiration Tester for testing colorfastness to perspiration, and to chlorinated pool, sea, and distilled water. Up to twenty specimens can be tested simultaneously. Courtesy of Atlas Electric Devices Company.

Figure 23-8. AATCC Wrinkle Recovery Tester.

FIBER IDENTIFICATION

In addition to the tests described which evaluate fabric characteristics and performance, a variety of procedures are used when it is necessary to identify the fiber composition of unknown fabrics.

The *Technical Manual* of AATCC test method 20-1973 "describes physical, chemical and microscopical techniques for identifying textile fibers used commercially in the United States."[2] Another useful publication for persons interested in laboratory techniques for use in identifying textile fibers is du Pont Bulletin No. X-156, "Identification of Fibers in Textile Materials."[3]

The identification of textile fibers generally follows these lines. A preliminary examination of the fibers or fabric is made. This may provide some clues as to the general category into which the fabric may fall. Experienced technologists may be able to exclude certain fibers or narrow the range of fibers into which the sample may fall simply by examining the fabric.

Burning a small sample of the fabric may help to distinguish its group still further. The odor and appearance of the fabric during and after burning, and the appearance of the residue may put it into a general category, such as cellulosic fiber, protein fiber, or synthetic. The results of this test help to determine the subsequent course of testing.

An examination with the microscope may also narrow the range of fibers with which the tester is working by providing a positive identification of those few fibers that have a distinctive appearance under the microscope. Wool or other animal hair is, for example, the only fiber with a scale structure. Generally, however, further analysis is required. Even if the identity of the fiber is reasonably certain, it may be desirable to verify the identification.

Different generic fiber types accept different types of dyes. Special fiber identification stains can be used to determine the fiber type, but this requires, of course, that the fiber being tested is a light shade or has been stripped of its color. These dye preparations come with a color shade chart showing the colors to which different generic fiber types will dye.

A further test of the solubility of the fiber in different chemicals can be made. Testing procedures specify the types of chemical solvents to be used, their concentrations, and the procedures to be used in handling the fibers and solvents. Many of these substances are hazardous and should be handled only in a laboratory under careful supervision. A comparison of the results of solubility testing with charts, such as those in the du Pont bulletin or AATCC test method, should provide a final confirmation of fiber identity.

A determination of specific gravity, melting point, and/or moisture regain of the specimen may also help to verify the identity of fibers.

[2] "Fibers in Textiles: Identification." Test method #20-1973, *Technical Manual*, Research Triangle Park, N.C.: AATCC, 1975, p. 50 ff.

[3] Available by writing to Textile Fibers Department, Technical Service Section, E. I. du Pont De Nemours & Company, Wilmington, Delaware, 19898.

IDENTIFICATION OF FINISHES

The identification of special finishes for textiles is difficult. Except for mechanical finishes that can easily be identified by eye (such as moiréing and napping), the determination of chemical finishes may require extensive laboratory procedures. AATCC Test Method 94-1973 outlines a variety of tests for the identification of textile finishes.

BABIARZ, R. S., V. D. LYON, F. L. SIEVENPIPER. "Colorfastness to Washing." *Textile Chemist and Colorist,* February 1976, p. 34.

Book of ASTM Standards, 1916 Race Street, Philadelphia, Penna.: American Society for Testing and Materials. (Published Annually)

"Compilation of Laws Administered by the U.S. Consumer Product Safety Commission." U. S. Consumer Product Safety Commission, Washington, D.C. 20207.

Catalog of American National Standards Institute, 1430 Broadway, New York, New York 10018.

GOBEIL, N. B., and B. J. MUELLER. "Evaluating Colorfastness to Perspiration: Lab Tests vs. Wear Tests." *Textile Chemist & Colorist.* November 1974, p. 46.

Identification of Fibers in Textile Materials, *Bulletin X-156,* Technical Service Department, E. I. du Pont de Nemours & Company, Wilmington, Delaware, 19898.

JOSEPH, M. *Introductory Textile Science.* New York: Holt, Rinehart, and Winston, Inc., Chapters 27, 31, and 34. 1972.

"The Physical Testing Laboratory in Weaving and Knitting." *International Textile Bulletin. World Edition: Weaving,* 1975 #1, p. 187, #3, p. 307.

PIZZUTO, J. *Fabric Science.* New York: Fairchild Publications, Inc., 1974, Chapter 10.

POTTER, M. D., and B. P. CORBMAN. *Textiles: Fiber to Fabric.* New York: McGraw-Hill, Inc., 1967, Chapter 2.

Technical Manual. American Association of Textile Chemists and Colorists, Research Triangle, N.C. 277099. (Published Annually)

Textile Handbook. American Home Economics Association, 2010 Massachusetts Avenue, N.W., Washington, D.C. 20036. 1974.

"U.S. Testing: Busier than Ever at 96." *Modern Textiles,* May 1976, p. 38.

Recommended References

24

FABRIC STRUCTURE: THE SUM OF ITS PARTS

This chapter is a summary of the preceding chapters. In previous chapters the many aspects of textile fabrics have been discussed at length, but a fabric is, in the final analysis, not a set of individual components; it is the sum of its various parts.

Fabrics are three-dimensional structures; they have length, width, and depth. A number of components must be assembled in different ways to create the structures. In the most complex fabric structures the components are the fiber content, yarn construction, fabric construction, and applied finishes. In simpler structures, such as fiber webs, the elements are more limited. They are fiber content, the method of distribution of fibers, the bonding medium, and applied finishes. Each of these aspects of textiles has been discussed before, but it is also important to consider them in relation to each other.

The Importance of the Fibers

"The properties of the single fiber are the basis on which fabric properties ultimately rest."[1] To recapitulate, these properties are length, density, crimp, surface character, diameter, luster, toughness, strength, elongation, elasticity, resilience, moisture regain, conductivity, dimensional stability, and resistance to heat and fire, sun, weathering, microorganisms, insects, acids, alkalis, and other solvents. Although special finishes can be applied that alter some of these properties, the fiber properties are an essential part of the ultimate character of a textile fabric, and an understanding of textile fabrics requires knowledge of fiber characteristics.

The Geometry of Yarns

When fibers are made into yarns, the construction of the yarn will impose certain characteristics and limitations. The aspects of yarn geometry (that is, the three-dimensional structure) are yarn diameter, the degree of fiber com-

---

[1]N. J. Abbott, "The Relationship between Fabric Structure and Ease of Care Performance of Cotton Fabrics," *Textile Research Journal* (December, 1964), p. 1050.

pactness, yarn twist, yarn cross-sectional shape, and yarn stiffness. Geometric characteristics of yarn are a product both of the type of fibers put into the yarn and of the yarn structure that is employed.

YARN DIAMETER AND FIBER COMPACTNESS

Yarn diameter can be increased by putting a larger number of fibers into a yarn or by using fibers of large diameter. Fibers with smooth, even surfaces will pack into a yarn more closely, giving the yarn a greater degree of fiber compactness. Fibers with rough or uneven surfaces will have the opposite effects.

YARN TWIST

The amount of twist given a yarn can be increased or decreased. However, the ability to incorporate more or less twist is affected to some extent by the fiber. Staple fibers require more twist to form them into a yarn than do filament fibers. Twist can have an effect on the diameter of the yarn. In two yarns with the same quantity of fiber in the yarn, the yarn that is given a higher degree of twist will have a smaller diameter. Yarn twist may also be used to produce fabrics with special geometric or aesthetic qualities. For example, crepe yarns with high twist are used in weaving crepe fabrics with their pebbly surface texture. Low twist, staple yarns are selected for use in fabrics that are to be napped. Low twist, bright filament yarns are used in some satin fabrics to produce a high luster.

YARN CROSS-SECTIONAL SHAPE

Twist, diameter, and yarn cross-sectional shape are related to fabric density and thickness. A yarn with a flat, ribbonlike cross section may be used to advantage in making a fabric with little depth. Round, thick yarns will increase fabric depth.

YARN STIFFNESS

Yarn stiffness is related to fiber stiffness. It is not possible to make a flexible yarn from an inflexible fiber. Moreover, the way in which fibers are combined in the yarn will affect yarn flexibility. "To take advantage of the inherent flexibility, it is necessary to give the individual fiber the greatest freedom of movement possible . . . the fibers should be able to slip over one another."[2] From this description it is easy to see that more tightly twisted yarns, in which fibers have less freedom of movement, will be less flexible. The most flexible yarn of all

[2] P. R. Lord and M. H. Mohamed, *Weaving: Conversion of Yarn to Fabric* (Watford, England: Merrow Publishing Company, Ltd., 1973), p. 129.

should be one in which the filament fibers are combined with little or no twist. The least flexible yarns should be those in which the fibers are bonded together by an adhesive or fused by heat or chemical means. An excellent example of this principle can be seen after a heavily sized fabric with a water-soluble sizing has been laundered. The fabric after laundering will be much softer and more flexible when the sizing that has held the fibers together has been removed.

Fabric Geometry

Just as yarn properties are governed in some respects by the properties of fibers, the properties of fabrics are in part a result of the properties of yarns. Other important factors that must also be considered are the fabric structure, that is, the specific weave, knit, or other method of construction; the number of threads per inch or degree of thread packing within the structure; yarn crimp; and yarn covering power.

YARN CRIMP

Yarn crimp is a factor in the thickness, flexibility, softness, and handle of the fabric. It may also affect the wear behavior and appearance of the fabric. Unbalanced crimp distribution may cause some portions of the fabric to be subjected to uneven wear, or may cause fabrics to have an uneven surface texture.

The term *crimp* has been used in relation to fiber properties. In this usage, it was defined as the undulating or wavy form of the fiber. Crimp is also an important characteristic in woven fabric structure. When warp and filling yarns cross each other, one or the other or both assume a wavy path. Certain generalizations about the effect of fabric weave on crimp can be made.

1. The greater the number of yarn intersections, the more crimp will be created in one or the other of the yarn directions. A logical outcome of this is that plain weave fabrics have greater crimp than satin, since yarns in plain weave fabrics intersect more often.

2. Thick, bulky yarns will produce greater yarn crimp than small diameter yarns. Obviously thick yarns will have to move further away from a straight path when they cross each other.

3. Double cloth fabric constructions in which yarns travel from one side of the fabric to the other will develop exceptionally great crimp as the yarns move from front to back of the fabric.

4. If there are a large number of fillings per inch and a small number of warps, then the crimp in the filling will be small, and the crimp in the warp will be large. Weavers can compensate for this by adjusting the tension on yarns during weaving. When tension is applied to the yarns in one direction,

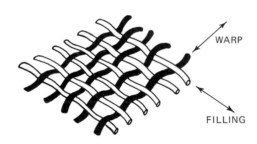

Figure 24-1. As warp and filling yarns pass over and under each other, they develop crimp. Smaller warp yarns (shown in black) develop greater crimp as they pass over larger filling yarns (shown in white).

they tend to straighten. But as the yarns in one direction become straighter and less crimped, the yarns in the opposite direction must develop a greater amount of crimp. This is known as *crimp transfer* or *crimp interchange*.

5. Stiffer yarns will develop less crimp than more flexible yarns when both are used in the same fabric. If a smooth surface is desired, the crimp must be adjusted to bring the crests of the yarns into the same level. If a ribbed or corded fabric is desired, crimp will be purposely decreased in the direction of the cord or rib and increased in the yarns that cross the cord or rib yarns.

Many aspects of fabric behavior are affected by crimp. Heat or water that may remove tensions applied to fabrics during weaving, for example, may produce crimp interchange and affect dimensional stability. Suppose that tension had been applied to the warp yarns during manufacture and that the fabric had been given no subsequent treatments to relax that tension. Warp crimp would be low, and the filling would be high. During laundering, relaxation of the tension on warp yarns may result in the transfer of some crimp from filling to warp, increasing warp crimp and decreasing filling crimp. The effect of this change would be to decrease the length of the fabric and increase the width. To the consumer, the effect would be that of shrinkage in the length.

COVERING POWER

Crimp is also related to the covering power of fabrics. The terms *covering power* and *cover factor* refer to both the optical and geometric properties of fabrics. Optical covering power is the ability of the fabric to hide that which is placed under it. Fiber characteristics affect the optical covering power. If the fibers used are translucent or transparent, the fabric will be more translucent or transparent. The same fiber may have greater opacity if it has been delustered, and will reflect more light, rather than allowing light to pass through the fiber. Yarn structure will be a factor. Smaller diameter yarns or smoother yarns will cover less well. Fabric structure will influence optical covering power. An open construction fabric will obviously cover less well than a densely constructed fabric. Dyeing and finishing will also have an effect on cover. Darker colors tend to cover better than lighter, for instance.

The geometric aspect of covering power is expressed as the *cover factor*, which is the ratio of fabric surface occupied by yarn to total fabric surface. A cover factor of 100 per cent would mean that all of the fabric surface is completely covered by yarn. It would require that the yarns be densely packed with no open spaces between the yarns. Few fabrics can actually achieve such complete cover, as there is generally some space, however small, between the yarns even in the most closely constructed fabrics.

Crimp is also related to covering power. As yarns in one direction cross and exert pressures on the yarns in the opposite direction, these yarns may be flattened somewhat. Flatter yarns provide better cover.

FABRIC DENSITY AND THICKNESS

Fabric density and thickness are achieved by the manipulation of yarn construction, fabric construction, and the application of some types of finishes. Fulling, used to produce a compact, denser fabric from wool fibers, is one such finish and napping of fabrics is another.

Fabric Behavior

Fabric geometry affects the behavior of fabrics in such areas as appearance, durability, comfort, and care.

APPEARANCE FACTORS

Crease Resistance and Wrinkle Recovery

When a crease forms in a woven or knitted fabric, the yarns bend. The fibers in the outer side of the yarn are strained, those on the inner side are compressed. Researchers who have investigated the factors of fabric structure that are related to crease resistance and crease recovery suggest that the following principles operate.

1. "The most important factor in crease resistance is the freedom of the yarns and fibers to relax."[3] Loosely woven fabrics generally allow more fiber redistribution and motion and therefore have better crease recovery. However, because loosely woven fabrics allow more fiber redistribution and motion, when these fabrics do become creased or wrinkled, the wrinkles may be more permanent. (Assuming, of course, that all other factors, such as fiber resiliency, yarn twist, and so on, are the same.)

2. Stiffer fabrics will become creased to a lesser degree than more flexible fabrics. Since greater pressure is required to form a crease in stiff fabrics, stiff fabrics will form fewer wrinkles during washing and drying. But once wrinkles have been formed, wrinkle recovery is less than for more flexible fabrics. Abbott recommends that in engineering fabrics for increased crease resistance *and* wrinkle recovery, fabrics be made in which "stiffness is high enough to prevent easy formation of wrinkles, but not so high that ability to recover from wrinkling is impaired."[4]

Drape and Handle

The draping qualities of fabrics are affected by the stiffness of the fiber and yarn, the size of the yarns, thread count, and method of fabric construction. Fabrics made from heavy, coarse yarns and in dense constructions do not drape well. Fabrics such as satin that have long floats in the weave can be more

[3] Lord, op. cit., p. 167.
[4] Abbott, op. cit., p. 1054.

flexible, bending more easily and making possible softer, smoother handle and improved draping qualities. If at the same time these fabrics are made from filament yarns with little twist, the draping quality is enhanced still more.

DURABILITY FACTORS

Abrasion Resistance

The abrasion resistance of fabrics is related to the yarn properties, fabric construction, and, particularly, the crimp distribution. The crown—the part of the yarn that protrudes above the surface of the fabric—receives the pressure of abrasion, whether it be surface, edge, or flex abrasion. The more crowns of the same height there are in a given area of cloth, the more evenly wear will be distributed over the surface of the fabric. Shantung, in which the uneven, slubbed yarns present higher crowns that are unevenly spaced, is an example of a fabric that has poor abrasion resistance.

Weave also enters into abrasion resistance. In fabrics with floats, yarns and fibers are more free to move and are less consistently exposed to abradants. For this reason, twill weave and some sateen fabrics may show superior abrasion resistance.

Tensile Strength and Tear Strength

The major factors in tensile strength and tear strength are the strength of the yarn and the strength of the fabric structure. Fiber tenacity is relatively less important, because strong yarn or fabric structures can compensate for low individual fiber tenacities.

Tear strength is more closely related to the serviceability of fabrics than is tensile strength. In testing tensile strength, all of the yarns share equally in the stress applied, but in tear-strength testing a few yarns, at most, are subject to stress. Fabric constructions in which groups of yarns are woven together, such as basket or rib weaves, will have the greatest tear strength, since more yarns will group together to share the stress. Any construction that restricts the ability of yarns to function together will decrease tear strength. Finishes that coat fabrics or restrict yarn movement will tend to isolate yarns and decrease tear strength.

Extensibility or Elongation

The elongation of fabrics takes place in two phases. First, as a fabric is stretched, the crimp in the direction of the stretch is removed, permitting the fabric structure to reach its maximum extensibility. The second phase is one in which the crimp of the yarn (as opposed to fabric crimp) is removed. The greater the yarn crimp, the more extensible the fabric will be. This may be readily understood if one remembers that crimped, textured yarns are often used to make stretch fabrics.

Dimensional Stability

Fibers, yarns, and fabric construction are all major factors in the dimensional stability of textiles. When the basic building block of the fabric, the fiber, exhibits progressive shrinkage, the end product will also exhibit progressive shrinkage. In other fabrics where the fiber is dimensionally stable, dimensional stability problems will be related to factors introduced in the manufacturing processes, particularly where stress is applied to yarns or fabrics that causes them to be elongated beyond their natural dimensions. Finishes may be applied to compensate for any of these factors.

COMFORT FACTORS

Thermal Conductivity

Fiber heat conductivity, the thickness of the fabrics, and the ability of the fabric to entrap still air within the fabric are related to thermal conductivity. Still air provides excellent insulation. If the yarn structure and the fabric structure permit the entrapment of still air, a fabric may provide warmth by insulating the body. Napped wool and acrylic sweaters are an instance of the application of this principle. However, if the wind blows hard, the same garment may allow the passage of moving air through the fabric, and its insulating qualities may be lost or diminished. Thermal properties are, therefore, also affected by air permeability.

Air Permeability

Air permeability is the ability of air to pass through a fabric. Obviously, where openings between yarns or between fibers within yarns are large, a good deal of air will pass through the fabric. Contrariwise, where compact yarns are packed tightly into fabrics with little air space between them, the flow of air through the fabric is diminished.

Some finishes for fabrics—such as ciréing of thermoplastic fabrics—decrease air permeability by causing fibers and yarns to fuse slightly. Fabrics may be coated with another material that closes up interstices in the fabric. To make garments that are warm enough for sports such as skiing in which moving air may cool the athlete, a fabric with low air permeability (such as closely woven nylon) may be combined with materials of low thermal conductivity (such as polyester or acrylic fiberfill or with pile fabrics) that trap air close to the body.

Moisture Vapor Transmission and Water Repellency

Like air permeability, water vapor transmission is closely related to the density of fabric construction. Tight, close constructions allow little transmission of water vapor. Hydrophobic fibers may act as a shield to prevent passage of water vapor, whereas, hydrophilic fibers allow some water vapor to pass through the fabric.

In some synthetic yarns, the empty spaces between the fibers may permit the wicking or spreading of water. These fibers are not, therefore, naturally water repellent, but must be given special treatments to render them water repellent. Dense cotton fabrics, by contrast, may provide better water repellency by virtue of the fact that they are hydrophilic. The fibers swell on exposure to water, jamming the construction and forming a barrier to keep out water.

CARE FACTORS

Drying Rate and Drying Time

Contrary to expectation, fabric drying rate and drying time once wet are more directly related to yarn and fabric construction than to fiber content. "A thin, low weight, low moisture regain synthetic filament fabric dries faster than a thick, heavy, high moisture regain spun yarn fabric because more water must be evaporated from the latter, not because it is hydrophilic."[5] Studies have shown that identical fabrics made from acrylics and wool will dry in the same length of time.[6]

Soiling

The ability of soil to penetrate a fabric is related to the fabric structure. Smooth-surfaced fabrics will allow soil to slide off the surface. Fuzzy, unevenly textured fabrics may serve as traps for dirt and dust. Some fabric structures may mask soil better than others by hiding it and do not appear soiled as quickly. Fibers with uneven surfaces such as wool or multilobal fibers may have this quality.

If soil is deeply embedded in fiber, yarn, or fabric structures it may be difficult to remove. Soil held inside a fabric structure may serve as an abradant and tend to cut or break yarns. Some finishes may tend to attract soil; others are applied to decrease soiling.

SUMMARY

The foregoing discussion shows clearly that no single characteristic of fibers, yarns, or fabrics can be judged by itself. All of these characteristics are subject to modification either intentionally or unintentionally and are mutually dependent on each other in the final product.

It is essential to analyze the factors that are at work in any particular textile product and to relate the various factors one to the other. Most of the paradoxical elements of fabric behavior can be accounted for by this means, and predictions of fabric performance and evaluations of textiles for specific end

[5] E. R. Kaswell, *Handbook of Industrial Textiles* (New York: Wellington Sears, 1964), p. 467.

[6] Ibid.

uses will be more satisfactory. It is the recognition of the interrelatedness of fiber, yarn, fabric, construction, and finishes that makes an understanding of textiles possible.

Recommended References

ABBOTT, N. J. "The Relationship between Fabric Structure and Ease of Care Performance of Cotton Fabrics." *Textile Research Journal,* December 1964, p. 1049.

BACKER, S., and S. J. TANNENHOUS. "The Relationship between the Structural Geometry of a Textile Fabric and Its Physical Properties. Part III: Textile Geometry and Abrasion Resistance." *Textile Research Journal,* September 1951, p. 635.

BERTOLI, P. "The Influence of Fibers and Yarn Properties on End-product Behavior." *Textile Month,* October 1975, p. 91.

GOLDBERG, J. B. "The Properties of Fabrics" in *Technology of Synthetic Fibers,* ed. S. B. McFarlane. New York: Fairchild Publications, Inc., 1953, p. 336 ff.

GOODINGS, A. C. "Air Flow Through Textile Fabrics." *Textile Research Journal,* August 1964, p. 713.

KASWELL, E. R. *Handbook of Industrial Textiles.* New York: Wellington Sears Co., Inc., 1963.

LORD, P. R., and M. H. MOHAMED. *Weaving: Conversion of Yarn to Fabric.* Watford, England: Merrow Publishing Co., Ltd., 1973.

ROBINSON, A. T. C., and R. MARKS. *Woven Cloth Construction.* Manchester, England; The Textile Institute, 1973.

Appendix A
BIBLIOGRAPHY

General References: Texts and Encyclopedias

ALEXANDER, P. R. *Textile Products: Selection, Use, and Care.* Boston: Houghton Mifflin Company, 1977.

American Fabrics Encyclopedia of Textiles. Englewood Cliffs, N.J.: Prentice-Hall, Inc. 2nd Ed.

COLLIER, A. M. *A Handbook of Textiles.* New York: Pergamon Press, 1970.

DEMBECK, A. *A Guide to Man-made Textile Fibers and Texture Yarns of the World.* New York: United Piece Dye Works, 1964.

DENNY, G. G. *Fabrics.* Philadelphia: J. B. Lippincott Co., 1962.

HARRIES, N. and T. HARRIES. *Textiles: Decision Making for the Consumer.* New York: McGraw-Hill, Inc., 1974.

HOLLEN, M. and J. SADDLER. *Textiles.* New York: Macmillan Publishing Co., Inc., 1973.

JOSEPH, M. *Introductory Textile Science.* New York: Holt, Rinehart, and Winston, Inc., 1976.

KLAPPER, M. *Fabric Almanac.* New York: Fairchild Publications, Inc., 1971.

LABARTHE, J. *Elements of Textiles.* New York: Macmillan Publishing Co., Inc., 1975.

LINTON, G. E. *The Modern Textile and Apparel Dictionary.* Plainfield, N.J.: Textile Book Service, 1972.

LYLE, D. S. *Modern Textiles.* New York: John Wiley & Sons, Inc., 1976.

POTTER, M. D. and B. P. CORBMAN. *Textiles, Fiber to Fabric.* New York: McGraw-Hill Book Co., 1967.

PIZZUTO, J. *Fabric Science.* New York: Fairchild Publications, Inc., 1974.

Textile Handbook. Washington, D.C.: American Home Economics Association, 1974.

WINGATE, I. B. *Dictionary of Textiles.* Fairchild Publications, Inc., 1967.

WINGATE, I. B. *Textile Fabrics and Their Selection.* Englewood Cliffs, N.J.: Prentice-Hall, Inc., 1970.

WINGATE, I. B., K. R. GILLESPIE, and B. C. ADDISON. *Know Your Merchandise.* New York: McGraw-Hill, Inc., 1975.

Historic Textiles

D'HARCOURT, R. *Textiles of Ancient Peru and Their Techniques.* Seattle: University of Washington Press, 1962.

Encyclopedia of Textiles. London: Ernest Benn, Ltd., 1928.

GOLDENBERG, S. L. *Lace: Its Origin and History.* New York: Brentano's, 1904.

LEWIS, E. *The Romance of Textiles.* New York: Macmillan Publishing Co., Inc., 1937.

PIANZOLA, M. and J. COFFINET. *Tapestry*. New York: Van Nostrand-Reinhold Co., Inc., 1974.

POLLEN, M. *Seven Centuries of Lace*. New York: Macmillan Publishing Co., Inc., 1908.

POWYS, M. *Lace and Lace-making*. Boston, Mass.: Charles T. Grandford Co., 1953.

SCHWAB, F. R. *The Story of Lace and Embroidery*. New York: Fairchild Publications, Inc., 1951.

SIEBER, R. *African Textile and Decorative Arts*. New York: Museum of Modern Art, 1972.

VOLBACH, W. F. *Early Decorative Textiles*. New York: Paul Hamlyn, 1969.

WALTON, P. *The Story of Textiles*. New York: Tudor Publishing Company, 1936.

WEIBEL, A. C. *Two Thousand Years of Textiles*. New York: Pantheon Books, 1952.

Textiles as an Art and Craft

ALBERS, A. *On Weaving*. Middletown, Ct.: Wesleyan University, 1965.

CLARK, L. J. *The Craftsman in Textiles*. New York: Praeger Publishers, Inc., 1968.

DENDEL, E. W. *African Pacific Crafts*. New York: Taplinger Publishing Company, 1974.

FANNIN, A. *Hand-spinning, Art and Technique*. New York: Van Nostrand-Reinhold Co., 1970.

HARVEY, V. *Macrame*. New York: Van Nostrand-Reinhold Co., 1967.

HELD, S. B. *Weaving*. New York: Holt, Rinehart and Winston, Inc., 1972.

KELLER, I. *Batik: The Art and Craft*. Rutland, Vermont: Charles Tuttle Co., 1966.

KLUGER, M. *The Joy of Spinning*. New York: Simon and Shuster, Inc., 1971.

KRAMER, J. *Natural Dyes, Plants, and Processes*. New York: Charles Scribner's Sons, 1972.

MELEN, L. *Knitting and Netting*. New York: Van Nostrand-Reinhold Co., 1971.

REGENSTEIN, E. *The Art of Weaving*. New York: Van Nostrand-Reinhold Co., 1970.

WARD, M. *Art and Design in Textiles*. New York: Van Nostrand-Reinhold Co., 1973.

Textile Care

Detergents in Depth. Proceedings of Symposium sponsored by Soap & Detergent Association, March, 1974, Washington, D.C.

MOSS, A. J. E. *Textiles and Fabrics: Their Care and Preservation*. New York: Chemical Publishing Company, 1961.

"Soaps and Detergents for Home Laundering." U.S. Department of Agriculture. Home and Garden Bulletin #139. Washington, D.C. Revised 1973.

The Technology of Home Laundering. Textile Monograph #108. New York: American Association for Textile Technology, 1973.

CARTER, M. E. *Essential Fiber Chemistry.* New York: Marcel Dekker, Inc., 1971.

MARK, H. F. and N. G. GAYLORD. *Encyclopedia of Polymer Science and Technology.* New York: Interscience Publishing, 1964–1971.

PETERS, R. H. *Textile Chemistry, Vol. 1.* New York: American Elsevier Publishing Co., Inc., 1967.

ROFF, W. J. *Handbook of Common Polymers.* Cleveland, Ohio: GRG Press, 1971.

Textile Chemistry

EMERY, I. *The Primary Structure of Fabric.* Washington, D.C.: The Textile Museum, 1966.

FORD, J. E. *Fibrillated Yarns.* Watford, England: Merrow Publishing Company, Ltd., 1975.

Handbook of Bonded and Laminated Fabrics. Triangle Park, N.C.: American Association of Textile Chemists and Colorists, 1974.

HATHORNE, B. L. *Woven Stretch and Textured Fabrics.* New York: John Wiley & Sons, Inc., 1964.

HENSHAW, D. E. *Self-twist Yarn.* Watford, England: Merrow Publishing Company, Ltd., 1971.

LENNOX-KERR, P. *Needle-felted Fabrics.* Plainfield, N.J.: Textile Book Service, 1971.

LORD, P. R. *Spinning in the 70's.* Watford, England: Merrow Publishing Company, Ltd., 1970.

LORD, P. R. and M. H. MOHAMED. *Weaving: Conversion of Yarn to Fabric.* Watford, England: Merrow Publishing Co., Ltd., 1973.

McDONALD, M. *Non-woven Fabric Technology.* Plainfield, N.J.: Textile Book Service, 1971.

REICHMAN, C. et al. *Knitted Fabric Primer.* New York: National Knitted Outerwear Association, 1967.

REICHMAN, C. Editor. *Knitting Encyclopedia.* National Knitted Outerwear Assn., 1972.

ROBINSON, A. T. C. and R. MARKS. *Woven Cloth Construction.* London: Butterworth, 1967.

ROHLENA, V. *Open-end Spinning.* New York: American Elsevier Publishing Co., 1975.

SELLING, A. J. *Twistless Yarns.* Watford, England: Merrow Publishing Company, Ltd., 1971.

Textile Construction (technical works)

AATCC Glossary of Printing Terms. Research Triangle Park, N.C.: American Association of Textile Chemists and Colorists, 1973.

Book of Papers, 1974 Technical Conference. Research Triangle Park, N.C.: American Association of Textile Chemists and Colorists, 1974.

HARPER, R. J. *Durable Press Cotton Goods.* Watford, England: Merrow Publishing Company, Ltd., 1971.

Textile Dyeing, Printing, and Finishing (technical works)

HEARLE, J. W. S. (Editor). *The Setting of Fibers and Fabrics.* Watford, England: Merrow Publishing Company, Ltd., 1971.

HALL, A. J. *Handbook of Textile Finishing.* New York: Chemical Publishing, 1957.

McPHEE, J. R. *The Moth-proofing of Wool.* Watford, England: Merrow Publishing Company, Ltd., 1971.

MARSH, J. T. *Introduction to Textile Finishing.* Plainfield, N.J.: Textile Book Service, 1966.

MILES, L. W. C. *Textile Printing.* Watford, England: Merrow Publishing Co., Ltd., 1971.

REEVES, W. A. and G. L. DRAKE. *Flame Resistance.* Watford, England: Merrow Publishing Company, Ltd., 1971.

Textile Printing: An Ancient Art and Yet So New. Research Triangle Park, N.C.: American Association of Textile Chemists and Colorists.

Textile Fibers (technical works)

BERGEN, W. B. *Wool Handbook.* New Jersey: Textile Book Service, 1963.

Bulk, Stretch and Texture. Manchester, England: The Textile Institute, 1966.

CARROL-PORCZYNSKI, C. Z. *Manual of Man-made Fibers.* New York: Chemical Publishing Company, 1961.

CHAPMAN, C. B. *Fibres.* Plainfield, N.J.: Textile Book Service, 1974.

COOK, C. G. *Handbook of Polyolefin Fibres.* Watford, England: Merrow Publishing Company, Ltd., 1967.

COOK, J. G. *Handbook of Textile Fibers. Volumes 1 and 2.* Watford, England: Merrow, Technical Library, 1968.

HAMBY, D. S. (Editor). *American Cotton Handbook.* 2 volumes. New York: Interscience Publishing, 1965–66.

HEARLE, J. W. S. and R. H. PETERS. *Fiber Structures.* London: Butterworth, 1963.

JEFFRIES, R. *Bicomponent Fibers.* Watford, England: Merrow Publishing Company, Ltd., 1971.

Man-made Fiber Fact Book. Washington, D.C.: Man-made Fiber Producers' Association, 1974.

MEREDITH, R. *Elastomeric Fibers.* Watford, England: Merrow Publishing Company, Ltd., 1971.

MONCRIEFF, R. W. *Man-Made Fibres.* New York: John Wiley and Sons, Inc., 1975.

PETUKOV, B. V. *Technology of Polyester Fibers.* New York: Pergamon Press, Inc., 1963.

ROLLINS, M. L. *Cotton Fiber Structure.* Watford, England: Merrow Publishing Company, Ltd.

SITTIG, M. *Acrylic and Vinal Fibers.* Plainfield, N.J.: Textile Book Service, 1972.

SITTIG, M. *Polyamide Fiber Manufacture.* Plainfield, N.J.: Textile Book Service, 1972.

VONBERGEN, W. (Editor) *Wool Handbook.* New York: Interscience Publishing, Volumes 1 and 2, 1963, 1970.

CONE, S. *The Textile Industry.* New York: Richards Rosen Press, Inc., 1969.
HOWELL, L. D. *The American Textile Industry.* Washington, D.C.: U.S. Department of Agriculture, 1964.

Textile Industry

Book of ASTM Standards. Philadelphia: American Society for Testing and Materials, published annually.
BOOTH, J. E. *Principles of Textile Testing.* New York: Chemical Publishing Company, 1969.
Technical Manual. Research Triangle Park, N.C.: American Association of Textile Chemists and Colorists, published annually.
Textile Flammability, A Handbook of Regulations, Standards, and Test Methods. Research Triangle Park, N.C.: American Association of Textile Chemists and Colorists.
WEAVER, J. W. *Analytical Methods for a Textile Laboratory.* Research Triangle Park, N.C.: American Association of Textile Chemists and Colorists, 1968.

Textile Testing, Standards, and Legislation

CROWN, F. *The Fabric Guide for People Who Sew.* New York: Grosset & Dunlap, Inc., 1973.
HOLT, J. M. *Fabrics and Clothing.* New York: Textile Book Service, 1957.
Proceedings of the American Chemical Society Symposium on Man-made Fibers. Washington, D.C., 1974.
RALSTON, V. H. *Textile Reference Sources.* Storrs, Ct.: University of Conn. Library, 1973.
ROBINSON, G. *Carpets and Other Textile Floor Coverings.* Plainfield, N.J.: Textile Book Service, 2nd ed.
SOMMAR, H. G. *A Brief Guide to Sources of Textile Fibers and Textile Information,* Washington, D.C.: Information Research Press, 1973.
Technical Bulletins of the DuPont Corporation, Wilmington, Delaware.

Miscellaneous

American Dyestuff Reporter
American Fabrics and Fashions
CIBA Review (until 1970)
America's Textiles: Reporter/Bulletin Edition
America's Textiles: The Knitter Edition
Family Economics Review
Fibre and Fabric
Handweaver and Craftsman
International Textile Bulletin: Dyeing, Printing, and Finishing
International Textile Bulletin: Knitting
International Textile Bulletin: Spinning
International Textile Bulletin: Weaving

Periodicals

Knitted Outerwear Times (to 1970)
Knitting Times (after 1970)
Modern Textiles
Textile Bulletin (until 1971)
Textile Chemist and Colorist
Textile Forum
Textile Industries
Textile Month
Textile Organon
Textile Research Journal
Textile Technology Digest
Textile World

Appendix B
GLOSSARY

Abrasion The rubbing or friction of fiber against fiber or fiber against other materials.

Absorption The taking of moisture into a fiber or fabric.

Adsorption The holding of moisture on the surface of a fiber, rather than its being taken into the fiber.

Amorphous areas (in the fiber structure) Areas within fibers in which long-chain molecules are arranged in a random or unorganized manner.

Appliqué Attaching, usually by sewing, small pieces of cloth or other materials to the surface of a larger textile.

Bandanna Indian textiles decorated by the tie-and-dye method.

Bast fibers Fibers found in the woody stem of plants.

Batik Indonesian technique of resist printing in which areas of fabric that are to resist the dye are covered with wax.

Bicomponent fibers Paired fibers made from two generically similar fibers, that is, two types of nylon, two types of acrylic, and the like.

Biconstituent fibers Paired or matrix fibers made from two generically different fibers, that is, nylon and polyester, vinal and vinyon, and the like.

Bleaching The removal of color from fabrics by means of a chemical agent.

Blend Two or more different fibers combined in the same yarn or fabric.

Block printing The application of printed designs by pressing dye-covered blocks onto a fabric.

Bobbin lace Lace made with a number of threads, each fastened to a spool. The pattern to be followed is anchored to a pillow, so that this lace is also called pillow lace.

Calendering The process of passing fabric between rollers with the application of heat and pressure.

Carbonization In the processing of wool, the treatment of fleeces with sulfuric acid to destroy vegetable matter remaining in the fleece after scouring.

Carding A hand or machine process for separating fibers to make them into a web of randomly aligned fibers.

Ciré A shiny, lustrous surface effect achieved by applying a wax finish or by heat treatment of thermoplastic fibers.

Cohesiveness The ability of fibers to cling together.

Combing A process that follows carding that pulls fibers into more parallel alignment.

Crimp Undulating or wavy fiber or yarn structure.

Crochet A technique of creating fabric by pulling one loop of yarn through another with a hook.

Cross-dyeing Coloring of fabric by dyeing in one dyebath a fabric in which two or more fibers with different affinity for the same dye are blended. The resulting fabric will have a multicolored effect as a result of each of the fibers taking up the dyestuff differently.

Cross-linking   The attachment of one long-chain molecule to another by chemical linkages.

Crystallinity (in fiber structure)   Orderly, parallel arrangements of molecules within a fiber.

Cystine linkages   Chemical cross-linkages in the wool fiber.

Delustered fiber   A man-made fiber that has had its natural luster decreased by the addition of a pigment to the solution.

Denier   The weight of 9,000 meters of fiber or yarn expressed in grams.

Density   The weight of a fiber expressed in grams per cubic centimeter.

Dimensional stability   The ability of a fiber or yarn to withstand shrinking or stretching.

Discharge printing   The application of design by applying a discharge material that removes color from treated areas of a dyed fabric.

Doupion or doupioni silk   A double strand of silk produced by two silkworms spinning a cocoon together.

Dry spinning   The formation of man-made textile fibers in which the polymer is dissolved in a solvent that is evaporated, leaving the filament to harden by drying in air.

Dull fiber   See delustered fiber.

Durable finishes   Those finishes that have good durability over a reasonably long period of use.

Elasticity   The ability of fibers to stretch and return to their original length.

Elongation   The ability of a fiber to be stretched or lengthened.

Embroidery   The use of yarns applied to fabrics with a needle in a variety of decorative stitches.

Fasciated yarns   Yarns made from a bundle of parallel fibers wrapped around by a surface wrapping of other fibers.

Felt   A compact sheet of matted fibers, usually wool.

Fiber dyeing   Dyeing of fibers before the spinning of yarns.

Filament   A continuous strand of fiber that may be many hundreds of feet in length.

Filet   An embroidered net, also known as lacis.

Filature   A factory in which silk fibers are processed.

Filling   The crosswise direction of a woven fabric.

Filling knit   A knit in which the loops interlace horizontally rather than vertically.

Flexibility   The ability of a fiber to be bent or folded.

Flock   Short staple fiber lengths that may be applied to a fabric by the use of adhesive.

Fulling   In the processing of wool or animal hair fabrics, treatment with moisture, heat, soap, and pressure that causes yarns to shrink, lie closer together, and give the fabric a more dense structure.

Generic name   Names assigned by the Federal Trade Commission to the various types of man-made fibers according to the chemical composition of the fiber-forming substance.

Gigging A synonym for napping or brushing up of loose fibers onto the surface of a fabric made from staple yarns.

Graft-polymers Polymers made by attaching short molecules (or monomers) to long-chain molecules.

Hackling A step in the processing of flax fibers that is comparable to combing.

Heat-setting The treatment of thermoplastic man-made fibers or fabrics with heat in order to set the fibers or fabrics into a specific shape or form.

Heat-transfer printing A system of textile printing in which dyes are applied to a paper base and then transferred from the paper to a fabric under heat and pressure.

Heddle A cord or wire eyelet through which warp yarns are passed on a loom.

Ikat A form of resist printing in which sections of warp yarns are made to resist dyes. Dye is applied to the warp yarns, and filling yarns are inserted. The resultant patterns have an indistinct, shimmering pattern. (A type of warp print.)

High-wet-modulus The quality in a fiber that gives that fiber very good stability when wet.

Kemp hairs Coarse, straight hairs in a wool fleece that do not absorb dye readily.

Lacis See filet.

Latch needle A needle used in knitting machines that has a latch that opens and closes in order to hold the yarn on the needle.

Linters Short cotton fibers that are too short to be spun into yarns.

Loft The ability of fibers to return to their original thickness after being flattened or compressed.

Luster The sheen or light reflectance of a fiber or yarn.

Macramé A technique for creating fabric by knotting yarns together.

Malimo See stitch-through.

Man-made fibers Fibers created through technology either from natural materials or from chemicals.

Matrix fiber A fiber in which one fiber-forming component is dispersed discontinuously within the other.

Melt-spinning The formation of man-made textile fibers in which the polymer is melted for extrusion and hardened by cooling.

Mercerization The treatment of cellulose fibers with sodium hydroxide in order to increase luster, strength, and dye affinity.

Micron A measurement that is 1/1000th of a millimeter or .000039 of an inch.

Mildew A fungus that grows on some fibers under conditions of heat and dampness.

Moiré A ribbed cloth which has a water-marked or wavy pattern on the surface.

Moisture regain The ability of a bone-dry fiber to absorb moisture at 70 degrees F. and 65 per cent relative humidity.

Monofilament yarn Yarn made from a single filament.

Monomer The simple, unpolymerized form of a compound.

Multifilament yarn Yarn made from two or more, usually more, filament fibers.

Nap   The "fuzzy," raised fibers that have been brushed up on the surface of a fabric.

Needlepoint lace   Lace made by embroidering over other threads held in a pattern across a sheet of parchment.

Needlepunching   Fabric formation technique in which fabric is formed by the entangling that results when a series of needles are punched through a bat of fiber.

Netting   A technique of creating fabric by looping and knotting a continuous strand of thread into an open mesh.

Novelty yarns   Yarns made to create interesting decorative effects.

Open end spinning   A new method of spinning yarns from staple fibers in which the fibers move directly from the sliver into a spinning device where twist is imparted.

Orientation (of molecules within a fiber)   Arrangement of polymers in a position parallel to the length of the fiber.

Permanent finish   A finish that will last for the lifetime of the fabric.

Pilling   The formation of small balls of fiber that have broken off from a yarn and cling to the surface of the fabric.

Pillow lace   See bobbin lace.

Pirns   Small metal pins around which yarns are wrapped. These pins are then inserted in a shuttle that carries the yarns across the fabric during weaving. (Also called quills)

Plissé   A puckered effect achieved on cotton fabrics by shrinking some areas of the fabric with sodium hydroxide.

Ply yarns   Yarns made by twisting together two or more primary yarns.

Polymer   A long-chain molecule.

Polymerization   The formation of a long-chain molecule (polymer) by joining together a number of small molecules (monomers).

Progressive shrinkage   Shrinkage that continues after the first laundering and/or dry cleaning through successive cleanings.

Pure dye silk   Silk with less than 10 per cent of weighting (or less than 15 per cent if it is black in color.)

Quills   See pirns.

Regenerated fibers   Fibers produced from natural materials that cannot be used for textiles in their original form but that can, through chemical treatment and processing, be made into textile fibers.

Relaxation shrinkage   Shrinkage that takes place during initial laundering and/or dry cleaning as a result of the relaxation of tensions applied to yarns or fabrics during manufacture.

Residual shrinkage   Shrinkage remaining in a fabric after it has been pre-shrunk. Residual shrinkage is generally expressed as a percentage.

Resiliency   The ability of a fiber to spring back to its natural position after folding, creasing, or deformation.

Resist printing   The achieving of designs by causing sections of fabric to resist dye.

Retting   The process of decomposing the woody stem and gums surrounding bast fibers in order to remove the fiber.

Ring spinning Method of spinning yarns from staple fibers in which the twist is imparted to the fibers by the concurrent movement of a spindle and a metal ring that moves around the spindle.

Roller printing The application of printed designs to fabrics by the use of engraved rollers over which the fabrics pass.

Roving An elongated strand of staple fibers with a very slight amount of twist that is ready for spinning in a ring spinner or spinning mule.

Scouring Removing soil or other impurities from fabrics.

Screen printing The application of printed design to fabrics by the use of screens coated with resist materials that permit dye to penetrate through the screen only in selected areas.

Seed hair fibers Those fibers that grow around the seeds of certain plants, such as cotton or kapok.

Sericin The gum that holds silk filaments together in a cocoon.

Sericulture The cultivation of the silkworm for the production of silk fiber.

Shed The passageway between the warp and the filling yarns through which the shuttle is thrown in weaving.

Shuttle The device that carries the yarn across the loom, through the shed, in weaving.

Shuttleless loom Loom in which the yarn is carried across the fabric by some means other than a shuttle. These looms may utilize jets of water, air, metal rapiers, metal grippers, or mechanical action.

Simple yarn Yarn with uniform size and regular surface.

Singeing Treatment of woven fabrics with heat or flame to remove surface fibers from fabric in order to produce a smooth finish.

Sizing A stiffening material, usually either starch or synthetic resins, coated onto yarns to give them extra body.

Sliver A loose, untwisted strand of fibers obtained after carding.

Solution-dyeing Addition of color pigment to the liquid solution of man-made fibers before the fiber is formed.

Specific gravity The weight of a fiber in relation to the weight of an equal volume of water.

Spindle A long, slender stick used in spinning to provide the necessary twist to fibers being formed into a yarn. Spindles may be hand devices or part of a spinning wheel.

Spring beard needle A needle used in knitting machines that holds yarns on the needle by means of a springlike action of the flexible hook.

Spunlace A fabric formation technique in which a fiber web is formed by air entanglement.

Spun-bonding A fabric formation technique in which extruded fiber filaments are randomly arranged and bonded together by heat or chemical means.

Staple fibers Fibers of short, noncontinuous lengths.

Stitch-through A fabric formation technique in which fibers or yarns are held together by stitching through the materials.

Stock dyeing See fiber dyeing.

Striations Lengthwise markings on the surface of the man-made fibers when seen through a microscope.

Tapa   Cloth made from bark.

Tapestry   Woven designs, created on a tapestry loom.

Temporary finishes   Those finishes that are removed through use and cleaning and must be renewed to be effective.

Tenacity   The strength of a textile fiber.

Tensile strength   A measure of strength of textile fabrics.

Tentering   Drying of wet fabrics after finishing or dyeing on a frame on which fabrics are stretched taut and flat.

Tex   A unit of measure of yarns and fibers in which one tex equals the weight in grams of 1,000 meters of yarn or fiber.

Textured fibers   Fibers that have had some alteration of their surface texture.

Thermoplastic   Subject to softening or melting when heat is applied.

Tow   Bundles of continuous multifilament fibers without twist. Tow is generally destined to be made into staple lengths.

Trademark   The name assigned by a manufacturer to a man-made fiber, finish, or process.

Triaxial weave   A type of weaving in which three sets of yarns are utilized, with two sets of yarns moving in a diagonal direction to the third, rather than at right angles.

Tussah silk   Silk fiber from wild silkworms.

Union dyeing   The dyeing to the same color of two different fibers with different affinities for dye.

Warp   The lengthwise direction of a woven fabric.

Warp knit   A hand or machine-made knit in which the loops interlace vertically.

Warp print   A print in which the design is printed on the warp yarns before the filling yarns are interlaced. (See ikat).

Weft   The crosswise direction of a woven fabric; the filling.

Weft knit   See filling knit.

Wet-spinning   The formation of man-made textile fibers in which the fibers are hardened by extruding the fibers into a chemical bath.

Wicking   The traveling of moisture along the surface of a fiber without its being absorbed into the fiber.

Woof   The lengthwise direction of the woven fabric; the warp.

Woolen yarns   Yarns made from wool fibers that have been carded but not combed.

Worsted yarns   Yarns made from wool fibers that have been both carded and combed.

Yarn-dyeing   The dyeing of yarns before they are woven or knitted into fabrics.

Appendix C
SUMMARY OF REGULATORY LEGISLATION APPLIED TO TEXTILES

The following summarizes *briefly* the major pieces of legislation and/or regulations that apply to textile products. Fuller details are provided about each of these acts or rulings in the body of the text.

PASSED 1960, AMENDED SUBSEQUENTLY

Textile Fiber Products Identification Act

This legislation requires that each textile product carry a label listing the generic names of fibers from which it is made. These generic fiber categories are established by the Federal Trade Commission, which can add new generic categories as needed. At present there are twenty-one generic fiber categories for man-made fibers, as well as the names for the natural fibers.

The listing of fibers is made in order of percentage by weight of fiber present in the product, with the largest amount listed first, the next largest second, and so on. Fiber quantities of less than 5 per cent must be labeled as "other fiber" unless they serve a specific purpose in the product. Fibers that cannot be identified must be listed as "X per cent of undetermined fiber content."

The law prohibits the use of misleading names that imply the presence of fiber not in the product. Labels must carry either the name, trademark, or registered identification number of the manufacturer. This law applies to imported manufactured goods as well as to domestic goods, but does not apply to imported raw materials. (For details, see Chapter 1, pages 7–9.)

PASSED 1939

Wool Products Labeling Act

This legislation regulates the labeling of sheep's wool and other animal hair fibers. The Wool Products Labeling Act requires that all wool products be labeled and the fibers, except for ornamentation, be identified as either new, reprocessed, or reused wool. The rules and regulations of the Federal Trade Commission established in relation to the act require that the terms *wool, new wool,* or *virgin wool* be applied only to wool that has never been used before. Reprocessed wool is wool that has never been utilized in any way by the ultimate consumer, but which has been spun into yarns or woven or knitted into cloth. These formed but unused pieces of yarns or fabrics are pulled apart and the fibers are reprocessed into fabrics. Reused wool has been used by consumers and is reclaimed by pulling the fabrics apart into fibers and spinning and weaving these fibers into other yarns and fabrics.

The law requires that the percentage of wool used in pile fabrics be identified as to the percentage of wool in the face and percentage of wool in the backing. The proportion of fiber used in face and backing must also be noted. Contents of paddings, linings, or stuffings are designated separately from the face fabric of products, but must be listed with the same items noted. (See Chapter 5, pages 72–74.)

Fur Products Labeling Act

PASSED 1951

This law requires that fur products carry the true English name of the fur-bearing animal from which it comes, and the name of the country of origin of the fur. (See Chapter 5, pages 86–87.)

Flammable Fabrics Act

ORIGINAL PROVISIONS ENACTED IN 1953

The original provisions of the act stated that wearing apparel (excluding hats, gloves, and footwear) and fabrics that are highly flammable may not be sold. Standards were established for testing to determine whether items were highly flammable. (See Chapter 20, page 322 for discussion of the standard.)

AMENDMENTS TO THE ACT, 1967

The scope of the act was broadened in 1967 to cover a wider range of clothing and interior furnishings. The act called for the establishment of standards for flammability for items covered by the act, and banned from sale those carpets, mattresses, and items of children's sleepwear, sizes infant to 14, that do not meet the established standards. (See Chapter 20, page 322 for discussion of the standards.) Some small carpets and one-of-a-kind carpets are exempt from the provisions of the act, but must be labeled indicating that they do not meet the standard. The responsibility for administering and implementing the act was given to the Consumer Product Safety Commission. (See Chapter 20 for full discussion of the legislation.)

Established 1972

This ruling requires that all wearing apparel and fabric sold by the yard must carry permanently affixed labels giving instructions for care. Exempt from the ruling are household textiles, retail items costing the consumer less than $3, footwear, head gear, and hand coverings, and all items that would be marred by affixing a label. (See Chapter 1, pages 19–20.)

Permanent Care Labeling Ruling of the Federal Trade Commission

Established 1938

No silk products containing more than 10 per cent weighting except those colored black may carry a label saying that they are "silk" or "pure dye silk." Black silks can contain 15 per cent of weighting. Fabrics not meeting these standards must be labeled as "weighted silk." (See Chapter 5, pages 90–91.)

Federal Trade Commission Ruling on the Weighting of Silk

Appendix D
MAN-MADE FIBERS AND TRADEMARKS

The following lists (alphabetically) the generic categories of man-made fibers, the FTC definition, and trademarks for fibers in each of these categories together with the name of the manufacturer and the types of yarns and fibers made under the trademark.[1]

acetate   A manufactured fiber in which the fiber-forming substance is cellulose acetate. Where not less than 92 per cent of the hydroxl groups are acetylated, the term *triacetate* may be used as a generic description of the fiber.

	Trademark	Type of Yarn or Fiber	Manufacturer
acetate:	Acele	filament	E. I. du Pont de Nemours & Co.
	Ariloft	filament	Eastman Kodak Co.
	Avicolor	solution-dyed filament	Avtex Fibers Inc.
	Celanese acetate	staple, filament, cigarette filter tow, fiberfill.	Celanese Corp.
	Chromespun	solution-dyed filament	Eastman Kodak Co.
	Estron	filament and cigarette filter tow.	Eastman Kodak Co.
	Estron SLR	filament	Eastman Kodak Co.
	Acetate by Avtex	filament	Avtex Fibers Inc.
	SayFR	fire-resistant filament	Avtex Fibers Inc.
triacetate:	Arnel	filament and staple	Celanese Corp.
	Arnel V	filament	Celanese Corp.

acrylic   A manufactured fiber in which the fiber-forming substance is any long-chain synthetic polymer composed of at least 85 per cent by weight of acrylonitrile units ($-CH_2-CH-$).
$$\underset{CN}{|}$$

	Trademark	Type of Yarn or Fiber	Manufacturer
acrylic:	A-Acrilan	staple and tow	Monsanto Co.
	Acrilan	staple and tow	Monsanto Co.
	Acrilan 2000 +	solution-dyed staple	Monsanto Co.
	Bi-loft	staple, bicomponent, filaments	Monsanto Co.
	Creslan	staple and tow	American Cyanamid Co.
	Orlon	staple and tow	E. I. du Pont de Nemours & Co.
	Zefran	staple in both dyeable and producer-colored fiber.	Dow Badische Co.

[1] Sources: "Man-made Fiber Desk Book" (*Modern Textiles*, March 1976). *Man-made Fiber Fact Book* (Washington, D.C.: Man-Made Fiber Producers Association, 1974).

anidex A manufactured fiber in which the fiber-forming substance is any long-chain synthetic polymer composed of at least 50 per cent by weight of one or more esters of a monohydric alcohol and acrylic acid. (CH_2=CH—COOH)
Not manufactured in the United States.

aramid A manufactured fiber in which the fiber-forming substance is a long-chain synthetic polyamide in which at least 85 per cent of the amide (—C—NH—) linkages are attached directly to two aromatic rings.
$\|$
O

	Trademark	Type of Yarn or Fiber	Manufacturer
aramid:	Kevlar	filament	E. I. du Pont de Nemours & Co.
	Nomex	filament and staple	E. I. du Pont de Nemours & Co.

azlon A manufactured fiber in which the fiber-forming substance is composed of any regenerated naturally occurring proteins.
Not manufactured in the United States.

	Trademark	Type of Yarn or Fiber	Manufacturer
ECTFE fluoro-polymer:	Nypel Halar	monofilament	Nypel, Inc.
fluorocarbon:	Teflon	filament, monofilament	E. I. du Pont de Nemours & Co.
fluoroplastic:	Kynar	monofilament	Monofilaments, Inc.

glass A manufactured fiber in which the fiber-forming substance is glass.

	Trademark	Type of Yarn or Fiber	Manufacturer
glass:	Beta	filament	Owens-Corning Fiberglas Co.
	Fiberglas	filament and staple	Owens-Corning Fiberglas Co.
	Modiglass	monofilament and filament	Reichhold Chemicals Inc.
	Trianti	filament	PPG Industries
	Unicomb	combination mat and woven	Ferro Corp.
	Uniformat	mat	Ferro Corp.
	Unirove	woven roving	Ferro Corp.
	Unistrand	roving	Ferro Corp.
	Vitro-flex	mat	Johns Manville Co.
	Vitron	woven roving	Johns Manville Co.
	Vitro-Strand	milled fiber	Johns Manville Co.

metallic A manufactured fiber composed of metal, plastic-coated metal, metal-coated plastic, or a core completely covered by metal.

	Trademark	Type of Yarn or Fiber	Manufacturer
metallic:	Alistan	flat, laminated yarn	Multi-Tex Corp.
	Brunsmet	stainless steel fiber in filament, staple, tow	Brunswick Co.
	Chromeflex	flat, monofilament	Metal Film Co.
	Dura-Stran	flat, laminated filament	Multi-Tex Corp.
	Fairtex	flat, monofilament	Rexham Corp.
	Hudstat	monofilament	Hudson Wire Co.
	Lurex	yarn of slit film	Dow Badische Co.
	Raybrite C.F.	metallic cellophane	Raybrite Inc.
	Raybrite MF	Mylar foil	Raybrite Inc.
	Raybrite MM	metalized Mylar	Raybrite Inc.

modacrylic A manufactured fiber in which the fiber-forming substance is any long chain synthetic polymer composed of less than 85 per cent but at least 35 per cent by weight of acrylonitrile units, ($-CH_2-CH-$), except fibers

$$CN$$

qualifying under subparagraph (2) of paragraph (j) of this section and fibers qualifying under paragraph (q) of this section.

	Trademark	Type of Yarn or Fiber	Manufacturer
modacrylic:	Elura	tow	Monsanto Co.
	Sef	staple, flame retardant	Monsanto Co.
	Verel	staple (assorted types for various uses)	Eastman Kodak Co.

novoloid A manufactured fiber containing at least 85 per cent by weight of a cross-linked novolac.

	Trademark	Type of Yarn or Fiber	Manufacturer
novoloid:	Kynol	staple fiber	Carborundum Co.

nylon A manufactured fiber in which the fiber-forming substance is a long-chain synthetic polyamide in which less than 85 per cent of the amide ($-C-NH-$) linkages are attached directly to two aromatic rings (as

$$O$$

amended January 11, 1974).

	Trademark	Type of Yarn or Fiber	Manufacturer
nylon:	Actionwear	textured filament	Monsanto Co.
	Anso	nylon filament and staple soil-resistant carpet yarn	Allied Chemical Corp.
	Antron	filament, staple, and tow	E. I. du Pont de Nemours & Co.
	Astroturf	ribbon	Monsanto Co.
	Ayrlyn	continuous filament	Rohm and Haas Co.

	Trademark	Type of Yarn or Fiber	Manufacturer
nylon (Cont.):	Beaunit nylon	multicolored filament, staple and tow	Beaunit Corp.
	Berkley nylon	flat and round monofilament	Berkley Co.
	Blue "C"	filament, staple	Monsanto Co.
	Cadon } C-cadon }	filament yarn and multilobal monofilament, staple	Monsanto Co.
	Camalon	filament yarn, solution-dyed	Camac Corp.
	Cantrece	bicomponent filament	E. I. du Pont de Nemours & Co.
	Caprolan	yarns, monofilaments, and textured yarns	Allied Chemical Corp.
	Cedilla	textured nylon filament yarn	Celanese Corp.
	Celanese nylon	filament	Celanese Corp.
	Cerex	spun-bonded	Monsanto Co.
	Chadolon	filament, monofilament	Chadbourn Industries
	Cordura	filament	E. I. du Pont de Nemours & Co.
	Courtaulds nylon	filament	Courtaulds North America Inc.
	Crepeset	patented continuous monofilament that develops a regular crimp, also anticling yarn	American Enka Co.
	Cumuloft	textured filament carpet yarn	Monsanto Co.
	Enka nylon	filament, staple	American Enka Co.
	Enkaloft	textured multilobal continuous filament carpet yarn and staple	American Enka Co.
	Enkalure	multilobal continuous filament apparel yarn and textured delayed soiling carpet yarn	American Enka Co.
	Enkalure II	textured multilobal soil hiding continuous filament carpet yarn and staple	American Enka Co.
	Enkalure III	anticling, fine denier	American Enka Co.
	Enkasheer	continuous monofilament torque yarn for ladies stretch hosiery	American Enka Co.
	Firestone nylon	monofilament, filament	Firestone Co.
	Hanover nylon	monofilament, filament	Hanover Co.
	Lo-Temp	fusible, adhesive filament	Fibrex Co.
	Metlon	variety of flat, staple, and monofilaments each with different letters following the trademark name	Metlon Co.
	Multisheer	multifilament, producer-textured stretch yarn for pantyhose	American Enka Co.
	MX-108	monofilament, round opaque high modulus for industrial use	Shakespeare Co.
	Nypel nylon	monofilament	Nypel Co.
	nylon by Amtech	round monofilament	Amtech Co.
	Qiana	filament	E. I. du Pont de Nemours & Co.
	Random-set	heat-set	Rohm & Haas Co.
	Random-tone	fashion and styling yarns	Rohm & Haas Co.
	Ruvea	monofilament ribbon	E. I. du Pont de Nemours & Co.
	S-3	monofilament, clear or melt-dyed	Shakespeare Co.
	Shakespeare nylon	round monofilament	Shakespeare Co.
	Shareen	monofilament textured yarn	Courtaulds North America, Inc.
	Shoeflex	monofilament	Shakespeare Co.
	Sooflex	monofilament	Shakespeare Co.
	Starbrite	staple	Star Fibers
	Stria	bulked nylon carpet yarn, modified twist	American Enka Co.
	Sunylon	clear or melt-dyed monofilament	Sunshine Cordage Co.
	Super Bulk	heat-set, high bulk continuous filament nylon carpet yarn	American Enka Co.
	Superflex	monofilament	Shakespeare Co.
	Synflex-N	monofilament	Wall Industries
	Twix	bulked nylon carpet yarn, modified twist	American Enka Co.

	Trademark	Type of Yarn or Fiber	Manufacturer
nylon (Cont.):	Ultron	filament	Monsanto Co.
	Vylor	monofilament	E. I. du Pont de Nemours & Co.
	Wellon	staple	Wellman, Inc.
	X-Static	filament, anti-static	Rohm & Haas, Co.
	Zefran nylon	filament, staple	Dow Badische Co.

nytril A manufactured fiber containing at least 85 per cent of a long-chain polymer of vinylidene dinitrile ($-CH_2-C(CN)_2-$) where the vinylidene dinitrile content is no less than every other unit in the polymer chain. Production discontinued in the United States.

olefin A manufactured fiber in which the fiber-forming substance is any long-chain synthetic polymer composed of at least 85 per cent by weight of ethylene, propylene, or other olefin units except amorphous (noncrystalline) polyolefins qualifying under category (1) of Paragraph (j) of Rule 7.

	Trademark	Type of Yarn or Fiber	Manufacturer
olefin:	Amco polyethylene	monofilament, slit film	American Mfg.
	Amco polypropylene	monofilament, slit film	American Mfg.
	Autotwine	slit film for twine	Indian Head Yarn and Thread Co.
	Beaunit olefin	monofilament, staple	Beaunit Co.
	Cala-lines	monofilament	Sunshine Cordage Co.
	Comforlon	monofilament, staple	Beaunit Co.
	Concorde polypropylene	textured, dyed filament	Concorde Fibers
	DLP polyethylene	monofilament ribbon	Thiokol Fibers
	DLP polypropylene	monofilament, filament	Thiokol Fibers
	Fibretex	spun-bonded	Crown-Zellerbach
	Fibri-Knit, Fibri-Cord	fibrillated filament for industrial use	Fibron Inc.
	Fibrilawn, Fibrilon	fibrillated filament	Fibron Inc.
	Goldcres	fibrillated filament	Shuford Mills
	GSI	ribbon, slit	Georgia Synthetics
	Hamlon	filament yarn	ACS Industries
	Herculon	continuous multifilament, bulked, continuous multifilament staple and tow	Hercules, Inc.
	H. L. polypropylene	solution-dyed filament	H. L. Industries
	Jackson	monofilament and slit film	Jackson Rope Corp.
	Kimkloth	spun-bonded	Kimberly-Clark Corp.
	Lo-Pic	flat monofilament	Fibron Inc.
	Marvess	staple and tow, filament	Phillips Fibers Corp.
	Montrel	low shrinkage, high modulus	Wellington Synthetic Fibres, Inc.
	Nypel polypro	monofilament	Nypel Inc.
	Oletex	monofilament	Poncar Plastic Co.
	Parapro	filament	Wall Industries
	Patlon	fibrillated film	Chevron Corp.
	Polyethylene by Amtech	round monofilament	Amtech Inc.
	Polypropylene by Amtech	round and flat monofilament	Amtech Inc.

	Trademark	Type of Yarn or Fiber	Manufacturer
olefin (Cont.):	Polytwine⎫ Polywrap⎭	slit-processed, high modulus monofilament	Indian Head Yarn and Thread Co.
	Poncar	monofilament	Poncar Plastic Co.
	Pro-tuft	plastic ribbon	Bemis Co.
	Shurti	fibrillated film	Shuford Mills
	Stronghold	filament	Bemis Co.
	Sunshine	monofilament	Sunshine Cordage
	Super Tuff	monofilament and slit film	Jackson Rope Corp.
	Supertuft	slit film	General Fabrics & Fibers
	Tenacitex	filament	Bemis Co.
	TW 6208	filament	Fibron Inc.
	TY EZ⎫ Tylon⎬ Tytite⎭	slit processed, high modulus	Indian Head Yarn and Thread Co.
	Tyvek	spunbonded	E. I. du Pont de Nemours & Co.
	Unifil	monofilament	Wall Industries
	Vectra	filament and staple	Vectra Corp.
	Voplex	round or flat monofilament	Voplex Co.
	Wall polypropylene	monofilament	Wall Industries
	Waltrich polypropylene	monofilament and ribbon	Waltrich Plastics Corp.
	Weve Bac	slit film	Moultire Textiles
	WSF PE	monofilament, round, high tenacity, and slit film	Wellington Synthetic Fibres, Inc.
	WSF PP	monofilament and fibrillated film	Wellington Synthetic Fibres, Inc.
polycarbonate:	Polycarbonate	monofilament	Monofilaments, Inc.
	Solvex	monofilament	Fibrex Co.

polyester A manufactured fiber in which the fiber-forming substance is any long-chain synthetic polymer composed of at least 85 per cent by weight of an ester of a substituted aromatic carboxylic acid, including but not restricted to substituted therephthalate units $p(-R-O-\underset{\underset{O}{\|}}{C}-C_6H_4-\underset{\underset{O}{\|}}{C}-O-)$

and parasubstituted hydroxybenzoate units, $p(-R-O-C_6H_4-\underset{\underset{O}{\|}}{C}-O-)$ (as

amended September 12, 1973).

	Trademark	Type of Yarn or Fiber	Manufacturer
polyester:	Avlin	filament yarn and staple	Avtex Fibers Inc.
	Beaunit polyester	filament, staple, tow	Beaunit Co.
	Bidim	spunbonded	Monsanto Co.
	Blue "C"	filament, staple	Monsanto Co.
	Dacron	filament yarn, staple, tow and fiberfill	E. I. du Pont de Nemours & Co.
	Ektafil	staple fiberfill	Eastman Kodak Co.
	Encron	continuous filament yarn, staple, fiberfill	American Enka Co.
	Encron 8	octalobal polyester that reduces glitter	American Enka Co.
	Enka polyester	filament and staple	American Enka Co.
	Firestone polyester	filament	Firestone Co.
	Fortrel	filament yarn, staple, tow and fiberfill	Celanese Corp.

Trademark	Type of Yarn or Fiber	Manufacturer
polyester (Cont.):		
Golden Touch Encron	high denier per filament	American Enka Co.
Goodyear polyester	filament	Goodyear Co.
Hanover polyester	staple, filament	Hanover Mills Inc.
Hoechst polyester	staple, filament, high tenacity, low pilling	Hoechst Co.
Kodel	filament yarn, staple, tow fiberfill	Eastman Kodak Co.
MX 6020 } MX 6020-H	monofilament- round, regular, medium, and low shrinkage for industrial use	Shakespeare Co.
Newton polyester	filament	Newton Filaments Inc.
Nypel polyester	monofilament	Nypel Inc.
PE 3100	monofilament	Monofilaments Inc.
Plyloc	textured, two-ply stretch	American Enka Co.
Polar Guard	filament, tow	Celanese Corp.
Polyester by IRC	filament	IRC Fibers
Polyester by Amtech	monofilament, round	Amtech Co.
Polyester by Allied Chemical		Allied Chemical Corp.
Polystrand	for industrial use	Wellman Corp.
Quintess	multifilament yarns	Phillips Fibers Corp.
Reemay	spunbonded	E. I. du Pont de Nemours & Co.
Shakespeare polyester	monofilament	Shakespeare Co.
Spectran	staple	Monsanto Co.
Strialine Encron	slub-effect, variable dyeing	American Enka Co.
Textura	producer textured	Rohm & Haas Co.
Trevira	filament, staple, high tenacity	Hoechst Fibers Inc.
Vycron	filament, staple, tow, and fiberfill	Beaunit Corp.
Wellstrand	monofilament	Wellman, Inc.
Wonderfeel	filament	Celanese Corp.
Zefran polyester	filament	Dow Badische Co.

rayon A manufactured fiber composed of regenerated cellulose, as well as manufactured fibers composed of regenerated cellulose in which substituents have replaced not more than 15 per cent of the hydrogens of the hydroxyl groups.

Trademark	Type of Yarn or Fiber	Manufacturer
rayon:		
Aviloc	adhesive treated high strength rayon yarn	Avtex Fibers Inc.
Avril	high wet modulus staple	Avtex Fibers Inc.
Beau-Grip	specially treated high tenacity viscose yarn	Beaunit Corp.
Beaunit rayon	filament and tow	Beaunit Corp.
Briglo	bright luster continuous filament yarn	American Enka Co.
Coloray	solution-dyed staple	Courtaulds North America Inc.
Enka rayon	staple fiber	American Enka Co.
Enkrome	patented acid-dyeable staple and continuous filament yarn	American Enka Co.
Fiber 40	high-wet-modulus staple	Avtex Fibers Inc.
Fiber 700	high-wet-modulus staple	American Enka Co.
Fibro	staple	Courtaulds North America Inc.
Rayon by Avtex	staple	Avtex Fibers Inc.
I.T.	improved tenacity staple	American Enka Co.
Jetspun	solution-dyed continuous filament yarn	American Enka Co.
Kolorbon	solution-dyed staple	American Enka Co.

	Trademark	Type of Yarn or Fiber	Manufacturer
rayon (Cont.):	Super White	optically brightened rayon	American Enka Co.
	Suprenka	extra high tenacity continuous filament industrial yarn	American Enka Co.
	Zantrel	high wet modulus staple	American Enka Co.

rubber A manufactured fiber in which the fiber-forming substance is comprised of natural or synthetic rubber, including the following categories: (1) a manufactured fiber in which the fiber-forming substance is a hydrocarbon such as natural rubber, polyisoprene, polybutadiene, copolymers of dienes and hydrocarbons, or amorphous (noncrystalline) polyolefins, (2) a manufactured fiber in which the fiber-forming substance is a copolymer of acrylonitrile and a diene (such as butadiene) composed of not more than 50 per cent but at least 10 per cent by weight of acrylonitrile units.

$$(-CH_2-\underset{\underset{CN}{|}}{CH}-)$$

The term *lastrile* may be used as a generic description for fibers falling within this category, (3) a manufactured fiber in which the fiber-forming substance is a polychloroprene or a copolymer of chloroprene in which at least 35 per cent by weight of the fiber-forming substance is composed of chloroprene units.

$$(-CH_2-\underset{\underset{Cl}{|}}{C}=CH-CH_2-)$$

saran A manufactured fiber in which the fiber-forming substance is any long-chain synthetic polymer composed of at least 80 per cent by weight of vinylidene chloride units.

$$(-CH_2-CCl_2-)$$

	Trademark	Type of Yarn or Fiber	Manufacturer
saran:	Saran by Amtech	round and flat monofilament	Amtech Inc.

spandex A manufactured fiber in which the fiber-forming substance is a long-chain synthetic polymer comprised of at least 85 per cent of a segmented polyurethane.

	Trademark	Type of Yarn or Fiber	Manufacturer
spandex:	Cleerspan	filament	Globe Co.
	Glospan	filament	Globe Co.
	Lycra	filament	E. I. du Pont de Nemours, Co.
	Numa	filament	Ameliotex Inc.

vinal A manufactured fiber in which the fiber-forming substance is any long-chain synthetic polymer composed of at least 50 per cent by weight of vinyl alcohol units ($-CH_2-CHOH-$) and in which the total of the vinyl alcohol units and any one or more of the various acetal units is at least 85 per cent by weight of the fiber.
Not manufactured in the United States.

vinyon A manufactured fiber in which the fiber-forming substance is any long-chain synthetic polymer composed of at least 85 per cent by weight of vinyl chloride units.

$$-CH_2-CHCl-$$

	Trademark	Type of Yarn or Fiber	Manufacturer
vinyon:	Vinyon by Avtex	filament or staple	Avtex Fibers Inc.
	Voplex	flat monofilament	Voplex Co.
Biconstituent Fibers			
	Mirafi	fabric made from spunbonded biconstituent of nylon and olefin	Celanese Corp.
	Monvelle	biconstituent nylon and spandex	Monsanto Co.
	Ultron	fabric made from nylon and biconstituent nylon and carbon black fiber	Monsanto Co.
Other trademarked blended yarns:			
	Lanese	acetate and polyester yarn	Celanese Corp.
	Fortron	polyester and nylon yarn	Celanese Corp.

INDEX

401

Coneprest finish, 313
Consumer Product Safety Commission, 356
Cord yarns, 176
Cordelan, 146, 151
Corduroy, 202–203
Core-spun yarns, 141, 177
Corkscrew yarns, 177
Coronizing, 100
Cotton fiber, 35–42
    botanical information, 36, 37
    care, 42
    chemical reactivity, 49
    cultivation, 37, 38
    economic importance, 36
    effect of environmental conditions on, 42, 49
    history of, 35, 36
    mercerization of, 319
    physical properties, 38–42, 49
    production, 38
    structure, 40
    thermal properties, 41
    uses, 42
Courses, in knits, 221
Covering power, 10, 371
Co-We-Nit knit-weave fabrics, 231
Cow hair fiber, 87
Crash, 193
Crease resistance, 372
Crepe yarns, 170
Creslan acrylic fiber, 129
Crimp, fiber, 11, 12
    yarn, 370–71
Crinoline, 192
Crochet, 240
Crocking, 260
Crockmeter, 364
Crompton, Samuel, 156
Cross dyeing, 257–59
Crosslinking of molecules, 27, 175
Cuperammonium rayon, 58, 59
Cut of knit fabrics, *see* Gauge of knits

D

Damask, 197
Dan-Press finish, 313
Degumming, 289–90

Delnet fabric, 249
Delustering of fiber, 293, 309
Denier, 13, 172
Denim, 195
Density of fibers, 14
    See also generic fiber listings
Department of Agriculture, 344
Detergents, 327, 328, 329–31
Dimensional stability of fabrics, 374
    of fibers, 17
    See also individual generic fiber listings
Dimity, 193
Direct dyes, 261
Direct spinning, 168
Dispersed dyes, 262, 276
Dobby loom, 187
Dobby weave, 197–98
Documentary print, 285
Double-cloth construction, 203
Double-faced satin, 197
Double knits, 224–25
Doup weave, *see* Leno weave
Dowicide finish, 308
Drill, 195
Dry cleaning, 342–43
    testing for colorfastness to, 364
Dual Action Scotchgard finish, 317
Dubblestretch fabric, 175
Duchesse satin, 197
Durable press finishes, 313–17
    care of, 315–17
    problems of, 315–17
Dye classes, 260–63
Dyeing, 251–63
    beam, 256–57
    beck, 256
    box, 256
    cross, 257–59
    fiber, 254–55
    history of, 251–53
    jet, 256
    jig, 256
    pad, 257
    piece, 256–57
    polychromatic, *see* Printing, polychromatic
    solution, 253–54
    stock, *see* Dyeing, fiber
    tone-on-tone, 259